Rust for Data Science

Maxwell Vector

Contents

1

9

14

Chapter 1

Memory-Optimized Data Structures for Scientific Computing

Foundations of Rust's Memory Management

The architectural underpinnings of Rust center on its distinctive ownership model, which enforces memory safety through compile-time analysis. This system, characterized by strict ownership and borrowing rules, precludes traditional issues such as dangling pointers and data races. The ownership model assigns each datum a single owner, while borrow checking ensures that references obey precise lifetime constraints. Such rigorous guarantees allow data structures to be designed without the overhead of runtime garbage collection, providing memory efficiency that is paramount when handling large-scale scientific datasets. The static analysis performed by the compiler is reminiscent of formal verification techniques in theoretical computer science, where invariants are maintained with mathematical precision.

1 Ownership and Borrowing Mechanisms

Within Rust, every memory allocation is coupled with an ownership annotation that mandates unique responsibility for resource deallocation. The borrowing mechanism further refines this paradigm by allowing temporary, immutable, or mutable references with well-defined lifetimes. In mathematical terms, these lifetimes can be thought of as intervals during which the invariant

$$\text{Validity} \implies \text{Memory Safety}$$

must hold. This discipline in resource management fosters the creation of data structures that are not only efficient in their memory footprint but also capable of supporting parallel computations without fear of undefined behavior.

2 Lifetime Analysis and Scope Enforcement

The systematic approach to lifetime analysis in Rust serves to limit the duration of data accessibility. By enforcing a clear demarcation of variable lifetimes, data structures can be constructed such that each element is valid only within its intended scope. This explicit constraint is instrumental in scientific computing, where the manipulation of multidimensional arrays or sparse matrices often involves temporary aggregation of large volumes of data. The compile-time verification of these lifetimes reduces runtime overhead and ensures that every data access is deliberate and safe.

Zero-Cost Abstractions and Their Impact on Performance

Central to Rust's performance ethos is the concept of zero-cost abstractions. These abstractions allow high-level constructs to be used without incurring additional runtime penalties, granting the expressiveness of modern programming tools while preserving the efficiency of lower-level languages. In practice, these abstractions are resolved at compile time, resulting in executable code that mirrors the efficiency of hand-optimized routines. The mathematical equivalence can be described by asserting that for an abstraction A,

$$\text{Runtime Overhead}(A) \approx$$

Runtime Overhead of a corresponding low-level implementation.

This principle permits the construction of generic and composable data structures that are both safe and performant.

1 Theoretical Underpinnings of Zero-Cost Abstractions

The notion that no additional cost is incurred when using high-level constructs is fundamental in the design of data structures for scientific computing. Compiler optimizations in Rust transform abstract representations into concrete machine instructions that execute with minimal latency. This phenomenon is analogous to the practice in algorithmic theory where the asymptotic cost of a high-level operation is equivalent to that of its most optimized, lower-level realization. Consequently, the utilization of iterators, closures, and generic types in the construction of data structures does not depreciate the computational efficiency critical for processing voluminous scientific data.

2 Implications for High-Performance Scientific Computation

The advantages conferred by zero-cost abstractions manifest in scenarios where complex data transformations are performed at scale. Data structures that encapsulate multidimensional data, such as arrays and trees, can be implemented so that their abstractions introduce no observable latency. This behavior is particularly significant in the context of large-scale numerical simulations and statistical analysis, where performance degradation directly translates into increased computational cost. The guarantee of zero-cost overhead ensures that even intricate operations, when composed of multiple abstractions, maintain a predictable and minimal performance profile.

Memory Layout, Data Alignment, and Cache Optimization

Optimizing memory layout is a critical concern when designing data structures for scientific computing. Efficient data alignment and cache-friendly organization are essential for reducing memory access latencies and enhancing throughput. By aligning data to boundaries that reflect the underlying hardware constraints, the performance of iterative numerical computations can be significantly improved.

1 Data Alignment and Access Patterns

A well-structured data layout maximizes spatial locality, a property that facilitates efficient cache utilization. In the realm of scientific computing, where operations frequently traverse large, contiguous memory regions, ensuring that data structures are aligned to suitable boundaries (typically multiples of 2^k) can lead to performance gains. Such an alignment minimizes cache misses and leverages prefetching mechanisms inherent in modern processor architectures. The result is a reduction in the effective memory latency and an improvement in the computational throughput required for handling extensive datasets.

2 Considerations in Numerical Computation

Numerical methods in scientific computing often involve repetitive operations on large arrays and matrices. In this setting, the choice of data structure directly influences the feasibility of vectorized computations and parallel processing routines. The meticulous organization of data into cache-aligned blocks can be quantified by performance metrics that measure the ratio of cache hits to cache misses. This optimization strategy is essential for algorithms that perform iterative sweeps over multidimensional data, where even marginal improvements in memory access patterns can yield substantial reductions in overall runtime.

Specialized Data Structures for Scientific Data Processing

The design of data structures tailored for scientific datasets necessitates a judicious balance between flexibility and efficiency. Such data structures must accommodate varying levels of data density, support rapid indexing, and facilitate efficient modification without compromising memory performance.

1 Sparse and Dense Array Representations

In many scientific applications, datasets exhibit a high degree of sparsity, where the majority of elements are zero or otherwise insignificant. Data structures that are capable of representing both dense arrays and their sparse counterparts allow for adaptive memory usage. Dense representations are optimal when dealing with contiguous numerical data, while sparse formats are indispensable for conserving memory in the presence of infrequent nonzero elements. The deliberate selection and design of these structures enable the implementation of algorithms that operate in linear or near-linear time, depending on the distribution of relevant data points.

2 Graph-Based Models and Hierarchical Structures

Complex scientific problems often involve relationships that are naturally expressed in the form of graphs or hierarchical trees. Data structures that encapsulate these models are formulated to support rapid traversal, dynamic modifications, and efficient query operations. Rust's memory safety paradigm ensures that even when intricate interconnections exist between nodes and edges, the integrity of data is preserved throughout modifications and concurrent operations. Hierarchical structures that articulate multi-level relationships are particularly effective in domains such as computational biology and network analysis, where the ability to model interdependent data components is paramount.

Rust Code Snippet

```rust
use std::fmt::Debug;
use std::ops::{Add, Mul};

/// A memory-optimized dense matrix structure for scientific
↪    computing.
/// This structure demonstrates zero-cost abstractions through
↪    iterator-based operations
/// and enforces memory safety via Rust's ownership, borrowing, and
↪    lifetime rules.
#[derive(Debug, Clone)]
struct DenseMatrix<T> {
    rows: usize,
    cols: usize,
    data: Vec<T>,
}

impl<T> DenseMatrix<T>
where
    T: Copy + Default + Add<Output = T> + Mul<Output = T> + Debug,
{
```

```rust
/// Constructs a new dense matrix with given dimensions,
↪   initializing all elements to T::default().
fn new(rows: usize, cols: usize) -> Self {
    DenseMatrix {
        rows,
        cols,
        data: vec![T::default(); rows * cols],
    }
}

/// Constructs a dense matrix from a vector.
/// Panics if the length of the vector does not match rows *
↪   cols.
fn from_vec(rows: usize, cols: usize, data: Vec<T>) -> Self {
    assert_eq!(rows * cols, data.len(), "Data length does not
        ↪   match matrix dimensions");
    DenseMatrix { rows, cols, data }
}

/// Returns the element at the specified row and column.
fn get(&self, row: usize, col: usize) -> T {
    self.data[row * self.cols + col]
}

/// Sets the element at the specified row and column to a new
↪   value.
fn set(&mut self, row: usize, col: usize, value: T) {
    self.data[row * self.cols + col] = value;
}

/// Returns an iterator over the elements of a given row.
/// Zero-cost abstraction: The iterator is inlined at
↪   compile-time,
/// ensuring no additional runtime overhead over a manual slice.
fn row_iter(&self, row: usize) -> impl Iterator<Item = &T> {
    let start = row * self.cols;
    let end = start + self.cols;
    self.data[start..end].iter()
}

/// Performs matrix multiplication between two dense matrices.
///
/// Implements the mathematical formula:
///    c[i][j] = \sum_{k=0}^{n-1} a[i][k] * b[k][j]
///
/// Zero-cost abstraction: The use of iterator combinators (map
↪   and fold) achieves
/// the same efficiency as a hand-optimized loop.
fn mul(&self, other: &DenseMatrix<T>) -> DenseMatrix<T> {
    assert_eq!(
        self.cols, other.rows,
        "Matrix dimensions must agree for multiplication"
    );
```

```rust
        let mut result = DenseMatrix::new(self.rows, other.cols);
        for i in 0..self.rows {
            for j in 0..other.cols {
                let sum = (0..self.cols)
                    .map(|k| self.get(i, k) * other.get(k, j))
                    .fold(T::default(), |acc, x| acc + x);
                result.set(i, j, sum);
            }
        }
        result
    }
}


/// Demonstrates memory safety and lifetime enforcement in Rust.
/// The function takes a slice of data and computes the sum of its
↪    first and second halves.
/// The borrow checker ensures that no dangling references occur,
↪    upholding the invariant:
///    Validity \implies Memory Safety
fn compute_sums<'a>(data: &'a [i32]) -> (i32, i32) {
    let mid = data.len() / 2;
    let sum_first: i32 = data[..mid].iter().sum();
    let sum_second: i32 = data[mid..].iter().sum();
    (sum_first, sum_second)
}

fn main() {
    // Example: Dense matrix multiplication.
    let a = DenseMatrix::from_vec(2, 3, vec![1, 2, 3, 4, 5, 6]);
    let b = DenseMatrix::from_vec(3, 2, vec![7, 8, 9, 10, 11, 12]);
    let c = a.mul(&b);

    println!("Matrix A: {:?}", a);
    println!("Matrix B: {:?}", b);
    println!("Matrix C (A * B): {:?}", c);

    // Demonstrate the use of a row iterator (zero-cost
    ↪    abstraction).
    for (i, row) in c.data.chunks(c.cols).enumerate() {
        println!("Row {}: {:?}", i, row);
    }

    // Example: Memory safety via ownership and borrowing.
    let data = vec![10, 20, 30, 40, 50, 60];
    let (first_half, second_half) = compute_sums(&data);
    println!("Sum of first half: {}", first_half);
    println!("Sum of second half: {}", second_half);

    // Illustration: Zero-cost abstraction in action.
    // The iterator-based computation in `mul` is optimized at
    ↪    compile-time to match the performance
    // of a manual loop, satisfying the equation:
    //
```

```
    //    Runtime_Overhead(Iterator Abstraction)
    ↪    Runtime_Overhead(Explicit Loop)
    //
    // This guarantees that high-level abstractions do not
    ↪    compromise the performance necessary for
    // large-scale scientific computations.
}
```

Chapter 2

Functional Iterators in Data Pipelines

Iterator Traits: An Abstract Framework

The iterator abstraction in Rust is formalized through a trait that encapsulates a method for sequential element retrieval. At its core, the trait defines a function that returns an element wrapped in an option type, aligning with the mathematical construct of a partial function. Formally, the behavior of an iterator may be expressed as

$$next : S \to \text{Option}(T),$$

where S represents the internal state space and T the type of elements. This abstraction permits the encapsulation of state transitions, such that every invocation of the *next* function yields either a new element or an indication of termination. The stringent type conditions and lifetime constraints that govern this mechanism ensure that the iterator conforms to robust safety and performance guarantees, laying a rigorous foundation for constructing efficient data pipelines.

Lazy Evaluation: Principles and Performance Characteristics

Lazy evaluation constitutes a central tenet in the design of functional iterators. Within this paradigm, computations are deferred until the specific moment when the corresponding result is required. This deferral aligns with non-strict semantics in functional programming, where the evaluation of an expression is postponed until its value is indispensable for a subsequent computation. The mathematical symbolism for deferred computation can be denoted by

$$f(x) \downarrow,$$

implying that the evaluation of $f(x)$ is suspended. Such a strategy minimizes unnecessary processing by ensuring that intermediate results are produced on-demand. The resultant performance benefits are particularly significant when processing large-scale datasets, since resource-intensive operations are only executed when the pipeline explicitly requests them. This approach harmonizes the dual imperatives of expressive transformation logic and the preservation of computational efficiency.

Functional Combinators and Their Algebraic Properties

The composition of functional iterators hinges on an array of combinators—operations that transform or aggregate the elements produced by iterators. Combinators such as mapping, filtering, and folding are realized as higher-order functions that accept an iterator as input and return a new iterator as output. For instance, a mapping operation may be characterized by a function

$$map : (T \rightarrow U) \times I \rightarrow I',$$

where I' is an iterator over a transformed element type U. This structure mirrors the principles of function composition in mathematics, where applying a cascade of functions $f \circ g$ is equivalent to executing g followed by f. The associativity and identity properties inherent in these operations provide an algebraic framework that supports both the seamless fusion of multiple transformations and the optimization of iterative processes. Through these compositional paradigms, iterator-based pipelines achieve a level of abstraction that permits the elegant expression of complex data transformations without incurring additional runtime overhead.

Pipeline Composition and Fusion Techniques

The construction of efficient data pipelines is actualized through the fusion of multiple iterator-based operations into an integrated execution sequence. Fusion techniques involve the combination of successive transformation steps into a composite operation that operates with minimal additional overhead. Conceptually, if two iterator transformations are represented by functions f and g, then their fusion into a single operation h is expressed as

$$h(x) = g(f(x)),$$

where the cost model of h is analogous to the combined costs of f and g, yet without the extraneous overhead incurred by intermediate state transitions. This property is critical in eliminating redundant computations and consolidating the operational steps within a data pipeline. The theoretical underpinnings of fusion are largely derived from category theory and the study of monads in functional programming, where the preservation of structure under composition is a principal attribute. Such insights facilitate the systematic design of pipelines that maintain high throughput while processing complex data transformations.

Algorithmic Efficiency in Lazy Data Pipelines

The efficiency of lazy data pipelines is governed by the interplay between deferred computation and the compositional fusion of iterator transformations. The overall runtime overhead incurred by an iterator chain can be characterized by the sum of the individual costs associated with each transformation step. In formal terms, if an iterator operation exhibits a cost function C, then a sequence of n operations is bounded by approximately

$$O\left(\sum_{i=1}^{n} C_i\right),$$

modulo constant factors introduced by the lazy evaluation process. Moreover, properties such as early termination in certain combinators, including folding operations, facilitate the suppression of unnecessary computations. This analytical framework provides a metric for assessing the trade-offs inherent in the design of functional data pipelines. Through the rigorous application of these principles, iterator-based pipelines attain a balance between expressive transformation capabilities and the preservation of low-level computational efficiency, thereby ensuring that complex data manipulations execute with predictably minimal overhead.

Rust Code Snippet

```rust
use std::iter::Iterator;

/// Custom iterator that exemplifies the abstract iterator trait.
/// Mathematical formulation:
///     next : S -> Option(T)
struct Counter {
    count: usize,
    max: usize,
}

impl Counter {
    /// Create a new Counter with a given maximum value.
    fn new(max: usize) -> Self {
        Counter { count: 0, max }
    }
}

impl Iterator for Counter {
    type Item = usize;

    /// The `next` method embodies the mathematical function:
    ///     next : S -> Option(T)
    /// where S is the internal state (here, 'count') and T is the
    ↪   current value.
    fn next(&mut self) -> Option<Self::Item> {
        if self.count < self.max {
            let current = self.count;
            self.count += 1;
            Some(current)
        } else {
            None
        }
    }
}

fn main() {
    // Define two transformation functions to illustrate function
    ↪   composition.

    // f: Squares the input.
```

```rust
// This function represents a deferred computation (lazy
↪    evaluation), marked by f(x) ↓.
let f = |x: usize| {
    x * x
};

// g: Increments the input by one.
let g = |x: usize| {
    x + 1
};

// Compose f and g to form h where:
//      h(x) = g(f(x))
// This demonstrates fusion: combining two steps into one.
let h = |x: usize| {
    g(f(x))
};

// Create a custom iterator instance over a state space S using
↪    our Counter.
let counter = Counter::new(10);

// Build a lazy data pipeline using functional combinators:
//    1. Map: Applies the composed function h to each element,
//       corresponding to: map : (T -> U) x I -> I'
//    2. Filter: Selects only even values.
//    3. Fold: Aggregates the resulting numbers.
// The entire chain follows a cost model of approximately:
//       O( sum(C_i) ) for each iterator operation, with fusion
↪    minimizing overhead.
let pipeline_result: usize = counter
    .map(|x| {
        // Lazy evaluation: h(x) is computed on demand.
        h(x)
    })
    .filter(|&x| x % 2 == 0)
    .fold(0, |acc, x| acc + x);

println!("Result of iterator pipeline (sum of even h(x) values):
↪    {}", pipeline_result);

// Demonstrate early termination with the 'find' combinator:
// The evaluation remains lazy until a matching element is
↪    found.
let counter2 = Counter::new(20);
if let Some(value) = counter2
    .map(|x| h(x))
    .find(|&x| x % 2 == 0 && x > 50)
{
    println!("First even h(x) value greater than 50 found: {}",
↪    value);
} else {
    println!("No even h(x) value greater than 50 found.");
```

```
}

// In summary:
// - The iterator abstraction (next : S -> Option(T)) ensures
↪    stateful data processing.
// - Lazy evaluation (f(x) ↓) defers computations until
↪    required.
// - Functional combinators such as map and filter allow for
↪    elegant function composition,
//    e.g., h(x) = g(f(x)).
// - The overall performance of the lazy pipeline is bounded by
↪    O(C_i),
//    benefiting from fusion techniques that eliminate
↪    intermediate overhead.
}
```

Chapter 3

Pattern Matching Techniques for Complex Data Parsing

Conceptual Foundations of Pattern Matching

Pattern matching in Rust constitutes a rigorously defined mechanism for decomposing values of algebraic data types into their constituent components. This mechanism operates as a mapping from the domain of input values to a set of outcomes and is mathematically characterized by an abstract function

$$\mu : D \to E,$$

where D denotes the domain of input data and E represents the ensemble of possible decompositions. Within the paradigm of complex data parsing, pattern matching provides a disciplined approach to both the extraction and validation of substructures embedded within raw inputs. The inherent coupling between the structure of a value and its pattern ensures that the deconstruction process preserves semantic integrity while enforcing a comprehensive treatment of all possible configurations through exhaustive matching.

Structural Decomposition of Composite Data Types

Intricate data formats often embody nested and heterogeneous structures that require methodical disassembly to reveal their underlying components. The pattern matching constructs in Rust facilitate a deep structural decomposition wherein composite entities, represented as tuples, enums, or custom data types, are systematically partitioned. For example, an entity defined as

$$C = (d_1, d_2, \ldots, d_n)$$

can be processed by recursively applying matching rules to extract each individual component d_i. This recursive strategy allows for the validation and transformation of each element in a manner that reflects the hierarchical organization of the data. The layered application of pattern matching thereby ensures that every level of a composite structure is accurately decomposed and semantically verified.

Guard Expressions and Conditional Matching

Beyond structural decomposition, the pattern matching framework in Rust is augmented by the inclusion of guard expressions that impose additional conditional constraints on the matching process. A guard expression supplements a base pattern by introducing a logical predicate that must hold simultaneously with the structural match. Formally, if $P(x)$ denotes a base pattern that matches an element x, then an augmented match may be conceptualized as the compound condition

$$P'(x) = P(x) \wedge G(x),$$

where $G(x)$ represents the guard predicate. This dual mechanism of pattern matching with an accompanying condition permits the selective deconstruction of data only when conforming numerical or logical invariants are satisfied. The integration of guard conditions elevates the expressiveness of the matching construct, enabling the precise extraction of subcomponents while affirmatively enforcing domain-specific validation constraints.

Exhaustiveness, Type Inference, and Semantic Guarantees

A critical aspect of the pattern matching design is the principle of exhaustiveness, which mandates that every potential form of the input data is explicitly addressed by the matching construct. This exhaustive handling is verified statically, thereby guaranteeing that no variant of the input data remains unconsidered. The formal requirement for exhaustiveness can be expressed by the logical assertion

$$\forall x \in D, \ \exists p \in P \text{ such that } p(x) \text{ holds,}$$

with D representing the data domain and P denoting the set of all defined patterns. Additionally, Rust's powerful type inference system intertwines with the matching process to propagate constraints across patterns, ensuring that the deconstruction of data adheres strictly to defined type relations. Together, these mechanisms confer robust semantic guarantees, providing both compile-time correctness and enhanced safety in the decomposition and validation of complex data formats.

The Formal Algebra of Pattern Matching

The operational semantics of pattern matching in Rust can be abstracted into an algebraic framework reminiscent of constructs in category theory and functional programming. Each pattern can be regarded as a morphism that transforms an input from a given data type into a structured collection of components. When multiple patterns are composed sequentially, the composite effect is analogous to function composition. This composition is formally represented by

$$P_{\text{comp}}(x) = P_2(P_1(x)),$$

where the application of P_1 and P_2 successively effectuates a systematic deconstruction and validation of the input x. The associative properties of such compositions, along with the existence of identity patterns, establish an algebraic structure that underpins the reliability and expressiveness of Rust's pattern matching system. This formalism not only elucidates the conceptual underpinnings of data decomposition but also reinforces the intrinsic relationship between type-driven design and the operational integrity of complex data parsing processes.

Rust Code Snippet

```rust
//! This code snippet demonstrates key concepts from the chapter on
//!     Pattern Matching in Rust,
//! including the abstract mapping function  : D → E, structural
//!     decomposition (e.g. decomposing
//! composite data types), guard expressions with conditional
//!     matching, and the algebra of
//! pattern composition (P_comp(x) = P(P(x))). The example defines a
//!     simple data domain and
//! functions to illustrate these principles.

// Import the standard formatting module.
use std::fmt;

// Define an enum to represent various data types (Domain D).
#[derive(Debug)]
enum Data {
    Number(i32),
    Text(String),
    Composite(Vec<Data>),
}

// Implement Display for pretty-printing Data.
impl fmt::Display for Data {
    fn fmt(&self, f: &mut fmt::Formatter) -> fmt::Result {
        match self {
            Data::Number(x) => write!(f, "Number({})", x),
            Data::Text(s) => write!(f, "Text(\"{}\")", s),
            Data::Composite(vec) => {
                let parts: Vec<String> = vec.iter().map(|d|
                    format!("{}", d)).collect();
                write!(f, "Composite([{}])", parts.join(", "))
            }
        }
    }
}

// The function `mu` represents the abstract mapping  : D → E.
// Here, we map input data to a vector of strings representing the
//     decomposition (Ensemble E).
fn mu(data: Data) -> Option<Vec<String>> {
    match data {
        // Pattern matching with guard expressions:
        // For a positive number we output one message, and for
        //     non-positive, another.
        Data::Number(x) if x >= 0 => Some(vec![format!("Positive
            number: {}", x)]),
        Data::Number(x) => Some(vec![format!("Non-positive number:
            {}", x)]),
        // For textual data, check the length to categorize as long
        //     or short text.
```

```rust
            Data::Text(ref s) if s.len() > 5 => Some(vec![format!("Long
  ↪    text: \"{}\"", s)]),
            Data::Text(s) => Some(vec![format!("Short text: \"{}\"",
  ↪    s)]),
            // For composite data, recursively decompose each element.
            Data::Composite(vec) => {
                let mut results = Vec::new();
                for d in vec {
                    if let Some(mut res) = mu(d) {
                        results.append(&mut res);
                    }
                }
                Some(results)
            }
        }
    }
}


// Demonstrate the algebra of pattern matching via function
  ↪  composition:
// P: Extract a number from the data.
fn extract_number(data: Data) -> Option<i32> {
    match data {
        Data::Number(x) => Some(x),
        _ => None,
    }
}

// P: Square the extracted number.
fn square_number(x: i32) -> i32 {
    x * x
}

// Compose P and P to yield P_comp(x) = P(P(x)).
fn composed_function(data: Data) -> Option<i32> {
    extract_number(data).map(|num| square_number(num))
}

// Main function demonstrating various pattern matching scenarios.
fn main() {
    // Create sample data covering multiple cases:
    let number_positive = Data::Number(42);
    let number_negative = Data::Number(-7);
    let short_text = Data::Text(String::from("Rust"));
    let long_text = Data::Text(String::from("PatternMatching"));

    // Composite data demonstrates structural decomposition
    let composite_data = Data::Composite(vec![
        number_positive,
        short_text,
        Data::Composite(vec![
            number_negative,
            long_text,
        ]),
```

34

```
    ]);

    // Apply the mapping function mu : D → E.
    if let Some(decomposition) = mu(composite_data) {
        println!("Decomposition Result:");
        for line in decomposition {
            println!("  {}", line);
        }
    }

    // Demonstrate the composed function P_comp(x) = P(P(x)).
    let data_for_composition = Data::Number(8);
    if let Some(result) = composed_function(data_for_composition) {
        println!("Result of composed function (square of number):
        ↪  {}", result);
    } else {
        println!("No valid pattern matched for composition.");
    }
}
```

Chapter 4

Time Series Data Manipulation with Chrono Library

Representation of Temporal Data

Temporal data in computational systems is rigorously modeled as an ordered pair that encapsulates both calendar and clock components. Within the Chrono library, time-indexed values are encapsulated as entities that conform to precise algebraic and chronological invariants. At the most fundamental level, a timestamp is an element of the Cartesian product $D \times T$, where D represents the set of calendar dates and T denotes the continuum of time within a given day. Chrono distinguishes between types that carry timezone information and those that are devoid of any offset context. The former are formally defined as instances where a timestamp is rendered as $t = d + \delta$, with $d \in D$ and $\delta \in T$, further refined by an associated timezone function $Z : T \to Z$, while the latter, the naive representations, are unencumbered by such mappings. This bifurcation allows for a mathematically coherent treatment of time series data and underpins the subsequent operations of manipulation, formatting, and analysis.

Parsing and Formatting of Timestamps

The precise interpretation of temporal strings into structured data as well as the inverse process of rendering time objects into human-readable formats constitute a central theme in Chrono's functionality. Parsing is conceptualized as a morphism $\pi : S \to T$, whereby an element from the set of string representations S is mapped into a structured temporal object $t \in T$. Correspondingly, formatting is characterized by the mapping $\phi : T \to S$, ensuring that each temporal data point is transformed into a standardized textual representation. These operations are defined with adherence to strict syntactic and semantic rules. The robustness of these transformations lies in the invariant that a well-formulated parse followed by a subsequent format operation recovers the original structure, i.e., $\phi\big(\pi(s)\big) = s$ for all valid strings $s \in S$, up to intrinsic locale-specific variations. Such mathematical precision is crucial when dealing with heterogeneous time formats that often appear in time series datasets.

Temporal Computations and Arithmetic

Central to time series analysis is the capacity to perform arithmetic on timestamps and durations. In a formalized setting, let $t \in T$ denote a timestamp and let Δt represent a duration, an element of the additive group $(D, +)$. The Chrono library facilitates operations such that the summation $t + \Delta t$ yields another valid timestamp in T. Similarly, the difference between two timestamps, expressed as $t_2 - t_1$, is defined within the space of durations and obeys the properties of a metric space. The algebraic framework imposed by Chrono ensures that operations such as scalar multiplication of durations and the computation of successive intervals $\Delta t_i = t_{i+1} - t_i$ are mathematically sound. Furthermore, these computations implicitly assume that the associativity and commutativity of addition hold, modulo adjustments necessitated by phenomena such as leap seconds and other calendrical irregularities that are inherent in real-world temporal data.

Handling Time Zones and Daylight Saving Transitions

The integration of timezone semantics into temporal data manipulation introduces a layer of complexity that is meticulously addressed by Chrono. Timezone-aware timestamps are represented as elements that are modified by an offset function Z, formally expressed as $t_Z = t + Z$, where Z is typically a function mapping a given t to a fixed offset value. The mapping between different timezone contexts can be characterized by a transformation $f : T \rightarrow T'$, ensuring that the intrinsic temporal order is preserved under conversion. Special consideration is accorded to the discontinuities introduced by daylight saving transitions, wherein the conventional linear progression of time is interrupted by sudden shifts. The library's design rigorously enforces the invariance of temporal computations by embedding corrective measures that realign time values with canonical representations. Such measures guarantee that the relational properties between timestamps continue to hold even across periods of non-linear temporal transitions.

Structural Analysis of Temporal Patterns

The manipulation and arithmetic of time-indexed data pave the way for an in-depth structural analysis of temporal patterns. Given a sequence of timestamps $\{t_i\}_{i=0}^n$, the computation of inter-event intervals $\Delta t_i = t_{i+1} - t_i$ yields a secondary sequence that is essential for detecting periodicity and trend shifts within the dataset. The statistical distribution of these intervals can be described by a function $\psi : \{\Delta t_i\} \rightarrow \mathbb{R}$, where analytical techniques are applied to quantify variance, skewness, and other moments of the distribution. Additionally, the segmentation of time series data into subintervals based on identifiable temporal features is facilitated by rigorous operations that partition the full dataset into aggregates that conform to predefined criteria. Such partitioning is often formalized as the operation $\Omega : T^n \rightarrow \bigcup_{k=1}^m T^{n_k}$, where each subset T^{n_k} is subject to further analysis. The Chrono library provides the structural scaffolding for these operations, ensuring that every transformation and aggregation maintains consistency within the defined temporal algebra.

Rust Code Snippet

```rust
use chrono::{DateTime, NaiveDateTime, Duration, Utc, Local,
    FixedOffset, TimeZone};

/// Parse a naive datetime from an ISO formatted string (without
    timezone).
fn parse_naive(datetime_str: &str) -> NaiveDateTime {
    NaiveDateTime::parse_from_str(datetime_str, "%Y-%m-%dT%H:%M:%S")
        .expect("Failed to parse naive datetime")
}

/// Format a naive datetime into a human-readable string.
fn format_naive(dt: NaiveDateTime) -> String {
    dt.format("%Y-%m-%d %H:%M:%S").to_string()
}

/// Convert a naive datetime to a timezone-aware datetime using a
    fixed offset.
/// This represents the mapping t = d +  with a fixed offset.
fn timezone_from_naive(dt: NaiveDateTime, offset_secs: i32) ->
    DateTime<FixedOffset> {
    let fixed_offset = FixedOffset::east(offset_secs);
    fixed_offset.from_local_datetime(&dt)
        .unwrap_or_else(|_| panic!("Invalid datetime with given
            offset"))
}

/// Computes the intervals (differences) between consecutive
    timestamps.
fn compute_intervals(timestamps: &Vec<DateTime<FixedOffset>>) ->
    Vec<Duration> {
    timestamps.windows(2)
        .map(|w| w[1] - w[0])
        .collect()
}

/// Calculates the average duration (in seconds) from a slice of
    durations.
fn average_duration(intervals: &[Duration]) -> f64 {
    let total_seconds: i64 = intervals.iter().map(|d|
        d.num_seconds()).sum();
    total_seconds as f64 / intervals.len() as f64
}

fn main() {
    // Parsing and formatting of temporal data.
    let datetime_str = "2023-10-12T14:30:00";
    let naive_dt = parse_naive(datetime_str);
    println!("Parsed NaiveDateTime: {}", naive_dt);
    let formatted_naive = format_naive(naive_dt);
    println!("Formatted NaiveDateTime: {}", formatted_naive);
```

```rust
// Handling timezone: Convert naive datetime to timezone-aware
↪ datetime.
let dt_with_tz = timezone_from_naive(naive_dt, 3600); // +1 hour
↪ offset
println!("Timezone-aware DateTime: {}", dt_with_tz);

// Temporal computations: Add a duration to a timestamp.
let added_duration = Duration::days(1) + Duration::hours(2); //
↪ 1 day and 2 hours later
let new_dt = dt_with_tz + added_duration;
println!("New DateTime after adding duration: {}", new_dt);

// Difference between two timestamps (t2 - t1).
let diff = new_dt - dt_with_tz;
println!("Difference in seconds: {}", diff.num_seconds());

// Demonstration of morphism in parsing and formatting:
// Parse an RFC3339 formatted string then format it back.
let rfc3339_str = "2023-10-12T13:30:00+01:00";
let dt_rfc3339 = DateTime::parse_from_rfc3339(rfc3339_str)
    .expect("Failed to parse RFC3339 datetime");
let formatted_rfc3339 = dt_rfc3339.to_rfc3339();
println!("RFC3339 parsed and formatted: {}", formatted_rfc3339);

// Structural Analysis of Temporal Patterns:
// Create a vector of timestamps at 15-minute intervals.
let mut timestamps = Vec::new();
for i in 0..5 {
    // Each element is dt_with_tz incremented by 15 minutes.
    timestamps.push(dt_with_tz + Duration::minutes(15 * i));
}

println!("\nTimestamps for Structural Analysis:");
for (i, ts) in timestamps.iter().enumerate() {
    println!("Timestamp {}: {}", i, ts);
}

// Compute the inter-event intervals t_i = t_{i+1} - t_i.
let intervals = compute_intervals(&timestamps);
for (i, interval) in intervals.iter().enumerate() {
    println!("Interval {} (in seconds): {}", i,
    ↪ interval.num_seconds());
}

// Calculate and output the average interval duration.
let avg_interval = average_duration(&intervals);
println!("Average interval duration (in seconds): {:.2}",
↪ avg_interval);

// Handling local datetime to illustrate timezone effects (e.g.,
↪ DST considerations).
let local_dt: DateTime<Local> = Local::now();
```

```
    println!("\nCurrent local datetime (system timezone): {}",
    ↪  local_dt);
}
```

Chapter 5

Numerical Arrays and Computation with ndarray

Representation of Multidimensional Arrays

Multidimensional arrays serve as a fundamental data structure for efficiently representing and manipulating numerical data in high-dimensional spaces. In a rigorous mathematical framework, an array is considered as an element of $\mathbb{R}^{d_1 \times d_2 \times \cdots \times d_n}$, where each d_i denotes the size along the ith dimension. The ndarray library implements these arrays with a layout that supports contiguous memory storage and constant-time access to array elements. Such a representation allows for direct correspondence between the logical dimensions of the data and the physical memory layout, thereby facilitating optimized indexing and traversal in performance-critical applications.

The abstraction encapsulated by the library is designed to capture both static and dynamic array shapes. By maintaining explicit shape metadata as an array of integers, the library ensures that operations such as reshaping, transposition, and dimensionality reduction are systematically well-defined. The invariants governing these arrays are expressed in terms of the array's dimensionality and shape, which are central to guaranteeing the consistency of mathematical operations performed on these data structures.

Element-wise Operations and Broadcasting

Element-wise operations lie at the core of numerical computation on arrays, whereby a given function is applied simultaneously to each element in parallel within a high-dimensional construct. Given two arrays $A, B \in \mathbb{R}^{m \times n}$, an element-wise addition operation corresponds to defining a new array C such that

$$C_{ij} = A_{ij} + B_{ij} \quad \forall\, i, j.$$

Such operations inherently respect the algebraic properties of the underlying scalar field, including associativity and distributivity.

Furthermore, the concept of broadcasting extends these operations to arrays of differing shapes, provided that the dimensions are compatible under well-established rules. For example, if one considers an array $A \in \mathbb{R}^{m \times n}$ and a vector $v \in \mathbb{R}^n$, broadcasting allows the vector to be implicitly expanded into an array $\tilde{v} \in \mathbb{R}^{m \times n}$, such that the operation

$$C_{ij} = A_{ij} + \tilde{v}_{ij}$$

remains valid. This mechanism eliminates the need for explicit replication of data, thereby optimizing both memory usage and computational efficiency.

Array Slicing and Subsetting

Slicing provides the capability to generate views or subsets of the original array without necessitating a deep copy of the underlying data. Formally, given an array $T \in \mathbb{R}^{m \times n}$, a slicing operation is defined by selecting index intervals along each dimension, which yields a sub-array $T' \in \mathbb{R}^{p \times q}$ where

$$T'_{ij} = T_{(i+i_0)(j+j_0)}$$

for appropriate offsets i_0 and j_0 and dimensions satisfying $p \leq m$ and $q \leq n$. This operation preserves the affine structure of the original array's index space and facilitates efficient partitioning of data for localized analysis.

The design of slicing routines emphasizes the need to maintain a lightweight interface, ensuring that the sub-array remains a view into the original data. Such an approach permits modifications and computations on the slice to be reflected in the parent array when necessary and minimizes overhead during repetitive slicing operations in large-scale numerical workflows.

Advanced Numerical Computations

In the realm of advanced numerical computations, the ndarray library enables the execution of sophisticated algorithms that are central to data analysis. Many operations, including reductions, aggregations, and transformations, are defined intrinsically over the array's dimensions. For instance, reduction operators may compute a scalar summary by aggregating over one or more axes:

$$s = \text{reduce}(T, \oplus, \text{axis})$$

where $\oplus$ denotes a binary associative operator. Such operators are critical in tasks ranging from statistical analysis to machine learning model evaluation.

Moreover, the library supports efficient element-wise transformation functions that can be composed with traditional linear algebra operations. The mathematical framework underlying these transformations is solidified by properties of linear maps and tensor contractions, thereby ensuring that composite operations retain both logical rigor and computational efficacy. In particular, the ability to combine slicing, broadcasting, and reduction into a single computational pipeline epitomizes the strength of the ndarray approach; the resulting formulations may be expressed as

$$R_{ij} = f\Big(\{T_{k\ell} \mid k \in I, \ell \in J\}\Big)$$

where I and J denote index subsets defined by prior slicing operations and f represents a function that encapsulates both an element-wise transformation and an aggregation over the specified dimensions.

The methodology is engineered to exploit modern hardware architectures by aligning memory access patterns with the intrinsic layout of multidimensional arrays. This correspondence permits advanced numerical computations to operate at high throughput, a necessity given the scale and complexity of contemporary data analysis tasks in computational science.

Rust Code Snippet

```rust
/// This Rust program demonstrates the usage of ndarray for
↪  numerical arrays and computations.
/// It covers the representation of multidimensional arrays,
↪  element-wise operations with broadcasting,
/// array slicing, and advanced numerical reductions.

use ndarray::prelude::*;

fn main() {
    // ==============================================
    // Representation of Multidimensional Arrays
    // ==============================================
    // Create a 3x4 array with contiguous memory layout.
    // This corresponds to an element in ^(3×4).
    let a = Array::from_shape_vec((3, 4), (1..=12).map(|x| x as
↪  f64).collect())
        .expect("Failed to create array 'a'");
    println!("Original array a:\n{:?}\n", a);

    // ==============================================
    // Element-wise Operations and Broadcasting
    // ==============================================
    // Element-wise addition:
    // Given two arrays A and B, we compute C such that C[i][j] =
↪  A[i][j] + B[i][j]
    let b = Array::from_elem((3, 4), 0.5);
    let c = &a + &b;
    println!("Element-wise addition (a + b):\n{:?}\n", c);

    // Broadcasting:
    // Add a 1D vector (of size 4) to each row of array 'a'.
    // The vector v is broadcasted to match the shape of 'a'.
    let v = array![10.0, 20.0, 30.0, 40.0];
    let d = &a + &v; // Broadcasting happens automatically since the
↪  vector shape is compatible.
    println!("Broadcasting addition (a + v):\n{:?}\n", d);

    // ==============================================
    // Array Slicing and Subsetting
    // ==============================================
    // Extract a sub-array (view) from 'a' without making a deep
↪  copy.
    // For instance, selecting rows 1..3 and columns 1..4:
    let slice = a.slice(s![1.., 1..]);
    println!("Sliced view of a (rows 1..3, columns 1..4):\n{:?}\n",
↪  slice);

    // ==============================================
    // Advanced Numerical Computations
    // ==============================================
```

```rust
    // Reduction: Compute a summary statistic such as row-wise sums.
    // For an array A   ^(3×4), the row sums correspond to summing
    ↪   over axis 1.
    let row_sums = a.sum_axis(Axis(1));
    println!("Row sums of a:\n{:?}\n", row_sums);

    // Combining slicing, broadcasting, and reduction:
    // 1. Slice sub-array: first 2 rows and first 3 columns.
    // 2. Broadcast addition of a constant (5.0) to each element.
    // 3. Compute the column sums of the modified sub-array.
    let sub_slice = a.slice(s![..2, ..3]);
    let sub_added = &sub_slice + 5.0; // Broadcasting the scalar 5.0
    ↪   to sub_slice.
    let col_sums = sub_added.sum_axis(Axis(0));
    println!("Column sums of (first 2 rows, first 3 columns after
    ↪   adding 5.0):\n{:?}", col_sums);
}
```

Chapter 6

Matrix Algebra using nalgebra

Matrix Representation and Fundamental Operations

A matrix $A \in \mathbb{R}^{m \times n}$ constitutes a primary construct in linear algebra, encapsulating a collection of elements arranged in m rows and n columns. The nalgebra crate adopts a representation optimized for contiguous memory storage and rapid indexed access, ensuring that the inherent mathematical structure is preserved while achieving high computational performance. Fundamental operations on matrices include addition, scalar multiplication, and the more elaborate matrix multiplication. For two matrices $A, B \in \mathbb{R}^{m \times n}$, the addition is defined element-wise by

$$(A + B)_{ij} = A_{ij} + B_{ij} \quad \forall i, j.$$

Scalar multiplication involves an element-wise product with a scalar $\lambda \in \mathbb{R}$, yielding

$$(\lambda A)_{ij} = \lambda \cdot A_{ij}.$$

Matrix multiplication, central to many algorithms, is rigorously defined by

$$(AB)_{ij} = \sum_{k=1}^{p} A_{ik} B_{kj},$$

requiring that the inner dimensions are compatible. The adherence to these algebraic definitions guarantees that properties such as associativity, distributivity, and the existence of identity elements are maintained, which is critical for both theoretical analyses and practical implementations.

Matrix Decompositions and Factorization Techniques

The decomposition of matrices into simpler, structured components is a cornerstone method for solving complex numerical problems and assessing the stability of computational algorithms. Among the various factorization techniques implemented within nalgebra, the LU, QR, and singular value decompositions offer robust avenues for matrix analysis. In the LU decomposition, a matrix A is factored as

$$A = LU,$$

where L is a lower triangular matrix and U is an upper triangular matrix. This factorization underpins efficient algorithms for solving linear systems as it facilitates forward and backward substitution. The QR decomposition expresses a matrix as

$$A = QR,$$

with Q being an orthogonal matrix and R an upper triangular matrix, rendering it particularly effective in the context of least-squares approximations. Furthermore, the singular value decomposition (SVD) decomposes A as

$$A = U\Sigma V^T,$$

where U and V are orthogonal matrices and Σ is a diagonal matrix whose entries are the singular values of A. Such decompositions are indispensable in mitigating numerical instability and reveal intrinsic properties of matrices that are exploited in a variety of data science algorithms.

Linear Transformations and Their Applications in Data Science

Linear transformations provide a rigorous framework for mapping between vector spaces, encapsulated by matrices that perform operations on vectors. Given a matrix $T \in \mathbb{R}^{m \times n}$ representing a linear transformation, the action on a vector $x \in \mathbb{R}^n$ is described succinctly by the product

$$y = Tx,$$

where $y \in \mathbb{R}^m$. These transformations preserve the structure of vector spaces, as encapsulated by the properties of additivity and homogeneity. In the context of data science, linear transformations are central to tasks such as dimensionality reduction, where they facilitate the projection of data into lower-dimensional subspaces without sacrificing critical information. The capacity to compute eigenvalues, eigenvectors, and to perform basis changes is fundamental for techniques such as principal component analysis and manifold learning. The nalgebra crate provides an efficient and precise environment for executing these operations, ensuring that linear transformations are implemented in a manner that is both mathematically rigorous and computationally optimized.

Rust Code Snippet

```
// Cargo.toml:
// [dependencies]
// nalgebra = "0.31"

extern crate nalgebra as na;
use na::{DMatrix, Vector3};

fn main() {
    // Matrix Representation and Fundamental Operations

    // Define two 3x3 matrices A and B using row-major order
    let data_a = vec![
        1.0, 2.0, 3.0,
        4.0, 5.0, 6.0,
        7.0, 8.0, 9.0,
    ];
    let data_b = vec![
        9.0, 8.0, 7.0,
        6.0, 5.0, 4.0,
        3.0, 2.0, 1.0,
    ];
    let a = DMatrix::from_row_slice(3, 3, &data_a);
    let b = DMatrix::from_row_slice(3, 3, &data_b);

    println!("Matrix A:\n{}", a);
    println!("Matrix B:\n{}", b);
```

49

```rust
// Matrix Addition: C = A + B
// According to (A + B)_{ij} = A_{ij} + B_{ij}
let c = &a + &b;
println!("\nMatrix Addition (A + B):\n{}", c);

// Scalar Multiplication: D = lambda * A
// Each element of A is scaled: (lambda * A)_{ij} = lambda *
↪  A_{ij}
let lambda = 2.0;
let d = a.scale(lambda);
println!("\nScalar Multiplication (2.0 * A):\n{}", d);

// Matrix Multiplication: E = A * B
// (AB)_{ij} = sum_{k} A_{ik} * B_{kj}
let e = &a * &b;
println!("\nMatrix Multiplication (A * B):\n{}", e);

// Linear Transformation Example:
// Let x be a 3-dimensional vector and compute y = A * x.
let x = Vector3::new(1.0, 2.0, 3.0);
let y = a * x;
println!("\nLinear Transformation (y = A * x):\n{}", y);

// Matrix Decompositions and Factorization Techniques

// LU Decomposition: A = L * U
// L is lower triangular and U is upper triangular.
let lu = a.lu();
let l = lu.l();
let u = lu.u();
println!("\nLU Decomposition of A:");
println!("Lower Triangular Matrix L:\n{}", l);
println!("Upper Triangular Matrix U:\n{}", u);

// QR Decomposition: A = Q * R
// Q is an orthogonal matrix and R is upper triangular.
let qr = a.clone().qr();
let q = qr.q();
let r = qr.r();
println!("\nQR Decomposition of A:");
println!("Orthogonal Matrix Q:\n{}", q);
println!("Upper Triangular Matrix R:\n{}", r);

// Singular Value Decomposition (SVD): A = U *  * V^T
// Here, U and V are orthogonal matrices and  is a diagonal
↪  matrix
// containing the singular values of A.
let svd = a.svd(true, true);
let u_svd = svd.u.unwrap();
let singular_values = svd.singular_values;
let vt_svd = svd.v_t.unwrap();
println!("\nSingular Value Decomposition (SVD) of A:");
println!("Matrix U:\n{}", u_svd);
```

```
    println!("Singular Values ():\n{}", singular_values);
    println!("Matrix V^T:\n{}", vt_svd);
}
```

Chapter 7

DataFrame Operations with Polars

Data Acquisition and Schema Inference

Tabular data is ingested and structured through well-defined abstractions that encapsulate the inherent complexity of external data sources. Polars provides a unified interface for loading data from various formats such as comma-separated values, binary storage structures like Parquet, and other delimited text representations. In this context, the schema of the dataset is either inferred automatically or declared explicitly by the implementer, resulting in a DataFrame whose columns are strongly typed according to Rust's rigorous type system. The process of schema inference involves the systematic examination of sample data to determine the most appropriate data type for each column, such that a matrix $X \in \mathbb{R}^{n \times m}$ is represented with structural consistency and minimal conversion overhead. Such mechanisms provide the groundwork for subsequent manipulation and enable the safe, compile-time verification of operations that are integral to efficient data handling.

Core DataFrame Manipulation Techniques

At the heart of the Polars library lies a robust framework for DataFrame manipulation, characterized by its columnar data storage and optimized memory management. The internal representation adheres to a design that prioritizes contiguous memory allocation, thereby accelerating access to data and enhancing cache utilization. Fundamental operations such as column-wise transformation, row filtering based on predicate expressions, and the reordering and renaming of columns are performed in a manner that supports both mutability and immutability in accordance with Rust's ownership semantics. The design facilitates complex operations including the resolution of missing data, the application of user-defined transformation functions, and the execution of vectorized computations that leverage parallel processing. The rigor in these operations is maintained by adherence to functional programming principles, whereby expressions are composed in a chainable paradigm that promotes both expressiveness and performance.

Advanced Querying and Aggregative Methodologies

Polars extends the DataFrame abstraction by incorporating a sophisticated query engine that enables the formulation of complex, SQL-like operations over tabular data. Within this architecture, operations such as grouping, filtering, and aggregated computations are articulated through an expressive syntax that abstracts the underlying execution details. Advanced querying processes utilize lazy evaluation techniques to defer computation until the full transformation pipeline has been specified; this results in an optimized execution plan that minimizes redundant data passes and conserves computational resources. Aggregative methods, including statistical summarization, pivot operations, and multi-level aggregation, are underpinned by algorithms that exploit parallelism and vectorized computation, ensuring that the computation of metrics such as means, variances, and frequency counts occur with minimal overhead. The formulation of these expressions, as well as their subsequent optimization, is achieved through a combination of declarative constructs and algebraic rewrites, which guarantee that the final physical execution plan is both efficient and scalable across large datasets.

Intrinsic Performance Characteristics of Polars

Performance optimization represents a fundamental design pillar of the Polars library. The implementation leverages the inherent strengths of Rust, including zero-cost abstractions and compile-time immutability guarantees, to provide deterministic and high-throughput data processing capabilities. The columnar storage model employed by Polars is specifically designed to exploit cache locality and to facilitate Single Instruction, Multiple Data (SIMD) operations. Such architectural choices reduce computational overhead and enhance the efficiency of operations that are otherwise computationally intensive. Moreover, the lazy evaluation paradigm ensures that only the essential computations are executed, thereby reducing unnecessary memory transfers and redundant aggregation steps. The resulting performance characteristics enable the processing of tabular data with high expressiveness, ensuring that operations remain both fast and semantically clear even when operating upon large-scale datasets.

Rust Code Snippet

```rust
use std::error::Error;
use polars::prelude::*;
use polars::lazy::dsl::*;
use ndarray::prelude::*;

fn main() -> Result<(), Box<dyn Error>> {
    // ==============================
    // Data Acquisition and Schema Inference
    // ==============================
    // Load CSV data from a file into a DataFrame, letting Polars
    // ↪ automatically infer the schema
    // based on a sample of the data. The resulting DataFrame will
    // ↪ have a strongly-typed schema.
    let file_path = "data.csv"; // Path to your CSV data file
    let df = CsvReader::from_path(file_path)?
        .infer_schema(Some(100)) // Use first 100 rows to infer
        // ↪ schema
        .has_header(true)
        .finish()?;

    println!("Inferred Schema:\n{}", df.schema());

    // ==============================
```

```
// Core DataFrame Manipulation Techniques
// ==============================
// Perform a series of operations including:
// - Renaming an existing column from "old_column" to
↪    "new_column".
// - Filtering rows based on a predicate (only rows where
↪    new_column > 10 are kept).
// These operations are defined using a lazy API that composes
↪    transformations.
let df = df.lazy()
    .with_column(col("old_column").alias("new_column"))
    .filter(col("new_column").gt(lit(10)))
    .collect()?;

println!("DataFrame after filtering and transformation:\n{}",
↪    df);

// ==============================
// Advanced Querying and Aggregative Methodologies
// ==============================
// Group the data by a categorical column 'category' and compute
↪    the mean
// of the 'new_column' for each group. Advanced aggregation is
↪    achieved by
// deferring computation through lazy evaluation.
let agg_df = df.lazy()
    .groupby(vec![col("category")])

    ↪    .agg(vec![col("new_column").mean().alias("mean_new_column")])
    .collect()?;

println!("Aggregated DataFrame:\n{}", agg_df);

// ==============================
// Intrinsic Performance Characteristics and Equation Simulation
// ==============================
// In this section we simulate the representation of a numerical
↪    matrix X  ^(n × m)
// by extracting two numerical features ('feature1' and
↪    'feature2') from the DataFrame,
// centering the data, and computing their covariance. The
↪    covariance is computed using:
//
//                         cov = (X_centered · X_centered) /
↪    (n - 1)
//
// For two feature vectors, the covariance simplifies to the dot
↪    product of their centered forms.

// Select the numeric features for covariance computation.
let df_cov = df.lazy()
    .select(vec![col("feature1"), col("feature2")])
    .collect()?;
```

```rust
// Extract the columns as vectors of f64 values.
let feature1 = df_cov.column("feature1")?
    .f64()?
    .into_no_null_iter()
    .collect::<Vec<f64>>();
let feature2 = df_cov.column("feature2")?
    .f64()?
    .into_no_null_iter()
    .collect::<Vec<f64>>();

// Ensure that data exists.
let n = feature1.len();
if n == 0 {
    return Err("No data available for covariance
    ↪   computation.".into());
}

// Convert the vectors to ndarray arrays.
let arr1 = Array::from(feature1);
let arr2 = Array::from(feature2);

// Compute the means () for each feature.
let mean1 = arr1.mean().unwrap();
let mean2 = arr2.mean().unwrap();

// Center the data by subtracting the mean from each observation
↪   (X_centered = X - ).
let centered1 = arr1 - mean1;
let centered2 = arr2 - mean2;

// Compute the covariance using the dot product of the centered
↪   vectors.
let covariance = centered1.dot(&centered2) / (n as f64 - 1.0);

println!("Covariance between feature1 and feature2: {}",
↪   covariance);

Ok(())
}
```

Chapter 8

Grouping, Joins, and Aggregations in Polars

Fundamentals of Grouping Operations in High-Dimensional Data

In the realm of large-scale data processing, grouping operations serve as an essential mechanism for partitioning datasets into distinct segments based on one or more categorical attributes. Within the Polars framework, the grouping process is formalized through a series of functional transformations, each of which applies a deterministic mapping from the original dataset to a collection of sub-dataframes. This methodology capitalizes on Polars' columnar storage model, where memory locality and contiguous allocation undergird rapid access to clustered data. The operational semantics rely on the mathematical abstraction of equivalence relations, in which elements are partitioned such that for a given grouping key function g, any two data entries x_i and x_j satisfy $g(x_i) = g(x_j)$ if, and only if, they belong to the same group. The design of these operations emphasizes both the expressiveness and verifiability ensured by the strong static typing of Rust, and builds upon chainable expressions that not only enhance readability but also simplify the debugging of intermediate states during the transformation pipeline.

Join Operations for Integrative Data Analysis

Join operations, by their very nature, embody the task of integrating multiple data sources into a unified representation. In Polars, joins are implemented as composable, functional transformations that blend the tabular data structures based on specified key columns. The underlying algebra is analogous to relational database management systems, where various forms of join—such as inner joins, left joins, and outer joins—are employed to produce a resultant dataset that preserves the referential integrity of the input collections. Each join operation can be viewed as a function $J : D_1 \times D_2 \to D_3$, where D_1, D_2, and D_3 represent the input and output dataframes, respectively. The chainable nature of these operations permits the sequential composition of multiple joins, thereby facilitating the construction of intricate data amalgamation schemes. In addition, the lazy evaluation strategy inherent in Polars defers the actual computation until the final stage of execution; this unique design feature allows for the optimization of join sequences by eliminating redundant data passes and consolidating intermediate transformations.

Aggregation Methodologies and Chainable Functional Transformations

Aggregation operations in Polars encapsulate the transformation of raw data segments into succinct statistical summaries. The procedure involves first grouping the dataset into meaningful clusters and then applying a suite of aggregative functions—such as sum, mean, count, and variance—to extract quantitative descriptors from each group. These functions are applied in a chainable manner, which promotes the development of declarative queries often reminiscent of algebraic expressions in functional programming. Specifically, if a dataframe is partitioned into groups defined by a key function g, the aggregation process can be formulated as a composite mapping $\mathcal{A}(x) = f(g(x))$, where the function f encapsulates the computation of statistical measures over each group. This formulation not only guarantees type safety but also supports the fusion of multiple aggregative transformations without sacrificing computational efficiency. Polars further enhances this paradigm by applying lazy evaluation to delay the execution of the aggregate functions until the transformation pipeline has been fully specified, thereby ensuring that the computational overhead is minimized through parallelized and vectorized operations across contiguous data blocks.

Chainable and Functional Transformation Pipelines

The central design philosophy behind Polars is the extensive use of chainable, functional transformation pipelines. Each operation in the pipeline adheres to a narrow interface, returning a new dataframe instance with a refined schema. This immutable model, reflective of functional programming principles, assures that the original data remains unaltered through every transformation step. The intermediate state of the dataset can be algebraically manipulated and recombined to form increasingly complex expressions, thus enabling both modularity and reusability. The transformation pipeline may be perceived as the composition of a series of functions, where the output of one function serves as the input to the next; mathematically, this can be written as $T = f_n \circ f_{n-1} \circ \cdots \circ f_1$. The composability intrinsic to such a design imbues the framework with the ability to optimize performance through operation fusion and elimination of superfluous data passes. With each operator defined in a declarative manner, the chainable approach not only clarifies the data flow but also leverages the compile-time guarantees provided by Rust, ensuring that any violation of type consistency or transformation logic is detected prior to runtime.

Rust Code Snippet

```
use polars::prelude::*;
use std::error::Error;

// Custom aggregation function to compute variance for each group.
// This computes variance using the formula: var(x) = E(x^2) -
↪  (E(x))^2.
fn custom_variance(s: Series) -> PolarsResult<Series> {
    // Convert the series to a slice of f64 values.
    let arr = s.f64()?;
    // Filter out any null values and collect the data into a Vec.
    let vals: Vec<f64> = arr.into_iter().filter_map(|v|
    ↪  v).collect();
```

```rust
    // If the group is empty, return 0.0 as variance.
    if vals.is_empty() {
        return Ok(Series::new(s.name(), vec![0.0]));
    }
    let count = vals.len() as f64;
    // Calculate mean: E(x)
    let mean = vals.iter().sum::<f64>() / count;
    // Calculate mean of the squares: E(x^2)
    let mean_sq = vals.iter().map(|x| x * x).sum::<f64>() / count;
    // Variance: E(x^2) - (E(x))^2
    let variance = mean_sq - mean * mean;
    Ok(Series::new(s.name(), vec![variance]))
}

fn main() -> PolarsResult<()> {
    // Create a sample DataFrame df1 with columns: id, group, and
    ↪  value.
    let df1 = df![
        "id" => &[1, 2, 3, 4, 5, 6],
        "group" => &["A", "A", "B", "B", "C", "C"],
        "value" => &[10.0, 20.0, 30.0, 40.0, 50.0, 60.0]
    ]?;

    // Create another DataFrame df2 with columns: id and category.
    let df2 = df![
        "id" => &[1, 2, 3, 7],
        "category" => &["X", "Y", "Z", "W"]
    ]?;

    // -----------------------------------------------------------------
    // Grouping Operations:
    // Group df1 by the "group" column and compute the sum and mean
    // of the "value" column. This represents the transformation:
    //    A(x) = [sum(value), mean(value)]
    // for each group defined by the key function g(x) = group.
    // -----------------------------------------------------------------
    let grouped = df1
        .lazy()
        .groupby([col("group")])
        .agg([
            col("value").sum().alias("sum_value"),
            col("value").mean().alias("mean_value")
        ])
        .collect()?;
    println!("Grouped DataFrame:\n{}", grouped);

    // -----------------------------------------------------------------
    // Join Operations:
    // Perform an inner join between df1 and df2 on the "id" column.
    // This implements the join function: J: D1 × D2 → D3, ensuring
    // referential integrity while merging related records.
    // -----------------------------------------------------------------
    let joined = df1
```

```rust
        .lazy()
        .join(df2.lazy(), col("id"), col("id"), JoinType::Inner)
        .collect()?;
    println!("Joined DataFrame:\n{}", joined);

    // ----------------------------------------------------------------
    // Chainable Transformation Pipeline:
    // Construct a pipeline that filters rows, groups data,
    // aggregates using sum, and sorts the result.
    // This sequential composition is expressed as:
    //    T = f  f  f  f
    // where each function represents one transformation step.
    // ----------------------------------------------------------------
    let pipeline = df1
        .lazy()
        .filter(col("value").gt(lit(20.0)))   // f: Filter rows where
        ↪ value > 20
        .groupby([col("group")])              // f: Group by
        ↪ "group"
        .agg([
            col("value").sum().alias("filtered_sum") // f: Aggregate
            ↪ with sum
        ])
        .sort("filtered_sum", false)          // f: Sort by the
        ↪ aggregated sum in descending order
        .collect()?;
    println!("Pipeline Result:\n{}", pipeline);

    // ----------------------------------------------------------------
    // Custom Aggregation Using Functional Transformation:
    // Apply a custom variance function on "value" for each group.
    // This operation embodies the composite mapping A(x) = f(g(x)),
    // where g(x) partitions the data by "group" and f(x) computes
    // the statistical variance using the formula: var = E(x²) -
    ↪ (E(x))².
    // ----------------------------------------------------------------
    let custom_agg = df1
        .lazy()
        .groupby([col("group")])
        .agg([
            col("value")
                .apply(custom_variance,
                ↪ GetOutput::from_type(DataType::Float64))
                .alias("variance")
        ])
        .collect()?;
    println!("Custom Aggregation (Variance) Result:\n{}",
    ↪ custom_agg);

    Ok(())
}
```

Chapter 9

Missing Data Handling and Imputation Patterns

Conceptual Underpinnings and Missing Data Paradigms

In any dataset D composed of n observations across m attributes, each datum is susceptible to being absent from the complete record. Formally, an indicator function $I : D \rightarrow \{0, 1\}$ can be defined such that for each element $x \in D$, $I(x) = 1$ if the observation is present and $I(x) = 0$ if it is absent. The mechanisms behind missing data are typically classified into three distinct paradigms: missing completely at random (MCAR), missing at random (MAR), and missing not at random (MNAR). The MCAR mechanism implies that the probability of a datum being missing is independent of both observed and unobserved data. In contrast, under MAR the missingness is conditionally independent of unobserved data given the observed data, and MNAR denotes that the mechanism of missingness is related to the unobserved data itself. The theoretical clarity provided by these classifications is fundamental, as each paradigm imposes particular constraints and implications on the subsequent algorithmic treatment and imputation of missing entries.

Detection and Quantification of Missingness

The detection of missing data involves the systematic characterization of the presence and pattern of absent values within D. A central metric in this analysis is the missingness rate, defined as

$$r = \frac{N_{\text{missing}}}{N_{\text{total}}},$$

where N_{missing} denotes the total number of missing entries and N_{total} represents the aggregate number of entries in the dataset. The process of detection is enriched by the deployment of various algorithmic techniques that perform a meticulous scan over individual columns and rows, identifying specific instances where data does not adhere to the expected schema. The outcome of this detection phase is the construction of a missingness pattern matrix that encapsulates the distribution of missing values and, in higher-dimensional settings, aids in revealing any systematic interdependencies or correlations between the absence in certain attributes and observed patterns in others.

Algorithmic Strategies for Handling Incomplete Data

The handling of incomplete data is governed by algorithmic strategies that seek to preserve the integrity and representativity of the original dataset. One elementary strategy involves the excision of rows or columns that exhibit a high proportion of missing entries; however, such an approach may induce bias if the missingness is not uniformly distributed. More sophisticated techniques incorporate the use of weighting schemes or iterative procedures that explicitly account for the uncertainty introduced by missingness. In an algorithmic context, methods such as iterative proportional fitting or model-based approaches aim to minimize a cost function

$$J = \sum_{i=1}^{n} \delta(x_i, \hat{x}_i),$$

where δ measures the discrepancy between the observed value x_i and its estimated counterpart $\hat{x}_i$, aggregated over the dataset. Such optimization formulations ensure that the handling mechanism reduces the error introduced by the absence of data while maintaining compliance with the inherent statistical properties of the dataset. Furthermore, these strategies are embedded within transformation pipelines that enforce immutability and type safety, thereby solidifying the computational guarantees provided by the implementation environment.

Imputation Techniques with Statistical Rigor

Imputation constitutes a pivotal stage where missing entries are replaced with estimated values that are statistically coherent with the observed data distribution. The simplest form of imputation, known as constant imputation, replaces missing values with a scalar representative of central tendency, such as the mean or median. More refined techniques, however, leverage the dependency structure across multiple features. In such approaches, the imputed value $\hat{x}$ for a missing entry is estimated by a function f that maps the vector of observed features $\mathbf{x}_{obs}$ to the imputed estimate, formally written as

$$\hat{x} = f(\mathbf{x}_{obs}).$$

Regression imputation strategies and nearest-neighbor approaches estimate $\hat{x}$ by modeling the relationships between the missing attribute and other covariates in D, thereby minimizing the residual error between the predicted and the true, albeit unobserved, values. Multiple imputation extends this framework by generating several imputed datasets, each reflecting a possible realization from the posterior distribution of the missing data, and by subsequently combining the results of analyses performed on these datasets to propagate the uncertainty due to imputation. Such statistical modeling ensures that the variance and bias originally present in the comprehensive data are tightly controlled, thus safeguarding data integrity during downstream analytical processes.

Rust Code Snippet

```
use std::fmt;

// A data structure representing a dataset row with multiple
↪   features.
```

```rust
// Each feature is wrapped in an Option to denote its presence
↳ (Some) or absence (None).
#[derive(Clone)]
struct DataRow {
    features: Vec<Option<f64>>,
}

impl fmt::Debug for DataRow {
    fn fmt(&self, f: &mut fmt::Formatter<'_>) -> fmt::Result {
        // Print row features in a user-friendly format.
        let feat_str: Vec<String> = self.features.iter()
            .map(|v| match v {
                Some(val) => format!("{:.2}", val),
                None      => "None".to_string(),
            })
            .collect();
        write!(f, "[{}]", feat_str.join(", "))
    }
}

/// Indicator function I(x):
/// Returns 1 if the data is present (Some) and 0 if it is missing
↳ (None).
fn missing_indicator(value: Option<f64>) -> u8 {
    match value {
        Some(_) => 1,
        None    => 0,
    }
}

/// Calculate the missingness rate r defined as:
/// r = N_missing / N_total,
/// where N_missing is the count of missing entries
/// and N_total is the total number of entries in the dataset.
fn missingness_rate(dataset: &[DataRow]) -> f64 {
    let mut missing_count = 0;
    let mut total_count = 0;
    for row in dataset.iter() {
        for &feature in row.features.iter() {
            total_count += 1;
            if feature.is_none() {
                missing_count += 1;
            }
        }
    }
    missing_count as f64 / total_count as f64
}

/// Compute column-wise means from the dataset ignoring missing
↳ values.
/// Returns a vector containing the mean for each column.
fn compute_column_means(dataset: &[DataRow]) -> Vec<f64> {
    if dataset.is_empty() {
```

```rust
        return vec![];
    }
    let num_cols = dataset[0].features.len();
    let mut sums = vec![0.0; num_cols];
    let mut counts = vec![0; num_cols];
    for row in dataset.iter() {
        for (i, feature) in row.features.iter().enumerate() {
            if let Some(val) = feature {
                sums[i] += val;
                counts[i] += 1;
            }
        }
    }
    sums.into_iter().zip(counts.into_iter())
        .map(|(sum, count)| if count > 0 { sum / count as f64 } else
        ↪  { 0.0 })
        .collect()
}


/// Mean imputation strategy (a form of constant imputation)
↪  replaces missing values
/// with the column mean computed from observed values. The imputed
↪  value  is given by:
///     = f(x_obs)
/// where f returns the column average.
fn mean_imputation(dataset: &[DataRow]) -> Vec<DataRow> {
    let column_means = compute_column_means(dataset);
    let mut imputed_data = Vec::with_capacity(dataset.len());

    for row in dataset.iter() {
        let new_features = row.features.iter().enumerate().map(|(i,
        ↪  feat)| {
            match feat {
                Some(val) => Some(*val),
                None => Some(column_means[i]),
            }
        }).collect();
        imputed_data.push(DataRow { features: new_features });
    }

    imputed_data
}


/// Cost function J defined as:
///     J =  (x, x)
/// where  measures the discrepancy between the observed value x and
↪  the imputed value x.
/// Here,  is implemented as the absolute difference.
/// Only non-missing original entries are evaluated.
fn cost_function(original: &[DataRow], imputed: &[DataRow]) -> f64 {
    let mut cost = 0.0;
    for (row_orig, row_imputed) in
        ↪  original.iter().zip(imputed.iter()) {
```

66

```rust
        for (orig, imputed_val) in
        ↪   row_orig.features.iter().zip(row_imputed.features.iter())
        ↪   {
            // Skip instances originally missing; these are the
            ↪   imputed entries.
            if orig.is_none() {
                continue;
            }
            if let (Some(x), Some(x_hat)) = (orig, imputed_val) {
                cost += (x - x_hat).abs();
            }
        }
    }
    cost
}

fn main() {
    // Sample dataset where each DataRow represents an observation
    ↪   with 3 features.
    // None represents a missing value.
    let dataset = vec![
        DataRow { features: vec![Some(1.0), None,        Some(3.0)]
        ↪   },
        DataRow { features: vec![None,      Some(2.0),   Some(3.5)]
        ↪   },
        DataRow { features: vec![Some(1.2), Some(2.2),   None      ]
        ↪   },
    ];

    // ------------------------------
    // Detection and Quantification
    // ------------------------------
    let rate = missingness_rate(&dataset);
    println!("Missingness rate r = {:.2}", rate);

    // ------------------------------
    // Imputation using Mean Imputation
    // ------------------------------
    // This technique replaces missing data with the column mean,
    // reflecting the equation: x = f(x_obs) = (sum of observed) /
    ↪   (count of observed)
    let imputed_dataset = mean_imputation(&dataset);

    println!("\nOriginal Dataset:");
    for row in &dataset {
        println!("{:?}", row);
    }

    println!("\nImputed Dataset (Mean Imputation):");
    for row in &imputed_dataset {
        println!("{:?}", row);
    }
```

```rust
    // -----------------------------
    // Compute the Cost Function J
    // -----------------------------
    // This value quantifies the discrepancy between the observed
    // ↪  and imputed values.
    let cost = cost_function(&dataset, &imputed_dataset);
    println!("\nCost Function J = {:.2}", cost);
}
```

Chapter 10

Data Transformation Pipelines in Rust

Architectural Foundations of Data Pipelines

A data transformation pipeline may be formally characterized as a sequence of composable functions that operate on a dataset D to yield a processed output D'. In this paradigm, the raw data undergoes a series of systematic transformations, each encoded as a function T_i such that the overall pipeline is represented by the composition

$$T = T_n \circ T_{n-1} \circ \cdots \circ T_1.$$

This construction emphasizes modularity and reusability while leveraging the strong static guarantees provided by Rust's type system. The pipeline's structure is architected in a manner that every transformation is isolated, deterministic, and amenable to formal reasoning about its correctness. Each stage of processing acts upon immutable data streams, ensuring that the integrity of D is maintained throughout the transformation process.

Iterator Combinators and Functional Composition

Iterators in Rust are endowed with a rich set of combinators that facilitate a functional style of composition. By deferring computations until a terminal operation is invoked, these iterators support lazy evaluation and contribute to the efficiency of the overall pipeline. When each transformation T_i is implemented as an iterator adapter, multiple operations such as mapping, filtering, or folding can be chained together seamlessly. This chaining is mathematically analogous to function composition, where the output of one iterator serves directly as the input to the next. The transformation obtained by iterating over the elements of D is therefore not only efficient but also expressed in a form that mirrors mathematical clarity, as every intermediate transformation adheres to the principle of compositionality.

Integrating Closures for Custom Transformations

Closures are employed within these pipelines to encapsulate bespoke transformation logic while retaining the capability to capture the ambient lexical scope. Serving as first-class functions, closures empower developers to define inline transformations of data elements without the overhead of function declarations. When a closure f is applied to an element x, it may produce a transformed element $\phi(x)$, and such operations can be composed in the form

$$\phi(x) = (f \circ g)(x),$$

where both f and g are closures that capture specific computational patterns. The integration of closures provides a powerful abstraction for parameterizing transformations and for embedding domain-specific logic directly into the data processing pipeline. This method of composition ensures that the transformation from raw data to refined outputs is both expressive and succinct.

Properties and Verification of Pipeline Composition

The design of data transformation pipelines in Rust is underpinned by properties that facilitate both reliability and correctness. The immutable nature of data within each iterator stage ensures that the transformations are free of side effects, a property that is crucial for formal verification. Associativity in function composition, expressed as

$$(h \circ g) \circ f = h \circ (g \circ f),$$

70

allows for the reordering of operations without altering the resultant data, provided that each function adheres to pure functional semantics. Furthermore, the static type system used in Rust enforces that each adapter in the pipeline accepts and returns data types that are mutually compatible, obviating the need for runtime type checks. This rigorous verification mechanism not only simplifies reasoning about pipeline behavior but also enhances the overall robustness of data preprocessing workflows.

Data Preprocessing Techniques within Transformation Pipelines

In the preprocessing phase of analytical tasks, raw data from heterogeneous sources is subjected to a series of normalization and filtering operations before it can be utilized in rigorous analysis. Transformation pipelines are architected to implement operations such as outlier removal, normalization, and type conversion, each of which is represented as a composable function. Formally, if f_i denotes a preprocessing function applied to an element $x \in D$, then the pipeline transforms the dataset by applying a sequence

$$x' = f_n(f_{n-1}(\cdots f_1(x) \cdots)),$$

where x' represents a sanitized and well-structured datum. Such a treatment guarantees that the data prepared for downstream analysis retains the semantic properties necessary for effective modeling. The careful orchestration of these transformations ensures that the pipeline performs not only as an efficient computational mechanism but also as a rigorous method for data curation in complex analytical contexts.

Rust Code Snippet

```
//! This Rust example demonstrates the construction of a data
↪    transformation pipeline
//! using functional composition, iterator combinators, and
↪    closures.
//! It encapsulates key mathematical representations such as:
//!
//! 1. Pipeline Composition: T = T_n   T_{n-1}   ...   T_1
//! 2. Closure-based transformation: (x) = (f   g)(x)
//! 3. Associativity of function composition: (h   g)   f = h   (g   f)
```

71

```rust
//! 4. Data preprocessing: x' = f_n(f_{n-1}(... f_1(x) ...))
//!
//! The example below defines a generic compose function to enable
//! function composition,
//! constructs a pipeline that filters a dataset, applies composed
//! transformations, and
//! demonstrates associativity of function composition as well as a
//! simple preprocessing chain.

/// A generic function to compose two functions.
/// Returns a new function that applies g first then f.
/// That is, compose(f, g)(x) = f(g(x))
fn compose<F, G, A, B, C>(f: F, g: G) -> impl Fn(A) -> C
where
    F: Fn(B) -> C,
    G: Fn(A) -> B,
{
    move |x: A| f(g(x))
}

fn main() {
    // Example 1: Simple Data Transformation Pipeline
    // Dataset: vector of integers.
    let data: Vec<i32> = vec![1, 2, 3, 4, 5, 6, 7, 8, 9, 10];

    // Transformation T1: Filter to retain only odd numbers.
    let is_odd = |x: i32| x % 2 != 0;

    // Transformation T2: Multiply each element by 2.
    let multiply_by_two = |x: i32| x * 2;

    // Transformation T3: Add 3 to each element.
    let add_three = |x: i32| x + 3;

    // Compose transformations T2 and T3:
    // This composition represents: (x) =
    // add_three(multiply_by_two(x))
    let transformation = compose(add_three, multiply_by_two);

    // Build the pipeline using iterator combinators:
    // Pipeline steps: Filter (T1) -> Apply composed transformation
    // (T3  T2)
    let pipeline_result: Vec<i32> = data.into_iter()
        .filter(is_odd)
        .map(transformation)
        .collect();

    println!("Result from pipeline (filter -> transform): {:?}",
        pipeline_result);

    // Example 2: Demonstrating Associativity of Function
    // Composition
    // Let f = add_three, g = multiply_by_two, and h = subtract_one.
```

72

```rust
    // Associativity property: (h ∘ g) ∘ f = h ∘ (g ∘ f)
    let subtract_one = |x: i32| x - 1;

    // First composition: (h ∘ g) ∘ f
    let first_composition = compose(compose(subtract_one,
    ↪  multiply_by_two), add_three);
    // Second composition: h ∘ (g ∘ f)
    let second_composition = compose(subtract_one,
    ↪  compose(multiply_by_two, add_three));

    // Test with a sample value
    let test_value = 5;
    let result1 = first_composition(test_value);
    let result2 = second_composition(test_value);

    println!("Associativity test with input {}: first = {}, second =
    ↪  {}",
            test_value, result1, result2);

    // Example 3: Data Preprocessing Pipeline for Normalization and
    ↪  Transformation
    // Raw dataset: vector of floating-point numbers representing
    ↪  raw measurements.
    let raw_data: Vec<f64> = vec![16.0, 25.0, 36.0, 49.0, 64.0];

    // Preprocessing function f1: Normalize the data to [0,1] by
    ↪  dividing by the maximum value.
    let normalize = |x: f64| x / 64.0;

    // Preprocessing function f2: Add a constant offset.
    let add_offset = |x: f64| x + 0.1;

    // Preprocessing function f3: Apply square root transformation.
    let sqrt_transform = |x: f64| x.sqrt();

    // Compose preprocessing functions: x' =
    ↪  sqrt_transform(add_offset(normalize(x)))
    let preprocessing = compose(sqrt_transform, compose(add_offset,
    ↪  normalize));

    let preprocessed_data: Vec<f64> = raw_data.into_iter()
        .map(preprocessing)
        .collect();

    println!("Preprocessed data: {:?}", preprocessed_data);
}
```

Chapter 11

Higher-Order Functions in Data Wrangling

Conceptual Framework of Higher-Order Functions in Data Manipulation

In the realm of data wrangling, higher-order functions serve as pivotal constructs that operate on functions as first-class entities. A higher-order function is formally defined as any function H for which either

$$H : (A \to B) \to C$$

or

$$H : A \to (B \to C),$$

where A, B, and C denote arbitrary types. This abstract formulation enables the encapsulation of transformation logic in such a manner that the functions being manipulated retain the properties of closure and composability. The primary significance of higher-order functions lies in their ability to abstract common transformation patterns, thereby fostering a separation between the mechanistic iteration over data and the logic that governs the individual data transformations.

Encapsulation of Transformation Logic in Data Wrangling

Data wrangling inherently involves operations such as filtering, mapping, and aggregating, each of which can be expressed as an elementary function. When these operations are encapsulated within higher-order functions, the underlying transformation logic is decoupled from the data flow mechanism. In rigorous mathematical terms, when a transformation function $f : X \to Y$ is passed as an argument to a higher-order function H, the resultant composition

$$H(f) : X \to Z$$

effectively encapsulates domain-specific logic while maintaining a clear boundary between procedural iteration and transformation. This encapsulation not only permits the reuse of transformation logic across varied contexts but also guarantees that such logic remains modular and amenable to formal reasoning. The immutability and purity of these functions, when strictly adhered to, result in a system where data is progressively transformed with an assurance of operational correctness.

Promotion of Code Reusability Through Functional Abstractions

The adoption of higher-order functions in complex data manipulation tasks engenders a significant enhancement in code reusability. By parameterizing operations and extracting common patterns into generic higher-order constructs, a coherent abstraction layer is established. For instance, consider a scenario where several disparate data cleaning operations share the underlying mechanism of transforming data elements. Instead of rewriting discrete loops or transformation pathways, a higher-order function T can be defined such that for any elementary transformation function f, the composite operation

$$T(f) = f \circ identity$$

yields a readily reusable transformation module. This abstraction not only simplifies the overall design but also allows for the composition of more complex transformations through sequential application of such higher-order functions. The mathematical clarity

secured by the operation of function composition, typically epito-
mized by the relation

$$(f \circ g)(x) = f(g(x)),$$

further corroborates the robustness of the reusable components,
ensuring that each transformation stage remains independent and
yet cohesively integrated within the broader pipeline.

Clarity in Complex Data Wrangling Routines

Complex data wrangling routines often necessitate the clear delineation of transformation stages, each with its own semantic purpose. Higher-order functions contribute substantially to this clarity by expressing transformation logic in a manner that aligns with
mathematical principles. When a sequence of transformations is
composed, the overall operation can be succinctly formalized as

$$T = T_n \circ T_{n-1} \circ \cdots \circ T_1,$$

where each T_i represents a fundamental transformation function.
This notation not only succinctly captures the modularity of the
individual operations but also affirms the associative property intrinsic to function composition:

$$(h \circ g) \circ f = h \circ (g \circ f).$$

Such formal properties permit reordering and refactoring of transformation logic without compromising the correctness of the data
processing pipeline. The transparency afforded by this approach
enables a rigorous verification of the compositional behavior, thereby
simplifying both the development and the maintenance processes
in sophisticated data wrangling tasks.

Rust Code Snippet

```rust
use std::fmt::Debug;

// Identity function: returns the same value.
fn identity<T>(x: T) -> T {
    x
```

```rust
}

// Compose two functions f and g to produce a new function h such
↪    that h(x) = f(g(x)).
// This mirrors the mathematical formulation of composition:
// (f ∘ g)(x) = f(g(x))
fn compose<A, B, C, F, G>(f: F, g: G) -> impl Fn(A) -> C
where
    F: Fn(B) -> C + Copy,
    G: Fn(A) -> B + Copy,
{
    move |x: A| f(g(x))
}


// A higher-order function that applies a transformation function to
↪    each element in the data slice.
fn apply_transformation<T, U, F>(data: &[T], transform: F) -> Vec<U>
where
    F: Fn(&T) -> U,
{
    data.iter().map(transform).collect()
}


// Example elementary transformation functions operating on &i32.
fn add_three(x: &i32) -> i32 {
    x + 3
}

fn double(x: &i32) -> i32 {
    x * 2
}

fn main() {
    // Define a sample dataset.
    let data = vec![1, 2, 3, 4, 5];

    // Compose two transformation functions using reference-based
    ↪    functions.
    // This composition represents the operation: add_three ∘ double,
    ↪    i.e.,
    // for any input x: composed_fn(x) = add_three(double(x)).
    let composed_fn = |x: &i32| add_three(&double(x));

    // Alternatively, to use our compose function, we define
    ↪    versions that own their arguments.
    let double_owned = |x: i32| x * 2;
    let add_three_owned = |x: i32| x + 3;
    let composed_owned = compose(add_three_owned, double_owned);

    // Apply the composed function to the dataset using our
    ↪    higher-order apply_transformation.
    let transformed_data: Vec<i32> = apply_transformation(&data,
    ↪    composed_fn);
```

77

```rust
    println!("Transformed data using reference functions: {:?}",
    ↪  transformed_data);

    // Alternatively, apply the composed_owned function to transform
    ↪  data using iterator mapping.
    let transformed_owned: Vec<i32> =
    ↪  data.clone().into_iter().map(composed_owned).collect();
    println!("Transformed data using owned functions: {:?}",
    ↪  transformed_owned);

    // Demonstrate the function composition property:
    // Evaluate f(g(x)) versus our composed function applied to x.
    let x = 10;
    let result1 = add_three_owned(double_owned(x));
    let result2 = composed_owned(x);
    println!("Result of add_three_owned(double_owned({})): {}", x,
    ↪  result1);
    println!("Result of composed_owned({}): {}", x, result2);

    // Demonstrate associativity of function composition:
    // Let f(x) = x + 3, g(x) = 2 * x, and h(x) = x - 1.
    let f = |x: i32| x + 3;
    let g = |x: i32| x * 2;
    let h = |x: i32| x - 1;

    // Compose functions in two different groupings to validate the
    ↪  associative property:
    // (f  (g  h))(x) should equal ((f  g)  h)(x).
    let comp1 = compose(f, compose(g, h)); // f(g(h(x)))
    let comp2 = compose(compose(f, g), h); // f(g(h(x)))

    let value = 5;
    let assoc1 = comp1(value);
    let assoc2 = comp2(value);

    println!("Associativity test with value {}: comp1 = {}", value,
    ↪  assoc1);
    println!("Associativity test with value {}: comp2 = {}", value,
    ↪  assoc2);

    // Further demonstration: using identity in higher-order
    ↪  function transformation.
    // Define a transformation that applies the identity function
    ↪  after a given transformation.
    let transform_with_identity = |f: fn(i32) -> i32, x: i32|
    ↪  f(identity(x));
    let test_value = 7;
    let transformed_value = transform_with_identity(double_owned,
    ↪  test_value);
    println!("Transformed value applying identity: {}",
    ↪  transformed_value);
}
```

Chapter 12

Statistical Metrics: Summaries and Distributions

Measures of Central Tendency

Consider a dataset represented by the collection $X = \{x_1, x_2, \ldots, x_n\}$. The arithmetic mean, denoted by $\bar{x}$, serves as a primary quantifier for the central location of the data and is computed via the expression

$$\bar{x} = \frac{1}{n} \sum_{i=1}^{n} x_i.$$

In contrast, the median constitutes an alternative measure of central tendency that emphasizes the inherent order within X. Its computation requires sorting the elements of X and selecting the middle value (or the average of the two central values when n is even). Such measures capture differing aspects of centrality, with the mean being sensitive to extreme values while the median tends to exhibit robustness in the presence of outliers.

Measures of Dispersion

Quantifying the spread of data is as essential as determining its central location. The variance, symbolized by σ^2, quantifies the average squared deviation of the data points from the computed mean, thus providing an index of dispersion. Formally, the variance is defined as

$$\sigma^2 = \frac{1}{n} \sum_{i=1}^{n} (x_i - \bar{x})^2.$$

Closely related is the standard deviation, σ, which is obtained by taking the square root of σ^2. In practice, when the dataset represents a sample from a larger population, an unbiased estimation of the population variance is often achieved through an adjusted formulation known as Bessel's correction:

$$s^2 = \frac{1}{n-1} \sum_{i=1}^{n} (x_i - \bar{x})^2.$$

These metrics collectively confer a quantitative narrative about the degree of heterogeneity present within the dataset.

Empirical Distribution Construction

A further dimension of statistical analysis involves the construction of empirical distributions, which encapsulate the frequency characteristics of the data elements. To accomplish this, the domain of X is partitioned into a series of non-overlapping intervals $\{I_1, I_2, \ldots, I_k\}$. For each interval I_j, the frequency count is defined by

$$f_j = |\{x_i \in X : x_i \in I_j\}|,$$

with the corresponding relative frequency given by

$$p_j = \frac{f_j}{n}.$$

This normalized approach ensures that

$$\sum_{j=1}^{k} p_j = 1.$$

The empirical distribution thus obtained provides a discrete approximation to the underlying probability density or mass function. Subsequent refinements may involve smoothing techniques, yet the fundamental methodology derives from the systematic quantification of frequency across the segmented domain.

Synthesis of Quantitative Summaries and Distributional Analysis

Integration of the aforementioned metrics yields a multidimensional statistical characterization of the dataset X. The arithmetic mean $\bar{x}$ and the median collectively offer insights into central location, while the variance σ^2 and its derivative metrics quantify data dispersion. The construction of an empirical distribution via calculated relative frequencies p_j augments these summary measures by delineating the spread of data across specified intervals. This synthesis permits a comprehensive portrayal of the dataset, encapsulating centrality, variability, and frequency characteristics in a unified framework. The quantitative analysis rests on these interrelated components, each contributing uniquely to the overarching description of the dataset's structural properties.

Rust Code Snippet

```
use std::cmp::Ordering;

/// Compute the arithmetic mean.
/// Formula: mean = (1/n) * (x_i)
fn mean(data: &Vec<f64>) -> f64 {
    let sum: f64 = data.iter().sum();
    sum / data.len() as f64
}

/// Compute the median of the dataset.
/// For an even number of observations, it returns the average of
↪   the two middle elements.
fn median(data: &mut Vec<f64>) -> f64 {
    data.sort_by(|a, b|
    ↪   a.partial_cmp(b).unwrap_or(Ordering::Equal));
    let n = data.len();
    if n % 2 == 0 {
        (data[n / 2 - 1] + data[n / 2]) / 2.0
    } else {
        data[n / 2]
    }
}

/// Compute the population variance.
/// Formula: variance = (1/n) * ((x_i - mean)^2)
fn variance(data: &Vec<f64>, m: f64) -> f64 {
    let n = data.len() as f64;
    data.iter().map(|&x| (x - m).powi(2)).sum::<f64>() / n
```

```rust
}

/// Compute the sample variance using Bessel's correction.
/// Formula: sample_variance = (1/(n-1)) * ((x_i - mean)^2)
fn sample_variance(data: &Vec<f64>, m: f64) -> f64 {
    let n = data.len() as f64;
    if data.len() > 1 {
        data.iter().map(|&x| (x - m).powi(2)).sum::<f64>() / (n -
        ↪    1.0)
    } else {
        0.0
    }
}

/// Compute the empirical distribution of the dataset.
/// The dataset is partitioned into non-overlapping intervals, and
/// ↪    for each interval [low, high),
/// the count of elements and relative frequency (p = count/total
/// ↪    elements) is calculated.
fn empirical_distribution(data: &Vec<f64>, intervals: &Vec<(f64,
↪    f64)>) -> Vec<(f64, f64, u32, f64)> {
    let n = data.len() as f64;
    let mut distribution = Vec::new();
    for &(low, high) in intervals {
        let count = data.iter().filter(|&&x| x >= low && x <
        ↪    high).count() as u32;
        let rel_freq = count as f64 / n;
        distribution.push((low, high, count, rel_freq));
    }
    distribution
}

fn main() {
    // Sample dataset X
    let data: Vec<f64> = vec![12.0, 15.0, 14.0, 10.0, 18.0, 20.0,
    ↪    17.0, 16.0, 13.0, 11.0];

    // Calculate the arithmetic mean.
    let mean_val = mean(&data);

    // Calculate the median (a clone is used since median() sorts
    ↪    the vector).
    let mut data_clone = data.clone();
    let median_val = median(&mut data_clone);

    // Calculate the population variance and its standard deviation.
    let pop_variance = variance(&data, mean_val);
    let pop_std = pop_variance.sqrt();

    // Calculate the sample variance (with Bessel's correction) and
    ↪    its standard deviation.
    let sam_variance = sample_variance(&data, mean_val);
    let sam_std = sam_variance.sqrt();
```

```
    println!("Dataset: {:?}", data);
    println!("Arithmetic Mean: {:.2}", mean_val);
    println!("Median: {:.2}", median_val);
    println!("Population Variance: {:.2}", pop_variance);
    println!("Population Standard Deviation: {:.2}", pop_std);
    println!("Sample Variance (Bessel's Correction): {:.2}",
    ↪   sam_variance);
    println!("Sample Standard Deviation: {:.2}", sam_std);

    // Define intervals for constructing the empirical distribution.
    // Example intervals: [10,12), [12,14), [14,16), [16,18),
    ↪   [18,20), [20,22)
    let intervals = vec![
        (10.0, 12.0),
        (12.0, 14.0),
        (14.0, 16.0),
        (16.0, 18.0),
        (18.0, 20.0),
        (20.0, 22.0)
    ];

    // Compute the empirical distribution over the defined
    ↪   intervals.
    let distribution = empirical_distribution(&data, &intervals);

    println!("\nEmpirical Distribution:");
    for (low, high, count, rel_freq) in distribution {
        println!(
            "Interval [{:.1}, {:.1}): Count = {}, Relative Frequency
            ↪   = {:.2}",
            low, high, count, rel_freq
        );
    }
}
```

Chapter 13

Correlation and Covariance Computation

Mathematical Foundations

Let X and Y be two quantitative variables for which finite first and second moments exist. The joint behavior of these variables is characterized by the covariance, a measure that quantifies the extent to which the variables vary in tandem. The theoretical definition of covariance is given by

$$\mathrm{Cov}(X, Y) = E\big[(X - E[X])(Y - E[Y])\big],$$

where $E[\cdot]$ denotes the expectation operator and $E[X]$, $E[Y]$ are the means of X and Y, respectively. In practice, when a finite sample of n paired observations $\{(x_1, y_1), (x_2, y_2), \ldots, (x_n, y_n)\}$ is considered, the unbiased estimator for covariance is commonly formulated as

$$s_{XY} = \frac{1}{n-1} \sum_{i=1}^{n} (x_i - \bar{x})(y_i - \bar{y}),$$

where $\bar{x}$ and $\bar{y}$ denote the sample means of X and Y. This estimator provides a robust measure of the overall linear relationship between the two variables.

Covariance Computation

The computation of covariance involves a sequential process that first determines the central tendency of each variable and subsequently quantifies the joint deviations. Notably, the variance of a single variable is a special case of covariance, as

$$\text{Var}(X) = \text{Cov}(X, X).$$

The covariance s_{XY} reflects the degree of joint variability: a positive value indicates that deviations of X and Y from their respective means tend to share the same sign, whereas a negative value suggests that the deviations are inversely related. A covariance value of zero, under appropriate conditions, implies that no linear relationship exists between the variables, albeit without precluding nonlinear dependencies. The sensitivity of covariance to the scales of X and Y necessitates careful interpretation in applied settings.

Correlation Coefficient Computation

To achieve a unitless measure that facilitates straightforward interpretation, the correlation coefficient is introduced by normalizing the covariance with the standard deviations of the constituent variables. The Pearson correlation coefficient, denoted by r, is defined as

$$r = \frac{\text{Cov}(X, Y)}{\sigma_X \sigma_Y},$$

where $\sigma_X = \sqrt{\text{Var}(X)}$ and $\sigma_Y = \sqrt{\text{Var}(Y)}$ represent the standard deviations of X and Y, respectively. By construction, the correlation coefficient is constrained within the interval $[-1, 1]$, with extremes of 1 and -1 signifying perfect linear association—either positive or negative, respectively—and a value near zero indicating the absence of linear correlation. This normalization mitigates the influence of the variables' scales, thereby rendering r a fundamental statistic in the analysis of linear dependence.

Covariance Matrix in Multivariate Analysis

In scenarios involving more than two variables, the covariance structure is encapsulated in a matrix framework. For a collection of p

variables $\{X_1, X_2, \ldots, X_p\}$, the covariance matrix $\Sigma \in \mathbb{R}^{p \times p}$ is defined by

$$\Sigma_{ij} = \text{Cov}(X_i, X_j)$$

for $i, j = 1, 2, \ldots, p$. The diagonal elements Σ_{ii} represent the variances of the respective variables, while the off-diagonal elements capture the pairwise covariances. The properties of symmetry and positive semi-definiteness inherent to Σ enable its use in a variety of multivariate statistical techniques, including eigen decomposition and factor analysis. The covariance matrix thus serves as a cornerstone for quantifying linear interdependencies and for subsequent dimensionality reduction methods in high-dimensional settings.

Numerical Stability and Computational Considerations

The practical computation of covariance and correlation coefficients in finite-precision arithmetic demands careful algorithmic design to circumvent numerical instability. A direct implementation based on the formula

$$\text{Cov}(X, Y) = E[XY] - E[X]E[Y]$$

can be susceptible to significant round-off errors, especially when the sample means are large relative to the variability in the data. Strategies to enhance numerical stability include employing a two-pass algorithm, wherein the sample means are computed in the first pass and the deviations summed in a subsequent pass. Furthermore, reordering computations to reduce the subtraction of nearly equal quantities and utilizing compensated summation techniques offer additional safeguards against floating-point inaccuracies. Such considerations are critical in environments handling large-scale data, ensuring that the computed covariance matrices and correlation coefficients faithfully reflect the true underlying relationships.

Rust Code Snippet

```rust
/// Compute the mean of a slice of f64 values.
/// Implements the equation: mean = (1/n) * x_i
fn mean(data: &[f64]) -> f64 {
```

```rust
    let sum: f64 = data.iter().sum();
    sum / data.len() as f64
}

/// Compute the variance of a dataset using a two-pass algorithm
/// for enhanced numerical stability. The variance is computed as:
/// variance = (1/(n-1)) * (x_i - mean)^2
fn variance(data: &[f64]) -> f64 {
    let n = data.len();
    if n < 2 {
        panic!("At least two data points are required to compute
        ↪   variance.");
    }
    let avg = mean(data);
    let sum_sq_diff: f64 = data.iter().map(|&value| {
        let diff = value - avg;
        diff * diff
    }).sum();
    sum_sq_diff / (n as f64 - 1.0)
}

/// Compute the covariance between two datasets x and y using the
/// two-pass method for numerical stability:
/// covariance = (1/(n-1)) * [(x_i - mean_x)*(y_i - mean_y)]
fn covariance(x: &[f64], y: &[f64]) -> f64 {
    let n = x.len();
    if n != y.len() {
        panic!("The two data slices must have the same length.");
    }
    if n < 2 {
        panic!("At least two paired observations are required to
        ↪   compute covariance.");
    }
    let mean_x = mean(x);
    let mean_y = mean(y);
    let cov: f64 = (0..n)
        .map(|i| (x[i] - mean_x) * (y[i] - mean_y))
        .sum();
    cov / (n as f64 - 1.0)
}

/// Compute the Pearson correlation coefficient between two datasets
/// ↪   x and y.
/// The formula is:
/// r = Cov(x,y) / (_x * _y)
fn correlation(x: &[f64], y: &[f64]) -> f64 {
    let cov = covariance(x, y);
    let std_x = variance(x).sqrt();
    let std_y = variance(y).sqrt();
    cov / (std_x * std_y)
}

/// Compute the covariance matrix for multiple variables.
```

87

```rust
/// Each variable is represented as a slice of f64 values, and the
↪   matrix is defined as:
/// [i][j] = Cov(variable_i, variable_j)
fn covariance_matrix(data: &[&[f64]]) -> Vec<Vec<f64>> {
    let p = data.len();
    if p == 0 {
        return vec![];
    }
    let n = data[0].len();
    // Ensure all variables have the same number of observations.
    for var in data {
        if var.len() != n {
            panic!("All variables must have the same number of
↪           observations.");
        }
    }
    let mut matrix = vec![vec![0.0; p]; p];
    for i in 0..p {
        for j in i..p {
            let cov_ij = covariance(data[i], data[j]);
            matrix[i][j] = cov_ij;
            matrix[j][i] = cov_ij; // Covariance matrix is
↪           symmetric.
        }
    }
    matrix
}

/// Helper function to print a matrix with formatted output.
fn print_matrix(matrix: &[Vec<f64>]) {
    for row in matrix {
        for val in row {
            print!("{:.4}\t", val);
        }
        println!();
    }
}

fn main() {
    // Example usage: Univariate computations for two quantitative
↪   variables.
    let x = vec![2.0, 4.0, 6.0, 8.0, 10.0];
    let y = vec![1.0, 3.0, 5.0, 7.0, 9.0];

    println!("--- Univariate Data Analysis ---");
    println!("Mean of x: {:.4}", mean(&x));
    println!("Mean of y: {:.4}", mean(&y));
    println!("Variance of x: {:.4}", variance(&x));
    println!("Variance of y: {:.4}", variance(&y));
    println!("Covariance of x and y: {:.4}", covariance(&x, &y));
    println!("Pearson Correlation between x and y: {:.4}",
↪       correlation(&x, &y));
```

```rust
    // Example usage: Multivariate analysis via covariance matrix.
    // Each variable is represented as a slice of f64.
    let var1 = vec![1.0, 2.0, 3.0, 4.0, 5.0];
    let var2 = vec![2.0, 4.0, 6.0, 8.0, 10.0];
    let var3 = vec![5.0, 4.0, 3.0, 2.0, 1.0];

    // Grouping the variables for covariance matrix computation.
    let data = vec![&var1[..], &var2[..], &var3[..]];

    println!("\n--- Covariance Matrix for Multivariate Data ---");
    let cov_matrix = covariance_matrix(&data);
    print_matrix(&cov_matrix);
}
```

Chapter 14

Probabilistic Models and Distributions

Mathematical Foundations of Probability Models

Within the domain of probabilistic modeling, a rigorous mathematical framework provides the basis for defining random variables, probability density functions, and cumulative distribution functions. A random variable is formalized as a measurable function from a sample space into the real numbers, where each outcome is assigned a probability via a measure. For continuous variables, the probability density function $f(x)$ satisfies

$$\int_{-\infty}^{\infty} f(x)\,dx = 1,$$

while for discrete variables, the probability mass function $P(X = x)$ conforms to

$$\sum_{x} P(X = x) = 1.$$

Expectation, variance, and higher-order moments are defined through integrals or sums over the support of the distribution. For example, the expectation of a continuous random variable is given by

$$E[X] = \int_{-\infty}^{\infty} x f(x)\,dx,$$

and the variance is formalized as

$$\text{Var}(X) = E\big[(X - E[X])^2\big].$$

This formalism underpins statistical models and serves as the guiding principle when translating theoretical concepts into computational constructs.

Key Probability Distributions

A comprehensive treatment of probabilistic models necessitates the examination of both discrete and continuous distributions. Among the discrete models, the Bernoulli distribution, which models binary outcomes, is characterized by

$$P(X = 1) = p \quad \text{and} \quad P(X = 0) = 1 - p,$$

where $0 \leq p \leq 1$. Extension to multiple independent trials leads to the binomial distribution with its probability mass function defined as

$$P(X = k) = \binom{n}{k} p^k (1 - p)^{n-k},$$

for $k = 0, 1, \ldots, n$. The Poisson distribution, suitable for modeling the occurrence of events over a fixed interval, is expressed as

$$P(X = k) = \frac{\lambda^k e^{-\lambda}}{k!},$$

where $\lambda > 0$ is the average event rate.

In the landscape of continuous distributions, the uniform distribution over an interval $[a, b]$ is defined by a constant density

$$f(x) = \frac{1}{b - a} \quad \text{for} \quad a \leq x \leq b.$$

The normal distribution, serving as a canonical model for many naturally occurring phenomena, possesses the probability density function

$$f(x) = \frac{1}{\sqrt{2\pi\sigma^2}} \exp\left(-\frac{(x - \mu)^2}{2\sigma^2}\right),$$

where μ and σ^2 represent the mean and variance, respectively. Additional continuous models, such as the exponential distribution with density

$$f(x) = \lambda e^{-\lambda x} \quad \text{for} \quad x \geq 0,$$

and variants thereof, further enrich the suite of probabilistic tools available for statistical analysis.

Simulation of Random Phenomena

The simulation of random phenomena relies on the generation of samples that adhere to the statistical properties dictated by the chosen probability distributions. This process is conventionally initiated by producing pseudorandom numbers drawn from the standard uniform distribution on the interval $[0, 1]$. Through methods such as the inversion method, where a uniform variate u is transformed via

$$x = F^{-1}(u),$$

with F^{-1} representing the inverse cumulative distribution function, sampling can be effectively extended to more complex distributions. For cases where the inverse function is not available in closed form, alternative strategies like rejection sampling or the Box-Muller transform are employed to generate samples that exhibit the desired statistical behavior. The simulation of multivariate random variables often involves the utilization of matrix decompositions, such as the Cholesky decomposition, to introduce and control correlations between variables in accordance with a specified covariance structure.

Translating Probabilistic Models into Rust

The imperatives of accuracy, efficiency, and maintainability in computational implementations of probabilistic models find a natural ally in the Rust programming language. Rust's robust type system and zero-cost abstractions facilitate the faithful transcription of mathematical formulations into code without compromising runtime performance. By encapsulating probability distributions as well-defined types with associated methods for computing densities, cumulative probabilities, and moments, implementations can remain closely aligned with their theoretical counterparts. Moreover, Rust's emphasis on memory safety and concurrency permits the development of simulation frameworks that are both reliable and scalable. The translation of concepts such as inverse transform sampling, rejection sampling, and variance reduction techniques into idiomatic Rust code is supported by language constructs that encourage modularity and reusability. The resulting implementations are well-suited for integration into larger statistical modeling pipelines, where precision and efficiency are paramount.

Rust Code Snippet

```rust
use std::f64::consts::PI;
use rand::Rng;

// ============================
// Mathematical Utilities
// ============================

/// Factorial computation for small k (used in discrete
↪   distributions)
fn factorial(k: u32) -> f64 {
    (1..=k).fold(1.0, |acc, x| acc * x as f64)
}

// ============================
// Discrete Distributions
// ============================

/// Bernoulli Distribution: Models binary outcomes.
/// PMF: P(X = 1) = p, P(X = 0) = 1 - p.
struct Bernoulli {
    p: f64,
}

impl Bernoulli {
    fn new(p: f64) -> Self {
        assert!(p >= 0.0 && p <= 1.0, "Probability must be between 0
        ↪   and 1");
        Bernoulli { p }
    }

    /// Returns the probability mass for the given outcome
    fn pmf(&self, x: u8) -> f64 {
        match x {
            0 => 1.0 - self.p,
            1 => self.p,
            _ => 0.0,
        }
    }

    /// Sample a random outcome from the Bernoulli distribution.
    fn sample<R: Rng>(&self, rng: &mut R) -> u8 {
        let u: f64 = rng.gen();
        if u < self.p { 1 } else { 0 }
    }
}

/// Binomial Distribution: Sum of n independent Bernoulli trials.
/// PMF: P(X = k) = C(n, k) * p^k * (1 - p)^(n - k)
struct Binomial {
    n: u32,
```

93

```rust
        p: f64,
}

impl Binomial {
    fn new(n: u32, p: f64) -> Self {
        assert!(p >= 0.0 && p <= 1.0, "Probability must be between 0
        ↪    and 1");
        Binomial { n, p }
    }

    /// Calculate the PMF for k successes
    fn pmf(&self, k: u32) -> f64 {
        if k > self.n {
            return 0.0;
        }
        let comb = factorial(self.n) / (factorial(k) *
        ↪    factorial(self.n - k));
        comb * self.p.powi(k as i32) * (1.0 - self.p).powi((self.n -
        ↪    k) as i32)
    }

    /// Sample by simulating n Bernoulli trials.
    fn sample<R: Rng>(&self, rng: &mut R) -> u32 {
        let mut count = 0;
        for _ in 0..self.n {
            if rng.gen::<f64>() < self.p {
                count += 1;
            }
        }
        count
    }
}

/// Poisson Distribution: Models the number of events in a fixed
↪    interval.
/// PMF: P(X = k) = (^k * exp()) / k!
struct Poisson {
    lambda: f64,
}

impl Poisson {
    fn new(lambda: f64) -> Self {
        assert!(lambda > 0.0, "Lambda must be positive");
        Poisson { lambda }
    }

    /// Calculate the PMF for k events.
    fn pmf(&self, k: u32) -> f64 {
        self.lambda.powi(k as i32) * (-self.lambda).exp() /
        ↪    factorial(k)
    }

    /// Generate a sample using the sequential product method.
```

```
        fn sample<R: Rng>(&self, rng: &mut R) -> u32 {
            let mut k = 0;
            let mut prod = 1.0;
            let threshold = (-self.lambda).exp();
            loop {
                prod *= rng.gen::<f64>();
                if prod < threshold {
                    break;
                }
                k += 1;
            }
            k
        }
    }


    // ==============================
    // Continuous Distributions
    // ==============================

    /// Uniform Distribution over [a, b]
    struct Uniform {
        a: f64,
        b: f64,
    }

    impl Uniform {
        fn new(a: f64, b: f64) -> Self {
            assert!(a < b, "Invalid interval: a must be less than b");
            Uniform { a, b }
        }

        /// PDF: f(x) = 1 / (b - a) if x in [a, b], 0 otherwise.
        fn pdf(&self, x: f64) -> f64 {
            if x >= self.a && x <= self.b {
                1.0 / (self.b - self.a)
            } else {
                0.0
            }
        }

        /// Sample uniformly from [a, b]
        fn sample<R: Rng>(&self, rng: &mut R) -> f64 {
            rng.gen_range(self.a..self.b)
        }
    }


    /// Exponential Distribution using inverse transform sampling.
    /// PDF: f(x) =  exp(x) for x  0.
    struct Exponential {
        lambda: f64,
    }

    impl Exponential {
```

95

```rust
    fn new(lambda: f64) -> Self {
        assert!(lambda > 0.0, "Lambda must be positive");
        Exponential { lambda }
    }

    /// Calculate the PDF for a given x.
    fn pdf(&self, x: f64) -> f64 {
        if x >= 0.0 {
            self.lambda * (-self.lambda * x).exp()
        } else {
            0.0
        }
    }

    /// Sample using the inverse transform method.
    /// x = F¹(u) = -ln(u) /
    fn sample<R: Rng>(&self, rng: &mut R) -> f64 {
        let u: f64 = rng.gen();
        -u.ln() / self.lambda
    }
}

/// Normal Distribution using the Box-Muller transform.
/// PDF: f(x) = 1/((2²)) exp((x)²/(2²))
struct Normal {
    mu: f64,
    sigma: f64,
}

impl Normal {
    fn new(mu: f64, sigma: f64) -> Self {
        assert!(sigma > 0.0, "Sigma must be positive");
        Normal { mu, sigma }
    }

    /// Calculate the PDF for a given x.
    fn pdf(&self, x: f64) -> f64 {
        (1.0 / ((2.0 * PI * self.sigma * self.sigma).sqrt()))
            * ( -((x - self.mu).powi(2)) / (2.0 * self.sigma *
            ↪  self.sigma) ).exp()
    }

    /// Generate a sample using the Box-Muller Transform.
    fn sample<R: Rng>(&self, rng: &mut R) -> f64 {
        let u1: f64 = rng.gen();
        let u2: f64 = rng.gen();
        let z0 = (-2.0 * u1.ln()).sqrt() * (2.0 * PI * u2).cos();
        self.mu + self.sigma * z0
    }
}

// ==============================
// Monte Carlo Estimation Utilities
```

```
// ================================

/// Estimate the expectation E[h(X)] by Monte Carlo integration.
/// For a function h and a sampling function sample_func that
↪   returns samples from the distribution.
fn estimate_expectation<F, G>(h: F, sample_func: G, num_samples:
↪   usize) -> f64
where
    F: Fn(f64) -> f64,
    G: Fn() -> f64,
{
    let sum: f64 = (0..num_samples).map(|_| h(sample_func())).sum();
    sum / (num_samples as f64)
}

/// Estimate the variance Var(h(X)) using Monte Carlo simulation.
fn estimate_variance<F, G>(h: F, sample_func: G, num_samples: usize,
↪   expectation: f64) -> f64
where
    F: Fn(f64) -> f64,
    G: Fn() -> f64,
{
    let sum: f64 = (0..num_samples)
        .map(|_| {
            let x = sample_func();
            let diff = h(x) - expectation;
            diff * diff
        })
        .sum();
    sum / (num_samples as f64)
}

// ================================
// Main Simulation Demonstrating Algorithms and Equations
// ================================

fn main() {
    let mut rng = rand::thread_rng();

    // ----- Exponential Distribution (Inverse Transform Sampling)
    ↪   -----
    let exp_dist = Exponential::new(1.5);
    let exp_sample = exp_dist.sample(&mut rng);
    println!("Exponential sample: {}", exp_sample);
    println!("Exponential PDF at sample: {}",
    ↪   exp_dist.pdf(exp_sample));

    // ----- Normal Distribution (Box-Muller Transform) -----
    let norm_dist = Normal::new(0.0, 1.0);
    let norm_sample = norm_dist.sample(&mut rng);
    println!("Normal sample: {}", norm_sample);
    println!("Normal PDF at sample: {}",
    ↪   norm_dist.pdf(norm_sample));
```

97

```
// ----- Uniform Distribution Expectation and Variance
↪ Estimation -----
let uniform_dist = Uniform::new(0.0, 1.0);
let num_samples = 100_000;
let uniform_expectation = estimate_expectation(|x| x, ||
↪ uniform_dist.sample(&mut rng), num_samples);
let uniform_variance = estimate_variance(|x| x, ||
↪ uniform_dist.sample(&mut rng), num_samples,
↪ uniform_expectation);
println!("Uniform Distribution: Estimated Expectation = {}",
↪ uniform_expectation);
println!("Uniform Distribution: Estimated Variance = {}",
↪ uniform_variance);

// ----- Bernoulli Distribution Sampling -----
let bernoulli = Bernoulli::new(0.3);
let bern_sample = bernoulli.sample(&mut rng);
println!("Bernoulli sample (0 or 1) with p=0.3: {}",
↪ bern_sample);
println!("Bernoulli PMF for 1: {}", bernoulli.pmf(1));

// ----- Binomial Distribution Sampling -----
let binom = Binomial::new(10, 0.5);
let binom_sample = binom.sample(&mut rng);
println!("Binomial sample (number of successes in 10 trials with
↪ p=0.5): {}", binom_sample);
println!("Binomial PMF for 5 successes: {}", binom.pmf(5));

// ----- Poisson Distribution Sampling -----
let poisson = Poisson::new(2.0);
let poisson_sample = poisson.sample(&mut rng);
println!("Poisson sample ( = 2.0): {}", poisson_sample);
println!("Poisson PMF for 3 events: {}", poisson.pmf(3));

// ----- Monte Carlo Estimation for Normal Distribution -----
let normal_expectation = estimate_expectation(|x| x, ||
↪ norm_dist.sample(&mut rng), num_samples);
let normal_variance = estimate_variance(|x| x, ||
↪ norm_dist.sample(&mut rng), num_samples,
↪ normal_expectation);
println!("Normal Distribution: Estimated Expectation = {}",
↪ normal_expectation);
println!("Normal Distribution: Estimated Variance = {}",
↪ normal_variance);

// The above implementations reflect key equations:
// 1. For continuous PDFs:  f(x) dx = 1, E[X] =  x f(x) dx and
↪  Var(X) = E[(X-E[X])^2].
// 2. For discrete models: Sum of PMFs equals 1, e.g., in the
↪  Binomial and Poisson distributions.
// 3. Sampling techniques: Inverse transform sampling for the
↪  Exponential distribution and
```

```
      //     Box-Muller for the Normal distribution, which transform
  ↪   uniform variates into targeted distributions.
}
```

Chapter 15

Random Sampling and Synthetic Data Generation

Foundations of Random Number Generation

Random number generation constitutes a critical underpinning in the construction of computational simulations and statistical experiments. In this context, a pseudo-random number generator (PRNG) is designed to produce a sequence of numbers $\{X_i\}_{i=1}^N$ that emulate the properties of independent and identically distributed random variables drawn from the continuous uniform distribution in the interval $[0, 1)$. The intrinsic quality of a PRNG is evaluated by its period, the degree of equidistribution across subintervals, and the minimal correlations among successive outputs. In contemporary systems, particularly within the Rust programming ecosystem, the implementation of PRNGs conforms to rigorous mathematical criteria that ensure both statistical uniformity and reproducibility. Such generators provide the computational substrate required for a variety of sampling applications, ranging from basic Monte Carlo estimation to complex bootstrapping procedures.

Techniques in Random Sampling

The process of random sampling leverages the raw output of PRNGs to simulate draws from diverse probability distributions. A common approach involves the use of the inversion method, whereby a continuous random variable X with cumulative distribution function (CDF) F is obtained through the transformation

$$X = F^{-1}(U),$$

where U denotes a sample from the standard uniform distribution. In circumstances where the inverse CDF cannot be expressed in closed form, alternative techniques such as rejection sampling are employed. Rejection sampling generates candidate samples from a proposal distribution and accepts them based on a criterion derived from the target distribution's probability density function (PDF).

A further refinement of sampling methodologies is observed in techniques that transform uniform variates into samples from the normal distribution. For example, the Box-Muller transform uses a pair of independent uniform samples U_1 and U_2 to produce a pair of independent standard normally distributed random variables via the equations

$$Z_0 = \sqrt{-2 \ln U_1} \cos(2\pi U_2),$$
$$Z_1 = \sqrt{-2 \ln U_1} \sin(2\pi U_2).$$

Techniques of this nature are underpinned by robust mathematical derivations that delineate error bounds, convergence rates, and the variance properties inherent to the sampling process. The statistical integrity of these methods is critical when they serve as the basis for simulation frameworks and inferential procedures where precise distributional characteristics are required.

Synthetic Data Generation for Simulation and Bootstrapping

Synthetic data generation represents a systematic framework for constructing artificial datasets that encapsulate the statistical properties of empirical observations. This process is of particular significance in simulation studies and resampling methods such as bootstrapping. Bootstrapping involves generating multiple synthetic datasets by resampling with replacement from an observed dataset. Such synthetic replicas facilitate the empirical estimation of sampling distributions, thereby providing insights into statistical variability and enabling the construction of confidence intervals for various estimators.

Beyond resampling, synthetic data can be generated parametrically by specifying a model with parameters θ and drawing samples $\{X_i\}_{i=1}^{N}$ from the associated probability distribution. This parameterized approach allows for the deliberate manipulation of feature correlations and distributional moments to mirror complex real-world phenomena. Techniques for synthetic data generation extend to the simulation of categorical, continuous, and mixed-type datasets, with strong emphasis on preserving inter-variable dependencies and higher-order statistical characteristics. The mathematical formalisms employed in these methodologies ensure that the resulting datasets maintain fidelity to the underlying statistical model, thereby supporting rigorous computational experiments and sensitivity analysis in both simulation and bootstrapping contexts.

Rust Code Snippet

```rust
use rand::Rng;
use rand::rngs::ThreadRng;
use std::f64::consts::PI;

/// Generates an exponentially distributed random number using the
↪    inversion method.
/// Equation: X = -ln(U) / , where U ~ Uniform(0,1)
fn exponential(lambda: f64, rng: &mut ThreadRng) -> f64 {
    let u: f64 = rng.gen_range(0.0..1.0);
    -u.ln() / lambda
}

/// Generates two independent standard normally distributed random
↪    numbers using
/// the Box-Muller transform.
/// Equations:
///    Z_0 = sqrt(-2 ln U_1) * cos(2 U_2)
///    Z_1 = sqrt(-2 ln U_1) * sin(2 U_2)
/// where U_1 and U_2 are independent samples from Uniform(0,1).
fn box_muller(rng: &mut ThreadRng) -> (f64, f64) {
    let u1: f64 = rng.gen_range(0.0..1.0);
    let u2: f64 = rng.gen_range(0.0..1.0);
    let magnitude = (-2.0 * u1.ln()).sqrt();
    let z0 = magnitude * (2.0 * PI * u2).cos();
    let z1 = magnitude * (2.0 * PI * u2).sin();
```

```
    (z0, z1)
}

/// Uses rejection sampling to generate a sample from a target
↪   probability density function.
/// Target PDF: f(x) = 6x(1-x) for x in [0,1], which has a maximum
↪   value of 1.5 at x = 0.5.
/// The algorithm generates candidates from a uniform proposal and
↪   accepts each candidate x
/// if a uniformly drawn y in [0,1.5] satisfies y < f(x).
fn rejection_sample(rng: &mut ThreadRng) -> f64 {
    loop {
        let x: f64 = rng.gen_range(0.0..1.0);
        let y: f64 = rng.gen_range(0.0..1.5);
        if y < 6.0 * x * (1.0 - x) {
            return x;
        }
    }
}

/// Generates a bootstrap sample from the given dataset by sampling
↪   with replacement.
/// This simulates the creation of a synthetic dataset for
↪   bootstrapping analysis.
fn bootstrap_sample<T: Clone>(data: &Vec<T>, rng: &mut ThreadRng) ->
↪   Vec<T> {
    let n = data.len();
    let mut sample = Vec::with_capacity(n);
    for _ in 0..n {
        let index = rng.gen_range(0..n);
        sample.push(data[index].clone());
    }
    sample
}

fn main() {
    let mut rng = rand::thread_rng();

    // Demonstrate the inversion method for exponential random
    ↪   number generation.
    let lambda = 1.5;
    let exp_value = exponential(lambda, &mut rng);
    println!("Exponential random sample ( = {}): {}", lambda,
    ↪   exp_value);

    // Generate a pair of standard normally distributed random
    ↪   numbers using Box-Muller.
    let (normal1, normal2) = box_muller(&mut rng);
    println!("Box-Muller normal samples: Z0 = {}, Z1 = {}", normal1,
    ↪   normal2);

    // Use rejection sampling to generate 10 samples from the target
    ↪   PDF f(x) = 6x(1-x).
```

103

```
    println!("Rejection Sampling (f(x) = 6x(1-x)) samples:");
    for i in 0..10 {
        let sample = rejection_sample(&mut rng);
        println!(" Sample {}: {}", i + 1, sample);
    }

    // Create a synthetic dataset and generate a bootstrap sample
    ↪   from it.
    let original_data = vec![10, 20, 30, 40, 50, 60, 70, 80, 90,
    ↪   100];
    let bootstrapped_data = bootstrap_sample(&original_data, &mut
    ↪   rng);
    println!("Original dataset: {:?}", original_data);
    println!("Bootstrap sample: {:?}", bootstrapped_data);
}
```

Chapter 16

Monte Carlo Integration and Simulation

Fundamentals of Monte Carlo Methods

Monte Carlo methods form a class of computational algorithms that rely on repeated random sampling to approximate numerical results. The core principle is based on the law of large numbers, where the approximation of an expected value or an integral converges to its true value as the number of independent samples increases. Consider a function $f(x)$ defined over a domain D with volume V. The integral

$$I = \int_D f(x)\, dx$$

can be approximated by drawing samples $x_1, x_2, \ldots, x_N$ uniformly from D and computing

$$I \approx V \frac{1}{N} \sum_{i=1}^{N} f(x_i).$$

The accuracy of this estimation is governed by the degree of variance in $f(x)$ and the number of samples N, with the standard error diminishing at a rate proportional to $1/\sqrt{N}$.

Monte Carlo Methods for Numerical Integration

Monte Carlo integration presents an elegant solution to the challenge of integrating functions over high-dimensional or irregular domains where traditional deterministic methods falter. The approach is particularly advantageous due to its independence from the dimensionality of D, as the convergence rate remains at $O(1/\sqrt{N})$. Crucial to this method is the statistical interpretation of integration as an expectation with respect to a uniform probability measure on D. When the function $f(x)$ exhibits high variability, variance reduction techniques—such as importance sampling, stratified sampling, or control variates—are introduced. These methods systematically redistribute sampling effort toward regions that contribute most significantly to the expected value and thereby enhance the accuracy of the estimate without a commensurate increase in computational overhead.

Monte Carlo Simulation of Stochastic Processes

Monte Carlo simulation extends beyond numerical integration to the emulation of stochastic processes and complex system dynamics. A stochastic process characterized by a state variable $X(t)$ is simulated by generating random samples that capture the probabilistic evolution of the system over time. The simulation typically involves iterative updating schemes where the transition from one state to the next is governed by a probability law. For instance, a discrete-time Markov process is simulated by generating a sequence

$$X_0, X_1, \ldots, X_T,$$

where each transition X_{t+1} is sampled according to a distribution that depends on X_t. This framework enables the construction of empirical distributions for system outcomes, facilitating the study of complex phenomena where analytical solutions are intractable.

Iterative Computational Strategies and Rust's Performance Considerations

The implementation of Monte Carlo methods is intrinsically iterative, involving the execution of extensive loops that perform independent sampling and evaluation tasks. In high-iteration, computation-
intensive contexts, the efficiency of the underlying programming
environment is paramount. Rust, with its emphasis on zero-cost
abstractions and rigorous memory safety guarantees, is well suited
for such tasks. The language allows for fine-grained control over
concurrency and parallelism, enabling the distribution of iterative computations across multiple cores while minimizing overhead.
The atomic and concurrent primitives in Rust ensure that iterative
sampling, the accumulation of sums, and the subsequent computation of averages are performed with optimal resource utilization
and minimal risk of data races.

Error Analysis and Convergence Properties

A detailed examination of error analysis within Monte Carlo integration reveals that the primary source of error is the variance of
the estimator. Denoting the standard deviation of the evaluated
function over the domain D by σ, the standard error in approxi-
mating the integral is given by

$$SE = \frac{\sigma}{\sqrt{N}}.$$

This statistical behavior is a direct consequence of the central limit
theorem applied to the sum of independent random variables. In
computational simulation, the convergence properties of the Monte
Carlo estimator are rigorously quantified, and strategies for variance reduction are critical to decrease the computational burden
for a specified accuracy. The balance between the number of iterations and the variance reduction techniques employed determines
the overall efficiency of the integration or simulation task. The iterative nature of Monte Carlo methods allows for adaptive strategies where convergence is monitored dynamically, ensuring that
the computational resources are optimally allocated to meet the
desired error thresholds.

Rust Code Snippet

```rust
use rand::Rng;
use rand_distr::{Normal, Distribution};

/// Performs Monte Carlo integration of a function `f` over the
↪ interval [a, b].
///
/// The integral is approximated by:
///     I   V * (1/N) * f(x_i)
/// where V = (b - a) is the length of the interval and the standard
↪ error is:
///     SE = V * sqrt(variance / N).
///
/// Returns a tuple (integral_estimate, standard_error).
fn monte_carlo_integration<F>(f: F, a: f64, b: f64, samples: usize)
↪ -> (f64, f64)
where
    F: Fn(f64) -> f64,
{
    let mut rng = rand::thread_rng();
    let mut sum = 0.0;
    let mut sum_sq = 0.0;

    // Generate samples and accumulate function values and their
    ↪ squares.
    for _ in 0..samples {
        // Sample x uniformly in the interval [a, b]
        let x = rng.gen_range(a..b);
        let fx = f(x);
        sum += fx;
        sum_sq += fx * fx;
    }

    // Calculate the volume of the domain (1D: length)
    let volume = b - a;
    let mean = sum / (samples as f64);
    let integral_estimate = volume * mean;

    // Estimate variance using the formula: Var = E[f^2] - (E[f])^2
    let variance = (sum_sq / (samples as f64)) - mean * mean;
    // Standard error: SE = volume * sqrt(variance/N)
    let standard_error = volume * (variance / (samples as
    ↪ f64)).sqrt();

    (integral_estimate, standard_error)
}

/// Simulates a discrete-time Markov process (e.g., a random walk)
↪ using Monte Carlo methods.
///
```

```rust
/// The process starts at `initial` and evolves for a given number
↪   of `steps`.
/// Each state transition is modeled as:
///     X_{t+1} = X_t +
/// where   is sampled from a normal distribution with mean 0 and
↪   standard deviation `sigma`.
///
/// Returns a vector of states representing the trajectory.
fn monte_carlo_markov(initial: f64, steps: usize, sigma: f64) ->
↪   Vec<f64> {
    let normal = Normal::new(0.0, sigma).unwrap();
    let mut rng = rand::thread_rng();

    // Create a vector to hold the states of the process.
    let mut states = Vec::with_capacity(steps + 1);
    let mut current_state = initial;
    states.push(current_state);

    // Iterate to simulate the evolution of the process.
    for _ in 0..steps {
        let step = normal.sample(&mut rng);
        current_state += step;
        states.push(current_state);
    }

    states
}

fn main() {
    // Monte Carlo Integration Example:
    // We integrate f(x) = x^2 over the interval [0, 1].
    // The analytical result is 1/3   0.333333.
    let f = |x: f64| x * x;
    let samples = 1_000_000;
    let (integral, std_error) = monte_carlo_integration(f, 0.0, 1.0,
↪       samples);

    println!("Monte Carlo Integration of f(x) = x^2 over [0, 1]:");
    println!("Estimated Integral = {:.6}", integral);
    println!("Standard Error     = {:.6}", std_error);

    // Monte Carlo Simulation of a Stochastic Process:
    // We simulate a random walk starting at 0, with step variations
↪       drawn from a N(0, sigma) distribution.
    let initial_state = 0.0;
    let steps = 100;
    let sigma = 1.0;
    let states = monte_carlo_markov(initial_state, steps, sigma);

    println!("\nMonte Carlo Simulation of a Random Walk:");
    for (i, state) in states.iter().enumerate() {
        println!("Step {}: {:.6}", i, state);
    }
```

}

Chapter 17

Graph-Based Data Structures for Network Analysis

Foundations of Graph Theory

Graph theory provides the mathematical framework for modeling complex relationships between discrete entities. A graph is defined as an ordered pair (V, E), where V is a set of vertices and E is a set of edges connecting pairs of vertices. Such structures may be undirected or directed, and edges may be assigned weights to represent the strength or capacity of connections. In the context of network analysis, these abstractions enable the rigorous study of connectivity, clustering, and flow within systems as diverse as social interactions and biological pathways. The structural properties of graphs, such as degree distributions, paths, cycles, and components, serve as fundamental indicators of the underlying network dynamics.

Adjacency List Representation

The adjacency list representation is particularly appropriate for sparse graphs where the number of edges is significantly lower than the maximum possible. In this structure, each vertex $v \in V$ is paired with a list that enumerates all vertices adjacent to v. Formally, given a graph $G = (V, E)$, an adjacency list is a mapping $\mathcal{L} : V \to \mathcal{P}(V)$, where $\mathcal{L}(v) = \{u \in V \mid (v, u) \in E\}$. This representation minimizes storage requirements by allocating memory proportional to $O(|V|+|E|)$. Such efficiency is critical when analyzing networks like social graphs, where the vast majority of entities maintain connections with only a small fraction of the total population, and in biological contexts, where interactions among proteins or genes form sparse yet highly significant networks.

Adjacency Matrix Representation

Alternatively, the adjacency matrix provides a dense representation of a graph that is especially suited to scenarios where constant time edge queries are paramount. For a graph with $n = |V|$ vertices, the adjacency matrix A is an $n \times n$ array defined by

$$A_{ij} = \begin{cases} 1, & \text{if there exists an edge from vertex } i \text{ to vertex } j, \\ 0, & \text{otherwise.} \end{cases}$$

In weighted graphs, the elements A_{ij} can be replaced by the corresponding weight of the edge (i, j), with an appropriate symbol (such as ∞ or 0) denoting the absence of a connection. Although this representation requires $O(n^2)$ memory, it allows for rapid implementation of operations such as matrix multiplication, which is instrumental in computing powers of the matrix to identify paths of varying lengths. The adjacency matrix is particularly useful in dense graphs or in settings where the overhead of sparse representations may hinder the performance of algebraic techniques for network analysis.

Applications in Social and Biological Networks

Within social networks, vertices typically represent individuals, while edges embody various forms of relationships such as friendship, collaboration, or information exchange. The use of adjacency lists in this domain enables efficient traversal of large-scale systems where each individual connects with only a limited subset of the entire network. Moreover, graph-based techniques facilitate the identification of community structures, influential nodes, and potential avenues for information diffusion.

In biological networks, vertices can denote elements such as proteins or genes, and edges may indicate interactions, regulatory influences, or metabolic connections. Both the adjacency list and matrix representations play pivotal roles in modeling these systems. For instance, the sparse nature of protein-protein interaction networks encourages the use of adjacency lists to efficiently store and process connection data, while the adjacency matrix offers a computationally tractable means for applying spectral analysis and other matrix-based methods to uncover modular structures within metabolic or gene regulatory networks.

The manipulation of these graph data structures forms the basis for numerous analytical algorithms. Techniques such as graph traversal, shortest path computation, and centrality measures are essential for quantifying the importance of nodes and relationships within the networks. The structural characteristics elucidated through these methods provide insight into the resilience and vulnerability of systems and contribute to the development of models that capture the complexity inherent in social and biological organizations.

Rust Code Snippet

```rust
use std::collections::VecDeque;

/// Adjacency List Representation for a directed (or undirected)
↪   graph.
/// We represent the graph as a vector of vectors, where each index
↪   corresponds
/// to a vertex and the inner vector lists the adjacent vertices.
/// This follows the mapping : V → (V) described in the chapter.
#[derive(Debug)]
struct AdjacencyListGraph {
    vertices: usize,
    adj_list: Vec<Vec<usize>>,
}

impl AdjacencyListGraph {
    /// Initialize a new graph with a given number of vertices.
    fn new(vertices: usize) -> Self {
        Self {
            vertices,
            adj_list: vec![Vec::new(); vertices],
        }
    }

    /// Add an edge from `src` to `dest`.
```

113

```rust
/// For an undirected graph, uncomment the second push.
fn add_edge(&mut self, src: usize, dest: usize) {
    self.adj_list[src].push(dest);
    // For undirected graphs, also add the reverse edge:
    // self.adj_list[dest].push(src);
}

/// Breadth-First Search (BFS) starting from a given vertex.
/// It computes the shortest-path distances (in number of edges)
↪  from the start vertex.
fn bfs(&self, start: usize) -> Vec<Option<usize>> {
    let mut visited = vec![false; self.vertices];
    let mut distance = vec![None; self.vertices];
    let mut queue = VecDeque::new();
    visited[start] = true;
    distance[start] = Some(0);
    queue.push_back(start);

    while let Some(v) = queue.pop_front() {
        // Traverse each adjacent vertex.
        for &w in &self.adj_list[v] {
            if !visited[w] {
                visited[w] = true;
                distance[w] = Some(distance[v].unwrap() + 1);
                queue.push_back(w);
            }
        }
    }
    distance
}
}

/// Adjacency Matrix Representation for a graph.
/// The matrix A is defined such that:
///    A[i][j] = 1 if there is an edge from vertex i to j,
///            = 0 otherwise.
/// For weighted graphs, these entries can represent weights.
#[derive(Debug)]
struct AdjacencyMatrixGraph {
    vertices: usize,
    matrix: Vec<Vec<i32>>, // 0 indicates no connection; positive
    ↪  numbers indicate weights
}

impl AdjacencyMatrixGraph {
    /// Initialize a new graph with a given number of vertices.
    fn new(vertices: usize) -> Self {
        Self {
            vertices,
            matrix: vec![vec![0; vertices]; vertices],
        }
    }
```

```rust
/// Add an edge from `src` to `dest` with the specified weight.
/// For an undirected graph, uncomment the second assignment.
fn add_edge(&mut self, src: usize, dest: usize, weight: i32) {
    self.matrix[src][dest] = weight;
    // For undirected graphs, also add the reverse edge:
    // self.matrix[dest][src] = weight;
}

/// Multiply two square matrices (used for computing matrix
↪    powers as per
/// algebraic techniques mentioned in the chapter).
fn matrix_multiply(a: &Vec<Vec<i32>>, b: &Vec<Vec<i32>>) ->
↪    Vec<Vec<i32>> {
    let n = a.len();
    let mut result = vec![vec![0; n]; n];
    for i in 0..n {
        for j in 0..n {
            for k in 0..n {
                result[i][j] += a[i][k] * b[k][j];
            }
        }
    }
    result
}

/// Compute the power of the adjacency matrix using
↪    exponentiation by squaring.
/// This corresponds to computing A^p, where the element at (i,
↪    j) indicates the number
/// of distinct paths of length p from vertex i to vertex j.
fn matrix_power(&self, power: usize) -> Vec<Vec<i32>> {
    let n = self.vertices;
    // Initialize the result as the identity matrix.
    let mut result = vec![vec![0; n]; n];
    for i in 0..n {
        result[i][i] = 1;
    }
    let mut base = self.matrix.clone();
    let mut p = power;
    // Exponentiation by squaring for efficient power
    ↪    computation.
    while p > 0 {
        if p % 2 == 1 {
            result = Self::matrix_multiply(&result, &base);
        }
        base = Self::matrix_multiply(&base, &base);
        p /= 2;
    }
    result
}
}

fn main() {
```

```rust
    // Demonstration of the Adjacency List Graph.
    println!("--- Adjacency List Representation ---");
    let mut graph_list = AdjacencyListGraph::new(6);
    // Adding edges to the graph (example: a sparse social or
    ↪ biological network)
    graph_list.add_edge(0, 1);
    graph_list.add_edge(0, 2);
    graph_list.add_edge(1, 3);
    graph_list.add_edge(2, 3);
    graph_list.add_edge(3, 4);
    graph_list.add_edge(4, 5);
    println!("Graph (Adjacency List): {:#?}", graph_list);

    // Compute BFS distances from vertex 0.
    let distances = graph_list.bfs(0);
    println!("BFS distances from vertex 0: {:?}", distances);

    // Demonstration of the Adjacency Matrix Graph.
    println!("\n--- Adjacency Matrix Representation ---");
    let mut graph_matrix = AdjacencyMatrixGraph::new(4);
    // Adding edges to form a cycle to illustrate dense connections.
    graph_matrix.add_edge(0, 1, 1);
    graph_matrix.add_edge(1, 2, 1);
    graph_matrix.add_edge(2, 3, 1);
    graph_matrix.add_edge(3, 0, 1);
    println!("Graph (Adjacency Matrix):");
    for row in &graph_matrix.matrix {
        println!("{:?}", row);
    }

    // Compute the square of the matrix (paths of length 2).
    let matrix_squared = AdjacencyMatrixGraph::matrix_multiply(
        &graph_matrix.matrix,
        &graph_matrix.matrix
    );
    println!("\nMatrix Squared (Paths of length 2):");
    for row in &matrix_squared {
        println!("{:?}", row);
    }

    // Compute the cube of the matrix using matrix_power method.
    let matrix_cubed = graph_matrix.matrix_power(3);
    println!("\nMatrix Cubed (Paths of length 3):");
    for row in &matrix_cubed {
        println!("{:?}", row);
    }
}
```

Chapter 18

Parallel Data Manipulation with Rayon

Fundamental Principles of Data Parallelism

Data manipulation tasks that involve large-scale datasets often exhibit a natural potential for parallel execution. Computational workloads that are intrinsically divisible can be reformulated so that independent sub-tasks are executed concurrently across multiple processing cores. In such scenarios, the overall computational effort is represented by a complexity of approximately $T(1)$ in serial execution, whereas the ideal parallel execution time approaches $T(p) \approx \frac{T(1)}{p}$ for p processing units, subject to overheads introduced by inter-thread communication and scheduling. This theoretical framework accentuates the importance of partitioning algorithms into granular, independent operations whose aggregated execution contributes to a significant reduction in wall-clock time.

Rayon as a Paradigm for Safe Concurrency

The Rayon crate embodies a modern approach to parallel data manipulation by leveraging Rust's guarantees for memory safety and data race prevention. By encapsulating low-level concurrency constructs within high-level abstractions, Rayon enables the decomposition of traditional iterator transformations into parallel counterparts without compromising correctness. The framework's architecture relies on the concept of parallel iterators, which mirror the semantics of sequential iterators while introducing mechanisms to distribute workloads safely. The design of Rayon ensures that closures, when executed in parallel, operate in isolation with respect to shared memory, thereby upholding Rust's strict ownership and borrowing principles. This combination of safety and expressiveness makes the crate particularly well-suited for complex data manipulation tasks that benefit from concurrent execution.

Strategies for Work Partitioning and Load Balancing

Efficiently partitioning data operations necessitates a detailed understanding of the inherent structure of the workload. Rayon employs a work-stealing scheduler that dynamically assigns tasks to available cores to mitigate imbalances arising from heterogeneous computation times. In practice, algorithms are transformed such that each segment of the data is independently processed and later merged to produce the final result. This process is commonly realized via a divide-and-conquer strategy, where an initial problem of size n is recursively split until sub-problems reach a threshold that optimizes the balance between parallelization overhead and computational gain. The theoretical benefits are tangible when the total workload exhibits minimal inter-dependencies, and thus the time complexity is effectively reduced by the concurrent evaluation of independently scheduled tasks.

Memory Safety and Synchronization Mechanisms

One of the foundational challenges in multi-core computations is the assurance of safe access to shared memory. Rayon circumvents potential pitfalls such as data races by establishing strict invariants governed by Rust's type system. The separation of compute tasks into isolated closures prevents inadvertent aliasing, and the explicit mechanisms for synchronization maintain a deterministic execution order where necessary. Critical sections, when required, are managed through atomic operations or lock-free data structures, ensuring that safe mutability can be achieved without incurring significant performance penalties. Such mechanisms are paramount when multiple threads are required to converge on a shared state after independent computation, and they are formalized within the abstraction layers provided by Rayon.

Scalability and Performance Trade-offs

The distribution of computational work across multiple cores not only reduces execution time but also introduces nuanced trade-offs in terms of overhead and resource contention. Rayon's design carefully balances the granularity of task splitting against the inherent costs of thread management and inter-thread communication. The performance model is intricately related to the overhead term α, which represents the synchronization and scheduling latency in relation to the total task execution time. As the number of cores p increases, the benefits of parallel computing are realized only if the ratio $\frac{T(1)}{p} \gg \alpha$. Consequently, the effective scalability of data manipulation operations using Rayon depends on both algorithmic characteristics and the underlying hardware architecture. The system must be architected to ensure that partitioning does not incur excessive overhead, thereby maintaining substantial net gains in throughput.

Rust Code Snippet

```
use rayon::prelude::*;
use std::time::Instant;

/// Computes the sum of elements sequentially.
/// This represents the serial execution time T(1).
fn sequential_sum(data: &[u64]) -> u64 {
    data.iter().sum()
}

/// Computes the sum of elements using a recursive
↪    divide-and-conquer
/// approach with Rayon's join for parallelism. This is an example
/// of how the workload can be partitioned safely to approximate
↪    T(p)  T(1)/p.
fn parallel_sum_recursive(data: &[u64]) -> u64 {
```

```rust
    const THRESHOLD: usize = 10_000;    // Granularity threshold for
    ↪  task splitting
    if data.len() <= THRESHOLD {
        // If small enough, perform sequentially to minimize
        ↪  overhead.
        sequential_sum(data)
    } else {
        let mid = data.len() / 2;
        let (left, right) = data.split_at(mid);
        // Recursively process each half in parallel using Rayon's
        ↪  join.
        let (sum_left, sum_right) = rayon::join(||
        ↪  parallel_sum_recursive(left),
            || parallel_sum_recursive(right));
        sum_left + sum_right
    }
}

fn main() {
    // Generate a large dataset of numbers 1 through n.
    let n: usize = 10_000_000;
    let data: Vec<u64> = (1..=n as u64).collect();

    // Serial computation using a standard iterator.
    let serial_start = Instant::now();
    let serial_result = sequential_sum(&data);
    let serial_duration = serial_start.elapsed();

    // Parallel computation using Rayon's parallel iterator.
    let par_iter_start = Instant::now();
    let parallel_result: u64 = data.par_iter().sum();
    let par_iter_duration = par_iter_start.elapsed();

    // Parallel computation using the recursive divide-and-conquer
    ↪  approach.
    let par_recursive_start = Instant::now();
    let recursive_result = parallel_sum_recursive(&data);
    let par_recursive_duration = par_recursive_start.elapsed();

    // Display the results of each computation.
    println!("Serial Result: {}", serial_result);
    println!("Parallel Iterator Result: {}", parallel_result);
    println!("Recursive Parallel Result: {}", recursive_result);

    println!("\n--- Timing Analysis ---");
    println!("Serial Duration: {:.6?}", serial_duration);
    println!("Parallel Iterator Duration: {:.6?}",
    ↪  par_iter_duration);
    println!("Recursive Parallel Duration: {:.6?}",
    ↪  par_recursive_duration);

    // Get the number of threads used by Rayon.
    let num_threads = rayon::current_num_threads() as f64;
```

```rust
    let serial_time_secs = serial_duration.as_secs_f64();

    // Compute the ideal parallel time according to the equation:
    // T(p)   T(1) / p
    let ideal_parallel_time = serial_time_secs / num_threads;
    println!("\nNumber of Threads: {}", num_threads);
    println!("Ideal Parallel Time (T(1)/p): {:.6} secs",
    ↪   ideal_parallel_time);

    // Estimate overhead as the additional time taken beyond the
    ↪   ideal time.
    let overhead_par_iter = par_iter_duration.as_secs_f64() -
    ↪   ideal_parallel_time;
    let overhead_recursive = par_recursive_duration.as_secs_f64() -
    ↪   ideal_parallel_time;
    println!("Overhead (Parallel Iterator): {:.6} secs",
    ↪   overhead_par_iter);
    println!("Overhead (Recursive Parallel): {:.6} secs",
    ↪   overhead_recursive);

    // Note: The overhead () signifies synchronization and
    ↪   scheduling latencies that arise
    // during parallel execution, reinforcing the trade-off
    ↪   discussed in the chapter.
}
```
<hr />

Chapter 19

Asynchronous Data Streams with Rust Futures

Foundations of Asynchronous Programming Concepts

Asynchronous programming constitutes a paradigm shift from traditional blocking models by decoupling the initiation of an operation from its execution and eventual completion. This model is predicated on the use of non-blocking primitives that permit the suspension and resumption of tasks without stalling the operating system threads. The central concept underpinning asynchronous execution is encapsulated in the notion of a future, which represents a value that may become available at some later point in time. In the context of high-throughput data streams, the asynchronous approach mitigates the latency inherent in Input/Output operations by allowing the system to continue processing other tasks while awaiting the readiness of a resource. Such a non-blocking architecture is critical for processing large volumes of incoming data concurrently, especially when the workload is predominantly bound by external events rather than by computation.

The Rust Futures Abstraction and Async/Await Syntax

Rust emphasizes safety and concurrency through a clearly defined abstraction for futures, which are implemented as an inherent trait within the language. The futures model in Rust operates on a poll-based mechanism wherein each future is repeatedly polled until it is ready to yield a result. The integration of the async/await syntax enables an intuitively linear coding style that is transformed by the compiler into state machines capable of cooperative multitasking. This syntactic sugar abstracts away the complexities of manually handling the state transitions between the pending and complete states of a task. The design of these constructs ensures that the memory safety guarantees offered by Rust remain intact even when multiple asynchronous tasks are executed concurrently. The resulting system seamlessly integrates with the ownership and borrowing rules, thereby negating data races and ensuring that resources are managed deterministically.

Asynchronous Execution in the Context of Streaming Data

Streaming data environments impose unique challenges due to the continuous influx and potentially unbounded nature of data elements. The asynchronous model lends itself particularly well to scenarios where the arrival rate of data is high and the processing must accommodate variable latencies. In such systems, data streams are treated as sequences of events that can be processed independently and concurrently. Each element or batch of elements can be associated with its own future, which is scheduled for execution based on the availability of computational resources. The async/await constructs facilitate seamless context switching between tasks, ensuring that while one future is in a waiting state, others actively contribute to the overall throughput. This approach effectively balances the computational workload across the available processing units, thereby optimizing response times and ensuring scalable handling of data streams characterized by sporadic burstiness and high variability in inter-arrival times.

Task Scheduling and Concurrency Dynamics

The execution of asynchronous tasks within Rust is governed by sophisticated scheduling mechanisms that rely on event-driven paradigms and efficient task wakeup strategies. The asynchronous runtime employs an event loop that continuously polls active futures, invoking their progress even when individual tasks encounter blocking operations. This process is akin to cooperative multitasking where the executor voluntarily yields control after a task indicates the inability to proceed. The schedulers are designed to minimize context switching overhead and to maintain high levels of concurrency by leveraging lightweight task representations. In rigorous computational models, the performance of such scheduling can be expressed in terms of the ratio $\frac{T(n)}{p} + \alpha$, where $T(n)$ denotes the total workload, p represents the number of concurrently executing tasks, and α encapsulates the intrinsic overhead associated with task management. By optimizing this ratio, the asynchronous model ensures that the system maximizes computational throughput even under conditions of high contention and resource diversity.

Implications for Large-Scale Concurrency in Streaming Data

The application of asynchronous programming to streaming data architectures transforms the method by which data is ingested, processed, and disseminated. Under this paradigm, large-scale concurrency is achieved not through the instantiation of numerous operating system threads but by multiplexing a large number of futures over a limited pool of threads. This results in significant reductions in memory footprint and context switching delays. When processing continuous streams, the efficiency of the async/await model allows for the aggregation, filtering, and transformation of voluminous datasets with minimal latency. The decoupling of task initiation from execution permits a system design wherein each incoming event is immediately encapsulated into a future, dispatched for processing, and then reassembled into the final data pipeline without necessitating synchronous blocking operations. This efficient orchestration of tasks is pivotal in applications where throughput, responsiveness, and the reliability of concurrent operations are of paramount importance.

Rust Code Snippet

```rust
// Import necessary crates and modules
use std::time::Duration;
use tokio::time::sleep;
use futures::stream::{FuturesUnordered, StreamExt};
use rand::Rng;

/// Asynchronously process an event from a streaming data source.
/// This function simulates variable processing time to mimic
/// ↪    workload variability.
///
/// # Parameters
/// - event_id: A unique identifier for the event.
///
/// # Returns
/// A floating-point value representing the simulated work done (in
/// ↪    milliseconds).
async fn process_event(event_id: usize) -> f64 {
    // Simulate processing time between 100 and 500 milliseconds.
    let process_time = rand::thread_rng().gen_range(100..500);
    println!("Event {}: processing for {} ms", event_id,
    ↪    process_time);

    // Simulate asynchronous wait (non-blocking delay)
    sleep(Duration::from_millis(process_time)).await;

    // Return the process time as the work metric T_i for this
    // ↪    event.
    process_time as f64
}

/// Computes the performance metric based on the formula:
///      Performance = T(n)/p +
/// where:
/// - T(n) is the total workload (sum of processing times).
/// - p is the number of concurrently executed tasks.
/// -  (alpha) is the overhead associated with task scheduling.
///
/// # Parameters
/// - total_work: The total accumulated work from all events.
/// - concurrency: The number of concurrent tasks.
/// - overhead: The scheduling overhead (alpha) in milliseconds.
///
/// # Returns
/// The computed performance metric.
fn compute_performance(total_work: f64, concurrency: usize,
↪    overhead: f64) -> f64 {
```

```
        total_work / concurrency as f64 + overhead
}

#[tokio::main]
async fn main() {
    // Total number of simulated events in the streaming data.
    let num_events = 20;
    // Scheduling overhead alpha (in milliseconds).
    let overhead_alpha = 50.0;

    // Create a FuturesUnordered to handle a dynamic collection of
    ↪ asynchronous tasks.
    let mut processing_tasks = FuturesUnordered::new();

    // Simulate the arrival of events in a continuous data stream.
    for event_id in 0..num_events {
        processing_tasks.push(process_event(event_id));
    }

    // Accumulate the total work T(n) from processed events.
    let mut total_work = 0.0;

    // Process events as soon as they complete, demonstrating
    ↪ asynchronous execution.
    while let Some(work_done) = processing_tasks.next().await {
        total_work += work_done;
        println!("Completed an event with work: {:.2} ms",
        ↪ work_done);
    }

    // In this simulation, we equate concurrency p to the number of
    ↪ events processed.
    let concurrency = num_events;

    // Compute the performance metric using the formula: T(n)/p + .
    let performance = compute_performance(total_work, concurrency,
    ↪ overhead_alpha);

    // Display the results and internal metric values.
    println!("\n--- Performance Metrics ---");
    println!("Total Work T(n): {:.2} ms", total_work);
    println!("Concurrent Tasks p: {}", concurrency);
    println!("Scheduling Overhead : {:.2} ms", overhead_alpha);
    println!("Performance Equation (T(n)/p + ): {:.2} ms",
    ↪ performance);
}
```

Chapter 20

Optimized CSV Parsing for Large Datasets

Foundations of CSV Data Processing and Memory Efficiency

The Comma-Separated Values (CSV) format, while syntactically simple, poses considerable challenges when employed in the context of massive datasets. The inherent sequential structure of CSV data necessitates a processing framework that minimizes redundant memory allocations and circumvent unnecessary I/O overhead. The operational model centers on the decomposition of an input stream into discrete, parseable segments such that the entirety of the dataset is not required to reside in memory simultaneously. In formal terms, if the sequential processing of data is modeled as a mapping $S \colon \mathbb{N} \to D$, where each natural number index is associated with a segment of data D, then the primary objective becomes the minimization of the cost incurred per mapping, both in temporal and spatial dimensions. The implementation strategy leverages buffered I/O routines to aggregate data until a suitable processing boundary is encountered, thus limiting the number of system calls and reducing the latencies associated with disk access.

Streaming Mechanisms and Buffering Strategies

The design of high-performance CSV parsers invariably rests on the adoption of streaming techniques that facilitate incremental processing of the input. Instead of imposing a monolithic loading strategy, the system maintains a rolling buffer that aggregates a block of data from the input stream. Such a buffering strategy is governed by the relationship $\frac{F}{B}$, where F denotes the total file size and B signifies the buffer block size. Adjusting B directly affects the frequency of I/O operations, with larger buffers potentially reducing the overhead at the expense of increased memory consumption. The streaming mechanism is further complicated by the necessity of handling records that span buffer boundaries. To address this, stateful management of partial records is integrated within the parsing logic, ensuring that incomplete data fragments are seamlessly concatenated with subsequent read operations. This approach not only preserves data integrity but also permits continuous parsing without resorting to blocking operations.

Architectural Design and Pipeline Optimization

The architectural paradigm adopted in the parser design is inherently modular and is segmented into distinct stages such as tokenization, syntactic analysis, and post-processing. During tokenization, the raw byte stream is decomposed into logical units corresponding to CSV fields. This phase must account for the syntactic anomalies intrinsic to the CSV format, including field delimiters, quoting conventions, and escape sequences. Subsequent syntactic analysis validates these tokens against the corpus of expected format constraints, enforcing consistency and correctness across the data items. The entire pipeline is orchestrated in a manner that enables concurrent processing stages. By leveraging Rust's zero-cost abstractions, the parser can implement state machines that coordinate between the aforementioned phases without introducing extraneous overhead. The cumulative performance can be approximated by the relation

$$P = \frac{\sum_{i=1}^{n} t_i}{c} + \alpha,$$

where t_i represents the processing time for individual segments, c is the degree of concurrent task execution, and α embodies the fixed overhead associated with task scheduling and resource management.

Error Handling, Data Integrity, and Robustness

Robustness in CSV parsing is imperative, particularly when confronting the realities of heterogeneous and occasionally malformed datasets. The parser incorporates comprehensive error-handling protocols that are capable of detecting, annotating, and recovering from an array of syntactic violations. Let E denote the set of potential errors during parsing; the design objective mandates that the cardinality of acknowledged errors, $|E|$, remains asymptotically negligible in comparison to the total number of records n, expressed formally as $|E| \ll n$. This is achieved through a combination of strict invariants and the application of Rust's static type system to enforce memory safety semantics. The error recovery strategy is engineered to isolate spurious records without discontinuing the overall ingestion process, thereby ensuring that data integrity is maintained across iterative parsing cycles. The careful delineation of record boundaries and the judicious use of buffering techniques further contribute to the resilience of the parser in large-scale, production environments.

System Integration and Resource Optimization

The optimized CSV parsing routines are designed for seamless integration within larger data processing ecosystems, where they function as the initial stage in an end-to-end analytical pipeline. Resource utilization is optimized by ensuring that non-blocking I/O operations and dynamic memory buffers are coordinated in real time with the system's workload demands. This alignment with the underlying hardware architecture is critical, as efficient management of CPU caches, memory hierarchies, and parallel execution units directly influences throughput. The parser's internal scheduling mechanism is crafted to minimize context switching, thus reducing the latency induced by thread management in concurrent

129

environments. By adopting a model in which data is parsed in a streaming fashion and processed incrementally, the system is able to sustain high throughput even when confronted with terabyte-scale datasets. The resulting architecture is characterized by its scalability and robustness, achieved through meticulous alignment of algorithmic efficiency with system-level resource optimization.

Rust Code Snippet

```rust
use std::fs::File;
use std::io::{self, BufReader, BufRead, Read};
use std::time::{Instant};
use std::error::Error;

const BUFFER_SIZE: usize = 8 * 1024; // Define block size B as 8KB
↪    for buffered I/O

/// CSVParser is a simple, stateful CSV parser that reads data
↪    incrementally,
/// handling partial records that span across buffer boundaries.
struct CSVParser<R: Read> {
    reader: BufReader<R>,
    remainder: String,
}

impl<R: Read> CSVParser<R> {
    /// Creates a new CSVParser instance using a buffered reader
    ↪    with a custom capacity.
    fn new(inner: R) -> Self {
        CSVParser {
            reader: BufReader::with_capacity(BUFFER_SIZE, inner),
            remainder: String::new(),
        }
    }

    /// Parses the next complete CSV record from the input stream.
    /// It reads buffered data incrementally and manages partial
    ↪    records.
    fn parse_next_record(&mut self) ->
    ↪    io::Result<Option<Vec<String>>> {
        loop {
            // Check if the remainder already has a newline (record
            ↪    boundary)
            if let Some(pos) = self.remainder.find('\n') {
                let line = self.remainder[..pos].to_string();
                self.remainder = self.remainder[pos +
                ↪    1..].to_string();
                // Tokenize the line into CSV fields.
                let tokens = self.tokenize(&line);
```

130

```
                return Ok(Some(tokens));
            }

            // Read additional data into a temporary buffer.
            let mut temp_buf = String::new();
            let bytes_read = self.reader.read_line(&mut temp_buf)?;

            // If no more data is read from input, process what
            ↪   remains.
            if bytes_read == 0 {
                if self.remainder.is_empty() {
                    return Ok(None);
                } else {
                    let line = std::mem::take(&mut self.remainder);
                    let tokens = self.tokenize(&line);
                    return Ok(Some(tokens));
                }
            }

            // Append the newly read data to the remainder.
            self.remainder.push_str(&temp_buf);
        }
    }

    /// A simple tokenization function that splits a CSV record by
    ↪   comma.
    /// For demonstration purposes, this does not implement full CSV
    ↪   quoting semantics.
    fn tokenize(&self, record: &str) -> Vec<String> {
        let mut tokens = Vec::new();
        let mut current = String::new();
        let mut in_quotes = false;
        let mut chars = record.chars().peekable();

        while let Some(ch) = chars.next() {
            match ch {
                '"' => {
                    in_quotes = !in_quotes;
                    current.push(ch);
                }
                ',' if !in_quotes => {
                    tokens.push(current.trim().to_string());
                    current = String::new();
                }
                _ => current.push(ch),
            }
        }

        if !current.is_empty() {
            tokens.push(current.trim().to_string());
        }
        tokens
    }
```

```rust
}

/// Main function demonstrating the optimized CSV parsing,
/// streaming, and performance calculation based on the equation:
///    P = ( t / c) +
/// where:
///    t: processing time per record segment,
///    c: degree of concurrent task execution (simulated here),
///    : fixed scheduling/resource overhead.
fn main() -> Result<(), Box<dyn Error>> {
    // Specify the CSV file path; ensure the file exists in your
    // ↪ working directory.
    let file_path = "large_dataset.csv";
    let file = File::open(file_path)?;
    let mut parser = CSVParser::new(file);

    // Performance tracking: total processing time for all records.
    let overall_start = Instant::now();
    let mut record_count = 0;
    let mut total_processing_time = 0u128;

    // Process CSV records one-by-one while streaming from the file.
    while let Some(record) = parser.parse_next_record()? {
        let record_start = Instant::now();

        // Simulate record processing: here we simply count and
        // ↪ print the number of fields.
        println!("Record {}: {} fields", record_count + 1,
        ↪ record.len());

        record_count += 1;
        let elapsed = record_start.elapsed().as_micros();
        total_processing_time += elapsed;
    }

    // Simulate performance metric calculation.
    // Assume c (concurrent tasks) = 4 and alpha (overhead) = 500
    // ↪ microseconds.
    let c: u128 = 4;
    let alpha: u128 = 500;
    let performance_metric = total_processing_time / c + alpha;

    println!("Processed {} records.", record_count);
    println!("Total processing time (µs): {}",
    ↪ total_processing_time);
    println!("Computed Performance Metric P: {}",
    ↪ performance_metric);
    println!("Total elapsed time (ms): {}",
    ↪ overall_start.elapsed().as_millis());

    Ok(())
}
```

Chapter 21

JSON Serialization and Deserialization for Data Interchange

Foundations of JSON-Based Data Interchange

The JSON format serves as a ubiquitous medium for data interchange across diverse computing systems, characterized by its lightweight, text-based representation. JSON employs a minimalistic syntax comprising objects and arrays, where objects represent unordered collections of key–value pairs and arrays denote ordered sequences of values. This restricted syntax facilitates a straightforward mapping to native data structures while retaining human readability. The expressiveness of JSON is, however, counterbalanced by its simplicity; the absence of explicit type definitions necessitates meticulous consideration when aligning JSON data with the statically typed paradigms inherent in languages such as Rust. The transformation process from JSON to native data forms must preserve data integrity, ensuring that the hierarchical structure and relational semantics embedded within the JSON document are faithfully reproduced in memory. In mathematical terms, if the mapping from JSON representations to native data types is denoted as $M : J \rightarrow D$, then the objective is to guarantee that M is both surjective and injective with respect to the well-defined, finite subsets of J and D.

Serde Framework: Architecture and Type System Integration

The Serde framework offers a sophisticated mechanism for handling JSON serialization and deserialization that leverages Rust's robust type system. At the core of Serde lies a set of well-defined traits that facilitate the translation between complex, user-defined data structures and their JSON counterparts. This trait-based mechanism enables the derivation of conversion functionalities at compile time, thus eliminating runtime overhead associated with dynamic type checks. The integration with Rust's type system is achieved via generics and procedural macros that auto-generate serialization logic, ensuring that the function $S : T \to J$, where T represents a set of native data types, adheres to strict type invariants. This process ensures that only those data structures that satisfy the required contracts are eligible for conversion, thereby enforcing a discipline that minimizes the risk of runtime errors. The zero-cost abstractions provided by Serde ensure that the abstraction overhead is effectively optimized away, resulting in performance characteristics that closely align with handwritten serialization routines.

Mapping Complex Data Structures to JSON

Complex data structures in Rust, such as nested structs, enums, and collections, require a highly nuanced approach when being mapped to and from JSON. The serialization process addresses these intricacies by performing a comprehensive traversal of the data structure, which involves unfolding nested components and reconciling them with JSON's hierarchical model. Product types, represented by structs or tuples, are naturally converted to JSON objects, with each field corresponding to a key–value pair. In contrast, sum types, often expressed as Rust enums, are mapped onto discriminated unions where an explicit tag identifies the variant in use. This conversion, formally represented as the mapping $\mathcal{M} : D \to J$, must ensure that for any data structure $d \in D$, the corresponding JSON representation $\mathcal{M}(d)$ encapsulates all semantic nuances and inter-field relationships. The reverse process, or deserialization, requires an equally meticulous approach where the

134

JSON document is parsed and then recursively reconstructed into the native data model, ensuring that the operation $\mathcal{M}^{-1} : J \to D$ reliably restores the original structure without loss of fidelity.

Robust Mechanisms for Error Handling and Type Safety

Robust error handling constitutes a critical aspect of the serialization and deserialization processes, particularly when interfacing with external JSON data sources. In the conversion process, discrepancies arising from type mismatches, unexpected field formats, or incomplete data are managed through a comprehensive error propagation system. Serde implements an extensive error enumeration that categorizes potential failures and provides granular diagnostic information. This mechanism is designed such that if E represents the set of errors associated with the transformation from native data to JSON and vice versa, then for any well-formed data structure $d \in D$, the condition $E(\mathcal{M}(d)) = $ holds under ideal circumstances. When irregularities are detected, the error handling framework ensures that such events are encapsulated in well-defined error types, thereby preventing propagation of corrupt state through the system. The interplay between robust error management and Rust's static analysis guarantees that the serialization and deserialization logic not only preserves type safety but also maintains consistency under the stringent requirements of distributed data interchange.

Rust Code Snippet

```rust
use serde::{Deserialize, Serialize};
use serde_json;
use std::error::Error;

// Define a nested data structure to represent a User's Address.
#[derive(Serialize, Deserialize, Debug)]
pub struct Address {
    street: String,
    city: String,
    zip: u32,
}

// Define a sum type using an enum to represent different user
    roles.
```

```rust
// This demonstrates mapping for Rust enums (sum types) to
//   discriminated unions in JSON.
#[derive(Serialize, Deserialize, Debug)]
pub enum Role {
    Admin,
    User,
    Guest,
}

// Define a composite data structure for a User,
// incorporating a nested Address and a vector of Roles,
// illustrating the mapping of product types (structs) to JSON
//   objects.
#[derive(Serialize, Deserialize, Debug)]
pub struct User {
    id: u32,
    name: String,
    address: Address,
    roles: Vec<Role>,
}

/*
In this example, we demonstrate key mappings discussed in the
↪   chapter:

    1. Serialization Mapping (M):
        Let D represent our native data structures (e.g., User), and J
        ↪   be the JSON representation.
        The mapping M: D -> J is implemented as:
            M(d) = JSON string obtained from serializing d.
        In Rust, this is achieved through serde_json::to_string_pretty.

    2. Deserialization Mapping (M^{-1}):
        Conversely, the mapping M^{-1}: J -> D converts a JSON string
        ↪   back into the native data structure.
        This is accomplished using serde_json::from_str.

    These mappings ensure one-to-one correspondence between the data
    ↪   as represented in memory
    and its JSON interchange format, preserving type safety and
    ↪   structural integrity.
*/

// Function to serialize a User to a JSON string.
fn serialize_user(user: &User) -> Result<String, Box<dyn Error>> {
    // Convert the native data structure (User) to its JSON
    //   representation.
    let json_str = serde_json::to_string_pretty(user)?;
    Ok(json_str)
}

// Function to deserialize a JSON string back to a User object.
```

```rust
fn deserialize_user(json_str: &str) -> Result<User, Box<dyn Error>>
↪  {
    // Parse the JSON string into the User data structure.
    let user: User = serde_json::from_str(json_str)?;
    Ok(user)
}

fn main() -> Result<(), Box<dyn Error>> {
    // Create a sample User instance to demonstrate the process.
    let user = User {
        id: 1,
        name: String::from("Alice"),
        address: Address {
            street: String::from("123 Maple Street"),
            city: String::from("Wonderland"),
            zip: 12345,
        },
        roles: vec![Role::Admin, Role::User],
    };

    // Serialization: Convert the native User object to a JSON
    ↪  string.
    // This implements the mapping M: D -> J.
    println!("Serializing User data...");
    let json_data = serialize_user(&user)?;
    println!("Serialized JSON:\n{}", json_data);

    // Deserialization: Reconstruct the native User object from the
    ↪  JSON string.
    // This implements the reverse mapping M^{-1}: J -> D.
    println!("\nDeserializing JSON data back to User object...");
    let deserialized_user = deserialize_user(&json_data)?;
    println!("Deserialized User:\n{:#?}", deserialized_user);

    // Demonstrate robust error handling: attempt deserialization of
    ↪  malformed JSON.
    let malformed_json = "{ \"id\": \"invalid_id\", \"name\":
    ↪  \"Bob\" }"; // Intentional type mismatch.
    println!("\nAttempting to deserialize malformed JSON...");
    match deserialize_user(malformed_json) {
        Ok(u) => println!("Unexpected Success: {:#?}", u),
        Err(e) => println!("Error encountered: {}", e),
    }

    Ok(())
}
```

Chapter 22

XML Data Manipulation for Structured Data

XML Document Structure and Parsing Techniques

XML is defined by a hierarchical markup that organizes data in a tree-like structure, where each element can nest other elements and attributes. Parsing such documents in Rust involves transforming the raw text format into an in-memory tree representation that accurately encapsulates the nested nature of the XML. Let X denote the set of all well-formed XML documents and T represent the corresponding set of tree structures. The transformation function $\mathcal{P} : X \rightarrow T$ must account for both the sequential ordering of elements and the semantic relationships inherent in tag nesting. Parsing algorithms in Rust, designed with zero-cost abstractions, utilize deterministic state transitions and recursive descent techniques. These methods support early error detection and precise control flow management, ensuring that each subtree is constructed with strict adherence to the intended schema of the XML document.

Hierarchical Data Transformation and Manipulation

The transformation of the parsed XML tree into structures that are amenable to downstream analytics necessitates a careful and systematic approach. In this phase, hierarchical data is dissected into constituent components that may be further reassembled or aggregated. The operation $\mathcal{T} : T \to D$, where D symbolizes the set of data models tailored for analytic processing, is implemented through a series of tree traversals and node reconfigurations. These traversals, typically executed via recursion or iterative state machines, isolate and transform the vital segments of the XML data. The manipulation of nodes, their attributes, and inter-node relationships is performed by applying formal rules that preserve the inherent data integrity. In this context, the maintenance of invariants such as parent-child consistency and ordered attribute mappings is critical, as even minor discrepancies can propagate to significant analytic errors in later stages of the data pipeline.

Schema-Aware Validation and Data Integrity

A significant aspect of XML manipulation lies in the verification of input against predetermined schema definitions. Where an XML Schema Definition (XSD) is available, the validity of the XML document is assessed through a validation function $V : X \to \{0, 1\}$, which yields a binary outcome corresponding to the adherence or non-adherence to the schema. The integration of schema-aware logic within the Rust environment leverages the language's robust type system to ensure that parsing and subsequent transformation operations are performed only on valid data. In practice, the parser incorporates rigorous consistency checks that validate complex hierarchical relationships, optional elements, and attribute constraints. The resulting internal representation respects the structural contracts imposed by the schema, thereby eliminating potential corruption or ambiguity in the data model. This meticulous approach to data integrity fosters reliable analytic operations by ensuring that the transformation of XML to domain-specific representations does not compromise semantic precision.

Analytical Mapping of Structured XML Data

The final phase involves converting the structurally rich XML tree into a format that is optimized for analytic processing. This mapping is formalized by the composite function $\phi = \mathcal{F} \circ \mathcal{T}$, where $\phi : T \rightarrow A$ and A denotes the analytic data domain. The process begins with the extraction of salient features from the hierarchical structure, identifying key-value pairs and subtrees that encapsulate the essential information. Subsequent reorganization of these elements into flat or semi-structured data models is performed with an eye toward minimizing redundancy and maximizing access efficiency. The transformation process incorporates sophisticated techniques for data normalization and type inference, ensuring that the extracted values conform to analytical requirements such as statistical compatibility and aggregation readiness. The design of these operations in Rust benefits from intrinsic language features that enforce memory safety and concurrency without incurring significant overhead. This results in an analytical mapping that retains the full complexity of the original XML while rendering it in a mathematically tractable form, thus facilitating downstream data analytics.

Rust Code Snippet

```rust
use std::collections::HashMap;

/// Representation of an XML node as a tree structure.
/// This corresponds to the set T in the transformation function : X
↪    → T,
/// where X is the set of all well-formed XML documents.
#[derive(Debug)]
struct XmlNode {
    tag: String,
    attributes: HashMap<String, String>,
    children: Vec<XmlNode>,
    text: Option<String>,
}

/// Domain-specific data model extracted from the XML tree.
/// This represents the set D in the transformation function : T →
↪    D,
/// where D is a data model tailored for downstream analytical
↪    processing.
```

```rust
#[derive(Debug)]
struct DomainData {
    data: HashMap<String, String>,
}

/// Analytic data representation as a vector of (key, numeric value)
↪ pairs.
/// This corresponds to the analytic domain A in the composite
↪ mapping =  : T → A.
type AnalyticData = Vec<(String, f64)>;

///
/// Function: parse_xml
/// Purpose: Implements a simplified version of a recursive descent
↪ parser
/// that converts a raw XML document (from X) into a tree structure
↪ (T).
/// (Transformation function : X → T)
///
fn parse_xml(input: &str) -> Result<XmlNode, String> {
    // For illustration, we simulate the parsing process with basic
    ↪ validation.
    let input_trimmed = input.trim();
    if !input_trimmed.starts_with("<") ||
    ↪ !input_trimmed.ends_with(">") {
        return Err("Input is not a valid XML document.".into());
    }

    // In a full implementation, recursive descent methods would be
    ↪ applied here
    // to process nested elements and attributes with early error
    ↪ detection.
    // For this code snippet, we return a dummy XML tree that mimics
    ↪ the expected structure.

    let mut attributes = HashMap::new();
    attributes.insert("version".to_string(), "1.0".to_string());

    let child_node = XmlNode {
        tag: "child".to_string(),
        attributes: HashMap::new(),
        // In a real parser, there could be multiple children with a
        ↪ recursive call
        children: Vec::new(),
        // This text node simulates a leaf containing numeric data
        ↪ for further analytics.
        text: Some("42".to_string()),
    };

    let root_node = XmlNode {
        tag: "root".to_string(),
        attributes,
        children: vec![child_node],
```

```
        text: None,
    };

    Ok(root_node)
}


///
/// Function: validate_schema
/// Purpose: Validates the XML document against predetermined schema
↪  rules
/// (Validation function V: X → {0,1}). Here, we ensure the presence
/// of a <root> element as a simple schema check.
///
fn validate_schema(input: &str) -> bool {
    input.contains("<root>") && input.contains("</root>")
}


///
/// Function: transform_tree_to_domain
/// Purpose: Traverses the XML tree (T) and extracts data into a
↪  domain-specific model (D).
/// This implements the transformation function : T → D which
↪  carefully assembles
/// analytic-ready data while preserving hierarchies and invariants.
///
fn transform_tree_to_domain(node: &XmlNode) -> DomainData {
    let mut data = HashMap::new();

    // For simplicity, we traverse only the immediate children of
    ↪   the root node.
    for child in &node.children {
        if let Some(text) = &child.text {
            data.insert(child.tag.clone(), text.clone());
        }
    }

    DomainData { data }
}


///
/// Function: analytic_mapping
/// Purpose: Converts domain-specific data (D) into an analytic
↪  structure (A)
/// by filtering and mapping values into numerical representations.
/// This embodies the composite function  =   : T → A.
///
fn analytic_mapping(domain: DomainData) -> AnalyticData {
    domain
        .data
        .into_iter()
        .filter_map(|(key, value)| {
            // Attempt to parse the textual data into a
            ↪   floating-point number.
```

142

```rust
                if let Ok(num) = value.parse::<f64>() {
                    Some((key, num))
                } else {
                    None // Skip non-numeric entries to maintain
                    ↪    analytical integrity.
                }
            })
            .collect()
    }

    fn main() {
        // Sample XML document (element of X)
        let xml_input = r#"
    <root version="1.0">
        <child>42</child>
        <child>Not a Number</child>
    </root>
    "#;

        // Step 1: Validate the XML document against schema (V: X →
        ↪  {0,1})
        if !validate_schema(xml_input) {
            eprintln!("XML does not conform to the expected schema.");
            return;
        }

        // Step 2: Parse the XML string to build the tree (: X → T)
        let xml_tree = match parse_xml(xml_input) {
            Ok(tree) => tree,
            Err(err) => {
                eprintln!("Error parsing XML: {}", err);
                return;
            }
        };
        println!("Parsed XML Tree: {:#?}", xml_tree);

        // Step 3: Transform the XML tree into domain-specific data (: T
        ↪  → D)
        let domain_data = transform_tree_to_domain(&xml_tree);
        println!("Domain Data: {:#?}", domain_data);

        // Step 4: Map the domain data into an analytic format ( =   : T
        ↪  → A)
        let analytic_data = analytic_mapping(domain_data);
        println!("Analytic Data Mapping: {:#?}", analytic_data);
    }
```

Chapter 23

Building Robust Data Pipelines with Composable Iterators

Iterator Abstractions and Theoretical Foundations

The iterator abstraction represents a foundational construct in both theoretical computer science and functional programming. In formal terms, an iterator may be viewed as a mechanism that encapsulates a sequence of elements drawn from a data source, with each element produced on demand. This abstraction is characterized by properties of laziness and stateless transformation, where an iterator does not require the immediate materialization of an entire collection. Instead, the iterator is governed by a state transition function, often conceptualized as a mapping $\sigma : S \to S \times F$, where S denotes the state space and F represents the yielded element. Such a characterization enables the encapsulation of sequential data flows without incurring the overhead of intermediate data structures. The mathematical foundation of iterators establishes a direct analogy to sequences defined over a domain D, where each element undergoes transformation through functions that maintain the zero-cost abstraction principle inherent in modern systems programming.

Modular Composition Through Transformation Operators

In the context of composable iterators, modularity arises from the ability to combine distinct transformation operators into a coherent processing pipeline. Each individual operator can be formalized as a function mapping between sets; for instance, given a transformation $f : A \to B$ and a subsequent transformation $g : B \to C$, the composite operation is defined by $g \circ f : A \to C$. This compositional structure is directly applicable to iterator-based transformations such as mapping, filtering, and flattening. The operators are designed to interact in a manner that is both associative and distributive over the data flow, thereby allowing multiple stages to be connected in a chain without compromising the integrity or efficiency of the process. The design of these operators emphasizes immutability and purity, ensuring that each transformation remains isolated and verifiable in isolation, yet fully integrable as part of a larger modular framework.

Pipeline Architecture and Lazy Evaluation

The construction of robust data pipelines is predicated on a layered architecture where each stage of the process is implemented as an iterator-based transformation. A key principle in this architecture is lazy evaluation, in which computations are deferred until the final results are required. Through lazy evaluation, pipelines are able to chain operations without generating intermediate collections, an optimization strategy often referred to as iterator fusion. This fusion process combines multiple transformation stages into a single pass over the data, thereby reducing both computational overhead and memory footprint. Formally, the overall transformation performed by a pipeline may be expressed as a composition $\phi = f_n \circ f_{n-1} \circ \cdots \circ f_1$, where each f_i corresponds to an individual iterator transformation. The associativity of function composition in this setting guarantees that the manner in which these stages are grouped does not affect the final output, thus ensuring both correctness and scalability.

145

Scalable Data Processing in Multi-Step Workflows

The scalability afforded by composable iterators is central to the design of data pipelines intended for processing complex, multi-step workflows. By decoupling the individual stages of data transformation, it is possible to construct pipelines that are highly adaptive to changing data volumes and computational requirements. Each iterator-based module operates as an independent unit, facilitating selective reordering and incremental processing of data elements. The modular nature of these pipelines permits a high degree of parallelism, as independent transformation stages can be executed concurrently when the underlying data dependencies allow it. This approach not only minimizes the propagation of errors through isolated stages but also enables a systematic allocation of system resources in response to real-time performance metrics. The abstract framework of iterator composition, combined with rigorous formalism, thus provides a scalable and efficient model for orchestrating multi-step data workflows in large-scale data processing environments.

Rust Code Snippet

```rust
use std::iter::Iterator;

/// A custom iterator that simulates the state transition function:
/// : S → S × F, where S is the state (here an integer) and the
↪   yielded element F is computed
/// as a function of the state (for illustration, we use the square
↪   of the state).
struct StateIterator {
    state: i32,
    max: i32,
}

impl Iterator for StateIterator {
    type Item = i32;

    fn next(&mut self) -> Option<Self::Item> {
        // If the current state is within bounds, compute the next
        ↪   element.
        // Here, we view the operation as a state transformation:
        //   (s, f) where s is updated (s + 1) and f = s^2.
        if self.state < self.max {
            let output = self.state * self.state;
```

```rust
            self.state += 1;  // State transition: s -> s+1
            Some(output)
        } else {
            None
        }
    }
}

/// Transformation function representing a simple mapping.
/// This function implements: f(x) = 2 * x.
fn double(x: i32) -> i32 {
    2 * x
}

/// Transformation function representing an additional mapping.
/// This function implements: g(x) = x + 3.
fn add_three(x: i32) -> i32 {
    x + 3
}

/// Composite transformation representing the composition:
/// (x) = (g  f)(x) = add_three(double(x))
fn composite_transform(x: i32) -> i32 {
    add_three(double(x))
}

/// Demonstrates a robust data pipeline using iterator composition
/// ↳  and lazy evaluation.
/// The pipeline corresponds to the formal structure:
///     = f  f  ...  f,
/// where each transformation operator is isolated yet composable.
fn main() {
    // Create a stateful iterator that simulates lazy, on-demand
    // ↳  data production.
    let state_iter = StateIterator { state: 0, max: 10 };

    // Construct a multi-stage data pipeline:
    // 1. Map the composite transformation (combines "double" and
    // ↳  "add_three").
    // 2. Filter the transformed values, only passing those > 10.
    // 3. Apply a final transformation (simulate another processing
    // ↳  stage by subtracting 5).
    let pipeline = state_iter
        .map(|x| {
            // Debug output to trace computation in this stage.
            println!("Original value from iterator (x²): {}", x);
            let transformed = composite_transform(x);
            println!("After composite transform (x) =
            ↳  add_three(double(x)): {}", transformed);
            transformed
        })
        .filter(|&x| {
```

```
            println!("Evaluating filter condition (x > 10) for: {}",
            ↪   x);
            x > 10
        })
        .map(|x| {
            println!("Applying final transformation: subtracting 5
            ↪   from {}", x);
            // Final stage transformation.
            x - 5
        });

    // Collect results. The act of collecting triggers the lazy
    ↪   evaluation of the pipeline.
    let results: Vec<i32> = pipeline.collect();
    println!("Final results of the pipeline: {:?}", results);
}
```

148

Chapter 24

Memory Management Techniques for Large-Scale Datasets

Foundational Concepts in Rust Memory Management

Rust implements a memory model defined by an ownership system that eliminates many classes of memory errors without resorting to a garbage collector. In this paradigm, every resource is owned by a variable, and transfers of ownership are tracked at compile time. This mechanism enforces a strict discipline such that every allocated resource is deterministically deallocated when it goes out of scope. The language further introduces the notions of borrowing and lifetimes, where references are subject to compile-time verification to ensure that they do not outlive the data to which they refer. Formally, given a variable x with an associated lifetime ℓ, any reference $\&x$ or $\&mut x$ must satisfy the constraint that its lifetime is a subset of ℓ. This formalism underpins the static safety guarantees that Rust affords, rendering it particularly suitable for managing the memory requirements of large-scale datasets.

149

Advanced Allocation Strategies in High-Volume Contexts

Managing large datasets demands strategies that go beyond naive allocation and deallocation methodologies. Rust provides flexible allocation mechanisms that cater to both stack and heap allocations, with the latter being essential for dynamic data sizes encountered in large-scale analysis. The language's allocator interface, designed to be both efficient and safe, permits fine-grained control over memory allocation patterns. In scenarios where large contiguous blocks or segmented allocations are required, Rust permits the integration of custom allocators that are optimized for specific workload characteristics. This level of abstraction ensures that allocation routines embody a zero-cost philosophy; the abstractions incur negligible overhead compared to traditional manual memory management techniques, as the compiler is able to inline and optimize allocation patterns in accordance with the program's static structure.

Borrowing Semantics and Lifetime Analysis in Data-Intensive Applications

A central pillar of Rust's memory management is the borrowing mechanism, which allows for flexible data access without compromising safety. This mechanism is formally characterized by the rules that govern mutable and immutable references. For an object x, the model permits either multiple non-mutable references $\&x$ or a single mutable reference $\&mut x$ at any point in time. The static analysis performed by the borrow checker ensures that these constraints hold rigorously, thereby preventing data races and ensuring memory safety even under high concurrency. In large-scale data processing contexts, where data may be accessed and modified concurrently, these borrowing semantics become critical. They ensure that memory is not inadvertently aliased, which prevents undefined behaviors. Additionally, lifetime annotations provide an explicit mechanism to relate the scopes of various references mathematically, such that for every reference with lifetime ℓ_1 and an associated resource with lifetime ℓ_2, the condition $\ell_1 \subseteq \ell_2$ is maintained. This formal approach results in verifiable guarantees of memory correctness across complex data transformation workflows.

Zero-Cost Abstractions: Design Philosophy and Practical Implications

The concept of zero-cost abstractions is a cornerstone of Rust's design, particularly in the domain of memory management where performance and safety must coexist. Zero-cost abstractions are designed such that the high-level constructs provided by the language and its standard libraries compile down to code that performs equivalently to hand-crafted low-level implementations. In mathematical terms, let C_{abstract} denote the computational overhead introduced by an abstraction and C_{manual} represent the overhead of a manually optimized implementation. Rust's optimization guarantees ensure that $C_{\text{abstract}} \approx C_{\text{manual}}$ under aggressive compiler optimizations. This is achieved by leveraging compile-time inlining, monomorphization, and static dispatch. In the context of large-scale datasets, these optimizations are critical; they reduce the memory footprint and improve cache locality without sacrificing the expressiveness and safety provided by higher-level abstractions. The synthesis of these strategies results in a system where advanced memory management concepts are implemented without incurring runtime penalties, thereby enabling scalable data processing pipelines that are both robust and efficient.

Rust Code Snippet

```rust
use std::fmt;

// A struct to represent a large-scale dataset stored in a
↪   heap-allocated array.
// This simulates advanced allocation strategies, where the data is
↪   allocated in
// a contiguous block in memory.
struct LargeDataset {
    data: Box<[i32]>,
}

impl LargeDataset {
    // Creates a new dataset of a specified size, initializing all
    ↪   elements with a given value.
    // This function demonstrates allocation on the heap with
    ↪   zero-cost abstractions in mind.
    fn new(size: usize, init: i32) -> Self {
        // The vector is created on the heap and then converted to a
        ↪   boxed slice.
```

```rust
        let vec = vec![init; size];
        LargeDataset {
            data: vec.into_boxed_slice(),
        }
    }

    // Processes the dataset using a closure provided by the caller.
    // This generic function uses zero-cost abstractions. The
    ↪  closure 'func' is inlined
    // and optimized at compile time, ensuring that the
    ↪  computational overhead Cabstract
    // is nearly equivalent to a manually optimized loop Cmanual.
    fn process<F>(&self, func: F) -> Vec<i32>
    where
        F: Fn(i32) -> i32,
    {
        // The map and collect operations are optimized by the
        ↪  compiler (monomorphization)
        // leading to performance comparable to a manual
        ↪  implementation.
        self.data.iter().map(|&x| func(x)).collect()
    }

    // Returns an iterator over the dataset.
    // This method shows how borrowing is used safely with lifetime
    ↪  annotations.
    fn iter(&self) -> std::slice::Iter<'_, i32> {
        self.data.iter()
    }
}

// Custom iterator demonstrating explicit lifetime handling, which
↪  links the lifetime of
// the iterator's items to that of the underlying data. The lifetime
↪  'a ensures that any
// reference returned cannot outlive the data slice.
struct DataIterator<'a> {
    data: &'a [i32],
    index: usize,
}

impl<'a> DataIterator<'a> {
    // Constructs a new DataIterator from a slice of data.
    fn new(data: &'a [i32]) -> Self {
        DataIterator { data, index: 0 }
    }
}

impl<'a> Iterator for DataIterator<'a> {
    type Item = &'a i32;

    // The next() method returns a reference with the same lifetime
    ↪  'a as the slice.
```

```
        fn next(&mut self) -> Option<Self::Item> {
            if self.index < self.data.len() {
                let result = &self.data[self.index];
                self.index += 1;
                Some(result)
            } else {
                None
            }
        }
    }


    // A function to retrieve the first element of the dataset. The
    ↪    lifetime 'a in the function
    // signature enforces that the returned reference does not outlive
    ↪    the dataset it borrows.
    // This is a direct application of the concept that for any
    ↪    reference with lifetime ,
    // associated with data of lifetime , the condition    must hold.
    fn get_first_element<'a>(dataset: &'a LargeDataset) -> Option<&'a
    ↪    i32> {
        dataset.data.first()
    }


    // Implementing Display for LargeDataset for easy debugging and
    ↪    logging.
    impl fmt::Display for LargeDataset {
        fn fmt(&self, f: &mut fmt::Formatter<'_>) -> fmt::Result {
            let display_data: Vec<String> = self.data.iter().map(|v|
            ↪    v.to_string()).collect();
            write!(f, "[{}]", display_data.join(", "))
        }
    }


    fn main() {
        // Advanced Allocation Strategy: Create a large dataset with
        ↪    1000 elements, each initialized to 42.
        let dataset = LargeDataset::new(1_000, 42);

        // Borrowing Semantics: Retrieve and print the first element.
        if let Some(first) = get_first_element(&dataset) {
            println!("First element is: {}", first);
        }

        // Zero-Cost Abstraction: Process the dataset using a closure
        ↪    that increments each element.
        // The closure is inlined, ensuring the overhead is practically
        ↪    the same as a manual loop.
        let processed_data = dataset.process(|x| x + 1);
        println!(
            "Processed data first element: {}",
            processed_data.first().unwrap()
        );
```

153

```rust
// Custom Iterator Usage: Create an iterator over the dataset to
↪    print the first five elements.
let mut iter = DataIterator::new(&dataset.data);
for i in 0..5 {
    if let Some(value) = iter.next() {
        println!("Iterator value {}: {}", i, value);
    }
}


// Comparing Zero-Cost Abstractions:
// This section demonstrates that using high-level iterator
↪    methods (map, sum) has no
// significant overhead compared to a manual loop. Formally, we
↪    expect:
//     Cabstract   Cmanual
// where Cabstract is overhead from abstractions and Cmanual is
↪    from a hand-crafted loop.
let sum_via_map: i32 = dataset.data.iter().copied().map(|x| x *
↪    2).sum();

// Manual loop for summing up the processed data.
let mut sum_manual = 0;
for &x in dataset.data.iter() {
    sum_manual += x * 2;
}

// Assertion to verify that both strategies produce the same
↪    result.
assert_eq!(sum_via_map, sum_manual);
println!("Sum computed by both methods: {}", sum_via_map);
}
```

Chapter 25

Sparse Matrix Representations in Rust

Theoretical Constructs and Motivation

A sparse matrix is defined as a matrix $A \in \mathbb{R}^{n \times m}$ in which the number of nonzero elements, denoted by p, is significantly lower than the total number of elements $n \times m$. In contexts where $p \ll n \times m$, the storage of zeros in a dense representation results in substantial inefficiencies in both memory consumption and computational performance. The mathematical foundation underlying sparse matrix representations relies on the observation that many high-dimensional datasets, particularly those arising from scientific simulations and network analysis, exhibit a natural sparsity that can be exploited by tailored data structures. The reduction in storage requirements directly influences the efficiency of arithmetic operations, as the computational cost is more closely associated with the number of stored nonzero values than with the overall dimensions of the matrix.

Data Structures for Sparse Matrix Representation

The design of data structures for storing sparse matrices is predicated on the need to encapsulate both the nonzero values and their respective indices in an efficient manner. Among the commonly employed formats are the Coordinate (COO) format, the Compressed Sparse Row (CSR) format, and the Compressed Sparse Column (CSC) format. In the COO format, each nonzero element is stored along with its row and column indices, thereby providing a direct mapping between the matrix structure and its stored representation. The CSR format, on the other hand, aggregates nonzero elements row-wise with an auxiliary index array that delineates the boundaries between rows. Similarly, the CSC format organizes the nonzero entries in a column-oriented fashion. These representations reduce the memory footprint by eliminating the need to store zero entries and allow for the development of algorithms that operate on only the significant, nonzero components of the matrix.

Operational Aspects and Algorithmic Complexity

Operations on sparse matrices, including addition, multiplication, and transposition, inherently benefit from the reduced number of stored elements. In matrix multiplication, for example, the computational complexity can be expressed as $O(k)$, where k represents the number of nonzero entries rather than the product of the matrix dimensions. This reduction in effective complexity is particularly advantageous in iterative algorithms and large-scale optimization problems. Furthermore, specialized algorithms that traverse only the nonzero elements reduce unnecessary data movement and improve cache locality. The challenge in designing these operations lies in preserving the inherent structure of the sparse representation while ensuring that the overhead associated with index management does not negate the performance benefits gained by avoiding dense computations.

Rust-Specific Implementation Considerations

Rust offers a unique combination of compile-time safety guarantees and performance optimizations that are particularly conducive to the implementation of sparse matrix data structures. The language's ownership model and lifetime analysis enforce strict memory safety, ensuring that data deallocations and buffer manipulations are conducted without introducing memory leaks or unsafe access patterns. In designing sparse matrix representations, the use of heap allocation via managed pointers such as those provided by *Box* and *Vec* permits the creation of contiguous memory blocks that house nonzero values and index arrays with minimal overhead. Furthermore, the zero-cost abstractions championed by Rust guarantee that high-level operations on these data structures are compiled down to machine code that approaches the efficiency of hand-tuned implementations. In this paradigm, the abstraction layer presents an interface that is both expressive and conducive to rigorous formal analysis, while the underlying compiler optimizations, including inlining and monomorphization, remove any superfluous computational overhead. This symbiosis between theoretical robustness and practical efficiency positions Rust as a compelling choice for managing high-dimensional datasets in applications where sparsity is a defining characteristic.

Rust Code Snippet

```
use std::fmt;

/// A sparse matrix represented in Compressed Sparse Row (CSR)
↪    format.
/// The matrix is stored as:
/// - `values`: nonzero values in row-major order.
/// - `col_indices`: corresponding column indices for each value.
/// - `row_offsets`: indices in `values` at which each row starts.
#[derive(Debug)]
pub struct SparseMatrix {
    rows: usize,
    cols: usize,
    values: Vec<f64>,
    col_indices: Vec<usize>,
    row_offsets: Vec<usize>,
}
```

```rust
impl SparseMatrix {
    /// Constructs a new SparseMatrix given the CSR components.
    pub fn new(
        rows: usize,
        cols: usize,
        values: Vec<f64>,
        col_indices: Vec<usize>,
        row_offsets: Vec<usize>,
    ) -> Self {
        SparseMatrix {
            rows,
            cols,
            values,
            col_indices,
            row_offsets,
        }
    }

    /// Constructs a SparseMatrix from a Coordinate (COO)
    /// representation.
    /// Each entry in `entries` is a tuple (row_index, col_index,
    /// value).
    /// The function sorts the entries by row and column and
    /// converts them to CSR format.
    pub fn from_coo(rows: usize, cols: usize, mut entries:
        Vec<(usize, usize, f64)>) -> Self {
        // Sort the entries: first by row index, then by column
        //    index.
        entries.sort_by_key(|&(r, c, _)| (r, c));
        let nnz = entries.len();
        let mut values = Vec::with_capacity(nnz);
        let mut col_indices = Vec::with_capacity(nnz);
        // row_offsets has size rows+1; initialize with 0.
        let mut row_offsets = vec![0; rows + 1];

        // Count nonzero elements per row.
        for &(r, _, _) in &entries {
            row_offsets[r + 1] += 1;
        }
        // Compute cumulative sum to convert counts into starting
        //    indices.
        for i in 1..=rows {
            row_offsets[i] += row_offsets[i - 1];
        }
        // Temporary copy to track insertion positions per row.
        let mut current_offset = row_offsets.clone();
        // Resize vectors to have exact nnz elements.
        values.resize(nnz, 0.0);
        col_indices.resize(nnz, 0);

        // Insert each COO entry into the CSR arrays.
        for (r, c, v) in entries {
            let pos = current_offset[r];
```

```
            values[pos] = v;
            col_indices[pos] = c;
            current_offset[r] += 1;
        }

        SparseMatrix {
            rows,
            cols,
            values,
            col_indices,
            row_offsets,
        }
    }

    /// Multiplies the sparse matrix by a dense vector `x` and
    ↪  returns the result.
    /// This computes y = A * x, where A is the sparse matrix.
    pub fn mul_dense(&self, x: &[f64]) -> Vec<f64> {
        assert_eq!(
            x.len(),
            self.cols,
            "Dimension mismatch: vector length must equal number of
            ↪  matrix columns."
        );
        let mut result = vec![0.0; self.rows];
        for row in 0..self.rows {
            let start = self.row_offsets[row];
            let end = self.row_offsets[row + 1];
            for idx in start..end {
                result[row] += self.values[idx] *
                ↪  x[self.col_indices[idx]];
            }
        }
        result
    }
}

/// Implements a simple display for the sparse matrix to visualize
↪  its CSR structure.
impl fmt::Display for SparseMatrix {
    fn fmt(&self, f: &mut fmt::Formatter<'_>) -> fmt::Result {
        writeln!(f, "SparseMatrix in CSR Format:")?;
        writeln!(f, "Rows: {}, Columns: {}", self.rows, self.cols)?;
        writeln!(f, "Row Offsets: {:?}", self.row_offsets)?;
        writeln!(f, "Column Indices: {:?}", self.col_indices)?;
        writeln!(f, "Values: {:?}", self.values)?;
        Ok(())
    }
}

fn main() {
    // Example data in COO format:
    // Each tuple represents (row_index, col_index, value)
```

159

```rust
    let coo_entries = vec![
        (0, 1, 3.0),
        (0, 3, 4.5),
        (1, 0, 2.1),
        (2, 2, 5.0),
        (3, 1, 6.2),
        (3, 3, 7.7),
    ];

    // Create a 4x4 sparse matrix from the COO representation.
    let sparse_matrix = SparseMatrix::from_coo(4, 4, coo_entries);

    // Print the CSR representation of the sparse matrix.
    println!("{}", sparse_matrix);

    // Create a dense vector to multiply with, e.g., x = [1.0, 2.0,
    ↪  3.0, 4.0].
    let dense_vector = vec![1.0, 2.0, 3.0, 4.0];

    // Carry out the multiplication y = A * x.
    let result = sparse_matrix.mul_dense(&dense_vector);

    // Display the result of the multiplication.
    println!(
        "Result of multiplying the sparse matrix with the vector
    ↪  {:?}:\n{:?}",
        dense_vector, result
    );
}
```

Chapter 26

Implementing Principal Component Analysis

Mathematical Foundations of Principal Component Analysis

Principal Component Analysis (PCA) is founded on the theory of linear algebra and statistical variance. Given a dataset represented as a matrix $X \in \mathbb{R}^{n \times m}$, where n denotes the number of observations and m the number of features, the initial step involves centerizing the data by subtracting the empirical mean computed along each feature dimension. The centering process yields a new matrix $\tilde{X}$ whose columns have zero mean. The next step is the formulation of the covariance matrix C, defined as

$$C = \frac{1}{n-1}\tilde{X}^T \tilde{X},$$

which encapsulates the pairwise variances and covariances among the features. The structure of C, a symmetric matrix in $\mathbb{R}^{m \times m}$, establishes the foundation upon which subsequent eigenvalue decomposition is performed. The inherent linearity and symmetry of the covariance matrix ensure that its eigenvalues are real and that the associated eigenvectors are orthogonal. This property is critical in deriving the directions along which the data exhibits maximum variance.

Eigenvalue Decomposition in the PCA Framework

The core computational task in PCA is the eigenvalue decomposition of the covariance matrix C. The decomposition involves solving the characteristic equation

$$Cv = \lambda v,$$

where λ represents an eigenvalue and v the corresponding eigenvector. In this context, the eigenvectors provide the directions or axes in feature space that capture the maximum variance, while the eigenvalues quantify the magnitude of variance along each direction. The decomposition yields a collection of pairs $\{(\lambda_i, v_i)\}_{i=1}^{m}$, which, once ordered by decreasing eigenvalue, enable the extraction of a lower-dimensional subspace that retains the most significant aspects of the original data. The numerical challenges associated with eigenvalue computation, including stability and efficiency of iterative methods, are addressed through the use of optimized algorithms embedded in robust numerical libraries.

Variance Maximization and Dimensionality Reduction

A central objective of PCA is to identify a set of orthogonal axes that maximize the variance of the projected data. Mathematically, this involves the search for a unit vector $w \in \mathbb{R}^m$ that maximizes the objective function

$$\max_{w} \; w^T C w \quad \text{subject to} \quad \|w\|_2 = 1.$$

The solution to this constrained optimization problem is given by the eigenvector corresponding to the largest eigenvalue of C. Subsequent principal components are determined similarly, with each new component requiring orthogonality to all previously selected components. The eigenvalues $\lambda_1 \geq \lambda_2 \geq \cdots \geq \lambda_m$ serve as measures of the variance captured along their corresponding eigenvectors. By retaining only the first k eigenvectors, where $k < m$, it becomes possible to form a reduced representation of the original dataset while preserving a substantial portion of the total variance. The cumulative sum of the eigenvalues provides a quantitative criterion for choosing the appropriate number of principal components, thus balancing between dimensionality reduction and information retention.

Leveraging Rust's Numerical Libraries for Principal Component Analysis

The implementation of PCA in Rust benefits significantly from the language's strong emphasis on safe memory management and performance optimization. Rust's numerical libraries provide high-performance routines for linear algebraic operations, including eigenvalue decomposition, matrix multiplication, and data transformation. The abstraction offered by these libraries enables the concise expression of mathematical operations in a manner that closely resembles their theoretical formulations. When executing eigenvalue decomposition, the robustness of the underlying algorithms is complemented by Rust's zero-cost abstractions, ensuring that high-level code translates into efficient machine instructions without compromising on safety. The integration of these numerical routines into a PCA implementation facilitates efficient handling of large-scale datasets, where the reduction of dimensionality is achieved through variance maximization. Through meticulous management of data structures, particularly dense and sparse representations, Rust provides an ideal environment for implementing the mathematically rigorous processes required for PCA while maintaining optimal computational performance.

Rust Code Snippet

```rust
use ndarray::prelude::*;
use ndarray_stats::SummaryStatisticsExt;
use ndarray_linalg::Eig;

fn main() {
    // Create a sample dataset: each row is an observation and each
    // ↪ column a feature.
    // For example, a 5 x 3 matrix.
    let data = array![
        [2.5, 2.4, 1.5],
        [0.5, 0.7, 1.3],
        [2.2, 2.9, 1.8],
        [1.9, 2.2, 1.4],
        [3.1, 3.0, 2.0]
    ];
```

```rust
let (n, m) = (data.nrows(), data.ncols());

// Compute the mean for each feature (column) and center the
↪ data.
let means = data.mean_axis(Axis(0)).expect("Failed to compute
↪ means");
let centered = &data - &means;

// Compute the covariance matrix:
// C = (1 / (n - 1)) * (centered)^T * (centered)
let covariance = centered.t().dot(&centered) / (n as f64 - 1.0);

// Perform eigenvalue decomposition on the covariance matrix.
// The eigenvalues quantify variance along corresponding
↪ eigenvectors.
let eig_result = covariance.eig().expect("Eigenvalue
↪ decomposition failed");
let (eigenvalues, eigenvectors) = eig_result; // eigenvalues:
↪ Array1<f64>, eigenvectors: Array2<f64>

// Sort eigenvalues and eigenvectors in descending order of
↪ eigenvalues.
let mut indices: Vec<usize> = (0..m).collect();
indices.sort_by(|&i, &j|
↪ eigenvalues[j].partial_cmp(&eigenvalues[i]).unwrap());

let sorted_eigenvalues =
↪ Array1::from_vec(indices.iter().map(|&i|
↪ eigenvalues[i]).collect());
// Reorder eigenvectors: each column corresponds to an
↪ eigenvector.
let sorted_eigenvectors = Array2::from_shape_vec(
    (m, m),
    indices.iter().flat_map(|&i|
    ↪ eigenvectors.column(i).to_vec()).collect()
)
.expect("Failed to reshape sorted eigenvectors");

// Choose the number of principal components to retain
↪ (dimensionality reduction).
let k = 2; // For example, reduce to 2 dimensions.

// Form the projection matrix using the first k eigenvectors.
let projection_matrix = sorted_eigenvectors.slice(s![..,
↪ 0..k]).to_owned();

// Project the centered data onto the new k-dimensional
↪ subspace.
let transformed_data = centered.dot(&projection_matrix);

// Display the results.
println!("Original Data:\n{}", data);
println!("Means:\n{}", means);
```

164

```
    println!("Centered Data:\n{}", centered);
    println!("Covariance Matrix:\n{}", covariance);
    println!("Sorted Eigenvalues:\n{}", sorted_eigenvalues);
    println!("Projection Matrix (first {} principal
    ↪   components):\n{}", k, projection_matrix);
    println!("Transformed Data:\n{}", transformed_data);
}
```

Chapter 27

Linear Regression from First Principles

Mathematical Model and Assumptions

Consider a dataset comprising n observations, each characterized by m features. The linear regression model postulates that the response variable can be expressed as a linear combination of the predictors. In formal terms, the model is defined by

$$y = X\beta + \varepsilon,$$

where $y \in \mathbb{R}^n$ is the vector of observed responses, $X \in \mathbb{R}^{n \times m}$ is the design matrix whose rows represent individual observations and columns denote the predictors, $\beta \in \mathbb{R}^m$ is the vector of unknown parameters, and $\varepsilon \in \mathbb{R}^n$ is the vector of random errors. The standard assumptions for this model include that the error vector satisfies $E[\varepsilon] = 0$ and that it possesses constant variance, conditions that are instrumental in establishing the statistical properties of the estimator.

Matrix Formulation of the Regression Problem

The utilization of matrix notation offers a compact and elegant framework for representing the regression problem. In this formulation, the design matrix X is constructed such that each row

166

corresponds to an observation, and its columns may include a column of ones to account for the intercept. The relationship between the predictors and the responses is encapsulated in the model

$$y = X\beta + \varepsilon.$$

This notation permits the expression of the objective function, namely the sum of squared residuals, in a concise form. The residual vector, given by $r = y - X\beta$, leads to the definition of the least squares criterion as

$$S(\beta) = \|y - X\beta\|_2^2.$$

This quadratic form not only quantifies the discrepancy between the observed and predicted outcomes but also sets the stage for the analytical derivation of the parameter estimates.

Derivation of the Normal Equations

The derivation of the optimal parameter vector $\hat{\beta}$ is founded on the minimization of the objective function

$$\hat{\beta} = \arg \min_{\beta} \|y - X\beta\|_2^2.$$

Expanding the squared Euclidean norm results in a quadratic function in the parameter vector β. The gradient of $S(\beta)$ with respect to β is computed as

$$\nabla S(\beta) = -2X^T (y - X\beta).$$

Setting this gradient to zero to achieve optimality yields the equation

$$X^T (y - X\beta) = 0,$$

which, upon reorganization, leads to the normal equations

$$X^T X \beta = X^T y.$$

Under the assumption that the matrix $X^T X$ is invertible (which holds when X has full column rank), the unique solution for the regression coefficients is given by

$$\hat{\beta} = \left(X^T X \right)^{-1} X^T y.$$

167

Analysis of the Least Squares Criterion

The least squares criterion defines a convex optimization landscape, ensuring that the minimization problem possesses a unique global optimum. The function

$$S(\beta) = \|y - X\beta\|_2^2$$

is quadratic and, thus, its curvature is governed entirely by the matrix $X^T X$. The optimal estimator $\hat{\beta}$, determined via the normal equations, represents the orthogonal projection of the response vector y onto the subspace spanned by the columns of the matrix X. This projection minimizes the residual sum of squares (RSS), given by

$$\text{RSS} = \|y - X\hat{\beta}\|_2^2,$$

and provides a quantitative measure of the fit of the linear model to the observed data.

Interpretation of Parameter Estimates

The expression

$$\hat{\beta} = \left(X^T X\right)^{-1} X^T y$$

yields the vector of coefficients that minimizes the projection error in a least squares sense. Each component of $\hat{\beta}$ quantifies the influence of the corresponding predictor variable on the response, assuming a linear relationship between them. The method of ordinary least squares elicits an estimator for which the residual vector is orthogonal to each column of the design matrix X, fulfilling the condition

$$X^T(y - X\hat{\beta}) = 0.$$

This orthogonality condition confirms that the deviations of the predictions from the actual responses are uncorrelated with the predictors, thereby ensuring that the estimator possesses desirable properties, including unbiasedness under the classical linear model assumptions.

Theoretical Implications and Computational Considerations

The computation of $\hat{\beta}$ requires executing several key matrix operations, foremost among which is the inversion of the matrix $X^T X$. The numerical stability of this inversion is governed by the conditioning of $X^T X$, and poor conditioning may necessitate alternative decomposition methods such as singular value decomposition (SVD) or QR decomposition. In theoretical terms, the ordinary least squares estimator is known to be the best linear unbiased estimator (BLUE) under the Gauss-Markov assumptions. The derivation of $\hat{\beta}$ via the normal equations epitomizes the elegant interplay between linear algebra and statistical estimation, linking the minimization of the quadratic error criterion directly to the projection properties inherent in Euclidean space. These theoretical insights also dictate the computational techniques deployed for large-scale linear regression, where the efficient execution of matrix multiplications and inversions is critical for scalability and precision.

Rust Code Snippet

```rust
extern crate ndarray;
extern crate ndarray_linalg;

use ndarray::{Array, Array1, Array2};
use ndarray_linalg::Inverse; // To compute the inverse of a matrix

/// Computes the Ordinary Least Squares (OLS) estimator for linear
↪  regression
///
/// The model is given by:
///     y = X * +
/// and the objective is to minimize the sum of squared residuals:
///     S() = || y - X ||².
///
/// The analytical solution (the normal equations) is:
///       = (XX)⁻¹ Xy
///
/// # Arguments
///
/// * `x` - The design matrix X of shape (n, m), where each row is
↪  an observation.
/// * `y` - The response vector y of length n.
///
/// # Returns
```

```rust
///
/// * `Array1<f64>` - The estimated coefficient vector .
///
/// # Panics
///
/// Panics if (XX) is non-invertible.
fn ordinary_least_squares(x: &Array2<f64>, y: &Array1<f64>) ->
↪  Array1<f64> {
    // Compute XX
    let xtx = x.t().dot(x);

    // Invert XX
    let xtx_inv = xtx.inv().expect("Matrix (XX) is
    ↪` non-invertible!");

    // Compute Xy
    let xty = x.t().dot(y);

    // Compute  = (XX)' * (Xy)
    let beta_hat = xtx_inv.dot(&xty);
    beta_hat
}

fn main() {
    // Example dataset:
    // Here, we have n = 4 observations and m = 2 predictors
    ↪  (including an intercept).
    // The design matrix X includes a column of ones for the
    ↪  intercept.
    let x = Array::from_shape_vec(
        (4, 2),
        vec![
            1.0, 1.1, // Observation 1: (intercept, x)
            1.0, 2.0, // Observation 2: (intercept, x)
            1.0, 3.0, // Observation 3: (intercept, x)
            1.0, 4.0, // Observation 4: (intercept, x)
        ],
    ).expect("Error creating the design matrix X.");

    // Response vector y with 4 observations
    let y = Array::from_vec(vec![2.0, 3.0, 5.0, 7.0]);

    // Display the design matrix and response vector
    println!("Design Matrix X:\n{:?}", x);
    println!("Response Vector y:\n{:?}", y);

    // Compute the regression coefficients using Ordinary Least
    ↪  Squares
    let beta_hat = ordinary_least_squares(&x, &y);
    println!("Estimated Coefficients ():\n{:?}", beta_hat);

    // Compute predicted responses: y = X *
    let y_hat = x.dot(&beta_hat);
```

170

```rust
    println!("Predicted Responses (ŷ):\n{:?}", y_hat);

    // Compute the residuals: r = y - ŷ
    let residuals = y - &y_hat;
    println!("Residuals (r):\n{:?}", residuals);

    // Compute the Residual Sum of Squares (RSS) = ||r||²
    let rss = residuals.dot(&residuals);
    println!("Residual Sum of Squares (RSS): {:.4}", rss);
}
```

Chapter 28

Logistic Regression for Classification Tasks

Mathematical Formulation and the Logistic Function

Logistic regression is a statistical model that formulates the probability of a binary outcome through a nonlinear transformation of a linear predictor. The model specifies that the conditional probability of the positive class, denoted by $Y = 1$, given a vector of predictor variables X, is captured by the logistic (or sigmoid) function. This function is defined as

$$\sigma(z) = \frac{1}{1 + e^{-z}},$$

where $z = X\beta$ represents the linear aggregation of the features with parameters β. Consequently, the probability of class 1 is expressed as

$$P(Y = 1 \mid X) = \sigma(X\beta),$$

and, by complement, the probability of class 0 is

$$P(Y = 0 \mid X) = 1 - \sigma(X\beta).$$

This formulation imposes a smooth, monotonic mapping from the entire real line to the bounded interval $(0, 1)$, thereby ensuring that the outputs are valid probabilities.

Cost Function and Maximum Likelihood Estimation

The logistic regression model is underpinned by a probabilistic framework that assumes each observation $y_i \in \{0,1\}$ is drawn independently from a Bernoulli distribution with success probability $\sigma(x_i\beta)$, where x_i represents the ith row of the design matrix X. The likelihood for a single observation is given by

$$P(y_i \mid x_i; \beta) = \sigma(x_i\beta)^{y_i} \left(1 - \sigma(x_i\beta)\right)^{1-y_i} .$$

Under the assumption of independence, the likelihood function for the entire dataset comprising n observations is

$$\mathcal{L}(\beta) = \prod_{i=1}^{n} \sigma(x_i\beta)^{y_i} \left(1 - \sigma(x_i\beta)\right)^{1-y_i} .$$

Maximization of this likelihood, or equivalently the minimization of the negative log-likelihood, yields the optimal parameter vector β. The corresponding cost function, known commonly as the cross-entropy loss, takes the form

$$J(\beta) = -\sum_{i=1}^{n} \left[y_i \log \sigma(x_i\beta) + (1 - y_i) \log \left(1 - \sigma(x_i\beta)\right)\right].$$

Due to the convex nature of this cost function with respect to β, a unique global minimum is guaranteed, and the optimization task is well-defined.

Gradient Descent Optimization for Logistic Regression

In the absence of a closed-form analytical solution for β, iterative numerical optimization methods, particularly gradient descent, are implemented to minimize the cost function $J(\beta)$. The gradient of the cost function with respect to the parameter vector β is derived by differentiating the cross-entropy loss. For each parameter β_j, the partial derivative is

$$\frac{\partial J(\beta)}{\partial \beta_j} = \sum_{i=1}^{n} \left(\sigma(x_i\beta) - y_i\right) x_{ij},$$

173

where x_{ij} denotes the jth feature of the ith observation. In vectorized notation, the gradient is expressed succinctly as

$$\nabla J(\beta) = X^T \left[\sigma(X\beta) - y\right],$$

where $\sigma(X\beta)$ is understood as the element-wise application of the sigmoid function to the vector $X\beta$. The gradient descent update rule is then formulated as

$$\beta^{(t+1)} = \beta^{(t)} - \alpha \nabla J(\beta^{(t)}),$$

where α represents the learning rate and t indexes the iteration. Iterative updates progress until the decrement in the cost function between successive iterations diminishes below a designated tolerance, signifying convergence.

Interpretation of Probabilistic Classification

By transforming the linear predictor through the logistic function, the model produces outputs that directly correspond to the estimated probability of a positive classification. The decision boundary is implicitly defined by the threshold on the predicted probability. Typically, an observation is classified as belonging to the positive class when

$$\hat{P}(Y = 1 \mid X) = \sigma(X\beta) \geq 0.5,$$

and to the negative class otherwise. This probabilistic interpretation facilitates not only the binary classification of observations but also provides a measure of confidence in the predictions. The logistic regression model, therefore, marries the rigors of maximum likelihood estimation with the computational tractability of gradient descent optimization, establishing a robust framework for binary outcome prediction in a variety of contexts.

Rust Code Snippet

```
extern crate ndarray;
use ndarray::{array, Array1, Array2};

/// Sigmoid function implementing the logistic function:
```

```
///  (z) = 1 / (1 + exp(-z))
///
/// This provides the mapping from any real value to (0, 1),
/// corresponding to the probability of the positive class.
fn sigmoid(z: &Array1<f64>) -> Array1<f64> {
    z.mapv(|v| 1.0 / (1.0 + (-v).exp()))
}


/// Compute the cost (cross-entropy loss) for logistic regression:
/// J() = - (1/m) *  [ y_i * ln((x_i·)) + (1 - y_i) * ln(1 - (x_i·))
↪   ]
///
/// A small epsilon is added inside the logarithm to avoid numerical
↪   issues.
fn compute_cost(X: &Array2<f64>, y: &Array1<f64>, beta:
↪   &Array1<f64>) -> f64 {
    let m = y.len() as f64;
    let z = X.dot(beta);
    let predictions = sigmoid(&z);
    let epsilon = 1e-10;
    let cost = y.iter()
                .zip(predictions.iter())
                .map(|(&yi, &pi)| {
                    -yi * (pi + epsilon).ln() - (1.0 - yi) * (1.0 -
↪   pi + epsilon).ln()
                })
                .sum::<f64>();
    cost / m
}


/// Compute the gradient of the cost function:
/// J() = (1/m) * X · ((X) - y)
fn compute_gradient(X: &Array2<f64>, y: &Array1<f64>, beta:
↪   &Array1<f64>) -> Array1<f64> {
    let m = y.len() as f64;
    let z = X.dot(beta);
    let predictions = sigmoid(&z);
    let errors = &predictions - y;
    X.t().dot(&errors) / m
}


/// Perform gradient descent to optimize parameters .
/// The update rule for each iteration is:
///  =  -  * J()
fn gradient_descent(
    X: &Array2<f64>,
    y: &Array1<f64>,
    beta: &mut Array1<f64>,
    alpha: f64,
    iterations: usize,
) {
    for iter in 0..iterations {
        let cost = compute_cost(X, y, beta);
```

```
        let grad = compute_gradient(X, y, beta);
        *beta = beta - &(grad * alpha);
        // Monitor convergence by printing the cost every 1000
        ↪  iterations.
        if iter % 1000 == 0 {
            println!("Iteration {}: Cost = {:.6}", iter, cost);
        }
    }
}

fn main() {
    // Example training data:
    // The feature matrix X has m = 4 samples and n = 3 features.
    // The first column is a bias term (all ones).
    let X: Array2<f64> = array![
        [1.0, 2.0, 3.0],
        [1.0, 3.0, 5.0],
        [1.0, 5.0, 8.0],
        [1.0, 7.0, 10.0]
    ];

    // Binary class labels (0 or 1) for each training sample.
    let y: Array1<f64> = array![0.0, 0.0, 1.0, 1.0];

    // Initialize parameter vector  (one parameter per feature) to
    ↪  zeros.
    let n_features = X.shape()[1];
    let mut beta = Array1::<f64>::zeros(n_features);

    // Hyperparameters: learning rate () and number of iterations.
    let alpha = 0.1;
    let iterations = 10_000;

    println!("Initial beta: {:?}", beta);
    gradient_descent(&X, &y, &mut beta, alpha, iterations);
    println!("Optimized beta: {:?}", beta);

    // Compute predictions using the optimized .
    // The predicted probability for the positive class is:
    // P(Y = 1 | X) = (X·)
    // Classify as 1 if probability  0.5; otherwise, classify as 0.
    let predictions = sigmoid(&X.dot(&beta))
        .mapv(|p| if p >= 0.5 { 1.0 } else { 0.0 });
    println!("Predictions: {:?}", predictions);
}
```

Chapter 29

Decision Boundary Computation and Visualization

Mathematical Formulation of Decision Boundaries

In classification theory, the decision boundary is defined as the locus of points in the feature space at which the classifier is indifferent between assigning either class label. For a binary classifier that defines a continuous score function $f : \mathbb{R}^n \to \mathbb{R}$, the decision boundary can be characterized by the equation

$$f(\mathbf{x}) = \theta,$$

where $\mathbf{x} \in \mathbb{R}^n$ represents the feature vector and θ is the decision threshold. In many models, particularly those in which the output is obtained via a transformation such as the logistic function, a natural choice is to set θ to the midpoint of the output scale. For instance, in logistic regression where the probability of a positive class is given by

$$P(Y = 1 \mid \mathbf{x}) = \sigma(\mathbf{x}\beta),$$

and the sigmoid function is defined as

$$\sigma(z) = \frac{1}{1 + e^{-z}},$$

selecting a threshold of 0.5 implies that the decision boundary satisfies

$$\sigma(\mathbf{x}\beta) = 0.5,$$

which is equivalent to the linear condition

$$\mathbf{x}\beta = 0.$$

This formulation generalizes to classifiers with nonlinear score functions, where the decision boundary may represent a complex hypersurface rather than a hyperplane.

Computational Techniques for Boundary Extraction

The extraction of decision boundaries depends critically on the mathematical properties of the classifier. In the case of linear classifiers, the decision boundary is readily obtained by solving a set of linear equations. For a classifier defined by a linear score function $f(\mathbf{x}) = \beta_0 + \sum_{i=1}^{n} \beta_i x_i$, the boundary reduces to the simple linear equation

$$\beta_0 + \sum_{i=1}^{n} \beta_i x_i = 0.$$

For nonlinear classifiers, however, no closed-form solution may exist. In these scenarios, numerical methods are employed to compute the boundary. One common approach involves a grid sampling of the feature space. The classifier is evaluated at a dense set of points, and the decision boundary is approximated by identifying the loci where the output transitions from one class region to another. More formally, if the classifier outputs a continuous value $f(\mathbf{x})$, contours corresponding to the isovalue θ can be extracted using algorithms for contour detection. The resulting set

$$\{\mathbf{x} \in \mathbb{R}^n \mid f(\mathbf{x}) = \theta\}$$

serves as a discrete approximation of the decision boundary. Additionally, by leveraging the differentiability of f, gradient-based methods can be applied to iteratively converge to points on the boundary, thereby refining the approximation in regions of high curvature or complex topology.

Visualization Techniques for Model Behavior

Visualization of decision boundaries plays a central role in interpreting model behavior in classification tasks. When the feature space is two-dimensional, the decision boundary can be directly overlaid on a scatter plot of the data. The procedure usually involves computing the classifier's prediction over a fine mesh grid covering the region of interest. The contour defined by

$$\{(x_1, x_2) \mid f(x_1, x_2) = \theta\}$$

is then superimposed on the data distribution to illustrate the separation between classes.

For higher-dimensional spaces, techniques such as dimensionality reduction are applied to project the data and the corresponding decision boundary into a two- or three-dimensional space amenable to visualization. The transformation must preserve the relative structure of the original data to ensure that the visualization accurately reflects model behavior. In some cases, color gradients are used to represent the output values of $f(\mathbf{x})$, thereby providing information not only about the location of the boundary but also about the classifier's confidence across the feature space. These approaches collectively provide insightful visual representations that elucidate the internal workings of the classifier, facilitating a deeper understanding of the decision-making process inherent in the model.

Rust Code Snippet

```
use std::f64;

/// Logistic (sigmoid) function: (z) = 1 / (1 + exp(-z))
fn logistic(z: f64) -> f64 {
    1.0 / (1.0 + (-z).exp())
}

/// Linear classifier function: f(x) =  +  * x +  * x
fn linear_classifier(x: &[f64; 2], beta: &[f64; 3]) -> f64 {
    beta[0] + beta[1] * x[0] + beta[2] * x[1]
}

/// Logistic regression output: (f(x))
fn classifier_output(x: &[f64; 2], beta: &[f64; 3]) -> f64 {
    logistic(linear_classifier(x, beta))
```

179

```
}

/// Grid sampling to extract the decision boundary approximation.
/// It scans a 2D feature space, estimates the classifier's output,
↪    and linearly interpolates
/// a crossing point when a transition over the threshold is found.
fn grid_sampling(beta: &[f64; 3], xmin: f64, xmax: f64, ymin: f64,
↪    ymax: f64, steps: usize) -> Vec<[f64; 2]> {
    let mut boundary_points = Vec::new();
    let dx = (xmax - xmin) / (steps as f64);
    let dy = (ymax - ymin) / (steps as f64);
    let threshold = 0.5; // For logistic regression, decision
↪    threshold is 0.5

    // Iterate over a 2D grid of points.
    for i in 0..steps {
        for j in 0..steps {
            let x1 = xmin + i as f64 * dx;
            let x2 = ymin + j as f64 * dy;
            let current_point = [x1, x2];
            let value = classifier_output(&current_point, beta);

            // Check horizontal neighbor for a sign change
            if i < steps - 1 {
                let x1_next = xmin + (i + 1) as f64 * dx;
                let neighbor_point = [x1_next, x2];
                let value_next = classifier_output(&neighbor_point,
↪    beta);
                // If the product (value - threshold) * (value_next
↪    - threshold) is negative,
                // a crossing occurs between these points.
                if (value - threshold) * (value_next - threshold) <
↪    0.0 {
                    // Linear interpolation along x-axis.
                    let t = (threshold - value) / (value_next -
↪    value);
                    let interpolated_x1 = x1 + t * dx;
                    boundary_points.push([interpolated_x1, x2]);
                }
            }

            // Check vertical neighbor for a sign change.
            if j < steps - 1 {
                let x2_next = ymin + (j + 1) as f64 * dy;
                let neighbor_point = [x1, x2_next];
                let value_next = classifier_output(&neighbor_point,
↪    beta);
                if (value - threshold) * (value_next - threshold) <
↪    0.0 {
                    // Linear interpolation along y-axis.
                    let t = (threshold - value) / (value_next -
↪    value);
                    let interpolated_x2 = x2 + t * dy;
```

180

```
                    boundary_points.push([x1, interpolated_x2]);
                }
            }
        }
    }
    boundary_points
}

/// Refines an approximated boundary point using gradient descent.
/// The optimization minimizes the error |(f(x)) - threshold| by
↪ adjusting the point in the input space.
/// The gradient with respect to x is computed via the chain rule:
/// d()/dz = (z) * (1 - (z))     and     dz/dx = [, ]
fn refine_boundary_point(mut point: [f64; 2], beta: &[f64; 3],
↪ learning_rate: f64, iterations: usize) -> [f64; 2] {
    let threshold = 0.5;
    let mut x = point;
    for _ in 0..iterations {
        // Compute the classifier's linear output and its logistic
        ↪ response.
        let linear_val = linear_classifier(&x, beta);
        let sigma = logistic(linear_val);
        let error = sigma - threshold;

        // Compute the gradient factor: derivative of logistic times
        ↪ error.
        let grad_factor = sigma * (1.0 - sigma) * error;

        // Update x: since f/x = and f/x = (for a linear
        ↪ function), adjust both coordinates.
        x[0] -= learning_rate * grad_factor * beta[1];
        x[1] -= learning_rate * grad_factor * beta[2];
    }
    x
}

fn main() {
    // Define classifier weights for a 2D logistic regression model
    ↪ (including bias).
    // For example, beta = [0, 1, -1] corresponds to the linear
    ↪ decision boundary x - x = 0.
    let beta: [f64; 3] = [0.0, 1.0, -1.0];

    // Set grid sampling parameters over a 2D feature space.
    let xmin = -5.0;
    let xmax = 5.0;
    let ymin = -5.0;
    let ymax = 5.0;
    let steps = 100;

    // Approximate decision boundary points via grid sampling.
    let boundary_points = grid_sampling(&beta, xmin, xmax, ymin,
    ↪ ymax, steps);
```

```
    println!("Estimated decision boundary points (before
    ↪  refinement):");
    for point in &boundary_points {
        println!("({:.4}, {:.4})", point[0], point[1]);
    }

    // Refine a sample of boundary points using gradient descent for
    ↪  improved precision.
    println!("\nRefined decision boundary points (first 10):");
    for point in boundary_points.iter().take(10) {
        let refined_point = refine_boundary_point(*point, &beta,
        ↪  0.1, 50);
        println!(
            "Original: ({:.4}, {:.4}) -> Refined: ({:.4}, {:.4})",
            point[0], point[1], refined_point[0], refined_point[1]
        );
    }
}
```

Chapter 30

k-Means Clustering Algorithm Implementation

Initialization of Cluster Centroids

The algorithm commences with the selection of initial centroids, fundamental points in the feature space denoted by $\mu_1, \mu_2, \ldots, \mu_k \in \mathbb{R}^d$, where k represents the number of clusters and d is the dimensionality of the data. These centroids may be chosen through simple random sampling from the dataset or by employing more sophisticated techniques such as the k-means++ probabilistic initialization. In the context of a Rust implementation, careful attention is paid to the efficient generation and storage of these centroid values, ensuring that each element is represented with precision and optimized for subsequent computations. The mathematical objective at this juncture is to provide an initial partitioning that allows the iterative process to refine these estimates towards minimization of within-cluster variance.

Iterative Assignment of Data Points

Following the initialization phase, the algorithm proceeds by assigning each data point $x \in \mathbb{R}^d$ to the cluster whose centroid is closest in terms of Euclidean distance. Formally, for each data point, the assignment is realized by identifying the index i satisfying

$$i = \arg \min_{j \in \{1,\ldots,k\}} \|x - \mu_j\|^2.$$

This distance measure is computed using the standard Euclidean norm, and serves as the criterion for class membership within the clustering framework. The assignment process is inherently iterative, as the clustering structure is dynamically adjusted based on the emergent distribution of data points. In an efficient Rust implementation, this phase is carefully engineered to leverage the language's concurrency primitives and memory safety guarantees, ensuring that the distance computations and comparisons are executed with both accuracy and speed. Each iteration re-evaluates point memberships in light of potentially updated centroids, thereby progressively leading the algorithm toward a stable partitioning.

Centroid Updating Mechanism

Upon completion of the assignment phase, the centroids are recalculated to better represent the current clusters. The update rule derives from the arithmetic mean of the points assigned to each cluster. For a given cluster C_i, the new centroid μ_i is computed as

$$\mu_i = \frac{1}{|C_i|} \sum_{x \in C_i} x,$$

where $|C_i|$ denotes the number of data points within the cluster. This recalibration serves both to reduce the distortion error and to steer the centroids closer to the underlying data distribution. The process, grounded in the principle of minimization of the squared error, is performed repeatedly in an iterative manner until the shifts in centroid positions fall below a predetermined threshold. The implementation in Rust emphasizes the utilization of zero-cost abstractions and effective memory management during the summation and division operations, ensuring that each centroid update is computed with minimal overhead and maximal precision. The iterative updates, in legal accordance with convergence criteria, culminate in a clustering configuration that approximates the optimal partitioning of the dataset with respect to the k-means objective function.

Rust Code Snippet

```rust
use rand::seq::SliceRandom;
use rand::thread_rng;

/// Computes the squared Euclidean distance between two points in
↪  ^d.
/// Squared distance is used to avoid the computational cost of the
↪  square root,
/// since the relative comparison remains valid.
fn squared_distance(a: &Vec<f64>, b: &Vec<f64>) -> f64 {
    a.iter()
     .zip(b.iter())
     .map(|(x, y)| (x - y) * (x - y))
     .sum()
}

/// Initializes centroids by randomly selecting k distinct data
↪  points.
/// This serves as the starting partition for the iterative k-means
↪  process.
fn initialize_centroids(data: &Vec<Vec<f64>>, k: usize) ->
↪  Vec<Vec<f64>> {
    let mut rng = thread_rng();
    data.choose_multiple(&mut rng, k)
        .cloned()
        .collect()
}

/// Assigns each data point to the closest centroid based on the
↪  squared Euclidean distance.
/// Returns a vector where each element is the index of the nearest
↪  centroid for the corresponding point.
fn assign_clusters(data: &Vec<Vec<f64>>, centroids: &Vec<Vec<f64>>)
↪  -> Vec<usize> {
    data.iter()
        .map(|point| {
            centroids.iter()
                     .enumerate()
                     .min_by(|&(_, cent_a), &(_, cent_b)| {
                         let dist_a = squared_distance(point,
                         ↪  cent_a);
                         let dist_b = squared_distance(point,
                         ↪  cent_b);
                         dist_a.partial_cmp(&dist_b).unwrap()
                     })
                     .unwrap()
                     .0
        })
        .collect()
}
```

```rust
/// Updates each centroid by computing the arithmetic mean of all
↪   points assigned to it.
/// This is performed for each cluster to reduce the within-cluster
↪   variance.
fn update_centroids(data: &Vec<Vec<f64>>, assignments: &Vec<usize>,
↪   k: usize, dim: usize) -> Vec<Vec<f64>> {
    let mut centroids = vec![vec![0.0; dim]; k];
    let mut counts = vec![0usize; k];

    // Sum all points belonging to the same cluster.
    for (point, &cluster) in data.iter().zip(assignments.iter()) {
        for j in 0..dim {
            centroids[cluster][j] += point[j];
        }
        counts[cluster] += 1;
    }

    // Compute the mean for each cluster.
    for i in 0..k {
        if counts[i] > 0 {
            for j in 0..dim {
                centroids[i][j] /= counts[i] as f64;
            }
        }
    }
    centroids
}


/// Executes the k-means clustering algorithm:
/// 1. Initialize centroids.
/// 2. Iteratively assign points to the nearest centroid (assignment
↪   step).
/// 3. Update centroids based on the current cluster memberships
↪   (update step).
/// The process repeats until the maximum centroid shift is below a
↪   specified tolerance,
/// indicating convergence, or until a maximum number of iterations
↪   is reached.
fn kmeans(data: &Vec<Vec<f64>>, k: usize, max_iter: usize, tol: f64)
↪   -> (Vec<Vec<f64>>, Vec<usize>) {
    // Initialize centroids via random sampling.
    let mut centroids = initialize_centroids(data, k);
    let mut assignments = vec![0; data.len()];

    for iter in 0..max_iter {
        // --- Iterative Assignment of Data Points ---
        // Each point is assigned to the nearest centroid.
        assignments = assign_clusters(data, &centroids);

        // --- Centroid Updating Mechanism ---
        // Recompute centroids as the mean of all points in each
        ↪   cluster.
```

```
        let new_centroids = update_centroids(data, &assignments, k,
        ↪   data[0].len());

        // Compute the maximum movement (shift) among all centroids
        ↪   to check for convergence.
        let mut max_shift = 0.0;
        for (old, new) in centroids.iter().zip(new_centroids.iter())
        ↪   {
            let shift = squared_distance(old, new).sqrt();
            if shift > max_shift {
                max_shift = shift;
            }
        }

        // Debug output to trace the iterative process.
        println!("Iteration {}: max centroid shift = {:.6}", iter,
        ↪   max_shift);

        centroids = new_centroids;

        // Terminate if the centroids have converged sufficiently.
        if max_shift < tol {
            println!("Convergence reached at iteration {}.", iter);
            break;
        }
    }
    (centroids, assignments)
}

fn main() {
    // Example dataset: a collection of 2D points.
    let data = vec![
        vec![1.0, 2.0],
        vec![1.5, 1.8],
        vec![5.0, 8.0],
        vec![8.0, 8.0],
        vec![1.0, 0.6],
        vec![9.0, 11.0],
        vec![8.0, 2.0],
        vec![10.0, 2.0],
        vec![9.0, 3.0],
    ];

    let k = 3;           // Number of clusters
    let max_iter = 100;  // Maximum iterations allowed
    let tol = 0.001;     // Tolerance for centroid movement
    ↪   (convergence criterion)

    let (centroids, assignments) = kmeans(&data, k, max_iter, tol);

    println!("Final centroids: {:?}", centroids);
    println!("Cluster assignments: {:?}", assignments);
```

}
_____

Chapter 31

Hierarchical Clustering Techniques in Rust

Agglomerative Clustering Algorithms

Agglomerative clustering constitutes a bottom-up paradigm in which each data point is initially regarded as a singleton cluster. At every iteration, pairs of clusters are merged according to a similarity or dissimilarity measure, thereby reducing the total number of clusters. Fundamental to this approach is the evaluation of inter-cluster distances, commonly defined by a chosen linkage criterion. For instance, given two clusters C_i and C_j, the single linkage distance is defined as

$$d_{\text{single}}(C_i, C_j) = \min_{x \in C_i, y \in C_j} \|x - y\|,$$

while the complete and average linkage criteria are expressed respectively as

$$d_{\text{complete}}(C_i, C_j) = \max_{x \in C_i, y \in C_j} \|x - y\|$$

and

$$d_{\text{average}}(C_i, C_j) = \frac{1}{|C_i| \cdot |C_j|} \sum_{x \in C_i, y \in C_j} \|x - y\|.$$

The algorithm recursively selects the pair of clusters exhibiting the smallest inter-cluster distance according to the evaluated metric. This recursive merging results in a hierarchical partitioning of the data, where each merge operation can be viewed as the formation of an internal node in the associated dendrogram. The recursive nature of the agglomerative process naturally lends itself to an implementation strategy that emphasizes clear and efficient memory management, with each merge operation abstracted as a composable function within the Rust ecosystem.

Divisive Clustering Strategies

Divisive clustering adopts a top-down methodology wherein the entire dataset is initially considered as a single cluster. The algorithm then recursively partitions this global cluster into smaller, more coherent sub-clusters. At each iteration, a splitting strategy is employed to identify the optimal bifurcation of a cluster. This process is often guided by measures of cluster quality that may include inter-point dissimilarities or the minimization of a certain cost function that quantifies intra-cluster variance. A common approach involves selecting a subset of data points within the current cluster, determining candidate split-points, and evaluating the resulting partitions based on an objective function. A typical recursive partitioning strategy may involve an initial extraction of a bipartition that maximizes the dissimilarity between the resultant clusters while preserving the internal cohesion of each group. The recursive splitting continues until a predetermined stopping condition is met, such as a minimal cluster size or a threshold on the improvement in the cost function. The divisive approach, while computationally more intensive than its agglomerative counterpart, offers enhanced flexibility particularly in scenarios where the natural structure of the data is globally non-convex.

Recursive Dendrogram Construction

The hierarchical relationships that emerge from both agglomerative and divisive methods are naturally represented in the form of a dendrogram. In this structure, each leaf node corresponds to an individual data point, and each internal node reflects the outcome of a merge or split operation. Construction of the dendrogram is inherently recursive: at every recursion step, the algorithm evaluates the current set of clusters, performing either a merge (in agglomerative clustering) or a split (in divisive clustering) to generate a new level of the hierarchy. The height of each node in the dendrogram is directly associated with the dissimilarity measure at the moment of the cluster combination or division. This height, denoted by h, is computed as

$$h = f\big(d(C_i, C_j)\big),$$

where f represents the mapping from the selected distance metric d to a scalar that signifies the level of separation within the hierarchical structure. The recursive construction of the dendrogram facilitates a granular analysis of the data grouping hierarchies, enabling not only the identification of distinct clusters at various levels of resolution but also the inspection of the underlying structural relationships between data points. The process exemplifies the power of recursive programming in building complex tree-like structures, and it leverages Rust's capabilities for safe memory management and efficient execution of recursive algorithms.

Rust Code Snippet

```rust
use std::f64;

#[derive(Debug, Clone)]
struct Point {
    coords: Vec<f64>,
}

impl Point {
    // Compute Euclidean distance between two points
    fn distance(&self, other: &Point) -> f64 {
        self.coords
            .iter()
            .zip(other.coords.iter())
            .map(|(a, b)| (a - b).powi(2))
            .sum::<f64>()
            .sqrt()
    }
}

#[derive(Debug, Clone)]
struct Cluster {
    points: Vec<Point>,
    // An identifier could be used to track clusters in the
    ↪   dendrogram.
    id: usize,
}

#[derive(Debug)]
enum Linkage {
    Single,
    Complete,
```

191

```rust
    Average,
}

// Dendrogram node representing either a leaf (single point)
// or an internal node with children resulting from a merge or
↪  split.
#[derive(Debug)]
struct DendrogramNode {
    left: Option<Box<DendrogramNode>>,
    right: Option<Box<DendrogramNode>>,
    cluster: Cluster,
    // Height corresponds to the dissimilarity measure at
    ↪  merge/split,
    // e.g., for agglomerative clustering it matches the computed
    ↪  distance:
    //   h = f(d(C_i, C_j)) with f as identity in this example.
    height: f64,
}

// Compute the inter-cluster distance based on the chosen linkage
↪  criterion.
// Implements the following formulas:
//   Single Linkage:    d_single(C_i, C_j) = min_{x in C_i, y in C_j}
↪  ||x - y||
//   Complete Linkage: d_complete(C_i, C_j) = max_{x in C_i, y in
↪  C_j} ||x - y||
//   Average Linkage:  d_average(C_i, C_j) = (1/(|C_i|*|C_j|)) *
↪  sum_{x in C_i, y in C_j} ||x - y||
fn inter_cluster_distance(cluster1: &Cluster, cluster2: &Cluster,
↪  linkage: &Linkage) -> f64 {
    match linkage {
        Linkage::Single => {
            let mut min_dist = f64::MAX;
            for p in &cluster1.points {
                for q in &cluster2.points {
                    let dist = p.distance(q);
                    if dist < min_dist {
                        min_dist = dist;
                    }
                }
            }
            min_dist
        }
        Linkage::Complete => {
            let mut max_dist = 0.0;
            for p in &cluster1.points {
                for q in &cluster2.points {
                    let dist = p.distance(q);
                    if dist > max_dist {
                        max_dist = dist;
                    }
                }
            }
```

```
                max_dist
            }
            Linkage::Average => {
                let mut sum = 0.0;
                let mut count = 0;
                for p in &cluster1.points {
                    for q in &cluster2.points {
                        sum += p.distance(q);
                        count += 1;
                    }
                }
                if count > 0 {
                    sum / count as f64
                } else {
                    0.0
                }
            }
        }
    }

// Implements the agglomerative clustering algorithm.
// Initially, each data point is its own cluster. Then recursively,
↪    the pair
// of clusters with the smallest inter-cluster distance is merged,
// forming a new node in the dendrogram.
fn agglomerative_clustering(mut clusters: Vec<DendrogramNode>,
↪    linkage: Linkage) -> DendrogramNode {
    while clusters.len() > 1 {
        let mut min_distance = f64::MAX;
        let mut merge_indices = (0, 0);

        // Find the pair of clusters with the smallest distance.
        for i in 0..clusters.len() {
            for j in i + 1..clusters.len() {
                let dist = inter_cluster_distance(
                    &clusters[i].cluster,
                    &clusters[j].cluster,
                    &linkage,
                );
                if dist < min_distance {
                    min_distance = dist;
                    merge_indices = (i, j);
                }
            }
        }

        // Remove clusters in order to merge them.
        let (index1, index2) = merge_indices;
        let (first, second) = if index1 < index2 {
            (index1, index2)
        } else {
            (index2, index1)
        };
```

```rust
        let left_node = clusters.remove(second);
        let right_node = clusters.remove(first);

        // Merge the points from both clusters.
        let mut merged_points = right_node.cluster.points.clone();
        merged_points.extend(left_node.cluster.points.clone());
        let merged_cluster = Cluster {
            points: merged_points,
            id: 0, // ID generation can be implemented as needed.
        };

        // Create a new dendrogram node representing this merge.
        let new_node = DendrogramNode {
            left: Some(Box::new(right_node)),
            right: Some(Box::new(left_node)),
            cluster: merged_cluster,
            height: min_distance, // Height is set to the minimal
            ↪   distance computed.
        };

        clusters.push(new_node);
    }

    clusters.pop().unwrap()
}

// Divisive clustering adopts a top-down approach. This example
↪   provides a naive
// implementation that recursively splits a cluster into two parts
↪   based on the median
// of the first coordinate. The stopping condition is determined by
↪   a minimal cluster size.
fn divisive_clustering(cluster: &Cluster, min_size: usize) ->
↪   DendrogramNode {
    if cluster.points.len() <= min_size {
        return DendrogramNode {
            left: None,
            right: None,
            cluster: cluster.clone(),
            height: 0.0,
        };
    }

    let mut points = cluster.points.clone();
    points.sort_by(|a, b|
    ↪   a.coords[0].partial_cmp(&b.coords[0]).unwrap());
    let mid = points.len() / 2;

    let left_points = points[..mid].to_vec();
    let right_points = points[mid..].to_vec();

    let left_cluster = Cluster { points: left_points, id: 0 };
```

194

```rust
        let right_cluster = Cluster { points: right_points, id: 0 };

        // Height is calculated as the absolute difference between the
        // ↪  last point in the left cluster
        // and the first point in the right cluster based on the first
        // ↪  coordinate.
        let height = if let (Some(last_left), Some(first_right)) = (
            left_cluster.points.last(),
            right_cluster.points.first(),
        ) {
            (first_right.coords[0] - last_left.coords[0]).abs()
        } else {
            0.0
        };

        let left_node = divisive_clustering(&left_cluster, min_size);
        let right_node = divisive_clustering(&right_cluster, min_size);

        DendrogramNode {
            left: Some(Box::new(left_node)),
            right: Some(Box::new(right_node)),
            cluster: cluster.clone(),
            height,
        }
    }
}

fn main() {
    // Create some sample points in 2D space.
    let points = vec![
        Point { coords: vec![1.0, 2.0] },
        Point { coords: vec![2.0, 3.0] },
        Point { coords: vec![10.0, 10.0] },
        Point { coords: vec![10.5, 9.5] },
        Point { coords: vec![5.0, 5.0] },
    ];

    // For agglomerative clustering, each point starts as an
    // ↪  individual cluster.
    let mut initial_nodes: Vec<DendrogramNode> = points
        .into_iter()
        .map(|p| DendrogramNode {
            left: None,
            right: None,
            cluster: Cluster { points: vec![p], id: 0 },
            height: 0.0,
        })
        .collect();

    // Perform agglomerative clustering using the Single Linkage
    // ↪  criterion.
    let dendrogram_agglomerative =
    ↪  agglomerative_clustering(initial_nodes.clone(),
    ↪  Linkage::Single);
```

```rust
    println!(
        "Agglomerative Clustering Dendrogram: {:#?}",
        dendrogram_agglomerative
    );

    // For divisive clustering, use a single cluster containing all
    ↪ points.
    let initial_cluster = Cluster {
        points: dendrogram_agglomerative.cluster.points.clone(),
        id: 0,
    };
    let dendrogram_divisive = divisive_clustering(&initial_cluster,
    ↪ 1);
    println!(
        "Divisive Clustering Dendrogram: {:#?}",
        dendrogram_divisive
    );
}
```
_____

Chapter 32

Support Vector Machines: Kernel Functions and Optimization

Mathematical Foundations of Support Vector Machines

The theoretical framework of support vector machines is rooted in the principles of statistical learning and convex optimization. At its core, the objective is to determine a separating hyperplane in a high-dimensional space that maximizes the margin between classes. Given a set of training examples (x_i, y_i), where x_i
in
$mathbbR^n$ and y_i
in
$-1, +1$, the classifier is constructed by determining a weight vector

$mathbfw$ and a bias b such that the decision function

$$f(x) = mathrmsgn(mathbfwcdotx + b)$$

exhibits a maximal separation between the classes. The primal optimization problem is typically formulated as the minimization of the functional

$$\min_{\mathbf{w},b} \frac{1}{2}|\mathbf{w}|^2,$$

subject to the constraint

$$y_i(\mathbf{w} \cdot x_i + b) \geq 1 \quad \text{for all } i.$$

This formulation guarantees maximization of the margin while minimizing the complexity of the classifier by controlling the norm of $\mathbf{w}$.

Kernel Functions and Feature Space Transformation

Kernel functions play an integral role when data are not linearly separable in the original input space. The strategy involves mapping the input data into a high-dimensional feature space via a nonlinear transformation
$\phi : \mathbb{R}^n \rightarrow \mathcal{H}$, such that inner products in the transformed space can be computed without explicit evaluation of ϕ. This is achieved through the definition of a kernel function

$$K(x_i, x_j) = \langle \phi(x_i), \phi(x_j) \rangle,$$

which encapsulates the similarity between pairs of input vectors. Common choices for the kernel function include the polynomial kernel, given by

$$K(x_i, x_j) = (\gamma(x_i \cdot x_j) + r)^d,$$

and the radial basis function (RBF) kernel, defined as

$$K(x_i, x_j) = \exp(-\gamma|x_i - x_j|^2).$$

These kernels enable the classifier to capture intricate patterns in the data while preserving the computational advantages of inner product evaluations.

Optimization Strategies and Theoretical Considerations

The constrained quadratic maximization presented in the dual formulation is subject to strict convexity properties, which guarantee a unique optimal solution. Solving this optimization problem necessitates the use of efficient numerical techniques, such as interior-point methods or iterative solvers like the sequential minimal optimization algorithm. The performance and convergence properties of these algorithms are strongly influenced by the handling of numerical precision and the sparsity characteristics of the kernel matrix. The trade-off between computational complexity and model expressiveness is managed through regularization parameters, which balance the violation of margin constraints against the robustness of the solution. An analytical understanding of the Karush-Kuhn-Tucker conditions is essential to ensure that the solution satisfies both primal and dual feasibility conditions, as well as the complementary slackness property.

Rust Implementation Considerations

Implementing a support vector machine classifier in Rust imparts several design advantages tied to the language's strong static type system and memory safety guarantees. The numerical routines required for efficient matrix operations and iterative solvers can be structured using Rust's trait system, thereby enabling polymorphic behavior across different kernel implementations. Special attention must be paid to the representation of floating-point arithmetic to minimize rounding errors in the evaluation of both the kernel function and the dual objective. Memory management plays a critical role when handling the potentially large and sparse kernel matrix, and Rust's ownership model aids in maintaining strict control over resource allocation. Furthermore, the modularity of the Rust implementation encourages the encapsulation of the optimization routines, allowing them to be unit tested independently and integrated seamlessly with the higher-level classification logic. This structured approach fosters the creation of a scalable and robust support vector machine classifier that can be extended or modified to accommodate various kernel functions and optimization strategies as dictated by the statistical properties of the data.

Rust Code Snippet

```rust
use std::f64::EPSILON;
use rand::Rng;

/// A single training example with feature vector `x` and label `y`
/// (-1.0 or +1.0)
#[derive(Debug)]
pub struct DataPoint {
    pub x: Vec<f64>,
    pub y: f64,
}

/// Trait representing a kernel function that computes the inner
/// product
/// in a transformed feature space.
pub trait Kernel {
    fn compute(&self, x1: &Vec<f64>, x2: &Vec<f64>) -> f64;
}

/// Polynomial kernel: K(x, y) = (gamma * <x, y> + coef0)^degree
pub struct PolynomialKernel {
    pub degree: usize,
    pub gamma: f64,
    pub coef0: f64,
}

impl Kernel for PolynomialKernel {
    fn compute(&self, x1: &Vec<f64>, x2: &Vec<f64>) -> f64 {
        let dot = x1.iter()
                    .zip(x2.iter())
                    .map(|(a, b)| a * b)
                    .sum::<f64>();
        (self.gamma * dot + self.coef0).powi(self.degree as i32)
    }
}

/// Radial Basis Function (RBF) kernel: K(x, y) = exp(-gamma * ||x -
/// y||^2)
pub struct RBFKernel {
    pub gamma: f64,
}

impl Kernel for RBFKernel {
    fn compute(&self, x1: &Vec<f64>, x2: &Vec<f64>) -> f64 {
        let sum_sq: f64 = x1.iter()
                    .zip(x2.iter())
                    .map(|(a, b)| (a - b).powi(2))
                    .sum();
        (-self.gamma * sum_sq).exp()
    }
}
```

200

```rust
/// Support Vector Machine model using the dual formulation and
↪ SMO-like optimization.
pub struct SVM<K: Kernel> {
    pub kernel: K,
    pub C: f64,                 // Regularization parameter
    pub tol: f64,               // Tolerance for error
    pub max_passes: usize,      // Max iterations without alpha updates
    ↪ before stopping
    pub alphas: Vec<f64>,       // Lagrange multipliers for each
    ↪ training sample
    pub b: f64,                 // Bias term
    pub data: Vec<DataPoint>,
}

impl<K: Kernel> SVM<K> {
    /// Initialize a new SVM with the given kernel, regularization
    ↪ parameter, tolerance, and max passes.
    pub fn new(kernel: K, C: f64, tol: f64, max_passes: usize) ->
    ↪ Self {
        SVM {
            kernel,
            C,
            tol,
            max_passes,
            alphas: Vec::new(),
            b: 0.0,
            data: Vec::new(),
        }
    }

    /// Fit the SVM model using a simplified Sequential Minimal
    ↪ Optimization (SMO) algorithm.
    pub fn fit(&mut self, data: Vec<DataPoint>) {
        self.data = data;
        let n = self.data.len();
        self.alphas = vec![0.0; n];
        self.b = 0.0;

        let mut passes = 0;
        let mut rng = rand::thread_rng();

        while passes < self.max_passes {
            let mut num_changed_alphas = 0;
            for i in 0..n {
                let E_i = self.decision_function(&self.data[i].x) -
                ↪ self.data[i].y;
                if (self.data[i].y * E_i < -self.tol &&
                ↪ self.alphas[i] < self.C) ||
                    (self.data[i].y * E_i > self.tol &&
                    ↪ self.alphas[i] > 0.0) {

                    // Select a random index j  i
```

201

```rust
    let mut j = i;
    while j == i {
        j = rng.gen_range(0..n);
    }
    let E_j =
    ↪    self.decision_function(&self.data[j].x) -
    ↪    self.data[j].y;
    let alpha_i_old = self.alphas[i];
    let alpha_j_old = self.alphas[j];

    // Compute bounds L and H for alpha[j]
    let (L, H) = if self.data[i].y != self.data[j].y
    ↪    {
        (f64::max(0.0, self.alphas[j] -
        ↪    self.alphas[i]),
         f64::min(self.C, self.C + self.alphas[j] -
         ↪    self.alphas[i]))
    } else {
        (f64::max(0.0, self.alphas[i] +
        ↪    self.alphas[j] - self.C),
         f64::min(self.C, self.alphas[i] +
         ↪    self.alphas[j]))
    };

    if (L - H).abs() < EPSILON {
        continue;
    }

    // Compute kernel evaluations
    let k_ii = self.kernel.compute(&self.data[i].x,
    ↪    &self.data[i].x);
    let k_jj = self.kernel.compute(&self.data[j].x,
    ↪    &self.data[j].x);
    let k_ij = self.kernel.compute(&self.data[i].x,
    ↪    &self.data[j].x);

    // Compute eta (second derivative of the
    ↪    objective function)
    let eta = 2.0 * k_ij - k_ii - k_jj;
    if eta >= 0.0 {
        continue;
    }

    // Update alpha[j]
    self.alphas[j] = self.alphas[j] -
    ↪    (self.data[j].y * (E_i - E_j)) / eta;
    if self.alphas[j] > H {
        self.alphas[j] = H;
    } else if self.alphas[j] < L {
        self.alphas[j] = L;
    }
```

202

```rust
                    if (self.alphas[j] - alpha_j_old).abs() <
                    ↪   EPSILON {
                        continue;
                    }

                    // Update alpha[i] based on the change in
                    ↪   alpha[j]
                    self.alphas[i] = self.alphas[i] + self.data[i].y
                    ↪   * self.data[j].y * (alpha_j_old -
                    ↪   self.alphas[j]);

                    // Update bias term b using computed thresholds
                    ↪   b1 and b2
                    let b1 = self.b - E_i
                        - self.data[i].y * (self.alphas[i] -
                        ↪   alpha_i_old) * k_ii
                        - self.data[j].y * (self.alphas[j] -
                        ↪   alpha_j_old) * k_ij;
                    let b2 = self.b - E_j
                        - self.data[i].y * (self.alphas[i] -
                        ↪   alpha_i_old) * k_ij
                        - self.data[j].y * (self.alphas[j] -
                        ↪   alpha_j_old) * k_jj;
                    if self.alphas[i] > 0.0 && self.alphas[i] <
                    ↪   self.C {
                        self.b = b1;
                    } else if self.alphas[j] > 0.0 && self.alphas[j]
                    ↪   < self.C {
                        self.b = b2;
                    } else {
                        self.b = (b1 + b2) / 2.0;
                    }
                    num_changed_alphas += 1;
                }
            }
            if num_changed_alphas == 0 {
                passes += 1;
            } else {
                passes = 0;
            }
        }
    }

    /// Compute the decision function for a given input vector.
    /// f(x) = sum(alpha[i] * y[i] * K(x_i, x)) + b
    pub fn decision_function(&self, x: &Vec<f64>) -> f64 {
        let mut sum = 0.0;
        for (i, data_point) in self.data.iter().enumerate() {
            sum += self.alphas[i] * data_point.y *
            ↪   self.kernel.compute(&data_point.x, x);
        }
        sum + self.b
    }
```

203

```rust
    /// Predict the class label for an input vector. Returns +1.0 if
    ↪ the decision function
    /// is non-negative and -1.0 otherwise.
    pub fn predict(&self, x: &Vec<f64>) -> f64 {
        if self.decision_function(x) >= 0.0 {
            1.0
        } else {
            -1.0
        }
    }
}

fn main() {
    // Define a simple dataset for binary classification.
    let data = vec![
        DataPoint { x: vec![2.0, 3.0], y: 1.0 },
        DataPoint { x: vec![1.0, 1.0], y: -1.0 },
        DataPoint { x: vec![2.0, 1.0], y: -1.0 },
        DataPoint { x: vec![3.0, 2.0], y: 1.0 },
    ];

    // Choose the kernel function.
    // Uncomment one of the following to select a kernel:
    // let kernel = PolynomialKernel { degree: 2, gamma: 1.0, coef0:
    ↪ 1.0 };
    let kernel = RBFKernel { gamma: 0.5 };

    // Instantiate the SVM with regularization parameter C,
    ↪ tolerance, and maximum passes.
    let mut svm = SVM::new(kernel, 1.0, 0.001, 5);
    svm.fit(data);

    // Test the trained SVM model with a new input.
    let test_point = vec![2.5, 2.0];
    println!("Prediction for {:?}: {}", test_point,
    ↪ svm.predict(&test_point));
}
```

Chapter 33

Naive Bayes Classification for Text Analytics

Probabilistic Foundations

The Naive Bayes classifier is derived from Bayes' theorem combined with the assumption of conditional independence among features. In this formulation, the posterior probability of a class c given a document d is expressed as

$$P(c \mid d) = \frac{P(d \mid c)\, P(c)}{P(d)},$$

where $P(c)$ indicates the prior probability of class c, $P(d \mid c)$ is the likelihood of document d given class c, and $P(d)$ serves as a normalizing constant independent of c. Under the assumption that the features extracted from the document are independent, the likelihood term factorizes into

$$P(d \mid c) = \prod_{i=1}^{N} P(w_i \mid c),$$

with w_i representing the individual features derived from the document. This simplification, although idealized, provides computational tractability and has been validated empirically in various text analytics applications.

Feature Extraction for Textual Data

The conversion of unstructured text into a structured format conducive to probabilistic modeling constitutes a critical step in the application of the Naive Bayes classifier. Text documents are typically represented as high-dimensional vectors constructed via a bag-of-words model. In this context, each document is transformed into a feature vector $\mathbf{x} = (x_1, x_2, \ldots, x_N)$, where each component x_i corresponds either to the count or a binary indicator of the presence of a corresponding term from a predefined vocabulary. Preprocessing techniques such as tokenization, stop word removal, and stemming are systematically applied to mitigate noise and reduce the dimensionality of the vocabulary space. Advanced weighting schemes, like term frequency-inverse document frequency (TF-IDF), may be incorporated to accentuate discriminative terms while attenuating the influence of ubiquitous words. The resultant feature representation provides a concise yet informative basis for subsequent probability estimation in the classification process.

Probability Estimation and Smoothing Techniques

Central to the Naive Bayes classifier is the estimation of the conditional probability of each feature given the class label. For each word w_i in the vocabulary and for each class c, the probability $P(w_i \mid c)$ is estimated using the maximum likelihood principle as

$$P(w_i \mid c) = \frac{\text{count}(w_i, c)}{\sum_{j=1}^{N} \text{count}(w_j, c)},$$

where $\text{count}(w_i, c)$ denotes the frequency with which the word w_i occurs in documents labeled with class c. In instances where $\text{count}(w_i, c)$ is zero, the probability estimate becomes problematic due to the complete omission of potentially informative features. To counteract this effect, Laplace smoothing (or additive smoothing) is utilized, modifying the estimate to

$$P(w_i \mid c) = \frac{\text{count}(w_i, c) + 1}{\sum_{j=1}^{N} [\text{count}(w_j, c) + 1]}.$$

This technique ensures that no probability is rendered zero and that the logarithmic transformation of these probabilities, which is commonly employed for numerical stability, remains well defined.

Additionally, the prior probability $P(c)$ is computed as the ratio of the number of documents in class c to the total number of documents in the training corpus,

$$P(c) = \frac{\text{number of documents in } c}{\text{total number of documents}}.$$

These computed probabilities form the basis for the classification decision, which is typically made by selecting the class c that maximizes the posterior probability $P(c \mid d)$.

Model Training and Inference in High-dimensional Spaces

During model training, document counts are aggregated to estimate the prior and conditional probabilities referred to in the previous sections. In the inference phase, the probability of a document belonging to a class c is evaluated in log-space to prevent underflow issues that arise from the product of many small probabilities. The log-transform leads to an additive scoring mechanism, expressed as

$$\log P(c \mid \mathbf{x}) \propto \log P(c) + \sum_{i=1}^{N} x_i \log P(w_i \mid c).$$

Here, the summation is taken over all components of the feature vector, with each term weighted by the corresponding feature value x_i. The decision rule assigns the document to the class with the highest score, effectively implementing a maximum a posteriori (MAP) selection.

The transition of computations into the logarithmic domain not only improves numerical stability but also simplifies the operations involved in optimization and parameter tuning. Despite the violation of the independence assumption in practical scenarios, the classifier often exhibits robust performance in text analytics tasks. The strategy of performing multiplicative probability calculations in log-space remains instrumental when dealing with high-dimensional data and a vast vocabulary, typical of document classification problems.

By virtue of these probabilistic and statistical techniques, the Naive Bayes classifier offers a computationally efficient and theoretically grounded approach for the classification of text documents.

Rust Code Snippet

```rust
use std::collections::{HashMap, HashSet};

/// A simple Naive Bayes classifier for text analytics.
struct NaiveBayesClassifier {
    /// Counts the number of documents for each class.
    class_counts: HashMap<String, usize>,
    /// For each class, stores the frequency of each word.
    word_counts: HashMap<String, HashMap<String, usize>>,
    /// Total number of documents seen during training.
    total_docs: usize,
    /// The set of all unique words observed (vocabulary).
    vocabulary: HashSet<String>,
    /// For each class, total number of words (used for probability
    ↪   normalization).
    total_word_counts: HashMap<String, usize>,
}

impl NaiveBayesClassifier {
    /// Creates a new NaiveBayesClassifier instance.
    fn new() -> Self {
        NaiveBayesClassifier {
            class_counts: HashMap::new(),
            word_counts: HashMap::new(),
            total_docs: 0,
            vocabulary: HashSet::new(),
            total_word_counts: HashMap::new(),
        }
    }

    /// Tokenizes input text into a vector of lower-cased words.
    fn tokenize(text: &str) -> Vec<String> {
        text.split_whitespace()
            .map(|s| s.to_lowercase())
            .collect()
    }

    /// Trains the classifier with labeled documents.
    /// Each training sample is a tuple (class_label,
    ↪   document_text).
    fn train(&mut self, data: Vec<(String, String)>) {
        for (label, doc) in data.into_iter() {
            self.total_docs += 1;
            *self.class_counts.entry(label.clone()).or_insert(0) +=
            ↪   1;

            let word_map =
            ↪   self.word_counts.entry(label.clone()).or_insert(
            HashMap::new());
            let total_words =
            ↪   self.total_word_counts.entry(label.clone()).or_insert(0);
```

```
        let tokens = NaiveBayesClassifier::tokenize(&doc);
        for token in tokens {
            self.vocabulary.insert(token.clone());
            *word_map.entry(token).or_insert(0) += 1;
            *total_words += 1;
        }
    }
}

/// Predicts the class label for a given document.
/// Uses Laplace smoothing and computes log probabilities to
↪   prevent underflow.
fn predict(&self, doc: &str) -> Option<String> {
    let tokens = NaiveBayesClassifier::tokenize(doc);
    let vocab_size = self.vocabulary.len() as f64;
    let mut best_class: Option<String> = None;
    let mut max_log_prob = std::f64::NEG_INFINITY;

    // Iterate over each class to compute its log-probability
    ↪   for the document.
    for (class, &doc_count) in &self.class_counts {
        // Prior probability: P(c) = (number of docs in class c)
        ↪   / (total docs)
        let prior = (doc_count as f64) / (self.total_docs as
        ↪   f64);
        let mut log_prob = prior.ln();

        // Get word frequency map and total word count for the
        ↪   class.
        let word_map = self.word_counts.get(class).unwrap();
        let total_words =
        ↪   *self.total_word_counts.get(class).unwrap() as f64;

        // Calculate log likelihood: sum_{i} log(P(w_i|c))
        // With Laplace smoothing: P(w|c) = (count(w, c) + 1) /
        ↪   (total_words + |vocab|)
        for token in tokens.iter() {
            let token_count = *word_map.get(token).unwrap_or(&0)
            ↪   as f64;
            let token_prob = (token_count + 1.0) / (total_words
            ↪   + vocab_size);
            log_prob += token_prob.ln();
        }

        if log_prob > max_log_prob {
            max_log_prob = log_prob;
            best_class = Some(class.clone());
        }
    }
    best_class
}
}
```

209

```rust
fn main() {
    // Example training data: each tuple is (class_label,
    // ↪ document_text).
    let training_data = vec![
        ("Sports".to_string(), "The team played a great game last
        ↪ night".to_string()),
        ("Sports".to_string(), "The coach was happy with the
        ↪ performance".to_string()),
        ("Politics".to_string(), "The parliament passed a new
        ↪ law".to_string()),
        ("Politics".to_string(), "The government is preparing for
        ↪ the election".to_string()),
    ];

    let mut classifier = NaiveBayesClassifier::new();
    classifier.train(training_data);

    // Test document to classify.
    let test_doc = "The team is preparing for a new season";
    match classifier.predict(test_doc) {
        Some(predicted_class) => println!("Predicted Class: {}",
        ↪ predicted_class),
        None => println!("Prediction could not be made."),
    }
}
```

Chapter 34

Ensemble Learning: Bagging and Boosting Techniques

Fundamental Concepts of Ensemble Methods

Ensemble methods are a class of machine learning algorithms that form predictions by aggregating the outputs of multiple base learners, each of which is typically a weak model with performance only marginally better than random chance. The underlying hypothesis is that the combination of several models, when their errors are uncorrelated, can produce a significantly more robust and accurate predictor than any individual component. Formally, if a set of weak learners is denoted by $h_1, h_2, \ldots, h_M$, the composite model can be expressed as

$$H(x) = \sum_{i=1}^{M} \alpha_i h_i(x),$$

where the weights α_i calibrate the contribution of each base learner. This aggregation is designed to leverage the strengths and mitigate the weaknesses inherent in each individual model, leading to enhanced predictive capability.

Bagging Techniques in Ensemble Learning

Bagging, an abbreviation for Bootstrap Aggregating, constructs multiple instances of a given base learner, each trained on a different bootstrap sample generated from the original training data. In this framework, each model $h_k(x)$ is trained on a dataset D_k obtained by random sampling with replacement. The predictions from these base learners are then aggregated through techniques such as averaging for regression tasks or majority voting for classification tasks. The aggregated prediction is mathematically represented as

$$H(x) = \frac{1}{K} \sum_{k=1}^{K} h_k(x),$$

where K is the total number of bagged models. The principal merit of bagging lies in its ability to reduce variance without increasing bias substantially, thereby yielding a predictor with enhanced stability and accuracy. Such variance reduction is achieved by decorrelating the individual learners, as the random resampling process ensures that each base learner is exposed to a distinct subset of the data, leading to diverse decision boundaries.

Boosting Techniques and Sequential Optimization

Boosting algorithms refine ensemble performance by sequentially training base learners in such a way that each subsequent model is designed to compensate for the errors of the preceding ensemble. The methodology involves assigning weights to the training instances to emphasize those that are difficult to classify. During each iteration, the weak learner is trained to minimize a cost function that reflects the misclassification error observed in the preceding iterations. The cumulative model is often expressed as

$$H(x) = \text{sign}\left(\sum_{t=1}^{T} \alpha_t h_t(x)\right),$$

where the parameters α_t are determined based on the performance of the corresponding weak learners $h_t(x)$, and T denotes the total number of boosting iterations. This sequential process inherently minimizes bias while also addressing the variance component, by focusing attention on the training instances that are mispredicted. The careful adjustment of the weights iteratively refines the decision boundaries and typically results in a strong classifier even when the individual base learners are prone to errors.

Ensemble Methodologies within the Rust Ecosystem

The integration of ensemble methods within a Rust-based data science framework capitalizes on the language's distinguishing features such as memory safety, concurrency, and performance. Rust permits the parallel training of multiple base learners, a characteristic that is particularly advantageous in bagging where independent models can be trained concurrently. The zero-cost abstractions and ownership model ensure that the computational overhead remains minimal while safeguarding the integrity of memory during parallel operations. Similarly, the iterative nature of boosting algorithms can benefit from Rust's efficient control flow constructs and safe concurrency paradigms. The modular design of Rust libraries facilitates the implementation of ensemble strategies by allowing complex data transformations and model evaluations to execute within a secure type system. Consequently, ensemble learning in Rust combines the theoretical robustness of bagging and boosting techniques with the practical benefits of high-performance, concurrent computing environments.

Rust Code Snippet

```rust
use rand::prelude::*;
use std::f64;

#[derive(Clone)]
struct Instance {
    features: Vec<f64>,
    label: i32,    // For classification: 1 or -1
    weight: f64,   // Used in boosting for weighted sampling
}

type Dataset = Vec<Instance>;
```

```rust
pub trait Classifier {
    fn predict(&self, x: &Vec<f64>) -> i32;
}

// A simple Decision Stump acting as a weak learner.
// It splits based on one feature, a threshold and a polarity.
#[derive(Clone)]
struct DecisionStump {
    feature_index: usize,
    threshold: f64,
    polarity: i32, // Either 1 or -1. Determines the direction of
    ↪   comparison.
}

impl Classifier for DecisionStump {
    fn predict(&self, x: &Vec<f64>) -> i32 {
        // The prediction rule:
        // if (polarity * x[feature_index]) < (polarity * threshold)
        ↪   then output -1, else 1.
        if (self.polarity as f64 * x[self.feature_index])
            < (self.polarity as f64 * self.threshold)
        {
            -1
        } else {
            1
        }
    }
}

// Function that creates a bootstrap sample (sampling with
↪   replacement)
// for bagging purposes.
fn bootstrap_sample(dataset: &Dataset) -> Dataset {
    let n = dataset.len();
    let mut rng = thread_rng();
    let mut sample = Vec::with_capacity(n);
    for _ in 0..n {
        let idx = rng.gen_range(0..n);
        sample.push(dataset[idx].clone());
    }
    sample
}

// Train a DecisionStump on the provided dataset.
// For boosting, the dataset instances come with their own weights.
fn train_decision_stump(dataset: &Dataset) -> DecisionStump {
    // Choose a random feature index.
    let num_features = dataset[0].features.len();
    let mut rng = thread_rng();
    let feature_index = rng.gen_range(0..num_features);

    // Determine threshold range based on feature values.
    let mut min_val = f64::INFINITY;
```

214

```rust
    let mut max_val = f64::NEG_INFINITY;
    for inst in dataset {
        let value = inst.features[feature_index];
        if value < min_val {
            min_val = value;
        }
        if value > max_val {
            max_val = value;
        }
    }
    // Randomly select a threshold between min and max.
    let threshold = rng.gen_range(min_val..=max_val);

    // For simplicity, randomly set polarity.
    let polarity = if rng.gen_bool(0.5) { 1 } else { -1 };

    DecisionStump { feature_index, threshold, polarity }
}

// ----------------------
// Bagging Ensemble
// ----------------------
struct BaggingEnsemble {
    models: Vec<Box<dyn Classifier>>,
}

impl BaggingEnsemble {
    // Predict using bagging.
    // Equation: H(x) = 1/K * sum_{k=1}^{K} h_k(x)
    // For classification, we take the sign of the aggregated
    // ↪ prediction.
    fn predict(&self, x: &Vec<f64>) -> i32 {
        let sum: i32 = self.models.iter().map(|m|
        ↪ m.predict(x)).sum();
        if sum >= 0 { 1 } else { -1 }
    }
}

// Train a Bagging Ensemble by creating K independent models
// on bootstrapped samples of the training dataset.
fn train_bagging(dataset: &Dataset, k: usize) -> BaggingEnsemble {
    let mut models: Vec<Box<dyn Classifier>> =
    ↪ Vec::with_capacity(k);
    for _ in 0..k {
        let sample = bootstrap_sample(dataset);
        let stump = train_decision_stump(&sample);
        models.push(Box::new(stump));
    }
    BaggingEnsemble { models }
}

// ----------------------
// Boosting Ensemble (AdaBoost)
```

```
// ----------------------
struct BoostingEnsemble {
    // Each element consists of a weight (alpha) and a weak learner.
    models: Vec<(f64, Box<dyn Classifier>)>,
}

impl BoostingEnsemble {
    // Predict using boosting.
    // Equation: H(x) = sign( sum_{t=1}^{T} alpha_t * h_t(x) )
    fn predict(&self, x: &Vec<f64>) -> i32 {
        let sum: f64 = self.models.iter()
            .map(|(alpha, model)| alpha * (model.predict(x) as f64))
            .sum();
        if sum >= 0.0 { 1 } else { -1 }
    }
}

// Train a Boosting Ensemble using a simple AdaBoost algorithm.
fn train_boosting(mut dataset: Dataset, t: usize) ->
↪   BoostingEnsemble {
    let n = dataset.len();
    // Initialize instance weights uniformly.
    for inst in dataset.iter_mut() {
        inst.weight = 1.0 / (n as f64);
    }

    let mut models: Vec<(f64, Box<dyn Classifier>)> =
    ↪   Vec::with_capacity(t);
    let mut rng = thread_rng();

    for _ in 0..t {
        // Sample the dataset according to current weights.
        let mut weighted_sample = Vec::with_capacity(n);
        for _ in 0..n {
            let mut r = rng.gen::<f64>();
            let mut cum_sum = 0.0;
            for inst in &dataset {
                cum_sum += inst.weight;
                if r <= cum_sum {
                    weighted_sample.push(inst.clone());
                    break;
                }
            }
        }

        let stump = train_decision_stump(&weighted_sample);

        // Compute weighted error of the stump on the full dataset.
        let mut error = 0.0;
        for inst in &dataset {
            if stump.predict(&inst.features) != inst.label {
                error += inst.weight;
            }
```

```rust
        }
        // Skip iteration if error is too high (must be <= 0.5 for
        ↪ AdaBoost)
        if error > 0.5 {
            continue;
        }
        // Avoid division by zero.
        if error == 0.0 {
            error = 1e-10;
        }

        // Compute alpha using: alpha = 0.5 * ln((1 - error) /
        ↪ error)
        let alpha = 0.5 * ((1.0 - error) / error).ln();

        // Update instance weights:
        // w_i = w_i * exp(-alpha * y_i * h(x_i))
        let mut weight_sum = 0.0;
        for inst in dataset.iter_mut() {
            let prediction = stump.predict(&inst.features) as f64;
            inst.weight *= (-alpha * (inst.label as f64) *
            ↪ prediction).exp();
            weight_sum += inst.weight;
        }
        // Normalize weights so they sum to 1.
        for inst in dataset.iter_mut() {
            inst.weight /= weight_sum;
        }

        models.push((alpha, Box::new(stump)));
    }

    BoostingEnsemble { models }
}

// ----------------------
// Main: Example usage
// ----------------------
fn main() {
    // Create a dummy dataset.
    let dataset: Dataset = vec![
        Instance { features: vec![2.5, 3.0], label: 1, weight: 0.0
        ↪ },
        Instance { features: vec![1.0, 2.0], label: -1, weight: 0.0
        ↪ },
        Instance { features: vec![3.5, 4.0], label: 1, weight: 0.0
        ↪ },
        Instance { features: vec![0.5, 1.0], label: -1, weight: 0.0
        ↪ },
    ];

    // Train a Bagging Ensemble with 5 models.
    let bagging = train_bagging(&dataset, 5);
```

217

```rust
    // For boosting, we clone the dataset as weights will be
    ↪ updated.
    let boosting = train_boosting(dataset.clone(), 5);

    // Define a test sample.
    let test_sample = vec![2.0, 3.0];

    // Make predictions using both ensemble methods.
    let bagging_pred = bagging.predict(&test_sample);
    let boosting_pred = boosting.predict(&test_sample);

    println!("Bagging Prediction: {}", bagging_pred);
    println!("Boosting Prediction: {}", boosting_pred);
}

/*
Important Equations and Formulas in this Chapter:

1. Ensemble Aggregation (General):
   H(x) =    * h(x)

2. Bagging Prediction:
   H(x) = (1/K) *   h(x)
   (For classification, taking the sign of the average yields the
   ↪ final prediction.)

3. Boosting Prediction (AdaBoost):
   H(x) = sign(   * h(x) )
*/
```

Chapter 35

Dimensionality Reduction using t-SNE

Mathematical Formulation of High-Dimensional Similarities

Let $X = \{x_1, x_2, \ldots, x_N\}$ denote a set of data points in a high-dimensional space. For each data point x_i, the similarity to another point x_j is quantified by a conditional probability that is computed using a Gaussian kernel. Specifically, the conditional probability is defined as

$$p_{j|i} = \frac{\exp\left(-\frac{\|x_i - x_j\|^2}{2\sigma_i^2}\right)}{\sum_{k \neq i} \exp\left(-\frac{\|x_i - x_k\|^2}{2\sigma_i^2}\right)},$$

where σ_i is a local bandwidth parameter that adapts to the density of the data around x_i. A symmetric joint probability is then obtained by symmetrizing the conditional probabilities, such that

$$p_{ij} = \frac{p_{j|i} + p_{i|j}}{2N}.$$

This formulation ensures that the similarity measure is both symmetric and appropriately normalized, thereby capturing the local structure inherent in the high-dimensional dataset.

Low-Dimensional Embedding Through a Heavy-Tailed Distribution

In the embedding phase, the set of high-dimensional points is mapped to a low-dimensional configuration $Y = \{y_1, y_2, \ldots, y_N\}$, typically in two or three dimensions. The similarity between points in the low-dimensional space is modeled using a heavy-tailed probability distribution. This is formally expressed as

$$q_{ij} = \frac{\left(1 + \|y_i - y_j\|^2\right)^{-1}}{\sum_{k \neq l} \left(1 + \|y_k - y_l\|^2\right)^{-1}},$$

where the choice of the Student's t-distribution with one degree of freedom (which is equivalent to a Cauchy distribution) provides a more forgiving decay in similarity with distance. The heavy-tailed nature of this distribution is critical in mitigating the crowding problem; it allocates a non-negligible probability to moderately distant points and thereby preserves local neighborhood relationships even when the intrinsic dimensionality of the data is compressed.

Cost Function and Optimization Scheme

The fidelity of the low-dimensional mapping is assessed by comparing the joint probability distributions from both the high-dimensional and low-dimensional spaces. This comparison is formalized by the Kullback-Leibler divergence, which serves as the cost function:

$$C = \sum_{i \neq j} p_{ij} \log \frac{p_{ij}}{q_{ij}}.$$

Minimization of C ensures that the pairwise similarities in the low-dimensional embedding approximate those in the original high-dimensional space as closely as possible. The optimization is typically performed via gradient descent, with the gradient of the cost function with respect to the coordinates y_i computed as

$$\frac{\partial C}{\partial y_i} = 4 \sum_j \left(p_{ij} - q_{ij}\right) \left(y_i - y_j\right) \left(1 + \|y_i - y_j\|^2\right)^{-1}.$$

This gradient provides the necessary information to adjust the positions of the low-dimensional points in order to minimize the divergence, iteratively refining the embedding toward an optimal configuration that preserves local similarities.

Parameter Selection and Considerations on Perplexity

A central parameter in the t-SNE algorithm is the perplexity, which controls the effective number of local neighbors considered for each data point during the computation of the high-dimensional similarities. Perplexity is defined as

$$\text{Perp}(P_i) = 2^{H(P_i)},$$

where the Shannon entropy $H(P_i)$ of the conditional probability distribution for x_i is given by

$$H(P_i) = -\sum_j p_{j|i} \log_2 p_{j|i}.$$

The perplexity acts as a smooth measure of the local scale and influences the selection of the bandwidth parameter σ_i for each data point. A carefully chosen perplexity ensures that the local neighborhood is neither overly concentrated nor excessively diffuse, thereby facilitating the maintenance of local structure in the resulting low-dimensional embedding. The interplay between perplexity and local similarity measures is crucial in achieving a balance that results in an informative and interpretable visualization of high-dimensional data.

Rust Code Snippet

```
// t-SNE implementation in Rust
//
// This code snippet demonstrates the computation of
↪    high-dimensional similarities,
// low-dimensional embeddings using a heavy-tailed Student's
↪    t-distribution,
// the Kullback-Leibler divergence cost function, gradient descent
↪    based optimization,
// and the calculation of perplexity as described in the chapter.
//
// External crate dependency (add to Cargo.toml):
// rand = "0.8"

use rand::prelude::*;

/// Computes the squared Euclidean distance between two vectors.
fn euclidean_distance_squared(a: &[f64], b: &[f64]) -> f64 {
```

```rust
    a.iter()
     .zip(b)
     .map(|(x, y)| {
         let diff = x - y;
         diff * diff
     })
     .sum()
}

/// Computes the conditional probabilities p_{j|i} for a given point
/// `i` in the high-dimensional dataset.
/// Uses a Gaussian kernel with bandwidth sigma.
/// Note: p_{i|i} is set to 0.
fn compute_conditional_probabilities_for_point(data: &Vec<Vec<f64>>,
    i: usize, sigma: f64) -> Vec<f64> {
    let n = data.len();
    let mut probabilities = vec![0.0; n];
    let mut sum = 0.0;
    for j in 0..n {
        if i == j {
            continue;
        }
        let dist_sq = euclidean_distance_squared(&data[i],
            &data[j]);
        let numerator = (-dist_sq / (2.0 * sigma * sigma)).exp();
        probabilities[j] = numerator;
        sum += numerator;
    }
    // Normalize probabilities so that they sum to 1.
    if sum > 0.0 {
        for j in 0..n {
            if i != j {
                probabilities[j] /= sum;
            }
        }
    }
    probabilities
}

/// Computes the perplexity of a conditional probability
/// distribution.
/// Perplexity is defined as 2 raised to the Shannon entropy (with
/// base 2).
fn compute_perplexity(probabilities: &Vec<f64>) -> f64 {
    let mut entropy = 0.0;
    for &p in probabilities.iter() {
        if p > 0.0 {
            entropy += -p * p.log2();
        }
    }
    2f64.powf(entropy)
}
```

```rust
/// Computes the symmetric joint probability matrix p_{ij} from the
↪   high-dimensional data.
/// p_{ij} is computed as (p_{j|i} + p_{i|j}) / (2N) where N is the
↪   number of data points.
fn compute_joint_probabilities(data: &Vec<Vec<f64>>, sigmas:
↪   &Vec<f64>) -> Vec<Vec<f64>> {
    let n = data.len();
    let mut conditional_probs: Vec<Vec<f64>> =
    ↪   Vec::with_capacity(n);
    // Compute conditional probabilities for each point.
    for i in 0..n {
        let p_i = compute_conditional_probabilities_for_point(data,
        ↪   i, sigmas[i]);
        conditional_probs.push(p_i);
    }

    // Optionally, print perplexity for each data point.
    for i in 0..n {
        let perplexity = compute_perplexity(&conditional_probs[i]);
        println!("Perplexity for point {}: {:.3}", i, perplexity);
    }

    // Compute symmetric joint probabilities.
    let mut joint_probs = vec![vec![0.0; n]; n];
    for i in 0..n {
        for j in 0..n {
            if i == j {
                joint_probs[i][j] = 0.0;
            } else {
                joint_probs[i][j] = (conditional_probs[i][j] +
                ↪   conditional_probs[j][i]) / (2.0 * n as f64);
            }
        }
    }
    joint_probs
}

/// Computes the low-dimensional similarities q_{ij} using a
↪   heavy-tailed Student's t-distribution.
/// q_{ij} = (1 + ||y_i - y_j||^2)^{-1} normalized over all i != j.
fn compute_low_similarities(embedding: &Vec<Vec<f64>>) ->
↪   Vec<Vec<f64>> {
    let n = embedding.len();
    let mut similarities = vec![vec![0.0; n]; n];
    let mut sum = 0.0;
    // Compute unnormalized similarities.
    for i in 0..n {
        for j in 0..n {
            if i == j {
                similarities[i][j] = 0.0;
            } else {
```

```
            let dist_sq =
            ↪   euclidean_distance_squared(&embedding[i],
            ↪   &embedding[j]);
            let value = 1.0 / (1.0 + dist_sq);
            similarities[i][j] = value;
            sum += value;
        }
    }
}
// Normalize similarities to obtain probabilities q_{ij}.
if sum > 0.0 {
    for i in 0..n {
        for j in 0..n {
            similarities[i][j] /= sum;
        }
    }
}
similarities
}


/// Computes the Kullback-Leibler divergence cost:
/// C = sum_{i != j} p_{ij} * log (p_{ij} / q_{ij})
fn compute_cost(p: &Vec<Vec<f64>>, q: &Vec<Vec<f64>>) -> f64 {
    let n = p.len();
    let mut cost = 0.0;
    for i in 0..n {
        for j in 0..n {
            if i == j {
                continue;
            }
            if p[i][j] > 0.0 && q[i][j] > 0.0 {
                cost += p[i][j] * (p[i][j] / q[i][j]).ln();
            }
        }
    }
    cost
}

/// Computes the gradient of the cost function with respect to the
↪   low-dimensional embedding.
/// C/y_i = 4 _j (p_{ij} - q_{ij}) * (y_i - y_j) / (1 + ||y_i -
↪   y_j||^2)
fn compute_gradient(p: &Vec<Vec<f64>>, embedding: &Vec<Vec<f64>>, q:
↪   &Vec<Vec<f64>>) -> Vec<Vec<f64>> {
    let n = embedding.len();
    let dim = embedding[0].len();
    let mut grad = vec![vec![0.0; dim]; n];

    for i in 0..n {
        for j in 0..n {
            if i == j {
                continue;
            }
```

```rust
            let mut diff = vec![0.0; dim];
            let mut dist_sq = 0.0;
            for d in 0..dim {
                diff[d] = embedding[i][d] - embedding[j][d];
                dist_sq += diff[d] * diff[d];
            }
            let factor = 4.0 * (p[i][j] - q[i][j]) / (1.0 +
            ↪ dist_sq);
            for d in 0..dim {
                grad[i][d] += factor * diff[d];
            }
        }
    }

    grad
}

/// Executes the t-SNE optimization.
/// - data: high-dimensional dataset (each point is a Vec<f64>).
/// - sigmas: vector of bandwidth parameters for each data point.
/// - iterations: number of gradient descent iterations.
/// - learning_rate: step size for gradient updates.
///
/// Returns the final low-dimensional embedding.
fn tsne(data: &Vec<Vec<f64>>, sigmas: &Vec<f64>, iterations: usize,
↪ learning_rate: f64) -> Vec<Vec<f64>> {
    let n = data.len();
    let dim = 2; // We project to 2D for visualization.
    let mut rng = rand::thread_rng();

    // Initialize low-dimensional embedding randomly.
    let mut embedding: Vec<Vec<f64>> = (0..n)
        .map(|_| (0..dim).map(|_|
        ↪ rng.gen_range(-0.5..0.5)).collect())
        .collect();

    // Precompute high-dimensional joint probabilities p_{ij}.
    let p = compute_joint_probabilities(data, sigmas);

    // Iteratively refine the embedding using gradient descent.
    for iter in 0..iterations {
        let q = compute_low_similarities(&embedding);
        let cost = compute_cost(&p, &q);
        let grad = compute_gradient(&p, &embedding, &q);

        // Update each coordinate in the embedding.
        for i in 0..n {
            for d in 0..dim {
                embedding[i][d] -= learning_rate * grad[i][d];
            }
        }

        // Optionally print cost every 10 iterations.
```

225

```rust
        if iter % 10 == 0 {
            println!("Iteration {}: cost = {:.6}", iter, cost);
        }
    }

    embedding
}

fn main() {
    // Example high-dimensional dataset: 5 points in 3D space.
    let data = vec![
        vec![0.0, 0.0, 0.0],
        vec![1.0, 1.0, 1.0],
        vec![0.5, 0.2, 0.3],
        vec![0.8, 0.9, 0.5],
        vec![0.2, 0.1, 0.4],
    ];

    // For simplicity, use a constant sigma for all points.
    // In practice, sigma could be optimized to achieve a target
    ↪ perplexity.
    let sigmas = vec![1.0; data.len()];

    // t-SNE parameters.
    let iterations = 100;
    let learning_rate = 0.1;

    // Run t-SNE to obtain a 2D embedding of the high-dimensional
    ↪ data.
    let embedding = tsne(&data, &sigmas, iterations, learning_rate);

    // Print the final low-dimensional embeddings.
    println!("\nFinal low-dimensional embedding:");
    for (i, point) in embedding.iter().enumerate() {
        println!("Point {}: {:?}", i, point);
    }
}
```

Chapter 36

Manifold Learning with Isomap Algorithms

Mathematical Foundations and Theoretical Background

Data observed in high-dimensional Euclidean spaces are often assumed to lie on an underlying low-dimensional manifold, denoted by $\mathcal{M}$. The intrinsic geometry of $\mathcal{M}$ is inadequately captured by the ambient Euclidean metric, as it neglects the nonlinear structure present in the data. Isomap addresses this shortcoming by estimating the geodesic distances between data points, rather than relying on direct Euclidean distances. Given two points x_i and x_j on $\mathcal{M}$, the ideal notion of distance is provided by the geodesic length, $d_{\mathcal{M}}(x_i, x_j)$, measured along the surface of the manifold. This formulation embeds the premise of non-linear dimensionality reduction by preserving the global geometry through the preservation of approximate geodesic distances.

Graph Construction and Neighborhood Selection

The first computational step involves the construction of a weighted graph $G = (V, E)$ that approximates the manifold structure. Each vertex in the set V corresponds to a data point in the high-dimensional space, and edges in the set E are constructed either through a k-nearest neighbor rule or by establishing connections within an ϵ-radius neighborhood. For a given data point x_i, the corresponding neighborhood is defined as

$$N(x_i) = \{x_j \mid \|x_i - x_j\|_2 \leq \epsilon\} \quad \text{or} \quad N(x_i) = k \text{ nearest neighbors of } x_i.$$

Edges are assigned weights based on the Euclidean distance, specifically,

$$w(x_i, x_j) = \|x_i - x_j\|_2.$$

This graph implicitly captures the local connectivity of the manifold. A judicious selection of the neighborhood criterion is crucial since it directly influences the connectivity of G and, consequently, the quality of the geodesic distance approximation.

Computation of Geodesic Distances

Once the neighborhood graph is established, the next step is to approximate the geodesic distance between any pair of data points. The geodesic distance $d_G(x_i, x_j)$ is estimated as the shortest path distance on the graph G, computed via algorithms such as Dijkstra's or Floyd-Warshall. Formally, the geodesic distance between data points x_i and x_j is given by

$$d_G(x_i, x_j) = \min_{\pi \in \Pi_{ij}} \sum_{(u,v) \in \pi} w(u, v),$$

where Π_{ij} denotes the set of all paths connecting x_i and x_j. This approximation benefits from the assumption that local Euclidean distances reliably reflect the manifold structure, thereby allowing the cumulative distances along the graph to serve as substitutes for true geodesic lengths. The accuracy of this approximation is paramount to preserving the manifold's intrinsic geometry in the subsequent low-dimensional embedding.

Embedding via Classical Multidimensional Scaling

Following the computation of the pairwise geodesic distances, the Isomap framework applies classical Multidimensional Scaling (MDS) to obtain a low-dimensional embedding that preserves these distances. Let D be the matrix containing the squared geodesic distances, where the element $D_{ij} = (d_G(x_i, x_j))^2$. The double-centered matrix B is computed as

$$B = -\frac{1}{2} H D H,$$

with the centering matrix defined by

$$H = I - \frac{1}{n} \mathbf{1} \mathbf{1}^T,$$

where n is the number of data points, I is the identity matrix, and $\mathbf{1}$ is a column vector of ones. An eigen-decomposition of B yields

$$B = V \Lambda V^T,$$

where the top d eigenvectors corresponding to the largest eigenvalues in Λ form the basis for the low-dimensional coordinates. The resulting embedding $\{y_1, y_2, \ldots, y_n\}$ in $\mathbb{R}^d$ is constructed as

$$Y = V_d \Lambda_d^{1/2}.$$

This process ensures that the Euclidean distances $\|y_i - y_j\|_2$ in the embedding space are as close as possible to the geodesic distances $d_G(x_i, x_j)$, thereby revealing the manifold's inherent structure.

Algorithmic Considerations and Computational Complexity

The Isomap algorithm integrates several computationally intensive components: construction of the neighborhood graph, computation of all-pairs shortest paths, and the eigen-decomposition necessary for MDS. The graph construction phase typically scales as $O(n \log n)$ per data point when employing efficient nearest neighbor searches, while the all-pairs shortest path computation can scale up to $O(n^2)$ or higher depending on the chosen algorithm. Eigen-decomposition of the centered distance matrix further contributes a computational burden that is approximately $O(n^3)$ in the worst case.

Implementation in a language such as Rust offers significant advantages with respect to execution speed and memory safety. The static type system in Rust ensures that errors are minimized during compilation, while features such as concurrency and low-level memory management facilitate the optimization of critical algorithmic components. Effective handling of large-scale data thus necessitates careful algorithmic design and exploitation of Rust's performance-oriented constructs. A balance between numerical precision and computational efficiency is essential, particularly in the context of the eigen-decomposition step where perturbations in the distance matrix can propagate to the low-dimensional embedding.

Rust Code Snippet

```
use petgraph::graph::NodeIndex;
use petgraph::Graph;
use petgraph::algo::dijkstra;
use nalgebra::{DMatrix, SymmetricEigen};
use std::f64;

/// A simple structure representing a high-dimensional data point.
#[derive(Debug, Clone)]
struct Point {
    coords: Vec<f64>,
}

impl Point {
    /// Compute the Euclidean distance between self and another
    ↪    point.
    fn euclidean_distance(&self, other: &Point) -> f64 {
        self.coords.iter()
            .zip(other.coords.iter())
            .map(|(a, b)| (a - b).powi(2))
            .sum::<f64>()
            .sqrt()
    }
}

/// Build an undirected weighted graph where each node corresponds
↪    to a data point.
/// An edge is added between two nodes if the Euclidean distance is
↪    within the epsilon threshold.
/// The weight on each edge is the Euclidean distance.
///
/// This corresponds to the neighborhood selection step:
///    N(x_i) = { x_j | ||x_i - x_j||_2    }
fn build_graph(points: &[Point], epsilon: f64) -> Graph<usize, f64>
↪    {
    let mut graph = Graph::<usize, f64>::new_undirected();
```

```
// Add nodes to the graph.
let nodes: Vec<_> = (0..points.len()).map(|i|
↪    graph.add_node(i)).collect();

// Connect each pair of points by an edge if the distance is
↪    below epsilon.
for i in 0..points.len() {
    for j in (i + 1)..points.len() {
        let d = points[i].euclidean_distance(&points[j]);
        if d <= epsilon {
            graph.add_edge(nodes[i], nodes[j], d);
        }
    }
}
graph
}

/// Compute the all-pairs approximate geodesic distances on the
↪    graph using Dijkstra's algorithm.
/// The geodesic distance between points is approximated as the
↪    shortest path distance on the graph.
/// The resulting matrix D has elements D_{ij} = (d_G(x_i,x_j))^2,
↪    according to the formula:
///    D_{ij} = (min_{\pi _{ij}} _{(u,v)  } w(u,v))^2
fn compute_geodesic_distances(graph: &Graph<usize, f64>, num_points:
↪    usize) -> DMatrix<f64> {
    let mut distance_matrix =
    ↪    DMatrix::<f64>::from_element(num_points, num_points,
    ↪    f64::INFINITY);
    for i in 0..num_points {
        let source = NodeIndex::new(i);
        let distances = dijkstra(&graph, source, None, |edge|
        ↪    *edge.weight());
        for j in 0..num_points {
            let target = NodeIndex::new(j);
            if let Some(&dist) = distances.get(&target) {
                // Store the squared geodesic distance.
                distance_matrix[(i, j)] = dist * dist;
            }
        }
    }
    distance_matrix
}

/// Perform classical Multidimensional Scaling (MDS) to compute a
↪    low-dimensional embedding.
/// The procedure is as follows:
///    1. Compute the centering matrix H = I - (1/n)*11^T.
///    2. Compute B = -1/2 * H * D * H, where D is the matrix of
↪    squared geodesic distances.
///    3. Perform eigen-decomposition of B: B = V  V^T.
///    4. Compute the coordinates in lower dimensional space as Y =
↪    V_d * _d^(1/2),
```

231

```
///        where V_d contains the top d eigenvectors and _d the
↪    corresponding eigenvalues.
fn mds(distance_matrix: &DMatrix<f64>, target_dim: usize) ->
↪    DMatrix<f64> {
    let n = distance_matrix.nrows();
    // Construct the centering matrix H.
    let identity = DMatrix::<f64>::identity(n, n);
    let ones = DMatrix::<f64>::from_element(n, n, 1.0 / n as f64);
    let h = identity - ones;

    // Compute the double-centered matrix B.
    let b = -0.5 * (h.clone() * distance_matrix * h);

    // Compute the eigen-decomposition of B.
    let eigen = SymmetricEigen::new(b);

    // Pair eigenvalues with corresponding eigenvectors.
    let mut eigen_pairs: Vec<(f64, Vec<f64>)> =
    ↪    eigen.eigenvalues.iter()
        .cloned()
        .zip(eigen.eigenvectors.column_iter().map(|col|
        ↪    col.iter().cloned().collect()))
        .collect();
    // Sort the pairs in descending order of eigenvalues.
    eigen_pairs.sort_by(|a, b| b.0.partial_cmp(&a.0).unwrap());

    // Construct the embedding: for each of the top target_dim
    ↪    eigenpairs,
    // multiply the eigenvector by the square root of its
    ↪    eigenvalue.
    let mut embedding = DMatrix::<f64>::zeros(n, target_dim);
    for (i, (e_val, vec)) in
    ↪    eigen_pairs.into_iter().take(target_dim).enumerate() {
        let sqrt_lambda = if e_val > 0.0 { e_val.sqrt() } else { 0.0
        ↪    };
        for j in 0..n {
            embedding[(j, i)] = vec[j] * sqrt_lambda;
        }
    }
    embedding
}


fn main() {
    // Example: Define high-dimensional data points believed to lie
    ↪    on a low-dimensional manifold.
    let points = vec![
        Point { coords: vec![0.0, 0.0, 0.0] },
        Point { coords: vec![1.0, 0.0, 0.0] },
        Point { coords: vec![0.0, 1.0, 0.0] },
        Point { coords: vec![1.0, 1.0, 0.0] },
        Point { coords: vec![0.5, 0.5, 1.0] },
    ];
```

232

```rust
    // Neighborhood parameter (epsilon) for graph construction.
    let epsilon = 1.5;

    // Build the weighted neighborhood graph approximating the
    ↪  manifold structure.
    let graph = build_graph(&points, epsilon);

    // Compute the all-pairs geodesic distances (squared) using
    ↪  Dijkstra's algorithm.
    let distance_matrix = compute_geodesic_distances(&graph,
    ↪  points.len());

    // Apply classical Multidimensional Scaling (MDS) to reduce to
    ↪  target dimension.
    let target_dim = 2;
    let embedding = mds(&distance_matrix, target_dim);

    // Output the low-dimensional embedding.
    println!("Low-dimensional embedding (each row corresponds to a
    ↪  data point):");
    for i in 0..embedding.nrows() {
        let coords: Vec<f64> = (0..embedding.ncols()).map(|j|
        ↪  embedding[(i, j)]).collect();
        println!("Point {}: {:?}", i, coords);
    }
}
```

Chapter 37

Neural Network Building Blocks in Rust

Layer Architecture and Design

Neural network models are composed of interconnected layers that perform distinct mathematical operations, transforming high-dimensional input data into representations amenable to downstream tasks. Each layer is mathematically characterized by an affine transformation followed by a non-linear mapping, which can be expressed as

$$z = Wx + b,$$

where W denotes the weight matrix, x is the input vector, and b represents the bias vector. The design of a layer requires deliberate consideration of dimensional compatibility and data propagation. In Rust, the explicit management of memory and strong type systems serve to ensure that these linear operations are both efficient and verifiable at compile time. Layers are organized sequentially or in more complex topological arrangements where the output of one layer serves as the input to subsequent layers. Special attention is paid to maintaining clear abstraction boundaries, such that each layer encapsulates its respective transformation and state.

Activation Function Dynamics

Activation functions introduce non-linearity into neural networks, enabling the model to capture complex patterns that cannot be represented by a mere composition of linear operations. These functions are applied element-wise after the affine transformation and play a pivotal role in determining the expressiveness of the network. Common activations include the rectified linear unit (ReLU), sigmoid, and hyperbolic tangent functions, each characterized by unique mathematical properties. For instance, the ReLU function is defined as

$$\mathrm{ReLU}(x) = \max(0, x),$$

and is favored in many deep learning applications due to its simplicity and empirical performance. The selection of an activation function is informed by factors such as differentiability, gradient propagation, and the mitigation of issues like vanishing gradients. In the Rust programming environment, these functions must be implemented with a focus on numerical stability and computational efficiency, ensuring that floating-point operations adhere to the rigorous standards required for training deep models.

Weight Initialization Techniques

Proper weight initialization is critical to the successful training of neural networks, as it directly affects the behavior of gradient descent and the convergence properties of the model. The initialization of weights is performed before any training iterations, and its purpose is to set the network on a favorable trajectory in the parameter space. Mathematically, if weights are initialized too large, the activations may explode exponentially; if initialized too small, the gradients might vanish. Techniques such as Xavier initialization and He initialization adopt principles derived from the preservation of signal variance across layers. Specifically, Xavier initialization establishes the variance of the weights as

$$\mathrm{Var}(W) = \frac{2}{n_{\mathrm{in}} + n_{\mathrm{out}}},$$

where n_{in} and n_{out} denote the number of input and output neurons, respectively. In contrast, He initialization, which is particularly suited for layers followed by ReLU activations, uses

$$\mathrm{Var}(W) = \frac{2}{n_{\mathrm{in}}}.$$

When these principles are applied within the Rust ecosystem, the advantages of compile-time safety and performance optimization come to the forefront, permitting the generation of weight matrices that conform to both statistical prerequisites and memory safety guarantees. The explicit allocation and initialization patterns in Rust help to mitigate errors often encountered in lower-level implementations, all while achieving near-optimal runtime performance.

Integration of Neural Components in Rust

The assembly of neural network building blocks in Rust involves a deliberate interplay between abstraction and performance. Layers, activation functions, and weight initialization schemes constitute the fundamental components that are integrated into a cohesive model architecture. The language's emphasis on zero-cost abstractions ensures that high-level representations of these mathematical constructs do not incur a performance penalty. Moreover, Rust's strict handling of mutable state and ownership semantics facilitates the development of efficient backpropagation routines and forward propagation mechanisms. The careful design of data structures and algorithms guarantees that operations such as matrix multiplication and element-wise function evaluation are executed with optimal resource utilization. The modular design encouraged by the language promotes reusable and testable components, ultimately contributing to the construction of robust and scalable neural network models.

Rust Code Snippet

```rust
use ndarray::prelude::*;
use ndarray_rand::RandomExt;
use rand_distr::Normal;

// Define a structure representing a neural network layer.
// The layer encapsulates its weight matrix, bias vector,
// and a pointer to its activation function.
pub struct Layer {
    // Weight matrix with dimensions (n_out, n_in)
```

```rust
    weights: Array2<f64>,
    // Bias vector of length n_out
    bias: Array1<f64>,
    // Activation function applied element-wise after the affine
    ↪   transformation
    activation: fn(&Array1<f64>) -> Array1<f64>,
}

// Activation Functions

// ReLU activation: ReLU(x) = max(0, x)
pub fn relu(input: &Array1<f64>) -> Array1<f64> {
    input.mapv(|x| if x > 0.0 { x } else { 0.0 })
}

// Sigmoid activation: sigmoid(x) = 1 / (1 + exp(-x))
pub fn sigmoid(input: &Array1<f64>) -> Array1<f64> {
    input.mapv(|x| 1.0 / (1.0 + (-x).exp()))
}

// Hyperbolic Tangent activation: tanh(x)
pub fn tanh(input: &Array1<f64>) -> Array1<f64> {
    input.mapv(|x| x.tanh())
}

// Weight Initialization Functions

// Xavier initialization: Ensures variance preservation across
↪   layers.
// Var(W) = 2 / (n_in + n_out)
pub fn initialize_weights_xavier(n_in: usize, n_out: usize) ->
↪   Array2<f64> {
    let stddev = (2.0 / (n_in as f64 + n_out as f64)).sqrt();
    Array2::random((n_out, n_in), Normal::new(0.0, stddev).unwrap())
}

// He initialization: Suitable for layers using ReLU activation.
// Var(W) = 2 / n_in
pub fn initialize_weights_he(n_in: usize, n_out: usize) ->
↪   Array2<f64> {
    let stddev = (2.0 / n_in as f64).sqrt();
    Array2::random((n_out, n_in), Normal::new(0.0, stddev).unwrap())
}

impl Layer {
    // Create a new neural network layer.
    // use_he flag determines if He initialization is used;
    ↪   otherwise, Xavier is applied.
    pub fn new(n_in: usize, n_out: usize, activation:
    ↪   fn(&Array1<f64>) -> Array1<f64>, use_he: bool) -> Self {
        let weights = if use_he {
            initialize_weights_he(n_in, n_out)
        } else {
```

237

```rust
            initialize_weights_xavier(n_in, n_out)
        };
        let bias = Array1::zeros(n_out);
        Layer { weights, bias, activation }
    }

    // Forward pass through the layer.
    // Computes the affine transformation z = W * x + b and then
    // ↪  applies the activation function.
    pub fn forward(&self, input: &Array1<f64>) -> Array1<f64> {
        // Compute affine transformation: z = W * x + b
        let z = self.weights.dot(input) + &self.bias;
        // Apply the activation function element-wise on z
        (self.activation)(&z)
    }
}

fn main() {
    // Define a simple layer with 3 input neurons and 4 output
    // ↪  neurons.
    let n_in = 3;
    let n_out = 4;

    // Instantiate the layer using He initialization since we plan
    // ↪  to use ReLU activation.
    let layer = Layer::new(n_in, n_out, relu, true);

    // Define an example input vector.
    let input = array![0.5, -1.2, 3.3];

    // Perform forward propagation: compute z = W*x + b and apply
    // ↪  ReLU activation.
    let output = layer.forward(&input);

    // Print the resulting output vector.
    println!("Layer output: {:?}", output);
}
```

Chapter 38

Backpropagation Algorithm Implementation

Mathematical Foundations and Notation

The backpropagation algorithm is grounded in the principles of multivariable calculus, serving as a systematic procedure for computing the gradient of a loss function with respect to the parameters of a neural network. In a network with multiple layers, each layer is characterized by an affine transformation given by

$$z^l = W^l a^{l-1} + b^l,$$

where W^l represents the weight matrix, b^l the bias vector of layer l, and a^{l-1} the activation output from the preceding layer. The activation function σ, applied to z^l, yields

$$a^l = \sigma(z^l),$$

which introduces the necessary nonlinearity into the system. The loss function L is defined over the network output and the corresponding target values, and the objective is to compute the derivatives $\frac{\partial L}{\partial W^l}$ and $\frac{\partial L}{\partial b^l}$ for every layer. These derivatives are central to adjusting the network's parameters during training.

Gradient Computation via the Chain Rule

The computation of gradients in deep neural architectures relies on the recursive application of the chain rule. For the output layer, the initial error signal is formulated as

$$\delta^L = \nabla_{a^L} L \odot \sigma'(z^L),$$

where $\odot$ denotes the Hadamard product and σ' is the derivative of the activation function. For each intermediate layer, the gradient with respect to the pre-activation becomes

$$\delta^l = \left((W^{l+1})^T \delta^{l+1}\right) \odot \sigma'(z^l).$$

This expression encapsulates two key concepts: the propagation of error through the transposed weight matrix from the subsequent layer, and the modulation of this error by the derivative of the activation function applied to the current layer's pre-activation values. Such recursive computations ensure that the contribution of each parameter to the final loss is meticulously accounted for.

Error Propagation Through Layered Architectures

Error propagation follows a reverse traversal of the network's architecture, starting from the output and moving backward through each layer. Having computed the local error δ^l for a given layer, the gradients of the loss function with respect to the network parameters are obtained via the relations

$$\frac{\partial L}{\partial W^l} = \delta^l (a^{l-1})^T \quad \text{and} \quad \frac{\partial L}{\partial b^l} = \delta^l.$$

These formulations highlight that the gradient for the weight matrix is the outer product of the current layer's error signal and the transpose of the activation vector from the previous layer, while the bias gradient is directly given by the error signal. Such structure ensures that the gradient computation adheres to both linear algebraic clarity and the intricate dependencies embedded within deep network structures.

Parameter Update Strategies in Rust-Based Implementations

Once the requisite gradients have been computed, the subsequent step involves updating the network parameters in a manner that minimizes the loss function. In the context of gradient descent, the weight and bias updates for layer l are articulated as

$$W^l \leftarrow W^l - \eta \frac{\partial L}{\partial W^l},$$

$$b^l \leftarrow b^l - \eta \frac{\partial L}{\partial b^l},$$

where η denotes the learning rate—a hyperparameter controlling the magnitude of each update. The iterative refinement of parameters is critical for converging towards an optimal configuration. When implementing these updates in Rust, the language's explicit memory management, zero-cost abstractions, and robust type system are leveraged to ensure that both the computation and modification of large-scale matrices and vectors are performed with exceptional efficiency and safety. Moreover, the systematic handling of mutable state and concurrency in Rust provides a conducive environment for integrating advanced optimization techniques, such as momentum-based methods or adaptive learning rate schemes, without compromising on runtime performance.

Rust Code Snippet

```rust
use ndarray::prelude::*;
use ndarray::{Array1, Array2};
use ndarray_rand::rand_distr::Uniform;
use ndarray_rand::RandomExt;

// Define a simple neural network structure for backpropagation.
pub struct NeuralNetwork {
    layers: Vec<usize>,         // Number of neurons per layer
    weights: Vec<Array2<f32>>,  // Weight matrices for each layer
    ↪   connection.
    biases: Vec<Array1<f32>>,   // Bias vectors for each layer.
    learning_rate: f32,         // Learning rate for gradient
    ↪   descent.
}

impl NeuralNetwork {
```

```rust
// Constructor: initialize weights and biases with random
↪   values.
pub fn new(layers: Vec<usize>, learning_rate: f32) -> Self {
    let mut weights = Vec::new();
    let mut biases = Vec::new();
    for i in 1..layers.len() {
        // For layer i, initialize W^i with dimensions
        ↪   (layers[i] x layers[i-1])
        // and b^i with length layers[i].
        let weight = Array2::random((layers[i], layers[i - 1]),
        ↪   Uniform::new(-1.0, 1.0));
        let bias = Array1::random(layers[i], Uniform::new(-1.0,
        ↪   1.0));
        weights.push(weight);
        biases.push(bias);
    }
    NeuralNetwork { layers, weights, biases, learning_rate }
}

// Sigmoid activation function: a = (z) = 1 / (1 + exp(-z))
fn sigmoid(x: &Array1<f32>) -> Array1<f32> {
    x.mapv(|v| 1.0 / (1.0 + (-v).exp()))
}

// Derivative of the sigmoid function: '(z) = (z) * (1 - (z))
fn sigmoid_prime(x: &Array1<f32>) -> Array1<f32> {
    let s = Self::sigmoid(x);
    s.mapv(|v| v * (1.0 - v))
}

// Forward propagation: computes all layer outputs and
↪   pre-activation values.
// Returns a tuple (activations, z_values), where activations[0]
↪   is the input.
pub fn forward(&self, input: &Array1<f32>) -> (Vec<Array1<f32>>,
↪   Vec<Array1<f32>>) {
    let mut activations = Vec::new();
    let mut zs = Vec::new(); // Store the pre-activation values:
    ↪   z = W*a + b.
    activations.push(input.clone());
    let mut a = input.clone();
    for (w, b) in self.weights.iter().zip(self.biases.iter()) {
        let z = w.dot(&a) + b;
        zs.push(z.clone());
        a = Self::sigmoid(&z);
        activations.push(a.clone());
    }
    (activations, zs)
}

// Backpropagation for a single training example.
// Computes the gradient of the loss with respect to each weight
↪   and bias,
```

242

```rust
// and then updates the parameters using gradient descent.
pub fn backprop(&mut self, input: &Array1<f32>, target:
↪ &Array1<f32>) {
    // Forward pass: compute activations and z values for each
    ↪ layer.
    let (activations, zs) = self.forward(input);

    // Initialize gradients for weights (nabla_w) and biases
    ↪ (nabla_b).
    let mut nabla_w: Vec<Array2<f32>> = self.weights
        .iter()
        .map(|w| Array2::<f32>::zeros(w.dim()))
        .collect();
    let mut nabla_b: Vec<Array1<f32>> = self.biases
        .iter()
        .map(|b| Array1::<f32>::zeros(b.dim()))
        .collect();

    // Compute error at the output layer:
    // ^L = (a^L - y)  '(z^L)
    let mut delta = (&activations.last().unwrap() - target)
        * Self::sigmoid_prime(zs.last().unwrap());
    let last_layer = self.weights.len() - 1;
    nabla_b[last_layer] = delta.clone();

    // Gradient for weights at the output layer:
    // L/W^L = ^L (a^(L-1))^T
    let a_prev = &activations[activations.len() - 2];
    let delta_matrix = delta.clone().insert_axis(Axis(1));
    ↪ // Convert to column vector.
    let a_prev_matrix = a_prev.clone().insert_axis(Axis(0));
    ↪ // Convert to row vector.
    nabla_w[last_layer] = delta_matrix.dot(&a_prev_matrix);

    // Backpropagate the error through the hidden layers.
    for l in (1..self.weights.len()).rev() {
        let z = &zs[l - 1];
        let sp = Self::sigmoid_prime(z);
        delta = self.weights[l].t().dot(&delta) * sp;
        nabla_b[l - 1] = delta.clone();
        let a_prev = &activations[l - 1];
        let delta_matrix = delta.clone().insert_axis(Axis(1));
        let a_prev_matrix = a_prev.clone().insert_axis(Axis(0));
        nabla_w[l - 1] = delta_matrix.dot(&a_prev_matrix);
    }

    // Update weights and biases using gradient descent:
    // W^l ← W^l  * (L/W^l)
    // b^l ← b^l  * (L/b^l)
    for i in 0..self.weights.len() {
        self.weights[i] = &self.weights[i] -
        ↪ &(self.learning_rate * &nabla_w[i]);
    }
```

```rust
            self.biases[i] = &self.biases[i] - &(self.learning_rate
            ↪    * &nabla_b[i]);
        }
    }
}

fn main() {
    // Define a simple network with 3 layers:
    // Input layer with 3 neurons, one hidden layer with 4 neurons,
    // ↪    and an output layer with 2 neurons.
    let layers = vec![3, 4, 2];
    let mut nn = NeuralNetwork::new(layers, 0.1);

    // Dummy input vector and desired target output.
    let input = array![0.5, 0.1, 0.4];
    let target = array![0.0, 1.0];

    // Display the network's output before any training.
    println!("Before training:");
    let (activations, _) = nn.forward(&input);
    println!("Output: {:?}", activations.last().unwrap());

    // Train the network on the single example using backpropagation
    // ↪    over multiple iterations.
    for _ in 0..1000 {
        nn.backprop(&input, &target);
    }

    // Display the network's output after training.
    println!("After training:");
    let (activations, _) = nn.forward(&input);
    println!("Output: {:?}", activations.last().unwrap());
}
```

Chapter 39

Activation Functions in Neural Networks

Mathematical Formulations of Activation Functions

Activation functions are instrumental in introducing nonlinearity into neural network architectures, thereby enabling the approximation of complex functions. Among the prevalent activation functions are the Rectified Linear Unit (ReLU), the logistic sigmoid, and the hyperbolic tangent (tanh). The mathematical properties of these functions and the behavior of their derivatives critically affect the dynamics of gradient propagation during training.

1 Rectified Linear Unit (ReLU)

The ReLU function is defined as

$$f(x) = \max(0, x),$$

where the max operator selects the greater value between 0 and x. In neural network computations, ReLU acts as a simple thresholding mechanism, passing through positive inputs unchanged while zeroing negative ones. Its derivative is characterized by a piecewise formulation:

$$f'(x) = \begin{cases} 1, & \text{if } x > 0, \\ 0, & \text{if } x \leq 0. \end{cases}$$

This piecewise constant derivative facilitates efficient computation and generally sustains gradient magnitudes for activations in the active regime. However, the abrupt transition at $x = 0$ may lead to a significant number of neurons becoming inactive, a phenomenon that has implications for the sparsity of gradient updates in deep architectures.

2 Logistic Sigmoid Function

The logistic sigmoid function is expressed by the equation

$$f(x) = \frac{1}{1 + e^{-x}},$$

which maps the entire real line into the bounded interval $(0, 1)$. This bounded output can be particularly useful when modeling probabilistic interpretations of neuron activations. Differentiation yields that the derivative of the sigmoid function is given by

$$f'(x) = f(x)\left[1 - f(x)\right].$$

The self-referential nature of the derivative, relying on the output of the function itself, results in a steep gradient only within a limited central region. For inputs of large magnitude, the derivative diminishes toward zero, a behavior that may contribute to gradient saturation during backpropagation in deep networks.

3 Hyperbolic Tangent (tanh) Function

The hyperbolic tangent function is defined as

$$f(x) = \tanh(x) = \frac{e^x - e^{-x}}{e^x + e^{-x}},$$

which transforms real-valued inputs into the interval $(-1, 1)$. The symmetric output distribution around zero is advantageous in many training contexts, particularly for balancing positive and negative signals. The derivative is analytically derived to be

$$f'(x) = 1 - \tanh^2(x).$$

This expression implies that the derivative remains appreciably high over a broad central region but, analogous to the sigmoid function, tends toward zero for inputs with large absolute value. The maintenance of a considerable derivative magnitude within the central operating range contributes to more stable gradient propagation relative to functions that saturate quickly.

Implications on Backpropagation and Gradient Dynamics

Within the framework of gradient-based optimization, the backpropagation algorithm leverages the chain rule to compute derivatives with respect to network parameters. The local derivative provided by an activation function directly affects the gradient signal transmitted from one layer to the previous layer. In this context, activation functions with derivatives that approach zero in regions of high activation magnitude can lead to significant diminishment of gradient information, a scenario commonly referred to as the vanishing gradient problem.

The ReLU function, with its constant derivative of 1 for positive inputs, generally preserves gradient magnitude in its active regime. This property renders it particularly useful in deep architectures where sustained gradient flow is paramount. In contrast, both the logistic sigmoid and tanh functions exhibit regions where their derivatives are small, thereby increasing the likelihood of gradient attenuation. The trade-offs inherent in each activation function, including the risk of saturation versus the benefits of smooth nonlinear transformations, underscore the need for careful selection in the context of specific network architectures and training regimes.

The propagation of errors in backpropagation is modulated by these derivatives. For a network layer employing a particular activation function, the local gradient is obtained by multiplying the incoming gradient with the activation derivative. This mechanism is central to the adjustment of weights and biases during optimization and determines the efficacy of learning in deep neural structures. The quantitative differences in the derivative properties of ReLU, logistic sigmoid, and tanh directly influence the convergence behavior and stability of the training process.

Comparative Analysis of Activation Function Roles

A comparative examination of the activation functions elucidates their distinct contributions to neural network training. The ReLU function is computationally efficient and supports a constant gradient in its non-zero regime, thereby facilitating robust propagation of error signals. Its susceptibility to rendering neurons inactive when inputs are non-positive, however, introduces the risk of dead units that may inhibit learning.

The logistic sigmoid function provides a smooth, bounded transformation that can be interpreted probabilistically, yet its inherent propensity for gradient saturation in extreme regions of the input space can slow convergence. Similarly, the tanh function offers the benefits of symmetry and zero-centered output, which can expedite convergence under certain conditions; nonetheless, it shares the limitation of diminishing gradients for large input magnitudes.

The interplay between activation functions and backpropagated gradients is a critical factor in the optimization of neural network parameters. A rigorous understanding of each function's derivative behavior and impact on gradient dynamics is essential for the design and tuning of deep learning models. The theoretical underpinnings provided by these mathematical formulations serve not only to explain the role of activation functions but also to guide empirical decisions in neural network architecture design.

Rust Code Snippet

```
// Comprehensive Rust implementation for activation functions and a
↪   basic neuron model
// demonstrating forward and backward propagation using ReLU,
↪   Sigmoid, and Tanh.
//
// The code defines an enum for the activation type with methods to
↪   compute the function
// and its derivative according to the mathematical formulations:
//    - ReLU:    f(x) = max(0, x);            f'(x) = 1 if x > 0 else
↪   0
//    - Sigmoid: f(x) = 1 / (1 + exp(-x));    f'(x) = f(x) * (1 -
↪   f(x))
//    - Tanh:    f(x) = tanh(x);              f'(x) = 1 - tanh(x)^2
//
// A simple Neuron struct utilizes one of these activation functions
↪   for its computation.
// The Neuron provides a 'forward' method for calculating the output
↪   and a 'train'
// method that performs a single gradient descent update using a
↪   mean squared error loss.

#[derive(Debug, Clone, Copy)]
enum ActivationType {
    ReLU,
    Sigmoid,
    Tanh,
```

248

```
}

impl ActivationType {
    // Applies the activation function based on the selected type.
    fn activate(&self, x: f64) -> f64 {
        match self {
            ActivationType::ReLU => {
                if x > 0.0 { x } else { 0.0 }
            },
            ActivationType::Sigmoid => 1.0 / (1.0 + (-x).exp()),
            ActivationType::Tanh => x.tanh(),
        }
    }

    // Computes the derivative of the activation function at input
    ↪  x.
    fn derivative(&self, x: f64) -> f64 {
        match self {
            ActivationType::ReLU => {
                if x > 0.0 { 1.0 } else { 0.0 }
            },
            ActivationType::Sigmoid => {
                let s = 1.0 / (1.0 + (-x).exp());
                s * (1.0 - s)
            },
            ActivationType::Tanh => 1.0 - x.tanh().powi(2),
        }
    }
}

// A simple neuron structure that encapsulates a single weight,
↪  bias, and the chosen
// activation function. It simulates both the forward activation
↪  computation and a
// one-step gradient descent update based on the mean squared error
↪  loss.
struct Neuron {
    weight: f64,
    bias: f64,
    activation: ActivationType,
}

impl Neuron {
    // Constructs a new neuron with the given weight, bias, and
    ↪  activation function.
    fn new(weight: f64, bias: f64, activation: ActivationType) ->
    ↪  Self {
        Neuron { weight, bias, activation }
    }

    // Computes the forward pass: z = weight * input + bias,
    ↪  followed by the activation.
    fn forward(&self, input: f64) -> f64 {
```

249

```rust
        let z = self.weight * input + self.bias;
        self.activation.activate(z)
    }

    // Trains the neuron using one training sample.
    // It computes the pre-activation value, applies the activation
    ↪ function,
    // calculates the error, and updates the parameters using
    ↪ gradient descent.
    fn train(&mut self, input: f64, target: f64, learning_rate: f64)
    ↪ -> f64 {
        // Compute linear combination (pre-activation)
        let z = self.weight * input + self.bias;
        // Compute the activated output
        let output = self.activation.activate(z);
        // Error derivative of mean squared error loss: (output -
        ↪ target)
        let error = output - target;
        // Chain rule: multiply error with derivative of activation
        ↪ function at z.
        let grad = error * self.activation.derivative(z);
        // Update parameters: gradient descent step.
        self.weight -= learning_rate * grad * input;
        self.bias   -= learning_rate * grad;
        output
    }
}

fn main() {
    // Example input and target for the neuron.
    let input = 1.0;
    let target = 0.0;
    let learning_rate = 0.1;

    // Create neurons with different activation functions.
    let mut neuron_relu    = Neuron::new(0.5, 0.0,
    ↪ ActivationType::ReLU);
    let mut neuron_sigmoid = Neuron::new(0.5, 0.0,
    ↪ ActivationType::Sigmoid);
    let mut neuron_tanh    = Neuron::new(0.5, 0.0,
    ↪ ActivationType::Tanh);

    println!("Training neurons with different activation
    ↪ functions:");
    // Run multiple training iterations to observe how each neuron
    ↪ adjusts.
    for epoch in 0..10 {
        let output_relu    = neuron_relu.train(input, target,
        ↪ learning_rate);
        let output_sigmoid = neuron_sigmoid.train(input, target,
        ↪ learning_rate);
        let output_tanh    = neuron_tanh.train(input, target,
        ↪ learning_rate);
```

```rust
    println!(
        "Epoch {}: ReLU Output = {:.4}, Sigmoid Output = {:.4},
        ↪ Tanh Output = {:.4}",
        epoch, output_relu, output_sigmoid, output_tanh
    );
}

// Demonstrate direct computation of each activation function
↪ and its derivative.
let test_value = 0.8;
println!("\nDirect activation function computations for test
↪ value {:.2}:", test_value);
println!(
    "ReLU({:.2}) = {:.4}, ReLU'({:.2}) = {:.4}",
    test_value,
    ActivationType::ReLU.activate(test_value),
    test_value,
    ActivationType::ReLU.derivative(test_value)
);
println!(
    "Sigmoid({:.2}) = {:.4}, Sigmoid'({:.2}) = {:.4}",
    test_value,
    ActivationType::Sigmoid.activate(test_value),
    test_value,
    ActivationType::Sigmoid.derivative(test_value)
);
println!(
    "Tanh({:.2}) = {:.4}, Tanh'({:.2}) = {:.4}",
    test_value,
    ActivationType::Tanh.activate(test_value),
    test_value,
    ActivationType::Tanh.derivative(test_value)
);
}
```

Chapter 40

Gradient Descent Optimization Techniques for Model Training

Theoretical Foundations of Iterative Optimization

Gradient descent constitutes an iterative method for minimizing a differentiable objective function $J(\theta)$, where θ represents the parameter vector. The update rule is formalized as

$$\theta^{(k+1)} = \theta^{(k)} - \eta \nabla J(\theta^{(k)}),$$

with η denoting the learning rate and $\nabla J(\theta^{(k)})$ being the gradient of the objective function evaluated at the kth iteration. The method operates under the assumption that $J(\theta)$ exhibits continuity and differentiability; conditions which guarantee the existence of its gradient over the domain of interest. Analyses within this framework often invoke the convexity properties of $J(\theta)$, although many modern applications extend to nonconvex regimes wherein local minima and saddle points might be present. The convergence properties of the gradient descent method are intimately related to the Lipschitz continuity of the gradient and the condition number of the Hessian matrix, both of which influence the rate at which successive iterates approach a stationary point.

Adjustable Learning Rates in Iterative Processes

The selection of an appropriate learning rate η is critical, as it determines the size of each parameter update and, consequently, affects the convergence speed and stability of the optimization process. Fixed learning rates may be susceptible to either overshooting or slow convergence, particularly in scenarios involving gradients with highly variable magnitudes. To address these challenges, adaptive strategies for adjusting the learning rate are employed. One common scheme introduces a decay mechanism governed by a relation of the form

$$\eta^{(k)} = \frac{\eta_0}{1 + \lambda k},$$

where η_0 represents the initial learning rate, λ is a decay coefficient, and k is the iteration index. Alternative approaches adjust η dynamically based on properties of the gradient, often leveraging historical information to modulate the step size in a manner that reduces oscillations and encourages efficient descent. The interplay between the magnitude of the gradient and the scheduled adjustments to η is central to mitigating adverse effects such as overshooting minima and exacerbating the impact of noise in stochastic approximations.

Convergence Criteria and Stability Analysis

The termination of the gradient descent process is governed by carefully defined convergence criteria that ensure the iterative method has reached a state near a stationary point. One widely adopted criterion stipulates that convergence is achieved when the norm of the gradient satisfies

$$\|\nabla J(\theta^{(k)})\| < \epsilon,$$

for a predetermined tolerance ϵ. An alternative approach considers the relative change in the objective function across successive iterations, encapsulated by the condition

$$\left| \frac{J(\theta^{(k+1)}) - J(\theta^{(k)})}{J(\theta^{(k)})} \right| < \delta,$$

where δ is a small positive threshold. This criterion is particularly effective in high-dimensional settings, where direct measurements of the gradient norm may become computationally burdensome. Stability analysis further examines the spectral properties of the Hessian matrix at critical points, whereby the convergence rate is determined by the eigenvalues of the Hessian. A well-conditioned Hessian, in which the spread between the largest and smallest eigenvalues is minimal, facilitates more uniform convergence across dimensions. In contrast, ill-conditioning necessitates more cautious adjustments to η, underscoring the importance of marrying adaptive learning rate schemes with rigorous convergence diagnostics.

Iterative Model Improvement Through Gradient Dynamics

The iterative refinement of model parameters via gradient descent is characterized by a sequence of approximations that progressively reduce the value of the objective function. Each update acts as a discrete approximation to the continuous trajectory traced by the underlying dynamical system defined by the negative gradient flow. In practice, the discrete update mechanism must account for the curvature of $J(\theta)$ to avoid pitfalls such as slow convergence in the vicinity of plateaus or divergence near steep ascents. The incorporation of adjustable learning rates and robust convergence criteria not only enhances the stability of the method but also accelerates the approach to optimality by dynamically modifying the step size in response to local geometrical features of the objective landscape. The mathematical rigor underlying the derivation of these techniques provides a solid foundation for algorithmic implementations that balance the computational cost per iteration against the overall convergence rate, thereby enabling efficient and effective model training in a variety of complex settings.

Rust Code Snippet

```rust
/// This Rust code implements a simple gradient descent algorithm
↪   with an adaptive
/// learning rate schedule. The objective function is defined as:
///     J(x) = (x - 3)^2,
/// whose derivative (gradient) is:
///     J'(x) = 2 * (x - 3).
///
/// The update rule for gradient descent is:
///     x = x -  * J'(x)
///
/// An adaptive learning rate is computed using a decay formula:
///      =  / (1 +  * k)
///
/// Convergence is declared when |J'(x)| < , ensuring the gradient
↪   is sufficiently small.

fn objective(x: f64) -> f64 {
    // Objective function: J(x) = (x - 3)^2
    (x - 3.0).powi(2)
}

fn gradient(x: f64) -> f64 {
    // Gradient of the objective function: dJ/dx = 2 * (x - 3)
    2.0 * (x - 3.0)
}

fn gradient_descent(
    initial_x: f64,
    eta_0: f64,
    lambda: f64,
    tolerance: f64,
    max_iter: usize,
) -> (f64, usize) {
    // Initialize parameter and iteration counter.
    let mut x = initial_x;
    let mut iter = 0;

    // Iterate until convergence criteria is met or max iterations
    ↪   is reached.
    while iter < max_iter {
        let grad = gradient(x);

        // Check convergence: if the gradient norm is smaller than
        ↪   tolerance, break.
        if grad.abs() < tolerance {
            break;
        }

        // Adaptive learning rate based on decay schedule.
        let eta = eta_0 / (1.0 + lambda * iter as f64);
```

```
        // Update rule: x = x -  * gradient
        x = x - eta * grad;

        iter += 1;
    }

    (x, iter)
}

fn main() {
    // Hyperparameters for the gradient descent algorithm
    let initial_x = 10.0;      // Initial parameter value.
    let eta_0 = 0.1;           // Initial learning rate.
    let lambda = 0.01;         // Learning rate decay coefficient.
    let tolerance = 1e-6;      // Gradient tolerance for
    ↪ convergence.
    let max_iter = 1000;       // Maximum number of iterations.

    // Execute gradient descent.
    let (optimal_x, iterations) = gradient_descent(initial_x, eta_0,
    ↪ lambda, tolerance, max_iter);

    // Output the results.
    println!("Optimal x found: {:.6} after {} iterations",
    ↪ optimal_x, iterations);
    println!("Objective function value at optimal x: {:.6}",
    ↪ objective(optimal_x));
}
```

Chapter 41

Regularization Techniques: L1 and L2 Norms in Rust

Mathematical Underpinnings of Regularization

In the context of statistical and machine learning models, regularization constitutes an essential strategy for mitigating overfitting by introducing an additional penalty term into the objective function. Formally, one considers an augmented objective function of the form

$$J(\theta) = \mathcal{L}(\theta) + \Omega(\theta),$$

where $\mathcal{L}(\theta)$ is the original loss function and $\Omega(\theta)$ represents the regularization term. The penalty term is crucial for constraining the complexity of the hypothesis space. Two prevalent forms of $\Omega(\theta)$ are based on the L1 and L2 norms, each imposing distinct geometric constraints upon the parameter vector θ.

L1 Regularization in Model Training Routines

The L1 norm regularization approach introduces a penalty that is proportional to the sum of the absolute values of the model parameters. This method is particularly noted for its ability to induce sparsity in the parameter vector, promoting models that are both parsimonious and resilient against overfitting.

1 Formulation of the L1 Norm

The L1 regularization term is mathematically defined as

$$\Omega_{L1}(\theta) = \lambda \sum_{j=1}^{n} |\theta_j|,$$

where λ is a hyperparameter that governs the strength of the regularization, and n denotes the dimensionality of the parameter space. The absolute value function in this formulation contributes a linear penalty that tends to shrink the parameters towards zero, thereby effectively performing feature selection within the model training routine.

2 Gradient Dynamics and Non-Differentiability Considerations

The utilization of L1 regularization introduces challenges related to the non-differentiability of the absolute value function at $\theta_j = 0$. In practice, subgradient methods are employed in place of classical gradients, allowing for the integration of this non-smooth regularization term into gradient descent frameworks. The subgradient for $|\theta_j|$ is defined as

$$\partial |\theta_j| = \begin{cases} \{1\} & \text{if } \theta_j > 0, \\ \{-1\} & \text{if } \theta_j < 0, \\ [-1, 1] & \text{if } \theta_j = 0, \end{cases}$$

which permits a well-defined notion of descent even at points of non-differentiability. The interplay between the L1 penalty and the iterative parameter update mechanics is critical in driving the emergence of sparse solutions within the high-dimensional parameter landscape.

L2 Regularization in Model Training Routines

L2 regularization, by contrast, incorporates a quadratic penalty on the model parameters. This technique is renowned for its ability to penalize large parameter values more severely than small ones, thereby yielding a smoother penalty landscape and fostering improved numerical stability in the optimization process.

1 Formulation of the L2 Norm

The L2 regularization term is delineated mathematically as

$$\Omega_{L2}(\theta) = \lambda \sum_{j=1}^{n} \theta_j^2,$$

with λ again operating as a regularization coefficient that adjusts the magnitude of the penalty. Unlike the L1 norm, the quadratic nature of the L2 norm favors the shrinkage of parameter values without forcing them to exactly zero. This intrinsic property is beneficial in contexts where retaining all features is desirable while controlling the overall magnitude of the parameter values.

2 Effect on Gradient Descent Dynamics

The gradient contribution from the L2 penalty is obtained in a straightforward manner by differentiating the quadratic term. Concretely, the derivative of θ_j^2 with respect to θ_j yields

$$\frac{\partial \Omega_{L2}(\theta)}{\partial \theta_j} = 2\lambda\theta_j.$$

This result effectively augments the gradient of the loss function with a proportional term that systematically discourages large weights. The continuous, differentiable nature of the L2 norm ensures that the standard gradient descent update rule remains applicable, contributing to smoother optimization trajectories and enhanced convergence properties in practice.

Integration of Regularization Techniques in Rust-Based Model Training

The implementation of regularization methodologies within model training routines leverages Rust's capacity for concise and efficient mathematical operations. The language's robust type system and zero-cost abstractions facilitate the translation of these mathematical formulations into high-performance code, wherein each arithmetic operation mirrors the theoretical underpinnings with minimal overhead.

1 Efficiency of Concise Mathematical Expressions in Rust

Rust enables the expression of complex mathematical operations in a manner that aligns closely with their algebraic representations. In the context of regularization, the summation of absolute values for L1 and squared terms for L2 can be formulated in a pseudo-vectorized style, ensuring that the computational structure remains highly optimized. The use of iterators and functional programming paradigms further contributes to reducing unnecessary computational overhead while maintaining clarity in the implementation of mathematical operations.

2 Structural Advantages of the Rust Type System

The static type system in Rust rigorously enforces correct usage of mathematical constructs and numerical types, thereby minimizing errors during the compilation and execution phases. The language's emphasis on immutability and explicit mutability control permits cautious management of stateful computations, ensuring that each modification to the parameter vector θ is traceable and verified against the intended regularization logic. This confluence of safety and performance establishes Rust as an optimal platform for implementing sophisticated regularization techniques in model training pipelines.

Rust Code Snippet

```rust
use std::fmt;

// A simple demonstration of gradient descent with L1 and L2
// regularization
fn main() {
    // Initialize the parameter vector theta
    let mut theta: Vec<f64> = vec![0.5, -1.2, 0.0, 2.3];
    let lambda: f64 = 0.1;
    let learning_rate: f64 = 0.01;
    let iterations: usize = 10;

    println!("Initial theta: {:?}", theta);

    // Perform gradient descent for a fixed number of iterations
    for iter in 0..iterations {
        // Compute gradient of the primary loss function.
        // For this example, we assume a simple quadratic loss:
        // L(theta) = 0.5 * sum(theta_j^2)
        // so the gradient is simply theta.
        let loss_grad = compute_loss_gradient(&theta);

        // Compute L1 subgradient and L2 gradient for regularization
        let l1_grad = l1_subgradient(&theta, lambda);
        let l2_grad = l2_gradient(&theta, lambda);

        // Combine gradients: total gradient = loss_grad + l1_grad +
        // l2_grad
        let total_gradient: Vec<f64> = loss_grad
            .iter()
            .zip(l1_grad.iter().zip(l2_grad.iter()))
            .map(|(g_loss, (g_l1, g_l2))| g_loss + g_l1 + g_l2)
            .collect();

        // Update parameters: theta = theta - learning_rate *
        // total_gradient
        for i in 0..theta.len() {
            theta[i] -= learning_rate * total_gradient[i];
        }

        println!("Iteration {}: theta = {:?}", iter + 1, theta);
    }

    // After optimization, compute the regularization penalty terms
    let l1_reg = l1_regularization(&theta, lambda);
    let l2_reg = l2_regularization(&theta, lambda);

    println!("Final L1 regularization term: {}", l1_reg);
    println!("Final L2 regularization term: {}", l2_reg);
}
```

```rust
// Dummy loss function: In this example, we use a quadratic loss
// L(theta) = 0.5 * sum(theta_j^2) whose gradient is simply theta.
fn compute_loss_gradient(theta: &Vec<f64>) -> Vec<f64> {
    theta.clone()
}


// L1 regularization term: Omega_{L1}(theta) = lambda *
↪ sum(|theta_j|)
fn l1_regularization(theta: &[f64], lambda: f64) -> f64 {
    lambda * theta.iter().map(|&x| x.abs()).sum::<f64>()
}


// L1 subgradient: For each theta_j, the subgradient is defined as:
//    1 if theta_j > 0, -1 if theta_j < 0, and 0 if theta_j == 0
↪ (choice within [-1,1])
fn l1_subgradient(theta: &[f64], lambda: f64) -> Vec<f64> {
    theta
        .iter()
        .map(|&x| {
            if x > 0.0 {
                lambda
            } else if x < 0.0 {
                -lambda
            } else {
                0.0   // Choosing 0 at zero for subgradient
            }
        })
        .collect()
}


// L2 regularization term: Omega_{L2}(theta) = lambda *
↪ sum(theta_j^2)
fn l2_regularization(theta: &[f64], lambda: f64) -> f64 {
    lambda * theta.iter().map(|&x| x * x).sum::<f64>()
}


// L2 gradient: For each theta_j, the derivative of theta_j^2 is 2 *
↪ theta_j,
// so the gradient contribution becomes 2 * lambda * theta_j.
fn l2_gradient(theta: &[f64], lambda: f64) -> Vec<f64> {
    theta.iter().map(|&x| 2.0 * lambda * x).collect()
}
```

Chapter 42

Custom Loss Functions: Design and Implementation

Mathematical Formulation of Loss Functions

The formulation of a loss function begins with the definition of a mapping from the predicted values of a model to a non-negative real number that quantifies the error between these predictions and the ground truth. In formal terms, if the model produces an output $f(x; \theta)$ for an input x with model parameters θ, and the true value is denoted by y, then a loss function is defined as

$$L(f(x; \theta), y) : \mathbb{R} \times \mathbb{R} \to \mathbb{R}_{\geq 0}.$$

Standard loss functions such as the mean squared error, defined as

$$L_{\mathrm{MSE}}(\theta) = \frac{1}{m} \sum_{i=1}^{m} (f(x_i; \theta) - y_i)^2,$$

or the cross-entropy loss used in classification tasks, serve as starting points for understanding the role that loss functions play in the determination of optimal model parameters. The design of a custom loss function can be seen as an extension of these traditional formulations, where the loss is modified or entirely redefined to capture domain-specific properties or to enforce particular behaviors within the training process.

Design Considerations and Customization Strategies

The customization of loss functions is driven by the need to address inherent biases, heteroscedastic errors, or imbalanced data distributions that are problem-specific. A custom loss function, denoted by

$$L_{\text{custom}}(\theta) = \sum_{i=1}^{m} \ell\big(f(x_i; \theta), y_i; \psi\big),$$

can incorporate additional parameters ψ that control aspects such as the degree of penalization for different types of errors. These parameters may modulate the curvature of the loss landscape or adjust the sensitivity to outliers. In designing such functions, the mathematical properties of the resulting optimization problem are of paramount importance. The loss function must be constructed to maintain desirable traits such as non-negativity, robustness, and, where possible, convexity over the parameter space.

Geometric interpretations of loss functions further illuminate their usability in practice. The contours of a loss function in the parameter space provide insights into the presence of multiple local minima or saddle points. This analysis is essential when extending standard objectives with terms that introduce asymmetry or non-linearity. In certain cases, the loss function may be enhanced with regularization terms, yielding an augmented objective

$$J(\theta) = L_{\text{custom}}(\theta) + \Omega(\theta),$$

where $\Omega(\theta)$ encapsulates additional penalties that promote model generalization and mitigate overfitting.

Differentiability and Optimization Considerations

For effective integration into gradient-based optimization algorithms, the custom loss function must be differentiable with respect to the model parameters θ. In many instances, the loss function is designed to be differentiable almost everywhere, thereby allowing the application of classical techniques such as gradient descent. The derivative, or more generally the gradient, is computed as

$$\nabla_\theta L_{\text{custom}}(\theta) = \left(\frac{\partial \ell\big(f(x_1; \theta), y_1; \psi\big)}{\partial \theta}, \ldots, \frac{\partial \ell\big(f(x_m; \theta), y_m; \psi\big)}{\partial \theta} \right).$$

When the loss function contains non-smooth components, the notion of subgradients is introduced. In these cases, the subdifferential provides a set of valid descent directions at points of non-differentiability. Such an approach ensures that the optimization process remains feasible, even in the presence of sharp transitions or piecewise linear elements. A meticulous analysis of the derivative properties and an assessment of convexity are central to guaranteeing convergence during training.

The interplay between the loss function and the gradient-based optimization method is critical. The choice of step size, the structure of the gradient updates, and the possible incorporation of momentum or adaptive learning rate strategies all depend on the analytical properties of the custom loss function. Robust theoretical analysis is required to ensure that the loss landscape facilitates efficient navigation towards a global or suitably optimal minimum, while also being resilient in the face of noise and irregularities in the data.

Integration into Rust-Based Training Pipelines

The integration of a custom loss function into a Rust-based training pipeline necessitates a translation of the mathematical formulation into an efficient computational model that leverages Rust's strengths in performance and safety. Given Rust's emphasis on zero-cost abstractions, the design of the loss function is implemented in such a way that the mathematical structure is preserved without incurring extraneous computational overhead. The precise alignment between the theoretical construct and its implementation is achieved through a careful mapping of mathematical operations to statically-typed functions that ensure correctness at compile time.

In this context, the loss function is embedded within the overall training loop, whereby each iteration computes the value of $L_{\text{custom}}(\theta)$ along with its gradient components. The functional composition of the custom loss with auxiliary operations—such as normalization or regularization—is harmonized using Rust's expressive iterator and combinatorial paradigms. This design facilitates the construction of a training process that mirrors the continuum of the theoretical model, ensuring that every arithmetic and analytic operation is executed with rigorous attention to efficiency and correctness.

The structural advantages of Rust, including its robust type system and memory safety guarantees, contribute to a reliable implementation where portfolio optimization of the training routine and loss function evaluation is achieved through meticulous abstraction and inlining of mathematical operations. The resulting system embodies a synthesis of advanced theoretical insights and practical engineering considerations, thereby enabling custom loss functions to be seamlessly integrated into the broader framework of data science model development.

Rust Code Snippet

```
use std::fmt::Debug;

/// A simple linear model defined as f(x; theta) = theta * x.
fn model(x: f64, theta: f64) -> f64 {
    theta * x
}

/// Computes the custom loss for a given prediction and target using
↪    a scaling parameter psi.
/// The loss function is defined as:
///     L_custom = psi * (f(x; theta) - y)^2,
/// which extends the standard mean squared error with a
↪    domain-specific scaling factor.
fn custom_loss(pred: f64, target: f64, psi: f64) -> f64 {
    psi * (pred - target).powi(2)
}

/// Computes the gradient of the custom loss with respect to theta
↪    for one data point.
/// Given the loss:
///     L_custom = psi * (theta * x - y)^2,
/// the derivative with respect to theta is:
///     dL/dtheta = 2 * psi * (theta * x - y) * x.
```

```
fn custom_loss_gradient(x: f64, theta: f64, target: f64, psi: f64)
↪   -> f64 {
    2.0 * psi * (model(x, theta) - target) * x
}


/// Computes the average custom loss and its gradient over the
↪   entire training dataset,
/// augmented with an L2 regularization term. The complete objective
↪   function is:
///
///     J(theta) = (1/m) * [psi * (theta*x_i - y_i)^2] + lambda *
↪   theta^2,
///
/// and its gradient is given by:
///
///     dJ/dtheta = (1/m) * [2 * psi * (theta*x_i - y_i) * x_i] + 2
↪   * lambda * theta.
fn compute_loss_and_gradient(xs: &[f64], ys: &[f64], theta: f64,
↪   psi: f64, lambda: f64) -> (f64, f64) {
    let m = xs.len() as f64;
    let mut total_loss = 0.0;
    let mut total_grad = 0.0;
    for (x, y) in xs.iter().zip(ys.iter()) {
        total_loss += custom_loss(model(*x, theta), *y, psi);
        total_grad += custom_loss_gradient(*x, theta, *y, psi);
    }
    // Average the loss over all samples and add the L2
    ↪   regularization term.
    let loss = total_loss / m + lambda * theta.powi(2);
    // Average the gradient and add the gradient from the
    ↪   regularization term.
    let grad = total_grad / m + 2.0 * lambda * theta;
    (loss, grad)
}


/// Performs gradient descent to optimize the model parameter theta.
/// In each epoch, the function computes the loss and gradient, then
↪   updates theta accordingly.
/// This routine demonstrates how the custom loss function and its
↪   derivatives can be integrated
/// into an iterative training pipeline using Rust's performance and
↪   safety features.
fn gradient_descent(
    xs: &[f64],
    ys: &[f64],
    initial_theta: f64,
    psi: f64,
    lambda: f64,
    learning_rate: f64,
    num_epochs: usize
) -> f64 {
    let mut theta = initial_theta;
    for epoch in 0..num_epochs {
```

267

```rust
        let (loss, grad) = compute_loss_and_gradient(xs, ys, theta,
        ↪  psi, lambda);
        theta -= learning_rate * grad;
        if epoch % 100 == 0 {
            println!("Epoch {}: Loss = {:.6}, Theta = {:.6}", epoch,
            ↪  loss, theta);
        }
    }
    theta
}

fn main() {
    // Define a simple dataset exhibiting a linear relationship: y =
    ↪  2 * x.
    let xs = vec![1.0, 2.0, 3.0, 4.0];
    let ys = vec![2.0, 4.0, 6.0, 8.0];

    // Define hyperparameters for the custom loss function and
    ↪  gradient descent.
    let psi = 1.5;              // Scaling factor for the loss
    ↪  function.
    let lambda = 0.01;         // L2 regularization coefficient.
    let initial_theta = 0.0;   // Initial guess for the model
    ↪  parameter.
    let learning_rate = 0.01;  // Learning rate for gradient
    ↪  descent updates.
    let num_epochs = 1000;     // Number of training epochs.

    // Execute the gradient descent training loop.
    let optimized_theta = gradient_descent(&xs, &ys, initial_theta,
    ↪  psi, lambda, learning_rate, num_epochs);
    println!("Optimized theta: {:.6}", optimized_theta);
}
```

Chapter 43

Bootstrapping Methods for Statistical Inference

Foundations of Bootstrapping

Bootstrapping is a resampling methodology that approximates the sampling distribution of a statistical estimator by repeatedly drawing samples with replacement from an observed dataset. Given an original sample of n independent observations drawn from an unknown probability distribution F, the empirical distribution function (EDF) is defined as

$$\hat{F}(x) = \frac{1}{n} \sum_{i=1}^{n} \mathbf{1}_{\{x_i \leq x\}},$$

where $\mathbf{1}_{\{x_i \leq x\}}$ denotes the indicator function. Resampling based on $\hat{F}$ allows the generation of new datasets, each of size n, from which an estimator of interest, denoted by $\hat{\theta}$, is recalculated to yield bootstrap replicates $\hat{\theta}_1^*, \hat{\theta}_2^*, \ldots, \hat{\theta}_B^*$. This procedure serves as the foundation for quantifying variability in statistical estimates without assuming a specific parametric model for the underlying data.

Theoretical Underpinnings and Asymptotic Properties

The bootstrap paradigm is deeply rooted in theoretical statistics and leverages asymptotic properties that justify its application. Under mild regularity conditions, the distribution of the estimator $\hat{\theta}$ computed from the original sample converges to a well-defined limit as n approaches infinity. Similarly, the empirical distribution $\hat{F}$ converges to the true distribution F, thereby ensuring that the bootstrap replicates $\hat{\theta}^*$ mimic the variability of $\hat{\theta}$. Mathematically, if T is a functional acting on the space of probability distributions, then

$$\hat{\theta} = T(\hat{F}) \quad \text{and} \quad \hat{\theta}_b^* = T(\hat{F}_b^*),$$

where $\hat{F}_b^*$ is the EDF associated with the bth bootstrap sample. The consistency and convergence in distribution of $\hat{\theta}_b^*$ to the true sampling distribution are rigorously supported by results stemming from the central limit theorem and weak convergence in probability theory.

Resampling Techniques and Algorithmic Structure

The essential algorithm of bootstrapping relies on generating bootstrap samples through sampling with replacement from the original dataset. For each bootstrap iteration, a resample of size n is drawn, and the estimator of interest is recalculated. This repeated computation leads to an empirical approximation of the sampling distribution. Formally, if the original dataset is denoted by $X = (x_1, x_2, \ldots, x_n)$, a bootstrap sample $X^* = (x_1^*, x_2^*, \ldots, x_n^*)$ is constructed by sampling from X with replacement. The collection of estimates $\{\hat{\theta}_1^*, \hat{\theta}_2^*, \ldots, \hat{\theta}_B^*\}$ provides a means to assess the variability of $\hat{\theta}$ and often underpins subsequent inferential procedures, such as the construction of confidence intervals or the estimation of standard errors.

Variance Estimation and Construction of Confidence Intervals

Central to bootstrapping is the capacity to quantify uncertainty in estimators. One of the main applications of bootstrap methods is the estimation of the variance of a statistical estimator. The bootstrap estimate of the variance can be expressed as

$$\widehat{\text{Var}}(\hat{\theta}) = \frac{1}{B-1} \sum_{b=1}^{B} \left(\hat{\theta}_b^* - \overline{\hat{\theta}^*} \right)^2,$$

where $\overline{\hat{\theta}^*} = \frac{1}{B} \sum_{b=1}^{B} \hat{\theta}_b^*$ is the mean of the bootstrap replicates. Building on this variability estimate, bootstrapping facilitates the construction of confidence intervals. For instance, the percentile method obtains a $(1-\alpha)$ confidence interval by identifying the $\alpha/2$ and $1-\alpha/2$ quantiles of the distribution of $\hat{\theta}^*$. In this framework, if $q_{\alpha/2}$ and $q_{1-\alpha/2}$ denote the lower and upper quantiles respectively, then the interval

$$\left[q_{\alpha/2}, \, q_{1-\alpha/2} \right]$$

serves as a nonparametric confidence interval for the parameter of interest. Alternative methods, such as the bias-corrected and accelerated (BCa) approach, further refine interval estimation by adjusting for both bias and skewness in the bootstrap distribution.

Numerical Considerations and Convergence Aspects

The practical implementation of bootstrapping necessitates careful consideration of numerical factors, particularly the number of bootstrap replications B. A sufficiently large B is critical for ensuring that the empirical distribution of the bootstrap estimates adequately approximates the true sampling distribution. However, the computational cost increases linearly with the number of replications, thereby imposing trade-offs between statistical accuracy and processing efficiency. Convergence properties of the bootstrap estimator are influenced by both the magnitude of n and the choice of B, with convergence to the true variance and quantile estimates being asymptotically guaranteed under appropriate conditions. In addition to the standard nonparametric bootstrap, alternative re-sampling schemes, such as the parametric bootstrap or block boot-strap for dependent data, are available. These methods extend the basic principles of resampling to accommodate complexities such as model-driven data generation or temporal dependence, thereby broadening the applicability of bootstrapping within statistically and computationally challenging contexts.

Rust Code Snippet

```rust
//! Bootstrapping implementation in Rust
//!
//! This code demonstrates the bootstrap algorithm for estimating
↪   the variance
//! and constructing a 95% confidence interval for an estimator,
↪   using the sample mean
//! as an example. The methodology follows these steps:
//!
//! 1. Compute the empirical mean as our estimator:
//!     estimator T(X) = mean(X)
//!
//! 2. Generate bootstrap samples by drawing, with replacement, from
↪   the original dataset
//!     to mimic the empirical distribution function (EDF):
//!     X* = {x_1*, x_2*, ..., x_n*}
//!
//! 3. Recalculate the estimator for each bootstrap sample to obtain
↪   replicates:
//!     T*(b) for b = 1, 2, ..., B
//!
//! 4. Estimate the variance of T using the bootstrap replicates:
//!     Var(T) = (1/(B-1)) *  (T*(b) - mean(T*))²
//!
//! 5. Construct a 95% confidence interval using the percentile
↪   method by identifying
//!     the 2.5th and 97.5th percentiles of the bootstrap replicates.
//!
//! Note: To run this code, add the following dependency in your
↪   Cargo.toml:
//!     rand = "0.8"

use rand::prelude::*;
use rand::seq::SliceRandom;

// Compute the mean of a collection of f64 values.
fn mean(data: &[f64]) -> f64 {
    data.iter().sum::<f64>() / (data.len() as f64)
}
```

```rust
// Compute the unbiased sample variance of a collection of f64
↪  values.
fn sample_variance(data: &[f64]) -> f64 {
    let m = mean(data);
    let sum_sq: f64 = data.iter().map(|x| (x - m).powi(2)).sum();
    sum_sq / ((data.len() - 1) as f64)
}

// Generate a bootstrap sample by sampling with replacement from the
↪  original data.
fn sample_with_replacement(data: &[f64]) -> Vec<f64> {
    let mut rng = thread_rng();
    // Sample exactly data.len() elements with replacement
    (0..data.len())
        .map(|_| *data.choose(&mut rng).expect("Dataset must not be
        ↪  empty"))
        .collect()
}

fn main() {
    // Example dataset: a vector of observations.
    let dataset: Vec<f64> = vec![10.0, 12.5, 9.8, 11.3, 13.7, 12.0,
    ↪  10.5, 11.9, 14.2, 9.6];

    // Calculate the original estimator (mean of the dataset).
    let orig_estimator = mean(&dataset);
    println!("Original estimator (mean): {:.4}", orig_estimator);

    // Number of bootstrap replications.
    let B = 1000;
    let mut bootstrap_estimates: Vec<f64> = Vec::with_capacity(B);

    // Generate bootstrap replicates.
    for _ in 0..B {
        let boot_sample = sample_with_replacement(&dataset);
        let boot_estimator = mean(&boot_sample);
        bootstrap_estimates.push(boot_estimator);
    }

    // Estimate the variance of the estimator using the bootstrap
    ↪  replicates.
    // Var(T) = (1/(B-1)) * (T*(b) - mean(T*))²
    let bs_variance = sample_variance(&bootstrap_estimates);
    println!("Bootstrap estimated variance: {:.4}", bs_variance);

    // Construct a 95% confidence interval using the percentile
    ↪  method.
    // Sort the bootstrap estimates.
    bootstrap_estimates.sort_by(|a, b| a.partial_cmp(b).unwrap());

    // Determine the indices for the 2.5th and 97.5th percentiles.
    let lower_index = ((0.025 * B as f64).floor() as usize).min(B -
    ↪  1);
```

```rust
    let upper_index = ((0.975 * B as f64).floor() as usize).min(B -
    ↪   1);

    let ci_lower = bootstrap_estimates[lower_index];
    let ci_upper = bootstrap_estimates[upper_index];

    println!("95% Bootstrap Confidence Interval: [{:.4}, {:.4}]",
    ↪   ci_lower, ci_upper);
}
```

Chapter 44

Cross-Validation Methods Implemented in Rust

Foundations of Cross-Validation

Cross-validation constitutes a statistically rigorous framework for estimating the generalization performance of learning models. The central objective is to approximate the prediction error incurred when a model, trained on a finite dataset, is applied to previously unseen data. Formally, let a dataset be denoted as $D = \{x_1, x_2, \ldots, x_n\}$, where n represents the number of observations. The methodology partitions D into mutually exclusive subsets and cyclically designates one subset as the validation set while the remaining observations form the training set. This systematic subdivision facilitates the estimation of error as

$$\bar{E} = \frac{1}{k} \sum_{i=1}^{k} E_i,$$

where E_i is the error computed on the ith partition and k designates the number of folds. Such an estimator provides empirical assurance regarding model performance and mitigates overfitting by ensuring that validation occurs on data not used during the training phase.

275

k-Fold Cross-Validation

In k-fold cross-validation, the dataset is divided into k roughly equal sized folds. For each fold i, the model is trained on the augmented dataset

$$D_{\text{train}}^{(i)} = D \setminus D_i,$$

and the performance is then validated on the held-out fold, D_i. The resulting error metric, E_i, reflects the performance on that specific fold. Aggregation of these metrics according to

$$\bar{E} = \frac{1}{k} \sum_{i=1}^{k} E_i,$$

yields a robust estimate that accounts for variability inherent in the data partitioning. This procedure effectively balances bias and variance in the error estimation. The stratification of the data across folds also permits the detection of heterogeneity in model performance, thereby enabling detailed diagnostic analysis. Moreover, the procedure benefits from theoretical guarantees that underpin its asymptotic consistency, particularly when the number of folds is selected judiciously in relation to n.

Leave-One-Out Cross-Validation

Leave-one-out cross-validation (LOOCV) is a specialized instance of k-fold cross-validation where $k = n$. In this setting, the full dataset D is partitioned into n subsets, each consisting of a single observation. For every iteration i, the training set is defined as

$$D_{\text{train}}^{(i)} = D \setminus \{x_i\},$$

and the corresponding validation set comprises the single observation $\{x_i\}$. This exhaustive procedure computes the prediction error for each observation and aggregates the errors according to

$$\bar{E}_{\text{LOO}} = \frac{1}{n} \sum_{i=1}^{n} E_i.$$

LOOCV is renowned for its nearly unbiased nature, as each model is trained on almost the entire dataset. However, the method entails considerable computational overhead, especially for large n.

The balance between computational demand and fidelity of error estimation renders LOOCV particularly valuable in scenarios where dataset sizes are limited and high precision is required.

Implementation Considerations in Rust

Rust's robust type system and stringent compile-time memory safety checks enable the development of cross-validation routines that are both efficient and reliable. The explicit control over memory management, coupled with fine-grained concurrency primitives, facilitates the execution of computationally intensive routines, such as k-fold and leave-one-out cross-validation, within an environment that minimizes runtime errors. An idiomatic Rust implementation can leverage iterative paradigms and immutable data structures to enforce the separation of training and validation phases. Moreover, the language's emphasis on zero-cost abstractions allows for the delineation of data partitions operatorially without compromising performance efficiency. This paradigm ensures that parallel execution models, such as those supported by high-level concurrency crates, can be employed to mitigate the computational complexity associated with repeated model training.

Statistical Considerations of Cross-Validation Estimations

From a statistical perspective, cross-validation routines yield empirical estimators for model performance that inherently encapsulate both bias and variance components. The standard error of the aggregated performance metric, $\bar{E}$, can itself be estimated by computing

$$\mathrm{SE}(\bar{E}) = \sqrt{\frac{1}{k(k-1)} \sum_{i=1}^{k} \left(E_i - \bar{E}\right)^2},$$

a measure that assists in ascertaining the precision of the performance estimate. For LOOCV, analogous formulations apply with $k = n$, and rigorous analysis of these estimators is supported by modern statistical learning theory. This statistical framework provides assurance regarding the reliability of the cross-validation results when used to guide model selection and calibration in data-driven decision making.

277

Rust Code Snippet

```rust
use rayon::prelude::*;
use std::error::Error;

/// Computes k-fold cross-validation error metrics using a simple
/// ↪  mean-based model.
/// The error for a fold is computed as the Mean Squared Error (MSE)
/// ↪  between the
/// model prediction (mean of training set) and the validation set
/// ↪  values.
///
/// # Arguments
/// * `dataset` - A slice of f64 observations.
/// * `k` - The number of folds for cross-validation.
///
/// # Returns
/// A tuple containing:
/// - The aggregated mean error over all folds.
/// - The standard error of the aggregated errors.
///
/// The formulas employed are:
///     Mean Error: ȳ = (1/k) E_i,
///     Standard Error: SE(ȳ) = sqrt(1/(k*(k-1)) * (E_i - ȳ)²).
fn k_fold_cross_validation(dataset: &[f64], k: usize) ->
↪  Result<(f64, f64), Box<dyn Error>> {
    let n = dataset.len();
    if k == 0 || k > n {
        return Err("Invalid number of folds".into());
    }

    // Partition the dataset into k folds.
    let mut folds: Vec<&[f64]> = Vec::with_capacity(k);
    let fold_size = n / k;
    let remainder = n % k;
    let mut start = 0;
    for i in 0..k {
        // Distribute the remainder among the first 'remainder'
        // ↪  folds.
        let extra = if i < remainder { 1 } else { 0 };
        let end = start + fold_size + extra;
        folds.push(&dataset[start..end]);
        start = end;
    }

    // Compute error for each fold in parallel.
    let errors: Vec<f64> = (0..k).into_par_iter().map(|i| {
        // Build the training set from all folds except the i-th
        // ↪  fold.
        let training: Vec<f64> = folds.iter()
            .enumerate()
            .filter(|&(j, _)| j != i)
```

278

```rust
            .flat_map(|(_, fold)| fold.to_vec())
            .collect();

        // Train a simple predictor: the average value of the
        ↪    training set.
        let model = mean(&training);

        // Calculate Mean Squared Error (MSE) on the validation
        ↪    fold.
        let mse = folds[i].iter()
            .map(|&x| (model - x).powi(2))
            .sum::<f64>() / (folds[i].len() as f64);
        mse
    }).collect();

    let mean_error = mean(&errors);
    let se = standard_error(&errors, mean_error, k);
    Ok((mean_error, se))
}

/// Computes Leave-One-Out Cross-Validation (LOOCV) error metrics.
/// In LOOCV each observation is used once as the validation set.
/// The model is trained on the remaining observations and the
↪    squared error
/// is computed for the left-out observation.
///
/// # Arguments
/// * `dataset` - A slice of f64 observations.
///
/// # Returns
/// A tuple containing:
/// - The aggregated mean error (MSE) over all leave-one-out
↪    iterations.
/// - The standard error computed with k = n (number of
↪    observations).
fn loocv(dataset: &[f64]) -> Result<(f64, f64), Box<dyn Error>> {
    let n = dataset.len();
    if n == 0 {
        return Err("Dataset is empty".into());
    }

    let errors: Vec<f64> = (0..n).into_par_iter().map(|i| {
        // Training set excludes the i-th observation.
        let training: Vec<f64> = dataset.iter()
            .enumerate()
            .filter(|&(j, _)| j != i)
            .map(|(_, &x)| x)
            .collect();

        // Train model based on the mean of the training set.
        let model = mean(&training);

        // Compute the squared error for the left-out observation.
```

279

```
            (model - dataset[i]).powi(2)
    }).collect();

    let mean_error = mean(&errors);
    let se = standard_error(&errors, mean_error, n);
    Ok((mean_error, se))
}

/// Helper function that calculates the mean of a slice of f64
↪   values.
fn mean(data: &[f64]) -> f64 {
    data.iter().sum::<f64>() / (data.len() as f64)
}

/// Computes the standard error of the aggregated performance
↪   metric.
/// Uses the formula:
///     SE(ȳ) = sqrt( 1/(k*(k-1)) *  (E_i - ȳ)² ),
/// where k is the number of folds (or n in LOOCV).
fn standard_error(data: &[f64], mean_val: f64, k: usize) -> f64 {
    let sum_sq: f64 = data.iter().map(|&x| (x -
    ↪   mean_val).powi(2)).sum();
    (sum_sq / ((k * (k - 1)) as f64)).sqrt()
}

fn main() -> Result<(), Box<dyn Error>> {
    // Generate a sample dataset of numerical observations.
    let dataset: Vec<f64> = vec![2.5, 3.0, 2.8, 3.2, 3.6, 2.9, 3.1,
    ↪   3.3, 2.7, 3.4];

    // Execute k-Fold Cross-Validation with k = 5.
    let k = 5;
    let (mean_error, se) = k_fold_cross_validation(&dataset, k)?;
    println!("k-Fold Cross-Validation (k = {}):", k);
    println!("Mean Error (MSE): {:.4}", mean_error);
    println!("Standard Error: {:.4}", se);

    // Execute Leave-One-Out Cross-Validation (LOOCV).
    let (mean_error_loocv, se_loocv) = loocv(&dataset)?;
    println!("\nLeave-One-Out Cross-Validation (LOOCV):");
    println!("Mean Error (MSE): {:.4}", mean_error_loocv);
    println!("Standard Error: {:.4}", se_loocv);

    Ok(())
}
```

Chapter 45

Bayesian Inference and Probabilistic Programming

Mathematical Foundations of Bayesian Inference

Bayesian inference is founded on the principle of updating probability distributions as evidence accumulates. Central to this framework is Bayes' theorem, which is formally expressed as

$$p(\theta \mid \mathcal{D}) = \frac{p(\mathcal{D} \mid \theta) \, p(\theta)}{p(\mathcal{D})}.$$

Here, θ represents the model parameters, while $\mathcal{D}$ denotes the observed dataset. The term $p(\theta)$ encapsulates prior beliefs about the parameters before observing data, and $p(\mathcal{D} \mid \theta)$ is the likelihood function, indicating the probability of the data given the parameters. The denominator $p(\mathcal{D})$, often referred to as the evidence, is a normalizing constant that ensures the posterior distribution integrates to one. This theorem establishes a systematic mechanism for incorporating new information into existing models, thereby updating the state of knowledge in a probabilistically coherent manner.

Techniques for Posterior Estimation

The practical estimation of the posterior distribution $p(\theta \mid \mathcal{D})$ involves the evaluation of integrals that are typically analytically intractable in high dimensions. Two principal categories of methods serve this purpose: simulation-based approaches such as Markov Chain Monte Carlo (MCMC) techniques and optimization-based methods including variational inference. In MCMC, a Markov chain is constructed with the target posterior as its stationary distribution, enabling the approximation of the distribution via successive samples. Variational inference, on the other hand, posits a family of candidate distributions and seeks to minimize the divergence between the candidate and the true posterior, effectively transforming the problem into one of optimization. Each approach balances computational efficiency with the need for precision in capturing the full complexity of the uncertainty described by the model.

Uncertainty Quantification in Probabilistic Models

Bayesian methods inherently facilitate uncertainty quantification through the analysis of the posterior distribution. The distribution itself not only provides point estimates, such as the posterior mean, but also conveys the uncertainty associated with these estimates through measures such as the variance and higher-order moments. Credible intervals are derived from the posterior and define ranges within which the parameter values reside with a specified probability. For example, a credible interval $[a, b]$ satisfies

$$\int_a^b p(\theta \mid \mathcal{D}) \, d\theta = \gamma,$$

where γ represents the desired probability mass. The utility of these intervals is augmented when the highest posterior density regions are determined, providing a concise representation of the most probable parameter values along with associated uncertainty. Such quantification is critical to evaluating the robustness of statistical inferences and ensuring that subsequent data-driven decisions appropriately account for inherent model variability.

Translation of Bayesian Methods into Rust

The translation of Bayesian statistical methods into Rust code benefits from the language's strong type system, explicit memory management, and zero-cost abstractions. Rust's design allows for the precise implementation of probabilistic models in a way that mirrors the mathematical structure of Bayesian inference. Each component—from defining prior distributions and likelihood functions to computing posterior estimates—can be modularized into robust units that leverage Rust's compile-time guarantees. Furthermore, efficient handling of numerical operations and a strong emphasis on concurrency facilitate the implementation of computationally intensive procedures such as MCMC sampling and variational optimization. The resultant system maintains high-performance standards while rigorously adhering to statistical and mathematical principles, thereby enabling the creation of probabilistic data models that are both reliable and scalable.

Integration of Statistical Methods with Data Models

The effective integration of Bayesian inference into probabilistic data models necessitates a meticulous mapping between theoretical constructs and their algorithmic counterparts. Statistical parameters are treated as random variables that are updated according to the posterior distribution estimated from the observed data. This process involves a careful choreography of these components, ensuring that the prior, likelihood, and evidence components interact in a coherent framework. By embedding these techniques into a probabilistic programming paradigm, each uncertain element within a data model is handled in a systematic and mathematically rigorous way. Such integration not only reinforces the interpretability of the entire system but also allows for the decomposition of complex data modeling tasks into smaller, composable Bayesian subroutines. This composability is essential for constructing multifaceted models that adhere to both the theoretical underpinnings of Bayesian reasoning and the demands of high-performance computation.

Rust Code Snippet

```
// Bayesian Inference Example in Rust
// This example demonstrates a simple Bayesian parameter estimation
↪   using the
// Metropolis-Hastings algorithm. The goal is to estimate the
↪   posterior distribution
// of a parameter (here, the mean of a Gaussian likelihood) given
↪   observed data,
// following Bayes' theorem:
//
//      p( | D)  p(D | ) · p()
//
// where p(D | ) is the likelihood and p() is the prior.
//
// The code below implements:
// 1. The Gaussian probability density and its logarithm.
// 2. Computation of the log-likelihood for given data.
// 3. A Gaussian prior log-probability function.
// 4. The log-posterior function (without the normalization
↪   constant).
// 5. A Metropolis-Hastings sampler to approximate the posterior
↪   distribution.
// 6. Extraction of the posterior mean and computation of a 95%
↪   credible interval.

extern crate rand;
extern crate rand_distr;

use rand::prelude::*;
use rand_distr::Normal;
use std::f64::consts::PI;

/// Computes the Gaussian probability density function at x for a
↪   given mean and variance.
/// Formula: (1 / (2²)) * exp( -((x - mean)² / (2²)) )
fn gaussian(x: f64, mean: f64, var: f64) -> f64 {
    (1.0 / ((2.0 * PI * var).sqrt())) * ( -((x - mean).powi(2)) /
    ↪   (2.0 * var) ).exp()
}

/// Computes the logarithm of the Gaussian probability density
↪   function.
/// This formulation is useful to avoid numerical underflow when
↪   dealing with small probabilities.
fn log_gaussian(x: f64, mean: f64, var: f64) -> f64 {
    -0.5 * ((2.0 * PI * var).ln() + ((x - mean).powi(2) / var))
}

/// Computes the log-likelihood of the data given the parameter.
/// For each observation d in data, it sums the log Gaussian
↪   probability
```

284

```
/// of observing d given the parameter (assumed to be the mean) and
↪   variance sigma².
fn log_likelihood(data: &Vec<f64>, param: f64, sigma2: f64) -> f64 {
    data.iter().map(|&d| log_gaussian(d, param, sigma2)).sum()
}


/// Computes the log-prior probability for the parameter.
/// Here, we assume a Gaussian prior with a given mean and variance.
fn log_prior(param: f64, prior_mean: f64, prior_var: f64) -> f64 {
    log_gaussian(param, prior_mean, prior_var)
}


/// Computes the log-posterior probability for the parameter given
↪   the observed data.
/// According to Bayes' theorem (ignoring the evidence):
/// log p( | D)  log p(D | ) + log p()
fn log_posterior(data: &Vec<f64>, param: f64, sigma2: f64,
↪   prior_mean: f64, prior_var: f64) -> f64 {
    log_likelihood(data, param, sigma2) + log_prior(param,
    ↪   prior_mean, prior_var)
}


/// Implements the Metropolis-Hastings algorithm to sample from the
↪   posterior distribution.
///
/// Parameters:
/// - data: Vector of observed data.
/// - initial: Initial guess for the parameter.
/// - iterations: Total number of MCMC iterations.
/// - sigma2: Variance of the likelihood function (data noise
↪   variance).
/// - prior_mean: Mean for the Gaussian prior of the parameter.
/// - prior_var: Variance for the Gaussian prior.
/// - proposal_std: Standard deviation of the proposal (jump)
↪   distribution.
fn metropolis_hastings(
    data: &Vec<f64>,
    initial: f64,
    iterations: usize,
    sigma2: f64,
    prior_mean: f64,
    prior_var: f64,
    proposal_std: f64
) -> Vec<f64> {
    let mut samples = Vec::with_capacity(iterations);
    let mut current = initial;
    let mut rng = rand::thread_rng();

    // Compute the log-posterior for the initial parameter value.
    let mut current_lp = log_posterior(data, current, sigma2,
    ↪   prior_mean, prior_var);

    for _ in 0..iterations {
```

```rust
        // Propose a new candidate parameter using a Gaussian random
        // walk.
        let proposal: f64 = current + rng.sample(Normal::new(0.0,
        // proposal_std).unwrap());
        let proposal_lp = log_posterior(data, proposal, sigma2,
        // prior_mean, prior_var);

        // Calculate the acceptance ratio (in probability space)
        // using exponentiation of the difference.
        let acceptance_ratio = (proposal_lp - current_lp).exp();

        // Accept the proposed parameter with probability equal to
        // the acceptance ratio.
        if acceptance_ratio >= rng.gen::<f64>() {
            current = proposal;
            current_lp = proposal_lp;
        }

        samples.push(current);
    }
    samples
}

fn main() {
    // Observed data: sample measurements assumed to be drawn from a
    // normal distribution
    // with a true mean near 5.0.
    let data = vec![4.8, 5.2, 5.0, 4.9, 5.1, 5.3, 4.7, 5.2, 5.0,
    // 5.1];

    // Likelihood variance (noise variance) assumed known.
    let sigma2 = 0.1;

    // Prior parameters: a Gaussian prior with mean 0.0 and a high
    // variance (low confidence).
    let prior_mean = 0.0;
    let prior_var = 10.0;

    // MCMC configuration: starting value, number of iterations, and
    // proposal standard deviation.
    let initial = 0.0;
    let iterations = 10000;
    let proposal_std = 0.5;

    // Run the Metropolis-Hastings sampler to generate posterior
    // samples.
    let samples = metropolis_hastings(&data, initial, iterations,
    // sigma2, prior_mean, prior_var, proposal_std);

    // Compute the posterior mean estimate from the samples.
    let posterior_mean: f64 = samples.iter().sum::<f64>() /
    // samples.len() as f64;
    println!("Posterior mean estimate: {}", posterior_mean);
```

```rust
    // Derive a 95% credible interval from the posterior samples.
    let mut sorted_samples = samples.clone();
    sorted_samples.sort_by(|a, b| a.partial_cmp(b).unwrap());
    let lower_index = (0.025 * sorted_samples.len() as f64) as
    ↪  usize;
    let upper_index = (0.975 * sorted_samples.len() as f64) as
    ↪  usize;
    let lower_bound = sorted_samples[lower_index];
    let upper_bound = sorted_samples[upper_index];
    println!("95% credible interval: [{}, {}]", lower_bound,
    ↪  upper_bound);
}
```

Chapter 46

Markov Chain Monte Carlo Algorithms

Mathematical Foundations of Markov Chain Monte Carlo Methods

Markov Chain Monte Carlo (MCMC) methods constitute a class of algorithms that construct a Markov chain whose equilibrium distribution converges to a target probability distribution. Fundamental to these methods is the Markov property, which asserts that the probability of transitioning to any future state depends solely on the present state and not on any past states. Formally, if $\{X_t\}$ denotes a discrete-time Markov chain defined over a state space $\mathcal{X}$, then the transition probabilities satisfy

$$\mathbb{P}[X_{t+1} = y \mid X_t = x, X_{t-1} = x_{t-1}, \ldots, X_0 = x_0] = \mathbb{P}[X_{t+1} = y \mid X_t = x].$$

A key requirement of a valid MCMC algorithm is that the chain must be ergodic; that is, it must be irreducible and aperiodic so that it eventually explores the entire state space with nonzero probability. The equilibrium, or stationary, distribution $\pi(x)$ is arrived at by enforcing the detailed balance condition

$$\pi(x) P(x, y) = \pi(y) P(y, x),$$

where $P(x, y)$ represents the transition probability from state x to state y. This condition guarantees that the target distribution remains invariant under the dynamics of the chain.

The Metropolis-Hastings Algorithm

The Metropolis-Hastings algorithm is an MCMC method that generates a sequence of sample states through a two-phase iterative scheme: proposal and acceptance. In the proposal phase, a candidate state is generated from a proposal distribution $q(y \mid x)$, which is often chosen for its symmetric or tractable properties. The acceptance probability, given by

$$\alpha(x, y) = \min \left(1, \frac{\pi(y)\, q(x \mid y)}{\pi(x)\, q(y \mid x)} \right),$$

ensures that the chain converges to the desired target distribution $\pi(x)$. The algorithm permits transitions that may lead to states with lower probability densities, thereby circumventing the limitations imposed by local maxima. The balance between exploration and exploitation is managed by careful calibration of the proposal distribution, and the logarithmic transformation of the acceptance ratio is often employed to mitigate numerical underflow issues when dealing with high-dimensional or complex distributions.

Gibbs Sampling

Gibbs sampling is a particular case of MCMC that simplifies the sampling process by iteratively sampling each component of a multivariate distribution from its conditional distribution. Assuming the state vector is represented as $\mathbf{x} = (x_1, \ldots, x_n)$, the Gibbs sampler updates each component sequentially according to the conditional probability

$$x_i^{(t+1)} \sim p \left(x_i \mid x_1^{(t+1)}, \ldots, x_{i-1}^{(t+1)}, x_{i+1}^{(t)}, \ldots, x_n^{(t)} \right)$$

for $i = 1, \ldots, n$. This process leverages the availability of tractable conditional densities even when the joint distribution $\pi(\mathbf{x})$ is analytically intractable. By systematically sampling from these full conditional distributions, the Gibbs sampler nests a simple sampling mechanism within the broader MCMC framework, ensuring that the resulting chain attains the stationary distribution associated with the target joint density. The efficiency of Gibbs sampling is heavily dependent on the ability to exactly compute and sample from these conditional distributions, a task that may be facilitated by exploiting conjugate priors and other structural properties of the model.

Computational Considerations in Rust Implementations of MCMC Algorithms

The translation of MCMC algorithms into the Rust programming language capitalizes on Rust's strong emphasis on performance and memory safety. Rust's zero-cost abstractions permit precise control over low-level details without compromising the clarity of algorithmic implementations. When implementing both the Metropolis-Hastings algorithm and Gibbs sampling in Rust, careful attention is paid to the efficient evaluation of probability densities and the manipulation of high-dimensional data structures. Rust's ownership model provides compile-time guarantees that eliminate common sources of runtime errors, leading to robust and efficient execution even in computationally intensive scenarios.

Rust's expressiveness allows the design of modular abstractions that encapsulate the mathematical elegance of MCMC methods. Each component—from probability density functions and transition kernels to acceptance criteria—can be implemented as composable units that are rigorously tested against theoretical expectations. Moreover, leveraging Rust's capabilities for concurrency and parallel computation further enhances the performance of MCMC simulations. In high-dimensional settings, where the cost per iteration may be significant, Rust's efficient memory management and support for multi-threading contribute to substantial speed-ups. Such attributes make Rust an attractive choice for executing statistically complex simulations while maintaining clear and maintainable code structures.

Rust Code Snippet

```
//! An example implementation of key MCMC algorithms in Rust.
//!
//! This code demonstrates the Metropolis-Hastings algorithm and
↪  Gibbs sampling,
//! incorporating the fundamental equations and concepts discussed
↪  in the chapter.
//!
//! Key Equations and Concepts:
//!   - Markov Property: For a discrete-time Markov chain {X_t} over
↪  state space ,
//!       P[X = y | X = x, X, ..., X] = P[X = y | X = x].
//!
//!   - Detailed Balance (Stationarity Condition):
```

```rust
//!       (x) · P(x, y) = (y) · P(y, x)
//!
//!   - Metropolis-Hastings Acceptance Probability:
//!       (x, y) = min(1, [(y) · q(x|y)] / [(x) · q(y|x)])
//!
//!     For a symmetric proposal distribution q, this simplifies to:
//!       (x, y) = min(1, (y) / (x))
//!
//!   - Gibbs Sampling Update for a multivariate state vector (x,
//! ↪ ..., x):
//!       For each component i (1  i  n):
//!          x^(t+1) ~ p(x | x^(t+1), ..., x^(t+1), x^(t), ...,
//! ↪ x^(t))
//!
//! External Crates:
//!   - rand and rand_distr are used for random number generation
//! ↪ and sampling from distributions.

use rand::prelude::*;
use rand_distr::{Normal, Distribution};

/// Computes an unnormalized target density function (x).
/// Here, we use the standard normal (excluding the normalization
/// ↪ constant):
///   (x)  exp(-x² / 2)
fn target_density(x: f64) -> f64 {
    (-0.5 * x * x).exp()
}


/// Metropolis-Hastings sampler for a one-dimensional target
/// ↪ distribution.
/// Uses a symmetric proposal distribution, so the acceptance
/// ↪ probability simplifies to:
///   (x, y) = min(1, (y) / (x))
///
/// Parameters:
///   - `initial`: the starting state
///   - `target`: function that computes (x)
///   - `proposal`: proposal function generating a candidate state
/// ↪ from the current state
///   - `iterations`: number of iterations to run the chain
fn metropolis_hastings<F, G>(
    initial: f64,
    target: F,
    proposal: G,
    iterations: usize
) -> Vec<f64>
where
    F: Fn(f64) -> f64,
    G: Fn(f64, &mut ThreadRng) -> f64,
{
    let mut samples = Vec::with_capacity(iterations);
    let mut rng = rand::thread_rng();
```

291

```rust
    let mut current = initial;
    for _ in 0..iterations {
        // Generate a candidate state y using the proposal
        ↪  distribution q(y | x)
        let candidate = proposal(current, &mut rng);
        // Compute the acceptance probability (x, y) = min(1,
        ↪  (candidate) / (current))
        let acceptance = (target(candidate) /
        ↪  target(current)).min(1.0);
        // Accept or reject the candidate based on a uniform random
        ↪  draw
        if rng.gen::<f64>() < acceptance {
            current = candidate;
        }
        samples.push(current);
    }
    samples
}


/// Proposal function for Metropolis-Hastings using a normal
↪  distribution centered at the current state.
/// This implements q(y | x) where q is symmetric.
fn normal_proposal(current: f64, rng: &mut ThreadRng) -> f64 {
    let proposal_std = 1.0; // Standard deviation of the proposal
    ↪  distribution
    let normal_dist = Normal::new(current, proposal_std).unwrap();
    normal_dist.sample(rng)
}


/// Gibbs sampler for a bivariate normal distribution with
↪  correlation coefficient .
/// The joint target distribution is given by:
///    p(x, y)  exp( - (x² - 2xy + y²) / (2(1 - ²)) )
///
/// The full conditional distributions are:
///    - x | y ~ Normal(·y, sqrt(1 - ²))
///    - y | x ~ Normal(·x, sqrt(1 - ²))
///
/// Parameters:
///    - `initial`: starting values for (x, y)
///    - `rho`: correlation coefficient (|| < 1)
///    - `iterations`: number of iterations to perform
fn gibbs_sampler(initial: (f64, f64), rho: f64, iterations: usize)
↪   -> Vec<(f64, f64)> {
    let mut samples = Vec::with_capacity(iterations);
    let mut rng = rand::thread_rng();
    let (mut x, mut y) = initial;
    let std_cond = (1.0 - rho * rho).sqrt(); // Standard deviation
    ↪  for the conditional distributions
    for _ in 0..iterations {
        // Sample x conditioned on y:
        //   x ~ Normal(·y, sqrt(1 - ²))
        let normal_x = Normal::new(rho * y, std_cond).unwrap();
```

292

```rust
        x = normal_x.sample(&mut rng);
        // Sample y conditioned on the new x:
        //    y ~ Normal(·x, sqrt(1 - ²))
        let normal_y = Normal::new(rho * x, std_cond).unwrap();
        y = normal_y.sample(&mut rng);
        samples.push((x, y));
    }
    samples
}

fn main() {
    // --- Metropolis-Hastings Demonstration ---
    let initial_state = 0.0;
    let iterations = 10000;
    let mh_samples = metropolis_hastings(initial_state,
    ↪   target_density, normal_proposal, iterations);
    println!("First 10 samples from Metropolis-Hastings:");
    for sample in mh_samples.iter().take(10) {
        println!("{:.5}", sample);
    }

    // --- Gibbs Sampling Demonstration ---
    let initial_pair = (0.0, 0.0);
    let rho = 0.8;
    let gibbs_iterations = 10000;
    let gibbs_samples = gibbs_sampler(initial_pair, rho,
    ↪   gibbs_iterations);
    println!("\nFirst 10 samples from Gibbs Sampling (x, y):");
    for (x, y) in gibbs_samples.iter().take(10) {
        println!("x: {:.5}, y: {:.5}", x, y);
    }
}
```

Chapter 47

Hidden Markov Models for Sequential Data

Mathematical Foundations of Hidden Markov Models

The theoretical framework of a Hidden Markov Model is predicated upon the concept of a stochastic process in which the underlying states are not directly observable. Let the set of hidden states be denoted by $S = \{s_1, s_2, \ldots, s_N\}$ and the sequence of observable symbols or measurements by $O = (o_1, o_2, \ldots, o_T)$. The model is parameterized by three elements. The first is the state transition probability matrix $A = \{a_{ij}\}$, where each element a_{ij} is defined as

$$a_{ij} = P(s_{t+1} = s_j \mid s_t = s_i).$$

The second is the observation or emission probability function B, where for each state s_j, the probability of observing a symbol o_t is given by

$$b_j(o_t) = P(o_t \mid s_j).$$

The final parameter is the initial state distribution $\pi = \{\pi_i\}$ with

$$\pi_i = P(s_1 = s_i).$$

These parameters collectively provide a complete probabilistic description of the system. Emphasis is placed on the chain's Markov property, which implies that the forthcoming state depends solely on the present state, and the conditional independence that ensures the observations are generated solely based on the current hidden state.

State Transition Estimation

Within the context of Hidden Markov Models, accurate estimation of the state transition probabilities is crucial for capturing the dynamics exhibited by the underlying process. In the idealized scenario, the transition probabilities encapsulate the likelihood of the system shifting from state s_i to state s_j over discrete time increments. The estimation process begins with formulating the likelihood function of the observation sequence O under the model parameters $\theta = \{A, B, \pi\}$, which is expressed as

$$L(\theta) = P(O \mid \theta).$$

In supervised settings, where an annotated sequence of hidden states is available, maximum likelihood estimates can be derived directly by counting the observed transitions. In more challenging unsupervised contexts, iterative algorithms such as the Baum-Welch method are employed. This technique leverages the forward-backward procedure to compute the expected frequencies of transitions in the hidden state sequence. The careful implementation of these estimation techniques is paramount in ensuring that the derived model reflects the intrinsic temporal dependencies of the sequential data.

Sequence Decoding

Decoding the most probable sequence of hidden states from a given sequence of observations constitutes one of the central challenges in the application of Hidden Markov Models. This task is framed as an optimization problem where the objective is to identify the sequence $S^* = (s_1^*, s_2^*, \ldots, s_T^*)$ that maximizes the joint probability

$$S^* = \arg \max_S P(S \mid O).$$

The Viterbi algorithm is the canonical method used for this purpose. It employs dynamic programming techniques to recursively compute the maximum probability path to each state at every time step, using recursion of the form

$$\delta_t(s_j) = \max_{s_i \in S} \{ \delta_{t-1}(s_i) \, a_{ij} \} \, b_j(o_t),$$

where $\delta_t(s_j)$ denoted the highest probability of any state sequence ending in state s_j at time t. The algorithm also maintains back-pointers that allow for the reconstruction of the optimal path once the final state probabilities are computed. The use of logarithmic transformations is common practice in these calculations, to mitigate issues related to numerical underflow in the computation of products of small probability values.

Rust Implementation Considerations

The robust type system inherent to Rust affords a distinctive advantage when translating the mathematical formalism of Hidden Markov Models into executable code. The stringent compile-time checks and expressiveness of Rust facilitate the design of abstractions whose safety and correctness are enforced without incurring additional runtime overhead. In implementing HMMs, each probabilistic component—ranging from state transition matrices to emission distributions—is encapsulated within explicit data structures, with immutable state representations where appropriate.

Rust's traits and generics enable the creation of modular interfaces for probability distributions, ensuring that the implementation of state transition estimation and sequence decoding adhere strictly to the theoretical specifications. Furthermore, Rust's ownership model guarantees memory safety during the execution of iterative procedures such as those found in the Viterbi algorithm and Baum-Welch estimation. This careful utilization of Rust's features mitigates risks associated with manual memory management and inadvertent data races in multithreaded contexts. In aggregate, the language's design paradigms and type safety mechanisms offer a powerful framework for ensuring that the intrinsic properties of Hidden Markov Models are preserved and effectively exploited during the analysis of sequential data.

Rust Code Snippet

```rust
/// A simple implementation of a Hidden Markov Model (HMM) in Rust.
///
/// In this model:
///    - The set of hidden states is represented as indices: 0, 1,
↪    ..., N-1.
///    - The state transition probability matrix A is stored in
↪    `transitions` such that:
///        a_{ij} = P(s_{t+1} = j | s_t = i)
///    - The emission probability matrix B is stored in `emissions`
↪    such that:
///        b_j(o_t) = P(o_t | s_j)
///    - The initial state distribution is stored in `initial` such
↪    that:
///        _i = P(s_1 = i)
///
/// Two primary algorithms are implemented:
///    1. The Forward Algorithm to compute the likelihood L() = P(O |
↪    )
///    2. The Viterbi Algorithm to decode the most probable sequence
↪    S* such that:
///        S^* = argmax_S P(S | O)
///    with recursion:
///        _t(j) = max_{i} [_{t-1}(i) * a_{ij}] * b_j(o_t)
#[derive(Debug)]
pub struct HMM {
    /// Transition probability matrix: transitions[i][j] = a_{ij}
    pub transitions: Vec<Vec<f64>>,
    /// Emission probability matrix: emissions[j][symbol] =
↪    b_j(symbol)
    pub emissions: Vec<Vec<f64>>,
    /// Initial state distribution: initial[i] = _i
    pub initial: Vec<f64>,
}

impl HMM {
    /// Computes the likelihood of an observation sequence using the
↪    Forward Algorithm.
    ///
    /// Observation indices should correspond to columns in the
↪    emission matrix.
    pub fn forward(&self, observations: &Vec<usize>) -> f64 {
        let n_states = self.initial.len();
        let t_len = observations.len();
        // alpha[t][i] will hold the probability of being in state i
↪    at time t given the observations up to time t.
        let mut alpha = vec![vec![0.0; n_states]; t_len];

        // Initialization: _0(i) = _i * b_i(o_0)
        for i in 0..n_states {
```

```
                alpha[0][i] = self.initial[i] *
                ↪   self.emissions[i][observations[0]];
        }

        // Recursion: _t(j) = [_i _{t-1}(i) * a_{ij}] * b_j(o_t)
        for t in 1..t_len {
            for j in 0..n_states {
                let mut sum = 0.0;
                for i in 0..n_states {
                    sum += alpha[t - 1][i] * self.transitions[i][j];
                }
                alpha[t][j] = sum *
                ↪   self.emissions[j][observations[t]];
            }
        }

        // Termination: the likelihood is the sum of the final alpha
        ↪   values.
        alpha[t_len - 1].iter().sum()
}

/// Implements the Viterbi Algorithm to find the most probable
↪   hidden state sequence.
///
/// Returns a vector of state indices corresponding to the most
↪   likely path.
pub fn viterbi(&self, observations: &Vec<usize>) -> Vec<usize> {
    let n_states = self.initial.len();
    let t_len = observations.len();
    // dp[t][j] will hold the probability of the most likely
    ↪   path ending in state j at time t.
    let mut dp = vec![vec![0.0; n_states]; t_len];
    // backpointer[t][j] stores the index of the previous state
    ↪   which led to state j at time t.
    let mut backpointer = vec![vec![0; n_states]; t_len];

    // Initialization: _0(i) = _i * b_i(o_0)
    for i in 0..n_states {
        dp[0][i] = self.initial[i] *
        ↪   self.emissions[i][observations[0]];
        backpointer[0][i] = 0; // Not used for t = 0.
    }

    // Recursion:
    // For each time t and each state j, compute:
    // _t(j) = max_i [_{t-1}(i) * a_{ij}] * b_j(o_t)
    // and record the corresponding argmax in backpointer.
    for t in 1..t_len {
        for j in 0..n_states {
            let mut max_prob = 0.0;
            let mut argmax_state = 0;
            for i in 0..n_states {
```

```rust
                let prob = dp[t - 1][i] *
                ↪   self.transitions[i][j];
                if prob > max_prob {
                    max_prob = prob;
                    argmax_state = i;
                }
            }
            dp[t][j] = max_prob *
            ↪   self.emissions[j][observations[t]];
            backpointer[t][j] = argmax_state;
        }
    }

    // Termination: find the state with the maximum probability
    ↪   at the last time step.
    let mut best_last_state = 0;
    let mut best_prob = 0.0;
    for i in 0..n_states {
        if dp[t_len - 1][i] > best_prob {
            best_prob = dp[t_len - 1][i];
            best_last_state = i;
        }
    }

    // Backtracking: reconstruct the most probable path.
    let mut best_path = vec![0; t_len];
    best_path[t_len - 1] = best_last_state;
    for t in (1..t_len).rev() {
        best_path[t - 1] = backpointer[t][best_path[t]];
    }

    best_path
    }
}

fn main() {
    // Example HMM definition with 2 states and 3 observable
    ↪   symbols.
    // States: 0 and 1.
    // Symbols: 0, 1, 2.
    let transitions = vec![
        vec![0.7, 0.3], // From state 0 to states {0, 1}
        vec![0.4, 0.6], // From state 1 to states {0, 1}
    ];
    let emissions = vec![
        vec![0.5, 0.4, 0.1], // Emission probabilities for state 0
        ↪   for symbols {0, 1, 2}
        vec![0.1, 0.3, 0.6], // Emission probabilities for state 1
        ↪   for symbols {0, 1, 2}
    ];
    let initial = vec![0.6, 0.4]; // Initial probability
    ↪   distribution over states {0, 1}.
```

299

```rust
    let hmm = HMM {
        transitions,
        emissions,
        initial,
    };

    // Define an observation sequence with symbol indices.
    let observations = vec![0, 1, 2]; // e.g., first observe symbol
    ↪   0, then 1, then 2.

    // Compute the likelihood of the observation sequence using the
    ↪   forward algorithm.
    let likelihood = hmm.forward(&observations);
    println!("Observation sequence likelihood: {}", likelihood);

    // Decode the most probable hidden state sequence using the
    ↪   Viterbi algorithm.
    let best_path = hmm.viterbi(&observations);
    println!("Most likely hidden state sequence: {:?}", best_path);
}
```

Chapter 48

Clustering in High-Dimensional Spaces

Mathematical Foundations

Clustering techniques in high-dimensional spaces aim to partition a set of data points $X = \{x_1, x_2, \ldots, x_n\} \subset \mathbb{R}^d$ into disjoint groups based on similarity. The most common formulation involves minimizing an objective function such as

$$J = \sum_{j=1}^{k} \sum_{x \in C_j} \|x - \mu_j\|_2^2,$$

where C_j represents the jth cluster and μ_j denotes the centroid of that cluster. In this context, the Euclidean distance $\|x - \mu_j\|_2$ is frequently used to quantify proximity, though its effectiveness may diminish as the dimensionality d increases. The mathematical framework necessitates careful treatment of distance metrics and the definition of cluster centers, as the high-dimensional geometry can introduce subtleties that are overlooked in lower-dimensional settings.

Challenges in High-Dimensional Data

In high-dimensional spaces, phenomena such as the curse of dimensionality and distance concentration profoundly affect the behavior of clustering algorithms. The volume of the space increases exponentially with d, rendering data points increasingly sparse. This sparsity hampers the discrimination between points, as pairwise Euclidean distances tend to converge to similar values. Such behavior can be formally described in terms of the ratio of the difference between the maximum and minimum distances over the minimum distance, which vanishes as d grows large. The resulting degradation in distance contrast necessitates the exploration of alternative metrics and adjustments in algorithmic strategy.

1 Curse of Dimensionality

The curse of dimensionality implies that standard intuitions based on low-dimensional data become misleading. In high-dimensional settings, not only do distances lose their discriminative power, but the number of parameters required to estimate cluster membership grows substantially. This situation forces a reevaluation of clustering assignments and the importance of incorporating dimensionality reduction or feature selection steps before the application of clustering algorithms. The trade-off between preserving information and reducing noise is a central consideration in this domain.

2 Concentration of Measure

Another critical phenomenon is the concentration of measure, which describes how, in high dimensions, the majority of a probability distribution's mass tends to concentrate in a narrow region of the space. Consequently, the differences between the distances of points to the cluster centers become marginal. This behavior challenges the assumption that the nearest centroid is necessarily a meaningful representative of similarity. Mathematical analyses in high-dimensional probability show that when data points are normalized, the variance of distances diminishes, leading to scenarios where even minute perturbations in data representation or metric choice can yield substantially different clustering outcomes.

Optimizing Distance Metrics

Optimizing the choice of distance metric is paramount to effective clustering in high-dimensional settings. While the Euclidean distance is traditional, alternatives such as Manhattan distance, cosine similarity, and Mahalanobis distance offer enhanced robustness by either incorporating directional information or accounting for data covariance. In many cases, a weighted distance metric can be formulated as

$$d_w(x,y) = \sqrt{\sum_{i=1}^{d} w_i (x_i - y_i)^2},$$

where the weights w_i are determined based on the variance or relevance of each feature. This adjustment aims to counteract the uniform contribution of each dimension that often leads to the deterioration of Euclidean-based methods. Systematic optimization of these weights, possibly via an iterative procedure or analytical estimation, is central to adapting clustering algorithms to the peculiarities of high-dimensional data.

Partitioning Strategies

Partitioning high-dimensional data into coherent clusters requires modifications in algorithm design. Traditional centroid-based methods, such as those derived from the k-means paradigm, may be augmented with initialization techniques that improve convergence properties and stability. For instance, refined seeding methods ensure that initial cluster centers are sufficiently separated in a space where distances tend to be homogenized. Alternatively, density-based clustering algorithms adapt to high-dimensional challenges by identifying regions where data points exhibit locally high density relative to their surroundings. Hierarchical clustering approaches also benefit from sophisticated linkage criteria that consider not only inter-point distances but also the geometric configuration of clusters. The interplay between these partitioning strategies and distance metric adjustments is critical for robust performance.

Utilizing the Rust Paradigm for High-Dimensional Clustering

The adoption of Rust as an implementation language introduces significant advantages in addressing the computational challenges inherent to high-dimensional clustering. Rust's static type system and zero-cost abstractions facilitate the expression of complex mathematical operations without sacrificing performance. Memory management strategies ensure that partitioning algorithms can handle large, sparse datasets prevalent in high-dimensional spaces with minimal overhead. Abstractions based on traits and generics permit the development of modular components for distance computations and iterative optimization. Such design paradigms enable rigorous static checking of algorithmic invariants, thereby reducing the risk of runtime errors and ensuring that the mathematical properties of clustering are faithfully preserved in the implementation. The inherent support for concurrent programming further allows the exploitation of parallelism, which is essential given the computational intensity of evaluating high-dimensional distance metrics and partitioning large datasets.

Rust Code Snippet

```
extern crate rand;

use rand::Rng;
use std::f64;

/// Compute the standard Euclidean distance between two points.
fn euclidean_distance(x: &Vec<f64>, y: &Vec<f64>) -> f64 {
    x.iter()
     .zip(y.iter())
     .map(|(a, b)| (a - b).powi(2))
     .sum::<f64>()
     .sqrt()
}

/// Compute the weighted Euclidean distance between two points.
/// The formula is: d_w(x, y) = sqrt( sum_{i=1}^{d} w_i * (x[i] -
↪ y[i])^2 )
fn weighted_distance(x: &Vec<f64>, y: &Vec<f64>, weights: &Vec<f64>)
↪    -> f64 {
    x.iter()
     .zip(y.iter())
     .zip(weights.iter())
```

```rust
        .map(|((a, b), w)| w * (a - b).powi(2))
        .sum::<f64>()
        .sqrt()
}

/// Compute the centroid of a cluster given a list of point
↪   references and the dimensionality.
fn compute_centroid(points: &Vec<&Vec<f64>>, dim: usize) -> Vec<f64>
↪   {
    let mut centroid = vec![0.0; dim];
    let num_points = points.len();

    for point in points {
        for i in 0..dim {
            centroid[i] += point[i];
        }
    }
    // Average each dimension to obtain the centroid
    for val in &mut centroid {
        *val /= num_points as f64;
    }
    centroid
}

/// k-Means clustering algorithm for high-dimensional data.
/// It minimizes the objective function:
///    J = sum_{j=1}^{k} sum_{x in C_j} ||x - _j||^2
/// where _j is the centroid of cluster C_j.
///
/// If `weights` is provided, the weighted distance metric is used.
fn k_means(
    data: &Vec<Vec<f64>>,
    k: usize,
    weights: Option<&Vec<f64>>,
    max_iter: usize
) -> (Vec<usize>, Vec<Vec<f64>>) {
    let n_points = data.len();
    if n_points == 0 {
        return (Vec::new(), Vec::new());
    }
    let dim = data[0].len();

    // Initialize centroids using the first k points.
    let mut centroids: Vec<Vec<f64>> =
    ↪   data.iter().take(k).cloned().collect();
    let mut assignments: Vec<usize> = vec![0; n_points];
    let mut rng = rand::thread_rng();

    for _iter in 0..max_iter {
        let mut changed = false;
        // Assignment step: assign each point to the nearest
        ↪   centroid.
        for (idx, point) in data.iter().enumerate() {
```

305

```
                let mut min_distance = std::f64::MAX;
                let mut best_cluster = 0;
                for (cluster_idx, centroid) in
                ↪   centroids.iter().enumerate() {
                    let dist = match weights {
                        Some(w) => weighted_distance(point, centroid,
                        ↪   w),
                        None => euclidean_distance(point, centroid),
                    };
                    if dist < min_distance {
                        min_distance = dist;
                        best_cluster = cluster_idx;
                    }
                }
                if assignments[idx] != best_cluster {
                    assignments[idx] = best_cluster;
                    changed = true;
                }
            }

            // Update step: recalculate centroids based on current
            ↪   cluster assignments.
            let mut clusters: Vec<Vec<&Vec<f64>>> = vec![Vec::new(); k];
            for (point, &cluster_idx) in
            ↪   data.iter().zip(assignments.iter()) {
                clusters[cluster_idx].push(point);
            }
            for i in 0..k {
                if clusters[i].is_empty() {
                    // In case a cluster gets no points, reinitialize
                    ↪   with a random point.
                    let rand_index = rng.gen_range(0..n_points);
                    centroids[i] = data[rand_index].clone();
                } else {
                    centroids[i] = compute_centroid(&clusters[i], dim);
                }
            }

            // Terminate early if no assignment changed
            if !changed {
                break;
            }
        }
        (assignments, centroids)
    }

    /// Compute the objective function value (sum of squared distances)
    /// given the current clustering.
    fn objective_function(
        data: &Vec<Vec<f64>>,
        assignments: &Vec<usize>,
        centroids: &Vec<Vec<f64>>
    ) -> f64 {
```

```
    let mut sum = 0.0;
    for (i, point) in data.iter().enumerate() {
        let centroid = &centroids[assignments[i]];
        sum += euclidean_distance(point, centroid).powi(2);
    }
    sum
}

fn main() {
    // Synthetic high-dimensional data for demonstration.
    // Here we use 3-dimensional points for simplicity.
    let data: Vec<Vec<f64>> = vec![
        vec![1.0, 2.0, 3.0],
        vec![1.1, 2.1, 2.9],
        vec![0.9, 2.2, 3.1],
        vec![8.0, 8.0, 8.0],
        vec![8.1, 7.9, 8.2],
        vec![7.9, 8.2, 7.8],
    ];

    // Define weights to optimize the distance metric.
    // The weighted distance metric is:
    //    d_w(x, y) = sqrt( sum_{i=1}^{d} w_i * (x[i] - y[i])^2 )
    let weights: Vec<f64> = vec![1.0, 0.5, 1.5];

    let k = 2; // Number of clusters
    let max_iter = 100;

    let (assignments, centroids) = k_means(&data, k, Some(&weights),
    ↪   max_iter);

    println!("Final cluster assignments: {:?}", assignments);
    println!("Final centroids: {:?}", centroids);

    let cost = objective_function(&data, &assignments, &centroids);
    println!("Objective function value (sum of squared distances):
    ↪   {:.4}", cost);
}
```

Chapter 49

Anomaly Detection Algorithms in Rust

Theoretical Underpinnings of Anomaly Detection

Anomaly detection is rooted in the identification of observations that diverge significantly from the statistical characteristics of a given dataset. In formal terms, consider a random variable X characterized by a probability density function $f(x)$; anomalies are defined as those data points for which $f(x)$ assumes exceptionally low values. The approach is steeped in statistical hypothesis testing and extreme value theory, wherein the tail behavior of the distribution is scrutinized to establish thresholds for unusual observations. Metrics such as the z-score, computed as $z = \frac{x-\mu}{\sigma}$ where μ denotes the mean and σ the standard deviation, serve as a quantitative measure of deviation. Such theoretical constructs provide a rigorous framework that underlies the analysis and systematic identification of outliers within complex datasets.

Statistical Techniques for Identifying Outliers

Statistical methodologies for anomaly detection encompass both parametric and non-parametric approaches to model the inherent structure of data. Parametric techniques typically assume that the underlying data distribution belongs to a specific family, such as the Gaussian distribution, which facilitates the determination of significance thresholds based on well-established probabilistic bounds. For instance, the empirical rule suggests that approximately 99.7% of data lie within three standard deviations from the mean. Robust estimators such as the median and the median absolute deviation (MAD) are employed to reduce sensitivity to extreme values. The MAD is defined by

$$\text{MAD} = \text{median}(|x_i - \text{median}(x)|),$$

and forms the basis for establishing threshold criteria that are less influenced by anomalous observations. Alternative techniques involve quantile-based assessments where the interquartile range (IQR) is calculated and data points that lie beyond a predefined multiple of the IQR are flagged as potential outliers. These statistical procedures provide a disciplined means to differentiate between normal variations in the data and genuine anomalies, ensuring that the underlying probabilistic structure is faithfully represented.

Machine Learning Approaches to Uncovering Unusual Patterns

Machine learning methodologies extend the scope of anomaly detection to encompass data sets of high dimensionality and intricate structure. In an unsupervised learning context, the absence of labeled instances necessitates the use of methods that infer intrinsic groupings within the data. Clustering techniques partition the dataset into groups based on similarity measures; anomalies are identified as those observations that exhibit a low degree of association with any cluster centroid. Density-based methods further refine this approach by comparing the local density of a point to that of its neighbors, thereby assigning an anomaly score on the basis of relative sparsity. Notable among these techniques is the isolation forest algorithm, which operates by recursively partitioning the data space and attributing higher anomaly scores to points that require fewer partitions to isolate. In addition, advanced models employing neural architectures, such as autoencoders and one-class classifiers, learn compact representations of normal data behavior, rendering deviations from these learned patterns as indicators of anomaly. The interplay between feature representation and the selection of appropriate distance metrics is critical in ensuring that

309

the subtle, non-linear patterns characteristic of anomalies are captured effectively.

Integration of Rust in Anomaly Detection Implementations

The implementation of anomaly detection algorithms in Rust leverages the language's unique combination of performance, memory safety, and expressive abstraction mechanisms. Rust's stringent type system and zero-cost abstractions ensure that core mathematical operations—such as the evaluation of density functions, computation of distance metrics, and iterative optimization procedures—are executed with minimal runtime overhead. The language's support for trait-based generics encourages the modular design of statistical and machine learning components, thereby facilitating the encapsulation and reuse of algorithmic primitives. Concurrent processing capabilities in Rust further enable the parallelization of computationally intensive tasks, such as the simultaneous evaluation of anomaly scores across large datasets. The seamless integration with low-level numerical routines and linear algebra libraries augments the precision of statistical estimators and enhances the overall robustness of the detection mechanics. In this paradigm, anomalies are not merely isolated incidents but emergent phenomena identified through a confluence of rigorous statistical analysis and advanced machine learning inference, all underpinned by Rust's systematic and efficient programming environment.

Rust Code Snippet

```
use std::vec::Vec;

/// Computes the mean of a slice of f64 numbers.
/// Equation:  = ( x) / N
fn mean(data: &[f64]) -> f64 {
    data.iter().sum::<f64>() / data.len() as f64
}

/// Computes the standard deviation of a slice of f64 numbers.
/// Equation:  = sqrt(( (x - )²) / N)
fn standard_deviation(data: &[f64]) -> f64 {
    let m = mean(data);
```

```rust
        (data.iter().map(|x| (x - m).powi(2)).sum::<f64>() / data.len()
     ↪   as f64).sqrt()
}

/// Computes the median of a slice of f64 numbers.
fn median(data: &[f64]) -> f64 {
    let mut sorted = data.to_vec();
    sorted.sort_by(|a, b| a.partial_cmp(b).unwrap());
    let n = sorted.len();
    if n % 2 == 0 {
        (sorted[n / 2 - 1] + sorted[n / 2]) / 2.0
    } else {
        sorted[n / 2]
    }
}

/// Computes the Median Absolute Deviation (MAD).
/// Equation: MAD = median(|x - median(x)|)
fn mad(data: &[f64]) -> f64 {
    let med = median(data);
    let deviations: Vec<f64> = data.iter().map(|&x| (x -
     ↪   med).abs()).collect();
    median(&deviations)
}

/// Computes the z-scores for each data point in the slice.
/// Equation: z = (x - ) /
fn z_scores(data: &[f64]) -> Vec<f64> {
    let m = mean(data);
    let sd = standard_deviation(data);
    data.iter().map(|&x| (x - m) / sd).collect()
}

/// Detects anomalies using the z-score method.
/// Flags data points where |z| > threshold.
fn detect_anomalies(data: &[f64], threshold: f64) -> Vec<usize> {
    let scores = z_scores(data);
    scores.iter().enumerate()
        .filter_map(|(i, &z)| if z.abs() > threshold { Some(i) }
         ↪   else { None })
        .collect()
}

/// Detects anomalies using the MAD based method.
/// Flags data points where |x - median| / MAD > threshold.
fn detect_anomalies_mad(data: &[f64], threshold: f64) -> Vec<usize>
 ↪   {
    let med = median(data);
    let mad_value = mad(data);
    data.iter().enumerate()
        .filter_map(|(i, &x)| if (x - med).abs() / mad_value >
         ↪   threshold { Some(i) } else { None })
        .collect()
```

311

```rust
}

/// Computes the percentile of a sorted slice using linear
↪    interpolation.
fn percentile(sorted: &[f64], percent: f64) -> f64 {
    let n = sorted.len();
    if n == 0 {
        return 0.0;
    }
    // rank in the sorted array [0, n-1]
    let rank = (percent / 100.0) * (n - 1) as f64;
    let lower_index = rank.floor() as usize;
    let upper_index = rank.ceil() as usize;
    if lower_index == upper_index {
        sorted[lower_index]
    } else {
        let weight = rank - lower_index as f64;
        sorted[lower_index] * (1.0 - weight) + sorted[upper_index] *
        ↪    weight
    }
}

/// Computes the first (Q1) and third (Q3) quartiles from the data.
/// Uses the 25th and 75th percentiles, respectively.
fn iqr(data: &[f64]) -> (f64, f64) {
    let mut sorted = data.to_vec();
    sorted.sort_by(|a, b| a.partial_cmp(b).unwrap());
    let q1 = percentile(&sorted, 25.0);
    let q3 = percentile(&sorted, 75.0);
    (q1, q3)
}

/// Detects anomalies using the Interquartile Range (IQR) method.
/// Flags data points below Q1 - factor*IQR or above Q3 +
↪    factor*IQR.
fn detect_anomalies_iqr(data: &[f64], factor: f64) -> Vec<usize> {
    let (q1, q3) = iqr(data);
    let iqr_value = q3 - q1;
    let lower_bound = q1 - factor * iqr_value;
    let upper_bound = q3 + factor * iqr_value;
    data.iter().enumerate()
        .filter_map(|(i, &x)| if x < lower_bound || x > upper_bound
        ↪    {
            Some(i)
        } else {
            None
        })
        .collect()
}

fn main() {
    // Sample dataset simulating typical values with potential
    ↪    outliers.
```

```
let data: Vec<f64> = vec![10.0, 12.0, 13.5, 14.0, 12.5, 11.0,
↪    50.0, 12.0, 12.2, 10.5, 11.5];
println!("Data: {:?}", data);

// Compute basic statistical metrics.
let m = mean(&data);
let sd = standard_deviation(&data);
let med = median(&data);
let mad_value = mad(&data);

println!("Mean: {:.2}", m);
println!("Standard Deviation: {:.2}", sd);
println!("Median: {:.2}", med);
println!("MAD (Median Absolute Deviation): {:.2}", mad_value);

// Calculate and display z-scores for each data point.
let z_vals = z_scores(&data);
println!("Z-scores: {:?}", z_vals);

// Detect anomalies using the z-score method (e.g., |z| > 3).
let anomalies_z = detect_anomalies(&data, 3.0);
println!("Anomalies detected by z-score method (|z| > 3): {:?}",
↪    anomalies_z);

// Detect anomalies using the MAD method (e.g., (|x -
↪    median|)/MAD > 3).
let anomalies_mad = detect_anomalies_mad(&data, 3.0);
println!("Anomalies detected by MAD method (|x - median|/MAD >
↪    3): {:?}", anomalies_mad);

// Detect anomalies using the IQR method with a factor of 1.5.
let anomalies_iqr = detect_anomalies_iqr(&data, 1.5);
println!("Anomalies detected by IQR method: {:?}",
↪    anomalies_iqr);
}
```

Chapter 50

Time Series Decomposition and Seasonal Adjustment

Mathematical Framework and Component Definitions

Time series data, denoted by Y_t for discrete time indices t, is conventionally modeled as a combination of constituent components that capture distinct aspects of temporal variation. In the additive model, the series is expressed as

$$Y_t = T_t + S_t + R_t,$$

where T_t represents the long-term trend, S_t denotes the seasonality that recurs with fixed periodicity, and R_t corresponds to the residual component containing irregular fluctuations. An alternative formulation, the multiplicative model, is given by

$$Y_t = T_t \times S_t \times R_t,$$

which is particularly useful when the amplitude of the seasonal fluctuations scales with the level of the series. The rigorous definition of each component relies on statistical principles and time series inference. The trend component T_t is typically characterized as a slowly varying function that captures the persistent evolution over time, while the seasonal component S_t aggregates repetitive cyclical patterns that may arise due to calendar effects or natural periodicity. The residual component R_t, assumed to be a stationary stochastic process, encapsulates the noise and other non-systematic variations of the series.

Algorithmic Methods for Trend Extraction

Depicting the underlying progression of the time series, the trend extraction process necessitates the application of smoothing techniques designed to attenuate high-frequency variations. One common approach involves the computation of moving averages, whereby the estimate at time t is obtained as the arithmetic mean over a window centered around t, effectively filtering out short-term fluctuations. Alternatively, regression-based strategies may be employed, where the trend is modeled as a parametric function—such as a polynomial or exponential function—with coefficients determined via least squares or robust estimation methods. In both cases, the algorithm must preserve the intrinsic temporal order and causal structure of the data. The calibration of parameters, such as window size in moving average filters or the degree of the polynomial function, plays a critical role in the accurate delineation of the underlying trend T_t.

Seasonal Adjustment Techniques and Implementation Details

The seasonal adjustment process is designed to isolate and remove the periodic cyclicality inherent in the data. This stage involves grouping observations according to equivalent positions within their repetitive cycle, thereby enabling the estimation of seasonal indices. For additive models, the seasonal adjustment is implemented by subtracting the estimated seasonal component, yielding an adjusted series $Y_t - S_t$, whereas in the context of a multiplicative model, the adjustment is achieved by dividing the observed data by the seasonal index, resulting in Y_t/S_t. A pivotal challenge in this context is the determination of the periodicity, which may vary depending on the domain—in many cases, the periodicity is defined on a monthly, quarterly, or even weekly basis. The estimation procedure must account for potential non-stationarity in the seasonal patterns and may require iterative refinement, such as the use of robust measures (e.g., medians) to minimize the influence of transient anomalies. This methodology ensures that the seasonal fluctuations are accurately captured and separated from the other systematic components of the time series.

Residual Analysis and Evaluation Metrics

Following the removal of trend and seasonal effects, the residual component R_t represents the irregular fluctuations and noise that remain in the time series. A detailed examination of these residuals is essential for validating the adequacy of the decomposition process. Statistical diagnostics applied to R_t include the computation of autocorrelation functions and the application of tests such as the Ljung-Box statistic to assess the randomness and independence of the residuals. Moreover, analysis of the residual variance provides a quantitative measure of the decomposition quality; a minimized variance in R_t indicates that the systematic variation in Y_t has been effectively captured by T_t and S_t. The algorithmic framework for residual analysis often incorporates optimization techniques to iteratively adjust the estimates of the trend and seasonal components. Such iterative procedures are grounded in error propagation theory and are vital in ensuring that the final componentization faithfully represents the granular temporal dynamics inherent in the original time series.

Rust Code Snippet

```
use rand::Rng; // Make sure to include rand = "0.8" in Cargo.toml
↪    dependencies

/// This example demonstrates a full decomposition of a synthetic
↪    time series
/// into trend, seasonal, and residual components using an additive
↪    model.
/// The model is given by:
///      Y_t = T_t + S_t + R_t
///
/// Where:
```

```
///     - T_t: Trend component (extracted via moving average
↪   smoothing)
///     - S_t: Seasonal component (estimated by averaging detrended
↪   seasonal groups)
///     - R_t: Residual component (remaining noise and irregular
↪   fluctuations)
///
/// The code also computes the residual variance to evaluate
/// how effectively the systematic variations have been captured.

fn main() {
    // Generate synthetic time series data
    // Settings:
    let n: usize = 100;           // Total number of observations
    let season_period: usize = 12;  // Define periodicity (e.g.,
    ↪   monthly seasonality)

    // Create a synthetic time series: Y[t] = Trend + Seasonal +
    ↪   Noise
    let mut time_series: Vec<f64> = Vec::with_capacity(n);
    let mut rng = rand::thread_rng();

    for t in 0..n {
        // Trend: a linear function (e.g., 0.5 * t)
        let trend = 0.5 * t as f64;
        // Seasonal: use a sine function to simulate periodic
        ↪   behavior.
        // The seasonal amplitude is modulated (e.g., amplitude =
        ↪   10)
        let season_angle = 2.0 * std::f64::consts::PI * (t %
        ↪   season_period) as f64 / season_period as f64;
        let seasonal = 10.0 * season_angle.sin();
        // Noise: random value in a range to simulate irregular
        ↪   fluctuations
        let noise: f64 = (rng.gen::<f64>() - 0.5) * 5.0;  // Noise
        ↪   in approximately [-2.5, 2.5]
        // Additive model: Y[t] = Trend + Seasonal + Noise
        time_series.push(trend + seasonal + noise);
    }

    // 1. Trend Extraction using Moving Average Smoothing.
    // This function computes the moving average over a window
    ↪   centered at each time point.
    fn moving_average(data: &Vec<f64>, window_size: usize) ->
    ↪   Vec<f64> {
        let n = data.len();
        let mut smoothed: Vec<f64> = vec![0.0; n];
        let half_window = window_size / 2;
        for i in 0..n {
            // Determine window boundaries while handling edge
            ↪   cases.
            let start = if i >= half_window { i - half_window } else
            ↪   { 0 };
```

```
            let end = if i + half_window < n { i + half_window }
            ↪  else { n - 1 };
            let sum: f64 = data[start..=end].iter().sum();
            let count = (end - start + 1) as f64;
            smoothed[i] = sum / count;
        }
        smoothed
}

// Choose window_size for moving average (tunable parameter)
let window_size: usize = 5;
let trend_component: Vec<f64> = moving_average(&time_series,
↪  window_size);

// 2. Seasonal Component Extraction.
// Estimate seasonal indices by subtracting the trend component
↪  from the original data,
// then averaging the detrended values by season.
let mut seasonal_sum: Vec<f64> = vec![0.0; season_period];
let mut seasonal_count: Vec<usize> = vec![0; season_period];

for (t, &value) in time_series.iter().enumerate() {
    let season_index = t % season_period;
    seasonal_sum[season_index] += value - trend_component[t];
    seasonal_count[season_index] += 1;
}

let mut seasonal_component: Vec<f64> = vec![0.0; season_period];
for i in 0..season_period {
    seasonal_component[i] = seasonal_sum[i] / seasonal_count[i]
    ↪  as f64;
}

// Reconstruct full seasonal series by repeating the seasonal
↪  pattern.
let seasonal_full: Vec<f64> = (0..n)
    .map(|t| seasonal_component[t % season_period])
    .collect();

// 3. Residual Computation.
// For an additive model: R_t = Y_t - T_t - S_t
let residuals: Vec<f64> = time_series.iter()
    .zip(trend_component.iter())
    .zip(seasonal_full.iter())
    .map(|((&y, &t), &s)| y - t - s)
    .collect();

// 4. Residual Analysis: Compute Residual Variance.
let mean_residual: f64 = residuals.iter().sum::<f64>() /
↪  residuals.len() as f64;
let residual_variance: f64 = residuals.iter()
    .map(|&r| (r - mean_residual).powi(2))
    .sum::<f64>() / residuals.len() as f64;
```

```rust
    // Output the results to inspect the decomposition.
    println!("Original Time Series: {:?}", time_series);
    println!("Trend Component: {:?}", trend_component);
    println!("Seasonal Component (repeated): {:?}", seasonal_full);
    println!("Residuals: {:?}", residuals);
    println!("Residual Variance: {:.4}", residual_variance);
}
```

Chapter 51

Fourier Transform Implementation for Signal Analysis

Mathematical Foundation of the Fourier Transform

The Fourier transform is a fundamental mathematical operation that maps a time-domain signal into its frequency-domain representation. The continuous Fourier transform of a function $f(t)$ is defined as

$$F(\omega) = \int_{-\infty}^{\infty} f(t)\, e^{-i\omega t}\, dt,$$

where $F(\omega)$ indicates the complex amplitude for each angular frequency ω, and i stands for the imaginary unit. In practical applications, signals are sampled at discrete intervals, and the discrete Fourier transform (DFT) converts a sequence of N time-domain samples, denoted $x_0, x_1, \ldots, x_{N-1}$, into a set of frequency coefficients according to the relationship

$$X_k = \sum_{n=0}^{N-1} x_n\, e^{-i\frac{2\pi}{N} kn},$$

with k representing the frequency bin index. This transformation enables the decomposition of a signal into its constituent sinusoidal components, thereby revealing information about periodicities and spectral content.

Algorithmic Considerations for FFT

The direct evaluation of the DFT requires $O(N^2)$ complex multiplications, which is computationally prohibitive for large values of N. The fast Fourier transform (FFT) algorithm addresses this limitation by exploiting the inherent symmetries of the complex exponential kernel. Through a divide-and-conquer strategy, the FFT recursively decomposes the DFT into smaller DFTs, typically employing a radix-2 decimation-in-time approach. In this method, the original sequence is partitioned into subsequences consisting of even and odd indexed elements. This recursive splitting results in the decomposition

$$X_k = E_k + e^{-i\frac{2\pi}{N}k}O_k,$$

where E_k and O_k denote the DFTs computed over the even and odd portions of the data, respectively. Such a recursive framework reduces the computational complexity to $O(N \log N)$, rendering the FFT highly effective for processing extensive time series and signal data.

Rust-Based Implementation Details

The selection of Rust as the implementation language provides significant advantages in terms of memory safety and efficient resource management. In the context of FFT, Rust's strong type system and ownership model facilitate the manipulation of contiguous arrays and vectors that represent signal data. These data structures are central to achieving high cache locality and reducing memory access overhead during the execution of the FFT algorithm. Rust's support for zero-cost abstractions allows for the inlining of critical computational routines, ensuring that the performance is comparable to implementations in lower-level languages. Additionally, Rust provides mechanisms for concurrent execution, which can be utilized to run independent sub-transforms in parallel. This capability becomes increasingly valuable when processing high-resolution signals, where the workload can be distributed over multiple processor cores to achieve substantial acceleration.

Computational Efficiency and Complexity Analysis

A rigorous analysis of the FFT algorithm demonstrates that the reduction of redundant arithmetic operations is central to its efficiency. Through recursive decomposition, the FFT reduces the total number of required arithmetic operations from the order of N^2 to the order of $N \log N$. Each level of recursion performs linear work, and the logarithmic depth of the recursion encapsulates the efficiency gain. The algorithm is designed to compute the so-called twiddle factors efficiently, where a twiddle factor is defined as

$$W_N^k = e^{-i\frac{2\pi}{N}k}.$$

The pre-computation and reuse of these factors contribute to the overall speed of the transform. Furthermore, the implementation in Rust is optimized by leveraging in-place computation strategies, which minimize allocation overhead and reduce the memory footprint. Compiler optimizations, such as loop unrolling and vectorization, further enhance the performance. A comprehensive complexity analysis confirms that the FFT implementation scales gracefully with increased signal lengths while maintaining numerical stability and precision across a wide range of sampling resolutions and frequency domains.

Rust Code Snippet

```rust
use std::f64::consts::PI;
use num_complex::Complex;

// Naive implementation of the Discrete Fourier Transform (DFT)
// This function computes the frequency coefficients X_k using the
↳   formula:
//    X_k = sum_{n=0}^{N-1} x_n * exp(-i * 2kn/N)
fn dft(input: &[Complex<f64>]) -> Vec<Complex<f64>> {
    let n = input.len();
    let mut output = Vec::with_capacity(n);
    for k in 0..n {
        let mut sum = Complex::new(0.0, 0.0);
        for (n, &x_n) in input.iter().enumerate() {
            let angle = -2.0 * PI * k as f64 * n as f64 / n as f64;
            // exp(-i * 2kn/N)
            let twiddle = Complex::from_polar(1.0, angle);
            sum = sum + x_n * twiddle;
```

```rust
        }
        output.push(sum);
    }
    output
}


// Fast Fourier Transform (FFT) using recursive radix-2
↪  decimation-in-time algorithm.
// This function uses the recursive decomposition:
//    X_k = E_k + exp(-i * 2k/N) * O_k
// where E_k and O_k are the DFTs of the even- and odd-indexed parts
↪  respectively.
fn fft(input: &[Complex<f64>]) -> Vec<Complex<f64>> {
    let n = input.len();
    // Base case: a single sample is its own DFT.
    if n <= 1 {
        return input.to_vec();
    }
    // For radix-2 FFT, the input length must be a power of 2.
    // Partition input into even and odd indexed elements.
    let even: Vec<Complex<f64>> =
    ↪  input.iter().step_by(2).cloned().collect();
    let odd: Vec<Complex<f64>> =
    ↪  input.iter().skip(1).step_by(2).cloned().collect();

    // Recursively apply FFT to the even and odd parts.
    let fft_even = fft(&even);
    let fft_odd = fft(&odd);

    let mut output = vec![Complex::new(0.0, 0.0); n];
    for k in 0..(n / 2) {
        // Compute the twiddle factor W_N^k = exp(-i * 2k/N)
        let twiddle = Complex::from_polar(1.0, -2.0 * PI * k as f64
        ↪  / n as f64);
        output[k] = fft_even[k] + twiddle * fft_odd[k];
        output[k + (n / 2)] = fft_even[k] - twiddle * fft_odd[k];
    }
    output
}


fn main() {
    // Sample input signal: 8 time-domain samples represented as
    ↪  complex numbers.
    // In practical applications, these samples might come from
    ↪  sensor readings or audio data.
    let signal: Vec<Complex<f64>> = vec![
        Complex::new(1.0, 0.0),
        Complex::new(0.0, 0.0),
        Complex::new(-1.0, 0.0),
        Complex::new(0.0, 0.0),
        Complex::new(1.0, 0.0),
        Complex::new(0.0, 0.0),
        Complex::new(-1.0, 0.0),
```

323

```
        Complex::new(0.0, 0.0),
    ];

    // Compute the FFT of the input signal.
    let fft_result = fft(&signal);
    println!("FFT Result:");
    for (i, value) in fft_result.iter().enumerate() {
        println!("Bin {}: {:.4} + {:.4}i", i, value.re, value.im);
    }

    // Optionally, compute the DFT using the naive implementation
    ↪  for verification.
    let dft_result = dft(&signal);
    println!("\nDFT Result (Naive Implementation):");
    for (i, value) in dft_result.iter().enumerate() {
        println!("Bin {}: {:.4} + {:.4}i", i, value.re, value.im);
    }
}
```

Chapter 52

Wavelet Transform for Multi-Resolution Data Analysis

Mathematical Foundations of Wavelet Transforms

The wavelet transform extends traditional Fourier analysis by enabling a simultaneous localization in both time (or space) and frequency domains. A wavelet is a function with finite duration and rapid decay that oscillates and has zero mean. The continuous wavelet transform (CWT) of a function $f \in L^2(\mathbb{R})$ is defined as

$$W(a,b) = \frac{1}{\sqrt{|a|}} \int_{-\infty}^{\infty} f(t)\,\psi\left(\frac{t-b}{a}\right) dt,$$

where $a \in \mathbb{R} \setminus \{0\}$ is the scale parameter, $b \in \mathbb{R}$ is the translation parameter, and $\psi(t)$ is the mother wavelet. The admissibility condition imposed on $\psi(t)$, notably that

$$\int_{-\infty}^{\infty} \psi(t)\,dt = 0,$$

ensures that the wavelet transform is invertible. In practice, the discrete wavelet transform (DWT) is preferred. The DWT samples the CWT on a dyadic grid, with scales and translations restricted to the forms $a = 2^j$ and $b = k \cdot 2^j$, where $j, k \in \mathbb{Z}$. This dyadic sampling underlies the efficient representation of signals by means of a filter bank structure, which decomposes the input into successive approximation and detail coefficients.

Multi-Resolution Analysis

Multi-resolution analysis (MRA) provides a systematic framework for decomposing functions into components at various scales. This approach is built upon a series of nested subspaces $\{V_j\}_{j \in \mathbb{Z}}$ of $L^2(\mathbb{R})$ satisfying

$$V_j \subset V_{j+1}, \quad \bigcup_{j \in \mathbb{Z}} V_j \text{ is dense in } L^2(\mathbb{R}), \quad \text{and} \quad \bigcap_{j \in \mathbb{Z}} V_j = \{0\}.$$

A fundamental element of this structure is the scaling function $\phi(t)$, which generates V_0 via integer translations and satisfies a two-scale difference (refinement) equation,

$$\phi(t) = \sqrt{2} \sum_{k \in \mathbb{Z}} h_k \, \phi(2t - k),$$

with $\{h_k\}$ representing the low-pass filter coefficients. The detail spaces W_j, defined as the orthogonal complement of V_j in V_{j+1}, capture the information lost between approximations at successive resolutions. That is, one has

$$V_{j+1} = V_j \oplus W_j.$$

This construction allows a signal $f(t)$ to be expressed as an approximation at a coarse resolution plus a sum of details across various scales. Such a hierarchical representation is the cornerstone of many applications in signal and image processing, where the ability to separately analyze coarse and fine features is essential.

Properties and Characteristics of the Wavelet Transform

The wavelet transform is distinguished by its ability to provide adaptive time-frequency resolution. In contrast to the global sinusoidal basis functions used in Fourier methods, wavelets are localized, which leads to superior performance in analyzing non-stationary signals. The time-frequency tiling inherent to the transform yields high temporal resolution at high frequencies, and conversely, high frequency resolution at low frequencies. This behavior is quantitatively related to the uncertainty principle, which imposes a lower bound on the product of time and frequency variances.

Energy compaction is another significant attribute of the wavelet transform. Well-designed wavelet bases tend to concentrate the significant components of a signal in a small number of coefficients. This property is instrumental in applications such as noise reduction, data compression, and feature extraction, where the goal is to retain only the most pertinent information while discarding insignificant details.

The invertibility of the wavelet transform further underscores its utility. Provided that the wavelet function satisfies the necessary admissibility conditions, both the continuous and discrete transforms allow for exact reconstruction. Quadrature mirror filters (QMF) form the backbone of the practical implementations in the discrete setting, ensuring that the decomposition and subsequent reconstruction processes are both stable and computationally efficient.

Application to Signal and Image Processing

In the realm of signal processing, the wavelet transform facilitates the decomposition of temporal signals into hierarchical components. The representation distinguishes between the low-frequency approximations, which capture the overall trend, and the high-frequency details, which reveal transient phenomena and abrupt changes. This decomposition supports tasks such as denoising, where noise components often manifest at certain scales and can be selectively suppressed without significantly affecting the underlying signal structure.

For image processing, the extension to two-dimensional wavelet transforms allows the analysis of spatial variations across different resolutions. The image is decomposed into sub-bands corresponding to various orientations and scales, which is particularly beneficial for edge detection, texture analysis, and compression. The multi-resolution property enhances the extraction of salient features and supports the development of hierarchical image representations that reflect both global structure and localized detail.

Implementation Considerations in Rust

The design of an efficient and robust wavelet transform implementation in Rust relies heavily on its system-level programming capabilities. Rust's ownership model, strong static type system, and zero-cost abstractions contribute to both the reliability and performance of numerical algorithms. In the context of the wavelet transform, these features are especially pertinent when manipulating large arrays of data representing signals or images.

Designing the filter bank architecture for the DWT in Rust typically involves the careful management of memory to minimize unnecessary allocations and to ensure optimal cache utilization. The recursive nature of multi-level decomposition demands a functionally pure approach to avoid side effects while also exploiting the potential for concurrent processing, especially when handling high-dimensional inputs. The interplay between the mathematical formulation—such as the representation of scaling functions and wavelets—and Rust's efficient data structures, like vectors and slices, underpins the development of a solution that is simultaneously precise and performant.

Advancements in the Rust ecosystem further support numerical computing through libraries that facilitate linear algebra operations and complex arithmetic. These libraries contribute to the elaboration of a wavelet transform that adheres to both the theoretical underpinnings and the practical demands of signal and image processing, ensuring that operations such as filtering, downsampling, and signal reconstruction are executed with the desired accuracy and efficiency.

Rust Code Snippet

```
use std::f64::consts::SQRT_2;

/// The `Wavelet` struct holds the low-pass and high-pass filter
↪   coefficients.
/// For the Haar wavelet, these are given by:
///   h = [1/2, 1/2]
///   g = [1/2, -1/2]
/// which satisfy the admissibility and reconstruction conditions.
```

328

```rust
/// In our implementation, these filters define the two-scale
↪   refinement relation:
///   (t) = 2 *  h[k] · (2t - k)
/// and correspond to the decomposition formulas in the discrete
↪   wavelet transform (DWT).
struct Wavelet {
    low_pass: Vec<f64>,
    high_pass: Vec<f64>,
}

impl Wavelet {
    /// Constructs a new Haar wavelet with predefined filters.
    fn new_haar() -> Self {
        let scale = 1.0 / SQRT_2;
        Wavelet {
            low_pass: vec![scale, scale],
            high_pass: vec![scale, -scale],
        }
    }
}

/// Performs a single level discrete wavelet transform (DWT) using
↪   the provided wavelet filters.
/// The algorithm processes the input signal in pairs (dyadic
↪   sampling) and computes:
///
///   Approximation coefficient: a[i] = x[2*i] * h[0] + x[2*i+1] *
↪   h[1]
///   Detail coefficient:        d[i] = x[2*i] * g[0] + x[2*i+1] *
↪   g[1]
///
/// This corresponds to the filter bank structure used in
↪   multi-resolution analysis.
fn dwt(signal: &[f64], wavelet: &Wavelet) -> (Vec<f64>, Vec<f64>) {
    let mut approx = Vec::new();
    let mut detail = Vec::new();
    let n = signal.len();

    // Process the signal in steps of 2 (dyadic sampling)
    for i in (0..n).step_by(2) {
        // Ensure we have a pair of samples.
        if i + 1 < n {
            let a = signal[i] * wavelet.low_pass[0] + signal[i + 1]
            ↪   * wavelet.low_pass[1];
            let d = signal[i] * wavelet.high_pass[0] + signal[i + 1]
            ↪   * wavelet.high_pass[1];
            approx.push(a);
            detail.push(d);
        }
    }
    (approx, detail)
}
```

```
/// Recursively applies the DWT for multiple levels, thereby
↪   performing multi-resolution
/// analysis of the input signal. At each level, the approximation
↪   coefficients become the
/// new input signal, and the detail coefficients are stored.
///
/// Returns a tuple containing the final coarse approximation and a
↪   vector of detail coefficient
/// vectors for each level (ordered from coarse to fine).
fn multi_level_dwt(mut signal: Vec<f64>, wavelet: &Wavelet, levels:
↪   usize) -> (Vec<f64>, Vec<Vec<f64>>) {
    let mut details = Vec::new();
    for _ in 0..levels {
        // Stop if the signal cannot be further decomposed.
        if signal.len() < 2 {
            break;
        }
        let (approx, detail) = dwt(&signal, wavelet);
        details.push(detail);
        signal = approx;
    }
    (signal, details)
}


/// Performs a single level inverse discrete wavelet transform
↪   (IDWT).
/// Given the approximation and detail coefficients, it reconstructs
↪   the original signal
/// using the synthesis formulas:
///
///    x[2*i]   = a[i] * h[0] + d[i] * g[0]
///    x[2*i+1] = a[i] * h[1] + d[i] * g[1]
fn idwt(approx: &[f64], detail: &[f64], wavelet: &Wavelet) ->
↪   Vec<f64> {
    let mut signal = Vec::with_capacity(approx.len() +
    ↪   detail.len());
    for (&a, &d) in approx.iter().zip(detail.iter()) {
        signal.push(a * wavelet.low_pass[0] + d *
        ↪   wavelet.high_pass[0]);
        signal.push(a * wavelet.low_pass[1] + d *
        ↪   wavelet.high_pass[1]);
    }
    signal
}


/// Reconstructs the original signal by successively applying the
↪   inverse DWT from the coarsest
/// level back to the original resolution. The reconstruction
↪   proceeds by merging the final
/// approximation with the detail coefficients at each level in
↪   reverse order.
fn multi_level_idwt(final_approx: Vec<f64>, details: Vec<Vec<f64>>,
↪   wavelet: &Wavelet) -> Vec<f64> {
```

330

```rust
    // Process detail levels in reverse order.
    details.into_iter().rev().fold(final_approx, |signal, detail| {
        idwt(&signal, &detail, wavelet)
    })
}

fn main() {
    // Define a sample signal. For demonstration purposes, we use a
    // ↪ signal of length 16.
    let signal: Vec<f64> = (0..16).map(|x| x as f64).collect();
    println!("Original Signal: {:?}", signal);

    // Initialize the Haar wavelet.
    let wavelet = Wavelet::new_haar();

    // Specify the number of decomposition levels.
    let levels = 3;
    // Perform multi-level DWT (decomposing the signal into coarse
    // ↪ approximations and details).
    let (final_approx, details) = multi_level_dwt(signal.clone(),
    ↪ &wavelet, levels);
    println!("\n--- DWT Decomposition ---");
    println!("Final Approximation Coefficients: {:?}",
    ↪ final_approx);
    for (lvl, detail) in details.iter().enumerate() {
        println!("Detail Coefficients Level {}: {:?}", lvl + 1,
        ↪ detail);
    }

    // Reconstruct the original signal from the DWT coefficients.
    let reconstructed_signal = multi_level_idwt(final_approx,
    ↪ details, &wavelet);
    println!("\nReconstructed Signal: {:?}", reconstructed_signal);

    // To verify accuracy, compute the reconstruction error.
    let error: f64 = signal.iter()
                        .zip(reconstructed_signal.iter())
                        .map(|(orig, recon)| (orig -
                        ↪ recon).abs())
                        .sum();
    println!("\nTotal Reconstruction Error: {:.6}", error);
}
```

Chapter 53

Feature Engineering with Rust: Text and Numeric Data

Textual Feature Extraction

1 Tokenization and Lexical Analysis

The initial stage in processing raw textual data involves the systematic decomposition of character streams into elementary components called tokens. This process, referred to as tokenization, partitions a continuous string into discrete lexical units based on delimiters such as whitespace and punctuation. In many cases, the tokenization mechanism incorporates Unicode normalization to ensure consistency across various language representations. This phase establishes the foundation for subsequent operations by producing a sequence of substrings whose frequencies and distributions can be rigorously analyzed. Frequently, the count of an individual token t in a document or corpus is denoted as $f(t)$ and serves as a basis for further statistical evaluation.

2 Normalization and Vectorization

Following tokenization, textual data is subjected to normalization techniques that mitigate variability due to orthographic differences. This normalization frequently involves case-folding, the stripping of extraneous punctuation, and the elimination of common stop words. Advanced techniques, such as stemming and lemmatization, reduce tokens to their base or root forms so that semantically equivalent terms are consolidated within the feature space. Once normalized, the tokens are transformed into a numerical representation through vectorization. Standard methods include the bag-of-words representation and the computation of term frequency-inverse document frequency. In the TF-IDF formalism, the weight of a token t in a document d with respect to a corpus D is given by

$$\mathrm{tfidf}(t, d, D) = \mathrm{tf}(t, d) \cdot \log \frac{|D|}{|\{d' \in D : t \in d'\}|},$$

where $\mathrm{tf}(t, d)$ represents the frequency of t in d, and $|D|$ denotes the total number of documents. Such vectorized representations enable rigorous mathematical analyses and facilitate the utilization of robust similarity metrics.

Numeric Data Transformation

1 Scaling, Normalization, and Imputation

The preprocessing of numeric data requires techniques that transform raw measurements into a form amenable to statistical and machine learning models. A prevalent approach involves the standardization of data via the z-score, defined for a value x as

$$z = \frac{x - \mu}{\sigma},$$

where μ is the arithmetic mean and σ is the standard deviation of the dataset. An alternative approach is min-max scaling, which transforms a feature x into a normalized value x' through the equation

$$x' = \frac{x - \min(x)}{\max(x) - \min(x)}.$$

These transformations not only promote convergence in training algorithms but also ensure that features contribute proportionally to distance-based metrics. Moreover, imputation methods address the presence of missing or inconsistent entries. Statistical imputation may involve replacement with the mean or median, while more sophisticated approaches may apply model-based predictions to estimate absent values.

2 Outlier Detection and Statistical Aggregation

The detection and handling of outliers represent critical steps in ensuring the integrity of numeric feature sets. Outlier detection methodologies often employ robust statistical measures, such as the interquartile range (IQR). Data points falling outside the interval

$$[Q1 - 1.5 \cdot IQR, \; Q3 + 1.5 \cdot IQR]$$

are systematically identified as anomalies. Following detection, various techniques may be applied to either transform or exclude these aberrant points. In addition, numerical features are frequently aggregated to construct composite descriptors that capture central tendencies and dispersion characteristics, including the computation of higher-order statistical moments. The synthesis of these metrics underpins subsequent procedures for feature selection and dimensionality reduction.

Integrated Processing of Text and Numeric Modalities

1 Feature Fusion and Interaction Terms

In many practical applications, both textual and numeric features contribute essential information that can be synthesized into a unified analytical framework. Feature fusion involves the concatenation of vectorized text representations with the normalized numeric attributes, thereby creating a multidimensional feature space. This integrated methodology facilitates the parameterization of latent interdependencies between the two modalities. Furthermore, the generation of interaction terms—constructed as non-linear combinations of individual features—can expose subtle correlations that are not evident in isolated feature analyses. Mathematically, an interaction term may be expressed as

$$x_{\text{interaction}} = f\left(x_{\text{text}}, x_{\text{numeric}}\right),$$

where the function f encapsulates the rule for combining features based on domain-specific criteria and statistical considerations.

2 Performance and Memory Optimization in Rust Computations

The execution of feature engineering tasks on extensive text corpora and large numeric datasets necessitates a computational environment that emphasizes performance and memory efficiency. Rust offers a compelling solution by providing control over low-level data management while enforcing strict safety constraints. The language's zero-cost abstractions permit the seamless deployment of concurrent processing pipelines, ensuring that tokenization, normalization, and vectorization procedures can be parallelized without incurring unnecessary runtime overhead. Furthermore, Rust's rigorous compile-time checks facilitate the development of algorithms that optimize cache utilization and minimize memory allocations. This confluence of factors is particularly advantageous when performing heavy preprocessing, as it enables the efficient transformation and integration of heterogeneous data sources into a coherent feature space.

Rust Code Snippet

```rust
use regex::Regex;
use std::collections::{HashMap, HashSet};
use rayon::prelude::*;

// --- Textual Feature Extraction ---

// Tokenization and Lexical Analysis:
// This function converts the input text to lowercase and uses a
//   regular expression to extract words.
fn tokenize(text: &str) -> Vec<String> {
    let re = Regex::new(r"\w+").unwrap();
    re.find_iter(&text.to_lowercase())
        .map(|mat| mat.as_str().to_string())
        .collect()
}

// Compute term frequency from a list of tokens.
fn term_frequency(tokens: &[String]) -> HashMap<String, usize> {
    let mut freq = HashMap::new();
    for token in tokens {
        *freq.entry(token.clone()).or_insert(0) += 1;
    }
    freq
}
```

```rust
// Compute Inverse Document Frequency (IDF) for a corpus.
// For each unique token in each document, count the document
↪   frequency and compute the log ratio.
fn compute_idf(corpus: &[Vec<String>]) -> HashMap<String, f64> {
    let total_docs = corpus.len() as f64;
    let mut doc_freq: HashMap<String, usize> = HashMap::new();
    for tokens in corpus {
        let unique_tokens: HashSet<&String> =
        ↪   tokens.iter().collect();
        for token in unique_tokens {
            *doc_freq.entry(token.clone()).or_insert(0) += 1;
        }
    }
    let mut idf = HashMap::new();
    for (token, count) in doc_freq {
        idf.insert(token, (total_docs / count as f64).ln());
    }
    idf
}


// Compute TF-IDF for a single document given its term frequency and
↪   the corpus IDF.
fn compute_tfidf(tf: &HashMap<String, usize>, idf: &HashMap<String,
↪   f64>) -> HashMap<String, f64> {
    let mut tfidf = HashMap::new();
    for (token, &freq) in tf {
        let weight = freq as f64 * idf.get(token).unwrap_or(&0.0);
        tfidf.insert(token.clone(), weight);
    }
    tfidf
}


// --- Numeric Data Transformation ---

// Z-score normalization function:
// For a given value x, mean , and standard deviation , computes z =
↪   (x - ) / .
fn z_score(x: f64, mean: f64, std: f64) -> f64 {
    (x - mean) / std
}

// Min-max scaling function:
// Converts a value x into x' = (x - min) / (max - min), scaling
↪   feature to [0, 1].
fn min_max_scale(x: f64, min: f64, max: f64) -> f64 {
    (x - min) / (max - min)
}

// Compute mean and standard deviation for a slice of numeric data.
fn compute_mean_std(data: &[f64]) -> (f64, f64) {
    let n = data.len() as f64;
    let mean = data.iter().sum::<f64>() / n;
```

```rust
    let variance = data.iter().map(|x| (x -
↪    mean).powi(2)).sum::<f64>() / n;
    (mean, variance.sqrt())
}


// Compute quartiles for a sorted slice of data.
// Returns (Q1, Median, Q3) necessary for IQR-based outlier
↪    detection.
fn compute_quartiles(data: &mut [f64]) -> (f64, f64, f64) {
    data.sort_by(|a, b| a.partial_cmp(b).unwrap());
    let n = data.len();
    let q1 = data[n / 4];
    let q2 = data[n / 2];
    let q3 = data[(3 * n) / 4];
    (q1, q2, q3)
}


// Outlier Detection using the IQR method.
// Data points that fall outside [Q1 - 1.5*IQR, Q3 + 1.5*IQR] are
↪    flagged as potential outliers.
fn detect_outliers(data: &Vec<f64>) -> (f64, f64) {
    let mut data_clone = data.clone();
    let (q1, _median, q3) = compute_quartiles(&mut data_clone);
    let iqr = q3 - q1;
    let lower_bound = q1 - 1.5 * iqr;
    let upper_bound = q3 + 1.5 * iqr;
    (lower_bound, upper_bound)
}


// --- Integrated Processing: Feature Fusion ---

// Feature Fusion and Interaction Terms:
// Combines vectorized textual features (e.g., TF-IDF values) with
↪    normalized numeric features into a single vector.
fn feature_fusion(text_features: &HashMap<String, f64>,
↪    numeric_features: &[f64]) -> Vec<f64> {
    let mut fused = Vec::new();
    // Sort the text feature keys to ensure consistent ordering.
    let mut keys: Vec<&String> = text_features.keys().collect();
    keys.sort();
    for key in keys {
        fused.push(*text_features.get(key).unwrap());
    }
    // Append normalized numeric features.
    fused.extend_from_slice(numeric_features);
    fused
}


// --- Main Function Demonstration ---
fn main() {
    // Example textual data for processing.
    let sample_text = "Rust is fast, memory-efficient, and safe. It
↪    enables concurrent processing and robust data handling.";
```

337

```rust
// Step 1: Tokenization and Lexical Analysis.
let tokens = tokenize(sample_text);
println!("Tokens: {:?}", tokens);

// Step 2: Compute term frequency.
let tf = term_frequency(&tokens);
println!("Term Frequency: {:?}", tf);

// Step 3: Prepare a small corpus.
let corpus_texts = vec![
    "Rust is a systems programming language.",
    "Memory management is crucial in Rust.",
    sample_text,
];
let corpus: Vec<Vec<String>> = corpus_texts.iter().map(|s|
↪   tokenize(s)).collect();

// Step 4: Compute IDF for the corpus.
let idf = compute_idf(&corpus);

// Step 5: Compute TF-IDF for the sample text.
let tfidf = compute_tfidf(&tf, &idf);
println!("TF-IDF: {:?}", tfidf);

// --- Numeric Data Transformation ---
let numeric_data = vec![10.0, 12.0, 14.0, 16.0, 100.0, 18.0,
↪   20.0];

// Compute mean and standard deviation.
let (mean, std) = compute_mean_std(&numeric_data);
let z_scores: Vec<f64> = numeric_data.iter().map(|&x| z_score(x,
↪   mean, std)).collect();
println!("Z-Scores: {:?}", z_scores);

// Compute min-max scaling.
let min = *numeric_data.iter().min_by(|a, b|
↪   a.partial_cmp(b).unwrap()).unwrap();
let max = *numeric_data.iter().max_by(|a, b|
↪   a.partial_cmp(b).unwrap()).unwrap();
let scaled_data: Vec<f64> = numeric_data.iter().map(|&x|
↪   min_max_scale(x, min, max)).collect();
println!("Min-Max Scaled Data: {:?}", scaled_data);

// Detect outliers using the IQR method.
let (lower_bound, upper_bound) = detect_outliers(&numeric_data);
println!("Outlier Bounds: Lower = {}, Upper = {}", lower_bound,
↪   upper_bound);

// --- Integrated Feature Fusion ---
// Fuse textual features (TF-IDF) with numeric features (min-max
↪   scaled).
let fused_features = feature_fusion(&tfidf, &scaled_data);
```

```rust
    println!("Fused Feature Vector: {:?}", fused_features);

    // Example of generating an interaction term:
    // For illustration, compute the product of the first text
    ↪ feature and the first numeric feature.
    if let (Some(&first_text_feature), Some(&first_numeric_feature))
    ↪ = (tfidf.values().next(), scaled_data.first()) {
        let interaction_term = first_text_feature *
        ↪ first_numeric_feature;
        println!("Interaction Term: {}", interaction_term);
    }
}
```

Chapter 54

Feature Scaling and Normalization Techniques

Mathematical Foundations and Rationale

The systematic standardization of data features constitutes a fundamental prerequisite in the training of machine learning models. The process of scaling and normalization transforms heterogeneous feature distributions into a common numerical domain. This transformation enhances the convergence properties of many optimization algorithms and mitigates the risk of one feature disproportionately influencing model parameters. In a formal sense, given a dataset comprised of features represented by the random variable x, the objective is to transform x into a new variable x' such that the statistical properties of the resulting feature space adhere to predetermined criteria—often involving measures of central tendency and dispersion.

Z-Score Standardization

One prevalent methodology for standardization is the application of z-score normalization. This technique operates by centering the data on the arithmetic mean and scaling according to the standard deviation. For any individual data point x, the z-score is computed via

$$z = \frac{x - \mu}{\sigma},$$

where μ denotes the mean of the dataset and σ its standard deviation. By imposing this transformation, the resulting variable approximates a standard normal distribution with zero mean and unit variance, provided that the original distribution is not significantly skewed. The reliance on z-score normalization is particularly advantageous in scenarios where parameter sensitivity is high, as it reduces numerical instabilities during iterative optimization processes.

Min-Max Scaling

An alternative approach to feature scaling is encapsulated by the min-max normalization technique. This method performs a linear transformation of the original feature values such that the minimum and maximum values of the dataset correspond to fixed bounds, typically 0 and 1. The transformed value x' is derived as

$$x' = \frac{x - \min(x)}{\max(x) - \min(x)},$$

where $\min(x)$ and $\max(x)$ represent the minimum and maximum feature values, respectively. The primary advantage of this method lies in its ability to preserve the relative distances between original data points, thereby maintaining the intrinsic structure of the dataset. However, the presence of outliers can significantly distort the scaling range, necessitating further consideration when selecting an appropriate normalization technique.

Robust Scaling Methods

In circumstances where extreme values considerably bias the arithmetic mean and standard deviation, robust scaling methods provide an alternative means to standardize data features. Such techniques replace the classical parameters with robust statistical measures. For instance, the median M supplants the mean, and the interquartile range (IQR), defined as $Q_3 - Q_1$ where Q_1 and Q_3 are the first and third quartiles respectively, replaces the standard deviation. A typical robust scaling transformation is expressed as

$$x' = \frac{x - M}{Q_3 - Q_1}.$$

This formulation ensures that the impact of outliers is minimized, thereby rendering the scaled features more representative of the central mass of the data distribution.

Normalization via Logarithmic and Power Transformations

Feature normalization strategies extend beyond linear transformations when the underlying data exhibit high degrees of skewness. Logarithmic transformations, for example, provide a means to compress the dynamic range of positively skewed distributions. Given a feature x with strictly positive entries, a logarithmic transformation can be implemented via

$$x' = \log(x + c),$$

where c is a constant introduced to avoid computational difficulties in the presence of zero values. In addition to logarithmic scaling, power transformations (such as the Box-Cox transformation) serve to stabilize variance and render the data more amenable to techniques which assume normality. These methods are particularly valuable when preparation for model training necessitates adjustments for multiplicative relationships or heteroscedasticity present in the raw features.

Unit Norm Normalization

A further normalization procedure involves the enforcement of a unit norm on feature vectors. In this approach, each data point is considered as a vector in the feature space, and is scaled such that its norm is equal to one. When employing the Euclidean norm, the transformation is determined according to

$$\hat{x} = \frac{x}{\|x\|},$$

provided that $\|x\| \neq 0$. This approach is especially critical in settings where similarity metrics, such as the cosine similarity, underpin the comparative analysis of data points. Unit norm normalization ensures that all feature vectors reside on the same hyperspherical manifold, thereby simplifying the geometric interpretation and subsequent analysis of the data.

Implications for Machine Learning Model Training

The rigorous application of scaling and normalization techniques is instrumental in harmonizing feature inputs prior to model training. A standardized feature space not only accelerates the convergence of learning algorithms but also contributes to enhanced numerical stability. The appropriate selection of a scaling method requires careful consideration of the underlying data distribution, the presence of outliers, and the intended application of the model. Each discussed approach—ranging from z-score standardization to robust scaling and unit norm normalization—represents a distinct strategy for addressing the intrinsic variability of raw features, thereby laying a robust foundation for subsequent algorithmic implementations in the realm of machine learning.

Rust Code Snippet

```rust
use std::f64;

/// Compute the arithmetic mean of a slice of f64 values.
fn compute_mean(data: &[f64]) -> f64 {
    let sum: f64 = data.iter().sum();
    sum / (data.len() as f64)
}

/// Compute the standard deviation of a slice of f64 values given
↪    the mean.
fn compute_std(data: &[f64], mean: f64) -> f64 {
    let variance = data.iter().map(|&x| (x - mean) * (x -
    ↪    mean)).sum::<f64>() / (data.len() as f64);
    variance.sqrt()
}

/// Z-Score Standardization:
/// Transform each value using z = (x - mean) / std.
```

```rust
fn z_score_normalization(data: &[f64]) -> Vec<f64> {
    let mean = compute_mean(data);
    let std = compute_std(data, mean);
    data.iter().map(|&x| (x - mean) / std).collect()
}

/// Min-Max Scaling:
/// Transform each value using x' = (x - min) / (max - min).
fn min_max_normalization(data: &[f64]) -> Vec<f64> {
    let min_value = data.iter().cloned().fold(f64::INFINITY,
    ↪    f64::min);
    let max_value = data.iter().cloned().fold(f64::NEG_INFINITY,
    ↪    f64::max);
    let range = max_value - min_value;
    if range == 0.0 {
        return data.to_vec();
    }
    data.iter().map(|&x| (x - min_value) / range).collect()
}

/// Utility function to compute the median of a sorted slice of f64
↪    values.
fn median(sorted: &[f64]) -> f64 {
    let n = sorted.len();
    if n % 2 == 0 {
        (sorted[n / 2 - 1] + sorted[n / 2]) / 2.0
    } else {
        sorted[n / 2]
    }
}

/// Robust Scaling:
/// Transform data using x' = (x - median) / IQR,
/// where IQR = Q3 - Q1 computed from the first and third quartiles.
fn robust_scaling(data: &[f64]) -> Vec<f64> {
    // Make a sorted copy of the data.
    let mut sorted = data.to_vec();
    sorted.sort_by(|a, b| a.partial_cmp(b).unwrap());

    // Compute the median.
    let med = median(&sorted);

    // Determine lower and upper halves for quartile calculation.
    let n = sorted.len();
    let mid = n / 2;
    let lower_half = &sorted[..mid];
    let upper_half = if n % 2 == 0 {
        &sorted[mid..]
    } else {
        &sorted[mid+1..]
    };

    let q1 = median(lower_half);
```

```rust
    let q3 = median(upper_half);
    let iqr = q3 - q1;

    // Prevent division by zero if IQR is zero.
    if iqr == 0.0 {
        return data.iter().map(|&x| x - med).collect();
    }

    data.iter().map(|&x| (x - med) / iqr).collect()
}

/// Logarithmic Transformation:
/// Apply x' = log(x + offset) to each data point.
/// The `offset` is added to avoid computation of log(0).
fn log_transform(data: &[f64], offset: f64) -> Vec<f64> {
    data.iter().map(|&x| (x + offset).ln()).collect()
}

/// Unit Norm Normalization:
/// Scale the vector so that its Euclidean norm equals 1.
/// For a vector x, each component is scaled with x' = x / ||x||.
fn unit_norm_normalization(data: &[f64]) -> Vec<f64> {
    let norm: f64 = data.iter().map(|&x| x * x).sum::<f64>().sqrt();
    if norm == 0.0 {
        data.to_vec()
    } else {
        data.iter().map(|&x| x / norm).collect()
    }
}

/// Main function demonstrating the feature scaling and
/// ↪ normalization methods.
fn main() {
    // Sample dataset for demonstration.
    let data: Vec<f64> = vec![1.0, 2.0, 3.0, 4.0, 5.0, 100.0];

    // 1. Z-Score Standardization
    let z_scores = z_score_normalization(&data);
    println!("Z-Score Normalization:\n{:?}", z_scores);

    // 2. Min-Max Scaling
    let min_max = min_max_normalization(&data);
    println!("\nMin-Max Normalization:\n{:?}", min_max);

    // 3. Robust Scaling (using median and IQR)
    let robust = robust_scaling(&data);
    println!("\nRobust Scaling (Median & IQR):\n{:?}", robust);

    // 4. Logarithmic Transformation with a small offset (e.g.,
    // ↪ 1e-6)
    let log_trans = log_transform(&data, 1e-6);
    println!("\nLogarithmic Transformation:\n{:?}", log_trans);
```

345

```rust
    // 5. Unit Norm Normalization
    let unit_norm = unit_norm_normalization(&data);
    println!("\nUnit Norm Normalization:\n{:?}", unit_norm);
}
```

Chapter 55

One-Hot Encoding and Embedding Implementations

Foundational Concepts in Categorical Data Encoding

Categorical data, by its very nature, consists of discrete elements drawn from a finite set $C = \{c_1, c_2, \ldots, c_k\}$. The transformation of these discrete elements into a numerical domain necessitates the design of an injective mapping that preserves the uniqueness of each category. One such mapping is defined by an encoding function $\varphi \colon C \to \{0, 1\}^k$ where for each $c_i \in C$, the image $\varphi(c_i)$ is a binary vector satisfying $\varphi(c_i)_j = 1$ if and only if $i = j$, and $\varphi(c_i)_j = 0$ otherwise. This construction provides a rigorous mathematical foundation for representing categorical variables in a vector space, enabling subsequent algebraic manipulations and integration with numerical optimization techniques.

One-Hot Encoding: Structure and Practical Considerations

One-hot encoding constitutes a direct method for encoding categorical variables by mapping each category to a unique canonical basis vector in $\mathbb{R}^k$. In this representation, the absence of any ordinal relationship is explicitly maintained since the inner product between two distinct one-hot vectors is zero. Despite its conceptual clarity and ease of interpretation, one-hot encoding is inherently associated with high-dimensionality when $|C|$ is large, leading to sparse vector representations. Such sparsity can adversely affect computational performance and memory utilization. When implementing one-hot encoding in a systems programming language such as Rust, meticulous attention is devoted to the design of data structures that leverage the language's features of static typing, memory safety, and zero-cost abstractions. The efficiency in transforming a categorical datum into its corresponding binary vector is critical in performance-sensitive applications, and the approach benefits from Rust's capability to optimize memory layout and concurrent data processing.

Embedding Techniques: A Dense Representation Approach

Embeddings offer a sophisticated alternative to one-hot encoding by representing each categorical value as a dense vector of real numbers. Rather than mapping a category to a high-dimensional sparse vector, embeddings associate each $c \in C$ with a vector in a lower-dimensional space $\mathbb{R}^d$, where $d \ll k$. This association is typically realized through an embedding matrix $E \in \mathbb{R}^{k \times d}$, in which each row corresponds to the dense representation of a specific category. A categorical variable c_i is thereby transformed to a vector $\mathbf{v} = E_{i,:}$, where $E_{i,:}$ denotes the ith row of E. Such dense representations not only reduce storage requirements and computational overhead but also enable the capture of semantic and relational similarities between categories in the learned vector space. Further refinement of the embedding process is achieved by optimizing a suitable loss function during training, which encourages the embedding space to reflect intrinsic structures within the data. In the context of Rust, the implementation of embedding techniques benefits from rigorous memory management and advanced type safety, ensuring that dense representations are computed efficiently and integrated seamlessly into broader data processing pipelines.

Rust Code Snippet

```
//! This example demonstrates two fundamental techniques discussed
↪   in the chapter:
//!
//! 1. One-Hot Encoding:
//!    For a categorical set C = { c, c, ..., c }, the encoding
↪   function
//!      : C → {0,1} is given by:
//!
//!        (c)_j = 1 if c == c, and 0 otherwise
//!
//! 2. Embedding Techniques:
//!    Instead of representing categories with sparse one-hot
↪   vectors,
//!    a dense embedding matrix E   ^(k×d) is used where each row
↪   E[i, :]
 //!    is the low-dimensional representation of the i-th category.
//!
//! The following Rust code implements both these techniques.

use std::fmt;

/// Performs one-hot encoding for the given category.
///
/// Given a slice of categories, this function returns a vector
/// where the position corresponding to the target category is set
↪   to 1 and
/// all others are 0. This implements the mapping:
///
///    : C → {0,1}, where
///   (c)_j = { 1, if c equals the j-th category; 0, otherwise }
///
fn one_hot_encode(category: &str, categories: &[&str]) -> Vec<u8> {
    categories.iter()
        .map(|&c| if c == category { 1 } else { 0 })
        .collect()
}

/// Embeddings structure represents the dense embedding matrix for
↪   categorical data.
///
/// The embedding matrix E   ^(k×d) is represented as a vector of
↪   vectors,
/// where k is the number of categories and d is the embedding
↪   dimension.
/// Each category is mapped to a dense representation (row in the
↪   matrix).
///
struct Embeddings {
    vocabulary: Vec<String>,
```

349

```
        embeddings: Vec<Vec<f32>>, // Each inner Vec is the dense
        ↪    representation for a category.
}

impl Embeddings {
    /// Creates a new Embeddings instance.
    ///
    /// # Arguments
    ///
    /// * `vocabulary` - Slice of category strings.
    /// * `embedding_dim` - The dimensionality d of each dense
    ↪    embedding.
    ///
    /// In this example, the embeddings are initialized with
    ↪    deterministic values for clarity.
    ///
    fn new(vocabulary: &[&str], embedding_dim: usize) -> Self {
        let vocabulary: Vec<String> = vocabulary.iter().map(|&s|
        ↪    s.to_owned()).collect();
        // Initialize the embedding matrix using a simple
        ↪    deterministic function.
        // In practice, embeddings are typically initialized
        ↪    randomly and optimized via training.
        let embeddings = vocabulary.iter().enumerate().map(|(idx,
        ↪    _)| {
            (0..embedding_dim)
                .map(|j| (idx as f32 + 1.0) * (j as f32 + 0.5))
                .collect()
        }).collect();
        Embeddings { vocabulary, embeddings }
    }

    /// Retrieves the dense embedding vector for a given category.
    ///
    /// # Arguments
    ///
    /// * `category` - The target category as &str.
    ///
    /// Returns an Option containing a slice to the dense vector if
    ↪    the category exists.
    ///
    fn get(&self, category: &str) -> Option<&[f32]> {
        self.vocabulary.iter()
            .position(|s| s == category)
            .map(|idx| &self.embeddings[idx][..])
    }
}

/// For a nicer printout of the Embeddings struct.
impl fmt::Display for Embeddings {
    fn fmt(&self, f: &mut fmt::Formatter<'_>) -> fmt::Result {
        for (cat, emb) in
        ↪    self.vocabulary.iter().zip(self.embeddings.iter()) {
```

350

```rust
            writeln!(f, "{}: {:?}", cat, emb)?;
        }
        Ok(())
    }
}

fn main() {
    // Define the set of categories.
    let categories = vec!["apple", "banana", "cherry"];

    // Example: One-Hot Encoding for a given category.
    let target_category = "banana";
    let one_hot_vector = one_hot_encode(target_category,
    ↪  &categories);
    println!("One-hot encoding for '{}': {:?}", target_category,
    ↪  one_hot_vector);
    // Expected output: One-hot vector such as [0, 1, 0] for
    ↪  "banana"

    // Create embeddings with an embedding dimension of 4.
    let embedding_dim = 4;
    let embeddings = Embeddings::new(&categories, embedding_dim);

    // Retrieve and print the embedding for the target category.
    match embeddings.get(target_category) {
        Some(embedding) => println!("Dense embedding for '{}':
        ↪  {:?}", target_category, embedding),
        None => println!("Category '{}' not found in embeddings.",
        ↪  target_category),
    }

    // Print the entire embedding matrix for verification.
    println!("\nComplete Embedding Matrix:");
    println!("{}", embeddings);
}
```

Chapter 56

Categorical Data Handling and Statistical Tests

Representation and Preprocessing of Categorical Data

The systematic treatment of categorical data necessitates an initial phase of representation and preprocessing that transforms symbolic or textual identifiers into structured, analyzable constructs. In many applications, categories are drawn from a finite set $C = \{c_1, c_2, \ldots, c_k\}$, where each c_i denotes a unique categorical entity. The transformation process may employ encoding schemes that preserve the discrete nature of the data; for instance, one-hot encoding maps each category to a canonical binary vector in $\{0,1\}^k$, ensuring that no implicit ordinal relationship is introduced. Preprocessing also includes verifying the integrity of the categorical labels, managing missing values, and ensuring consistency across different sources. The design considerations emphasize maintaining a transparent correspondence between the raw categorical entities and their numerical representations, thereby facilitating rigorous subsequent statistical analysis.

Construction of Contingency Tables

An integral aspect of analyzing categorical variables involves the aggregation of data into contingency tables, which succinctly summarize the joint frequency distribution of two or more categorical attributes. A contingency table organizes observed counts into cells defined by row and column indices that correspond to the categories of the variables under study. The structure of such a table serves as the foundation for many inferential techniques; each cell entry reflects the number of occurrences for a given combination of categorical states. In formal terms, consider a contingency table with cells indexed by $i \in \{1, \ldots, r\}$ and $j \in \{1, \ldots, c\}$, where r and c represent the number of categories for the two variables. The observed frequencies, denoted by O_{ij}, are then used to compute expected frequencies under the hypothesis of independence, generally given by

$$E_{ij} = \frac{R_i \cdot C_j}{N},$$

with R_i and C_j representing the marginal totals and N denoting the grand total of observations. The careful construction of contingency tables ensures that the subsequent statistical tests are grounded on reliable and structured frequency data.

Statistical Tests for Categorical Data Analysis

The analysis of categorical data frequently relies on the application of statistical tests that either validate or refute hypotheses concerning the independence or association between categorical variables. The selection of an appropriate test depends on the sample size, the distribution of observations within the contingency table, and the theoretical underpinnings of the hypothesis being tested.

1   The Chi-Square Test of Independence

The chi-square test of independence is a well-established method for assessing whether two categorical variables are statistically independent. The test statistic is defined by the formula

$$\chi^2 = \sum_{i=1}^{r} \sum_{j=1}^{c} \frac{(O_{ij} - E_{ij})^2}{E_{ij}},$$

where O_{ij} denotes the observed frequency in cell (i,j) and E_{ij} represents the expected frequency under the null hypothesis of independence. Under the assumption of adequate sample size, the distribution of the χ^2 statistic converges to a chi-square distribution with $(r-1)(c-1)$ degrees of freedom. The validity of the test depends on the condition that the expected counts are sufficiently high in each cell, a constraint that is typically met in large-scale datasets. The chi-square test thus provides a robust mechanism for validating observed differences in categorical data by quantifying the divergence between empirical and theoretical frequency distributions.

2 Fisher's Exact Test

In scenarios where the assumptions required by the chi-square test are violated—particularly in the presence of small expected frequencies—Fisher's exact test offers an alternative approach. Contrasting with the asymptotic behavior of the chi-square test, Fisher's exact test computes the exact probability of observing a contingency table at least as extreme as the one obtained, given fixed marginal totals. This computation is based on the hypergeometric distribution, which governs the probability structure of cell counts in a two-by-two table. Although the method is computationally intensive for larger tables, its exact nature renders it indispensable when analyzing sparse categorical datasets. Fisher's exact test thereby complements the chi-square test by extending the repertoire of statistical inference to settings where sample sizes are limited.

3 Measures of Association and Effect Size

Beyond the binary decision of rejecting or accepting the null hypothesis, quantifying the strength of association between categorical variables offers deeper insight into the data. Among the various metrics available, Cramer's V is frequently employed to assess the effect size. Cramer's V is calculated using the formula

$$V = \sqrt{\frac{\chi^2/N}{\min(r-1, c-1)}},$$

where N represents the total number of observations. This measure provides a normalized index of association ranging between 0 and

1, with values closer to 1 indicating stronger relationships. Additional measures, such as the Phi coefficient for two-by-two tables, further elucidate the nature and magnitude of associations in categorical data. Comprehensive evaluation of these metrics not only validates the statistical significance of observed differences but also contextualizes their practical relevance.

Implementation Considerations in Statistical Testing

The rigorous implementation of statistical tests for categorical data in computational frameworks demands meticulous attention to algorithmic efficiency and numerical stability. Techniques for aggregating frequency counts and constructing contingency tables must harness optimized data structures to ensure rapid computation and minimal memory overhead. Furthermore, the estimation of expected frequencies and the subsequent computation of test statistics require careful handling of floating point arithmetic to avert rounding errors, particularly when processing large datasets. The integration of these statistical procedures within a broader data processing pipeline involves modular design principles that support both scalability and maintainability. In environments where performance is paramount, such considerations inform the choice of low-level optimizations and parallel processing paradigms, thereby enabling the robust and accurate execution of statistical tests with minimal computational latency.

Rust Code Snippet

```rust
use std::f64;

// Compute row sums, column sums, and the total number of
//   observations from a contingency table.
fn compute_marginals(table: &Vec<Vec<usize>>) -> (Vec<usize>,
   Vec<usize>, usize) {
    let num_rows = table.len();
    let num_cols = table[0].len();
    let mut row_sums = vec![0; num_rows];
    let mut col_sums = vec![0; num_cols];
    let mut total = 0;

    for i in 0..num_rows {
```

```rust
        for j in 0..num_cols {
            row_sums[i] += table[i][j];
            col_sums[j] += table[i][j];
            total += table[i][j];
        }
    }
    (row_sums, col_sums, total)
}

// Compute expected frequencies for each cell in the contingency
↪ table using:
// E_{ij} = (row_sum_i * col_sum_j) / total
fn compute_expected(
    table: &Vec<Vec<usize>>,
    row_sums: &Vec<usize>,
    col_sums: &Vec<usize>,
    total: usize,
) -> Vec<Vec<f64>> {
    let num_rows = table.len();
    let num_cols = table[0].len();
    let mut expected = vec![vec![0.0; num_cols]; num_rows];

    for i in 0..num_rows {
        for j in 0..num_cols {
            expected[i][j] = (row_sums[i] as f64 * col_sums[j] as
            ↪ f64) / (total as f64);
        }
    }
    expected
}

// Compute the Chi-Square Statistic using:
// ² = ( (O_{ij} - E_{ij})² / E_{ij} )
fn chi_square_statistic(table: &Vec<Vec<usize>>, expected:
↪ &Vec<Vec<f64>>) -> f64 {
    let mut chi2 = 0.0;
    let num_rows = table.len();
    let num_cols = table[0].len();

    for i in 0..num_rows {
        for j in 0..num_cols {
            let observed = table[i][j] as f64;
            let exp = expected[i][j];
            if exp > 0.0 {
                chi2 += (observed - exp).powi(2) / exp;
            }
        }
    }
    chi2
}

// Compute Cramer's V as a measure of association:
// V = ( (²/N) / min(r-1, c-1) )
```

```rust
fn cramers_v(chi2: f64, total: usize, num_rows: usize, num_cols:
↪ usize) -> f64 {
    let phi_squared = chi2 / (total as f64);
    let min_dim = f64::min((num_rows - 1) as f64, (num_cols - 1) as
    ↪ f64);
    if min_dim == 0.0 {
        0.0
    } else {
        (phi_squared / min_dim).sqrt()
    }
}

// Helper function to compute factorial as f64 (suitable for small
↪ n)
fn factorial(n: usize) -> f64 {
    (1..=n).fold(1.0, |acc, x| acc * (x as f64))
}

// Compute the binomial coefficient "n choose k"
fn binom(n: usize, k: usize) -> f64 {
    if k > n {
        return 0.0;
    }
    factorial(n) / (factorial(k) * factorial(n - k))
}

// Fisher's Exact Test for a 2x2 contingency table.
// For table = [[a, b],
//              [c, d]],
// the hypergeometric probability is given by:
// p = [C(a+b, a) * C(c+d, c)] / C(total, (a+c))
fn fisher_exact_2x2(table: &Vec<Vec<usize>>) -> f64 {
    if table.len() != 2 || table[0].len() != 2 || table[1].len() !=
    ↪ 2 {
        panic!("Fisher's Exact Test is only applicable to 2x2
        ↪ tables.");
    }
    let a = table[0][0];
    let b = table[0][1];
    let c = table[1][0];
    let d = table[1][1];

    let row1 = a + b;
    let row2 = c + d;
    let col1 = a + c;
    let total = row1 + row2;

    binom(row1, a) * binom(row2, c) / binom(total, col1)
}

fn main() {
    // Example 1: Chi-Square Test and Cramer's V using a 2x3
    ↪ contingency table.
```

```rust
// Each cell represents the observed frequency for a combination
↪  of two categorical variables.
let observed_table = vec![
    vec![10, 20, 30],
    vec![20, 15, 25],
];

// Compute marginal totals and expected frequencies.
let (row_sums, col_sums, total) =
↪  compute_marginals(&observed_table);
let expected_table = compute_expected(&observed_table,
↪  &row_sums, &col_sums, total);

// Calculate the Chi-Square statistic.
let chi2 = chi_square_statistic(&observed_table,
↪  &expected_table);
println!("Observed Table: {:?}", observed_table);
println!("Row Sums: {:?}, Column Sums: {:?}, Total Observations:
↪  {}", row_sums, col_sums, total);
println!("Expected Frequencies Table: {:?}", expected_table);
println!("Chi-Square Statistic: {:.4}", chi2);

// Calculate Cramer's V.
let num_rows = observed_table.len();
let num_cols = observed_table[0].len();
let cramers = cramers_v(chi2, total, num_rows, num_cols);
println!("Cramer's V: {:.4}", cramers);

// Example 2: Fisher's Exact Test for a 2x2 contingency table.
let table_2x2 = vec![
    vec![8, 2],
    vec![1, 5],
];
let fisher_p = fisher_exact_2x2(&table_2x2);
println!("\n2x2 Table for Fisher's Exact Test: {:?}",
↪  table_2x2);
println!("Fisher's Exact Test p-value (observed probability):
↪  {:.6}", fisher_p);
}
```

358

Chapter 57

Linear Discriminant Analysis for Dimensionality Reduction

Mathematical Foundations

Linear Discriminant Analysis (LDA) is founded on a rigorous statistical framework that models the separation between classes by analyzing scatter within and between classes. Consider a dataset represented by a matrix $X \in \mathbb{R}^{n \times d}$, where each of the n observations is an element of a d-dimensional space, and let the corresponding class labels be denoted by $y \in \{1, 2, \ldots, C\}$. For each class indexed by c, the class-specific mean vector is defined as

$$\mu_c = \frac{1}{n_c} \sum_{x \in X_c} x,$$

where X_c denotes the set of observations belonging to class c and n_c is the number of observations in that class. The overall mean of the dataset is given by

$$\mu = \frac{1}{n} \sum_{i=1}^{n} x_i.$$

The within-class scatter matrix, which quantifies the variance of data points relative to their respective class means, is computed as

$$S_W = \sum_{c=1}^{C} \sum_{x \in X_c} (x - \mu_c)(x - \mu_c)^T.$$

Conversely, the between-class scatter matrix measures the dispersion of the class means with respect to the overall mean and is defined as

$$S_B = \sum_{c=1}^{C} n_c (\mu_c - \mu)(\mu_c - \mu)^T.$$

Optimization Criterion

The core objective of LDA is to determine a projection that maximizes class separability. This requirement is formalized by seeking a projection matrix W that maximizes the ratio of between-class scatter to within-class scatter. In the case of a single projection vector $\mathbf{w} \in \mathbb{R}^d$, the optimization criterion is expressed as

$$J(\mathbf{w}) = \frac{\mathbf{w}^T S_B \mathbf{w}}{\mathbf{w}^T S_W \mathbf{w}}.$$

The optimization of $J(\mathbf{w})$ leads to a generalized eigenvalue problem of the form

$$S_B \mathbf{w} = \lambda S_W \mathbf{w},$$

where λ denotes the eigenvalue corresponding to the eigenvector $\mathbf{w}$. The set of eigenvectors associated with the largest eigenvalues forms the columns of the projection matrix W. This matrix reduces the dimensionality of the original data while preserving maximal class-discriminative information.

Statistical Properties and Assumptions

The statistical underpinning of LDA assumes that the data within each class are drawn from a multivariate normal distribution. Under this assumption, the covariance matrices of the classes are considered approximately equal, an assumption that facilitates the pooling of variances into the within-class scatter matrix S_W. The criterion essentially maximizes Fisher's ratio, thereby optimizing the separation between classes in the projected subspace. The eigen-decomposition of $S_W^{-1} S_B$ yields eigenvalues that are indicative of the discriminatory power of each corresponding projection direction. A higher eigenvalue implies a more favorable trade-off between between-class variance and within-class variance. The stability of the computation is dependent on the invertibility of S_W, a condition that may require the application of regularization techniques in cases where the number of features exceeds the number of observations.

Implementation Considerations with Rust's Performance

The translation of LDA from theoretical formulation to an efficient computational implementation necessitates careful attention to numerical stability and algorithmic efficiency. The matrix operations inherent to the computation of S_W and S_B, as well as the subsequent eigenvalue decomposition, require tools that handle large datasets robustly. Rust, with its emphasis on memory safety and zero-cost abstractions, provides a potent platform for executing these operations at high speed. The integration of LDA within a Rust-based framework enables the exploitation of concurrent computing paradigms while ensuring that the precision of floating-point arithmetic is maintained. The implementation leverages optimized linear algebra routines to perform the eigen-decomposition of $S_W^{-1} S_B$, ensuring that the extraction of the projection matrix W is both accurate and expedient. Such integration of statistical rigor with the performance characteristics of Rust exemplifies the advanced nature of modern data processing pipelines in high-performance computing environments.

Rust Code Snippet

```
use ndarray::prelude::*;
use ndarray::{array, s};
use ndarray_linalg::{Eigh, UPLO};

use std::collections::HashMap;

fn main() {
    // Example dataset: 6 observations with 3 features each.
```

361

```
// The first three observations belong to class 0 and the next
↪    three to class 1.
let X = array![
    [4.0, 2.0, 3.0],
    [2.0, 3.0, 4.0],
    [3.0, 2.0, 5.0],
    [7.0, 9.0, 6.0],
    [8.0, 8.0, 7.0],
    [9.0, 10.0, 8.0]
];
let labels = vec![0, 0, 0, 1, 1, 1];

// Compute the overall mean of the dataset: μ = (1/n) Σ x_i
let mu = X.mean_axis(Axis(0)).expect("Failed to compute the
↪    overall mean");

// Group sample indices by their class labels
let mut class_indices: HashMap<usize, Vec<usize>> =
↪    HashMap::new();
for (i, &label) in labels.iter().enumerate() {
    class_indices.entry(label).or_insert_with(Vec::new).push(i);
}

// Compute class-specific mean vectors: μ_c = (1/n_c) Σ_{x ∈ X_c} x
let mut class_means: HashMap<usize, Array1<f64>> =
↪    HashMap::new();
for (label, indices) in &class_indices {
    let mut sum = Array1::<f64>::zeros(X.shape()[1]);
    for &i in indices {
        sum = sum + &X.slice(s![i, ..]);
    }
    let mean = sum / (indices.len() as f64);
    class_means.insert(*label, mean);
}

let d = X.shape()[1]; // Number of features

// Compute the Within-Class Scatter Matrix:
// S_W = Σ_{c=1}^{C} Σ_{x ∈ X_c} (x - μ_c)(x - μ_c)^T
let mut S_W = Array2::<f64>::zeros((d, d));
for (label, indices) in &class_indices {
    let mu_c = class_means.get(label).expect("Missing class
    ↪    mean");
    for &i in indices {
        let x_i = X.slice(s![i, ..]);
        let diff = &x_i - mu_c;
        let diff_col = diff.insert_axis(Axis(1)); // Convert to
        ↪    a column vector
        S_W = S_W + diff_col.dot(&diff_col.t());
    }
}

// Compute the Between-Class Scatter Matrix:
```

```rust
// S_B = _{c=1}^{C} n_c (_c - )(_c - )^T
let mut S_B = Array2::<f64>::zeros((d, d));
for (&label, mu_c) in &class_means {
    let n_c = class_indices.get(&label).unwrap().len() as f64;
    let diff = mu_c - &mu;
    let diff_col = diff.insert_axis(Axis(1));
    S_B = S_B + n_c * diff_col.dot(&diff_col.t());
}

// To solve the generalized eigenvalue problem S_B w =  S_W w,
// ↪ we transform it into a
// standard eigenvalue problem by forming T = S_W^(-1/2) S_B
// ↪ S_W^(-1/2).
// Compute S_W^(-1/2) by performing an eigen-decomposition of
// ↪ S_W.
let (eigvals_sw, eigvecs_sw) = S_W.eigh(UPLO::Lower)
    .expect("Eigenvalue decomposition failed for S_W. Is S_W
    ↪ positive definite?");

let mut D_inv_sqrt = Array2::<f64>::zeros((d, d));
for i in 0..d {
    D_inv_sqrt[[i, i]] = 1.0 / eigvals_sw[i].sqrt();
}
let S_W_inv_sqrt =
↪ eigvecs_sw.dot(&D_inv_sqrt).dot(&eigvecs_sw.t());

// Form the symmetric matrix T = S_W^(-1/2) S_B S_W^(-1/2)
let T = S_W_inv_sqrt.dot(&S_B).dot(&S_W_inv_sqrt);

// Solve the eigen-decomposition of T: T = U  U^T.
let (eigvals, eigvecs) = T.eigh(UPLO::Lower)
    .expect("Eigenvalue decomposition failed for T");

// Pair eigenvalues with their corresponding eigenvectors and
// ↪ sort them in descending order.
let mut eig_pairs: Vec<(f64, Array1<f64>)> = eigvals.iter()
    .cloned()
    .zip(eigvecs.columns().into_iter().map(|col|
    ↪ col.to_owned()))
    .collect();
eig_pairs.sort_by(|a, b| b.0.partial_cmp(&a.0).unwrap());

// Reconstruct the sorted eigenvector matrix.
let mut sorted_eigvecs = Array2::<f64>::zeros((d, d));
for (i, pair) in eig_pairs.iter().enumerate() {
    sorted_eigvecs.slice_mut(s![.., i]).assign(&pair.1);
}

// The final projection matrix W is computed as: W = S_W^(-1/2)
// ↪ * (sorted eigenvectors)
let W = S_W_inv_sqrt.dot(&sorted_eigvecs);
```

```
    println!("Projection matrix W (LDA transformation):\n{:#.4?}",
    ↪   W);
}
```

Chapter 58

Regression Trees and Model Splitting Algorithms

Mathematical Formulation of Regression Trees

Regression trees are a class of nonparametric models designed for the prediction of continuous outcomes by partitioning the feature space into disjoint regions. Consider a dataset denoted by

$$D = \{(x_i, y_i)\}_{i=1}^{N},$$

where each observation $x_i \in \mathbb{R}^d$ and the corresponding response $y_i \in \mathbb{R}$. The regression tree model approximates the response variable by assuming a piecewise constant function. In particular, the feature space is segmented into a collection of mutually exclusive regions

$$R_1, R_2, \ldots, R_M,$$

such that the prediction for an observation falling in region R_m is given by

$$\hat{y} = c_m,$$

with

$$c_m = \frac{1}{|R_m|} \sum_{x_i \in R_m} y_i.$$

The optimal partition is determined by minimizing the total sum of squared residuals across all regions, expressed as

$$\sum_{m=1}^{M} \sum_{x_i \in R_m} (y_i - c_m)^2.$$

This formulation establishes the foundation for the decision splitting methods that recursively partition the data space.

Decision Splitting Criteria and Impurity Measures

The core mechanism underlying regression trees is the evaluation of candidate splits based on their efficacy in reducing heterogeneity in the response variable. For any given node representing a subset of data R, a candidate split divides it into two disjoint subregions, R_L and R_R, based on a threshold value applied to one of the predictors. The effectiveness of the split is often quantified by the residual sum of squares (RSS) on each resulting subset. In formal terms, for a split that partitions region R into R_L and R_R, the impurity measure is defined as

$$Q(R) = \sum_{x_i \in R_L} (y_i - \bar{y}_L)^2 + \sum_{x_i \in R_R} (y_i - \bar{y}_R)^2,$$

where the mean responses are

$$\bar{y}_L = \frac{1}{|R_L|} \sum_{x_i \in R_L} y_i \quad \text{and} \quad \bar{y}_R = \frac{1}{|R_R|} \sum_{x_i \in R_R} y_i.$$

An alternative perspective is to consider the variance within a node, with the impurity measured as

$$\text{Var}(R) = \frac{1}{|R|} \sum_{x_i \in R} (y_i - \bar{y})^2,$$

where $\bar{y}$ denotes the average of y over region R. The reduction in impurity achieved by a candidate split is then computed as

$$\Delta Q = \text{Var}(R) - \left(\frac{|R_L|}{|R|} \text{Var}(R_L) + \frac{|R_R|}{|R|} \text{Var}(R_R) \right).$$

The optimal split is selected by exhaustively evaluating candidate splits over all features and threshold values, and choosing the one that maximizes the reduction in impurity.

Recursive Partitioning and Tree Construction

The construction of a regression tree proceeds by recursive partitioning of the dataset. Initially, the entire dataset forms the root node. At each internal node, the algorithm evaluates a set of candidate splits across all features. A candidate split is defined by an inequality of the form

$$x_j \leq t,$$

in which x_j is one of the predictors and t is a threshold value. The split that results in the largest decrease in the credible impurity measure is selected, yielding two child nodes. This recursive process is applied to each child node, leading to a hierarchical tree structure that reflects successive divisions of the feature space.

The recursion is halted according to predefined stopping criteria, such as a minimum number of observations per node or a maximum allowable tree depth. At each terminal (leaf) node, the predicted value is computed as the average of the responses y_i of the observations contained in that node. The recursive algorithm thus partitions the feature space into regions with relatively homogeneous responses, enabling nuanced predictions via a collection of locally optimal approximations.

Statistical Considerations and Model Complexity

The application of regression tree algorithms entails careful statistical considerations to mitigate overfitting and to control model complexity. The decision splitting criterion, as quantified by reduction in residual sum of squares, balances the fidelity of the fitted model with its capacity to generalize. A deeper tree, while potentially capturing subtle patterns in the training data, may also overfit by modeling noise rather than underlying signal. To address these concerns, constraints such as minimum leaf size and maximum depth inherently act as regularization mechanisms.

Further complexity arises from the inherent variability of the recursive partitioning process. The sensitivity of split selections to fluctuations in the input data may result in different tree structures. As a result, statistical analyses of tree-based methods often focus on the asymptotic properties of split decisions. For instance, under repeated sampling, the consistency and unbiasedness of tree estimators are significant facets of theoretical inquiry. The interplay between high-dimensional feature spaces and the criteria for splitting also warrants rigorous consideration, particularly with respect to the risk of selecting spurious splits in the presence of correlated predictors.

The recursive nature of tree construction implies that errors made at higher levels can propagate through subsequent splits. Thus, the careful calibration of splitting criteria is crucial, as it provides a balance between local fit and global model stability. The precise quantitative evaluation of impurity reduction at each node forms the backbone of the regression tree algorithm, ensuring that the final model reflects both statistical robustness and computational efficiency.

Rust Code Snippet

```
//! This Rust code snippet implements the core aspects of regression
↪   trees,
//! exemplifying the mathematical formulation and decision splitting
↪   criteria
//! outlined in the chapter "Regression Trees and Model Splitting
↪   Algorithms".
//!
//! Mathematical Formulation (refer to chapter):
//!
//! 1. Prediction in a region R_m is given by:
//!    c_m = (1/|R_m|) * (y_i) for x_i  R_m
//!
//! 2. Residual Sum of Squares (RSS) for a node R is:
//!    RSS(R) = (y_i - mean_R)², where mean_R = (1/|R|)* y_i
//!
//! 3. Impurity reduction for a split dividing R into R_L and R_R
↪   is:
//!    Q = Var(R) - (|R_L|/|R| * Var(R_L) + |R_R|/|R| * Var(R_R))
//!
//! The following code defines data structures for data points and
↪   tree nodes,
//! along with functions to compute the RSS, evaluate candidate
↪   splits, and construct
//! the regression tree recursively.

use std::fmt;

// Define a struct for each data point, with a vector of features
↪   and a target value.
#[derive(Debug, Clone)]
```

```rust
struct DataPoint {
    features: Vec<f64>,
    target: f64,
}

// Define the tree structure: internal nodes for splits and leaf
↪   nodes for predictions.
#[derive(Debug)]
enum TreeNode {
    Leaf {
        // At a leaf, the prediction is simply the average (mean) of
        ↪   the target values,
        // i.e., c_m = (1/|R_m|) * y_i
        prediction: f64,
    },
    Internal {
        // The split is defined by a feature index and a threshold
        ↪   value.
        split_feature: usize,
        threshold: f64,
        // Left and right child nodes.
        left: Box<TreeNode>,
        right: Box<TreeNode>,
    },
}

// Implement Display trait for pretty printing the tree structure.
impl fmt::Display for TreeNode {
    fn fmt(&self, f: &mut fmt::Formatter<'_>) -> fmt::Result {
        match self {
            TreeNode::Leaf { prediction } => write!(f,
            ↪   "Leaf(prediction: {:.3})", prediction),
            TreeNode::Internal { split_feature, threshold, left,
            ↪   right } => {
                write!(f, "Internal(split_feature: {}, threshold:
                ↪   {:.3}, left: {}, right: {})",
                    split_feature, threshold, left, right)
            }
        }
    }
}

// Compute the mean of the target values in a dataset.
// This corresponds to the constant prediction value c_m in region
↪   R_m.
fn mean(data: &[DataPoint]) -> f64 {
    data.iter().map(|d| d.target).sum::<f64>() / data.len() as f64
}

// Compute the Residual Sum of Squares (RSS) for the given dataset.
// Formula: RSS =  (y_i - mean)²
fn rss(data: &[DataPoint]) -> f64 {
    let avg = mean(data);
```

369

```
    data.iter().map(|d| (d.target - avg).powi(2)).sum()
}

// Partition the dataset based on a given feature index and
↪    threshold.
// Points with feature value <= threshold go to the left node,
↪    others to the right.
fn partition(data: &[DataPoint], feature_idx: usize, threshold: f64)
↪    -> (Vec<DataPoint>, Vec<DataPoint>) {
    let mut left = Vec::new();
    let mut right = Vec::new();
    for point in data {
        if point.features[feature_idx] <= threshold {
            left.push(point.clone());
        } else {
            right.push(point.clone());
        }
    }
    (left, right)
}


// Evaluate candidate splits over all features and thresholds to
↪    find the best split,
// based on the reduction of RSS (impurity measure).
// Returns Option with tuple: (best_feature, best_threshold,
↪    best_rss, left_subset, right_subset)
fn best_split(data: &[DataPoint], min_samples: usize) ->
↪    Option<(usize, f64, f64, Vec<DataPoint>, Vec<DataPoint>)> {
    let n_features = data[0].features.len();
    // Base impurity (RSS) for the current node
    let base_rss = rss(data);
    let mut best_feature = 0;
    let mut best_threshold = 0.0;
    let mut best_rss = std::f64::INFINITY;
    let mut best_left = Vec::new();
    let mut best_right = Vec::new();

    // Iterate over every feature
    for feature_idx in 0..n_features {
        // To determine candidate thresholds, compute all unique
        ↪    values for the feature.
        let mut feature_values: Vec<f64> = data.iter().map(|d|
        ↪    d.features[feature_idx]).collect();
        feature_values.sort_by(|a, b| a.partial_cmp(b).unwrap());
        feature_values.dedup();

        // Evaluate each candidate threshold
        for &threshold in &feature_values {
            let (left, right) = partition(data, feature_idx,
            ↪    threshold);

            // Enforce minimum sample requirement in each node
```

```
        if left.len() < min_samples || right.len() < min_samples
        ↪  {
            continue;
        }

        // Compute RSS for the split:
        // RSS_split = RSS(left) + RSS(right)
        let current_rss = rss(&left) + rss(&right);
        // A better split minimizes the RSS; i.e., maximizes
        ↪  impurity reduction:
        // Q = RSS(parent) - RSS_split
        if current_rss < best_rss {
            best_rss = current_rss;
            best_feature = feature_idx;
            best_threshold = threshold;
            best_left = left;
            best_right = right;
        }
    }
}
// If a better split is found (i.e., impurity reduction), return
↪  it.
if best_rss < base_rss {
    Some((best_feature, best_threshold, best_rss, best_left,
    ↪  best_right))
} else {
    None
}
}

// Recursively construct the regression tree.
// Stopping criteria include maximum depth and minimum number of
↪  samples per node.
fn build_tree(data: &[DataPoint], max_depth: usize, min_samples:
↪  usize) -> TreeNode {
    // If maximum depth is reached or insufficient data, create a
    ↪  leaf node with prediction.
    if max_depth == 0 || data.len() <= min_samples {
        return TreeNode::Leaf {
            prediction: mean(data),
        };
    }

    // Attempt to find the best split in the current region.
    if let Some((feature, threshold, _split_rss, left, right)) =
    ↪  best_split(data, min_samples) {
        // Create internal node with the optimal split and
        ↪  recursively build child subtrees.
        return TreeNode::Internal {
            split_feature: feature,
            threshold,
            left: Box::new(build_tree(&left, max_depth - 1,
            ↪  min_samples)),
```

```
                right: Box::new(build_tree(&right, max_depth - 1,
                ↪  min_samples)),
            };
        }
        // If no beneficial split is found, create a leaf node.
        TreeNode::Leaf {
            prediction: mean(data),
        }
    }

    // Predict the target value for a new observation given the
    ↪  constructed regression tree.
    fn predict(tree: &TreeNode, features: &Vec<f64>) -> f64 {
        match tree {
            TreeNode::Leaf { prediction } => *prediction,
            TreeNode::Internal { split_feature, threshold, left, right }
            ↪  => {
                if features[*split_feature] <= *threshold {
                    predict(left, features)
                } else {
                    predict(right, features)
                }
            }
        }
    }

    fn main() {
        // Example dataset: each DataPoint contains two predictor values
        ↪  and a continuous target.
        let data = vec![
            DataPoint { features: vec![2.5, 3.0], target: 10.0 },
            DataPoint { features: vec![1.0, 2.0], target: 8.0 },
            DataPoint { features: vec![3.5, 4.0], target: 12.0 },
            DataPoint { features: vec![3.0, 3.5], target: 11.0 },
            DataPoint { features: vec![2.0, 2.5], target: 9.0 },
            DataPoint { features: vec![5.0, 6.0], target: 15.0 },
        ];

        // Hyperparameters: maximum depth of the tree and minimum
        ↪  samples per node.
        let max_depth = 3;
        let min_samples = 2;

        // Build the regression tree using recursive partitioning.
        let tree = build_tree(&data, max_depth, min_samples);

        println!("Constructed Regression Tree:\n{}", tree);

        // Predict the target value for a new observation.
        let new_point = vec![3.0, 3.0];
        let prediction = predict(&tree, &new_point);
        println!("Prediction for point {:?} is {:.3}", new_point,
        ↪  prediction);
```

}

Chapter 59

Random Forest Implementation for Classification Tasks

Mathematical Foundations

A random forest classifier is formulated on the basis of an ensemble of decision trees that operate over a dataset

$$D = \{(x_i, y_i)\}_{i=1}^{N},$$

where each feature vector $x_i \in \mathbb{R}^d$ is associated with a class label $y_i \in \{1, 2, \ldots, K\}$. In this framework, the classifier is composed of a collection of B individual trees, denoted as $\{h_b(x)\}_{b=1}^{B}$. Each tree is constructed from a bootstrap sample of D and produces a class prediction for a given input x. The aggregated prediction is obtained through a majority voting scheme, which mathematically is represented as

$$\hat{y}(x) = \underset{c \in \{1, \ldots, K\}}{\arg\max} \sum_{b=1}^{B} \mathbf{1}\{h_b(x) = c\},$$

where $\mathbf{1}\{\cdot\}$ denotes the indicator function that evaluates to 1 when its argument is true and to 0 otherwise. This ensemble averaging mechanism integrates the strengths of multiple regression trees, each of which offers a weak classification tendency, thereby reducing variance and yielding improved predictive performance.

Ensemble Construction and Decision Tree Aggregation

The construction of the ensemble in a random forest leverages a dual randomization strategy. Initially, bootstrap sampling is employed to generate diverse training subsets from the original dataset. For each tree in the forest, a random sample with replacement is drawn from D, ensuring that each tree is trained on a variant of the data. Secondly, at each internal node during tree construction, a random subset of the available features is considered when determining the optimal split. This selective approach reduces the correlation among trees by limiting the dominance of highly predictive features, leading to an ensemble where individual decision structures capture different aspects of the feature space.

Within each regression tree, the recursive partitioning process is executed by iteratively segmenting the feature space. At every node, candidate splits are evaluated according to a measure of impurity reduction, commonly drawing on indicators such as the Gini index or cross-entropy, adapted for classification contexts. The impurity reduction resulting from a candidate split that partitions a region R into subregions R_L and R_R is quantified by

$$\Delta Q = Q(R) - \left(\frac{|R_L|}{|R|} Q(R_L) + \frac{|R_R|}{|R|} Q(R_R) \right),$$

where $Q(\cdot)$ denotes the chosen impurity measure. The optimal split is identified by maximizing ΔQ, and the tree is grown until a stopping criterion—such as a minimum number of observations per node or a predetermined maximum depth—is met.

Aggregation Techniques and Voting Mechanisms

Within the random forest framework, the integration of predictions from individual trees is achieved through an aggregation technique based on majority voting. Each regression tree renders a class prediction for an input instance x, and the final ensemble decision is arrived at by selecting the class that occurs with the highest frequency among all tree predictions. This process is succinctly captured by the expression

$$\hat{y}(x) = \text{mode} \left\{ h_b(x) \mid b = 1, 2, \ldots, B \right\}.$$

The strength of this aggregation technique lies in its capacity to diminish the impact of anomalous or incorrect predictions from individual trees. The averaging effect imparted by the ensemble leads to a robust classifier that exhibits reduced variance compared to any constituent tree, while maintaining a high degree of sensitivity to the intrinsic patterns within the data.

Statistical Properties and Performance Considerations

The statistical characteristics of a random forest classifier are deeply rooted in the bias-variance trade-off inherent to ensemble methods. Individual regression trees, by virtue of their highly adaptive nature, tend to have low bias; however, they also possess high variance due to their sensitivity to fluctuations in the training data. The ensemble mechanism, by aggregating predictions from multiple trees, effectively averages out these variances, thus yielding a classifier with improved stability and predictive accuracy.

The performance of the random forest is influenced by several factors, including the number of trees B, the size of the bootstrap samples, and the degree of randomness incorporated in the feature selection at each split. Increasing B generally leads to a reduction in variance, though empirical considerations suggest that the marginal improvement diminishes beyond a certain ensemble size. The calibration of additional hyperparameters—such as the maximum depth of each tree and the minimum number of observations per node—plays a pivotal role in controlling the complexity of individual trees and, by extension, that of the entire forest.

Furthermore, considerations of consistency and asymptotic behavior are integral to the statistical evaluation of the model. Under suitable conditions, as the number of training instances N and the ensemble size B grow, the aggregated classifier converges towards the true decision boundary. This property underscores the theoretical robustness of the random forest methodology and its capacity to effectively classify high-dimensional data with complex decision surfaces.

Characterization of Decision Structures within the Forest

Each regression tree within the forest embodies a decision structure that is defined by a hierarchy of partitions across the feature space. The intricacies of this structure are revealed through the recursive process of splitting, which fosters the formation of localized regions where the class labels exhibit high homogeneity. The segmentation of the feature space is intrinsically linked to the selection of splitting criteria that prioritize substantial impurity reduction. Although the trees are individually susceptible to variability arising from the randomness of bootstrap samples and feature subsets, the ensemble collectively encapsulates a diverse array of decision structures.

The heterogeneity among the trees contributes to the overall interpretability of the classifier by enabling the assessment of feature importance and the identification of key decision boundaries. While the aggregated output of the random forest is derived from a majority voting mechanism, the underlying structure of each tree provides valuable insights into the contributions of specific features and the interaction effects captured during the recursive partitioning process. This detailed characterization of decision structures enhances the understanding of how individual splits and subsequent node formations coalesce into a powerful ensemble capable of delineating complex class boundaries.

Rust Code Snippet

```rust
use rand::prelude::*;
use rand::seq::SliceRandom;
use std::collections::HashMap;

/// A data point representing a feature vector and its corresponding
/// ↪ class label.
#[derive(Debug, Clone)]
struct DataPoint {
    features: Vec<f64>,
    label: usize,
}

/// The decision tree node is either a Leaf (with a class label)
/// or an Internal node that splits on a feature with a given
/// ↪ threshold.
#[derive(Debug, Clone)]
enum DecisionNode {
```

```rust
    Leaf {
        label: usize,
    },
    Internal {
        feature_index: usize,
        threshold: f64,
        left: Box<DecisionNode>,
        right: Box<DecisionNode>,
    },
}

impl DecisionNode {
    /// Recursively predict the class label for the given feature
    ↪ vector.
    fn predict(&self, features: &Vec<f64>) -> usize {
        match self {
            DecisionNode::Leaf { label } => *label,
            DecisionNode::Internal { feature_index, threshold, left,
            ↪ right } => {
                if features[*feature_index] < *threshold {
                    left.predict(features)
                } else {
                    right.predict(features)
                }
            }
        }
    }
}

/// A DecisionTree encapsulates the root node of the tree.
#[derive(Debug, Clone)]
struct DecisionTree {
    root: DecisionNode,
}

impl DecisionTree {
    /// Train a decision tree recursively.
    /// It uses a splitting criterion based on Gini impurity
    ↪ reduction.
    /// The impurity reduction is computed as:
    /// Q = Q(R) - ( |R_L|/|R| * Q(R_L) + |R_R|/|R| * Q(R_R) )
    fn train(data: &[DataPoint], min_samples: usize, max_depth:
    ↪ usize, depth: usize) -> DecisionNode {
        // If the number of samples is less than or equal to
        ↪ min_samples
        // or maximum depth is reached, return a leaf node.
        if data.len() <= min_samples || depth >= max_depth {
            return DecisionTree::create_leaf(data);
        }

        let num_features = data[0].features.len();
        let mut best_gain = 0.0;
        let mut best_feature = None;
```

378

```rust
let mut best_threshold = 0.0;
let mut best_left: Vec<DataPoint> = Vec::new();
let mut best_right: Vec<DataPoint> = Vec::new();

// Randomly select a subset of features (e.g.,
↪    sqrt(num_features))
let num_rand_features = ((num_features as
↪    f64).sqrt().ceil()) as usize;
let mut feature_indices: Vec<usize> =
↪    (0..num_features).collect();
feature_indices.shuffle(&mut thread_rng());
let feature_indices = &feature_indices[..num_rand_features];

// Evaluate candidate splits for each randomly selected
↪    feature.
for &feature_index in feature_indices {
    // Sort data based on the current feature.
    let mut sorted_data = data.to_vec();
    sorted_data.sort_by(|a, b| {
        a.features[feature_index]
            .partial_cmp(&b.features[feature_index])
            .unwrap()
    });
    // Try candidate thresholds between consecutive data
    ↪    points.
    for i in 1..sorted_data.len() {
        let threshold = (sorted_data[i -
        ↪    1].features[feature_index]
            + sorted_data[i].features[feature_index])
            / 2.0;
        // Partition the data into left and right splits.
        let (left, right): (Vec<DataPoint>, Vec<DataPoint>)
        ↪    = sorted_data
            .iter()
            .cloned()
            .partition(|point| point.features[feature_index]
            ↪    < threshold);

        // Skip splits that fail to divide the data.
        if left.is_empty() || right.is_empty() {
            continue;
        }

        // Calculate the impurity reduction for this split.
        let gain = impurity_reduction(data, &left, &right);
        if gain > best_gain {
            best_gain = gain;
            best_feature = Some(feature_index);
            best_threshold = threshold;
            best_left = left;
            best_right = right;
        }
    }
}
```

```rust
    }

    // If no split yields a gain, create a leaf node.
    if best_gain == 0.0 || best_feature.is_none() {
        return DecisionTree::create_leaf(data);
    }

    // Recursively build left and right subtrees.
    DecisionNode::Internal {
        feature_index: best_feature.unwrap(),
        threshold: best_threshold,
        left: Box::new(DecisionTree::train(&best_left,
        ↪  min_samples, max_depth, depth + 1)),
        right: Box::new(DecisionTree::train(&best_right,
        ↪  min_samples, max_depth, depth + 1)),
    }
}

/// Creates a leaf node using the majority class label from the
↪  data.
fn create_leaf(data: &[DataPoint]) -> DecisionNode {
    let mut label_counts: HashMap<usize, usize> =
    ↪  HashMap::new();
    for point in data {
        *label_counts.entry(point.label).or_insert(0) += 1;
    }
    let majority_label = label_counts
        .into_iter()
        .max_by_key(|&(_label, count)| count)
        .map(|(label, _)| label)
        .unwrap_or(0);
    DecisionNode::Leaf { label: majority_label }
}

/// Predict the label for a given feature vector using the
↪  trained tree.
pub fn predict(&self, features: &Vec<f64>) -> usize {
    self.root.predict(features)
}
}

/// Compute the Gini impurity for a dataset.
/// Gini impurity is defined as: 1 -  (p_i)², where p_i is the
↪  probability of class i.
fn gini_impurity(data: &[DataPoint]) -> f64 {
    let mut counts: HashMap<usize, usize> = HashMap::new();
    for point in data {
        *counts.entry(point.label).or_insert(0) += 1;
    }
    let n = data.len() as f64;
    let mut impurity = 1.0;
    for &count in counts.values() {
        let prob = count as f64 / n;
```

```
        impurity -= prob * prob;
    }
    impurity
}

/// Calculate the impurity reduction from a candidate split.
/// This implements the formula:
/// Q = Q(R) - ( (|R_L|/|R| * Q(R_L)) + (|R_R|/|R| * Q(R_R)) )
fn impurity_reduction(parent: &[DataPoint], left: &[DataPoint],
↪    right: &[DataPoint]) -> f64 {
    let parent_impurity = gini_impurity(parent);
    let left_impurity = gini_impurity(left);
    let right_impurity = gini_impurity(right);
    let p_left = left.len() as f64 / parent.len() as f64;
    let p_right = right.len() as f64 / parent.len() as f64;
    parent_impurity - (p_left * left_impurity + p_right *
↪    right_impurity)
}

/// A RandomForest is composed of multiple decision trees.
/// Each tree is trained on a bootstrap sample of the data.
#[derive(Debug)]
struct RandomForest {
    trees: Vec<DecisionTree>,
}

impl RandomForest {
    /// Train a random forest classifier.
    /// For each tree, bootstrap sampling and feature subsetting are
    ↪    applied.
    pub fn train(
        data: &[DataPoint],
        num_trees: usize,
        min_samples: usize,
        max_depth: usize,
    ) -> RandomForest {
        let mut trees = Vec::new();
        let mut rng = thread_rng();
        for _ in 0..num_trees {
            // Bootstrap sampling: sample with replacement from the
            ↪    dataset.
            let bootstrap: Vec<DataPoint> = (0..data.len())
                .map(|_| data.choose(&mut rng).unwrap().clone())
                .collect();
            let root = DecisionTree::train(&bootstrap, min_samples,
            ↪    max_depth, 0);
            trees.push(DecisionTree { root });
        }
        RandomForest { trees }
    }

    /// Aggregated prediction using majority voting over individual
    ↪    tree predictions.
```

```
/// This aligns with the ensemble formula:
/// ŷ(x) = mode{ h_b(x) | b = 1,2,...,B }
pub fn predict(&self, features: &Vec<f64>) -> usize {
    let mut votes: HashMap<usize, usize> = HashMap::new();
    for tree in &self.trees {
        let pred = tree.predict(features);
        *votes.entry(pred).or_insert(0) += 1;
    }
    votes
        .into_iter()
        .max_by_key(|&(_label, count)| count)
        .map(|(label, _)| label)
        .unwrap_or(0)
    }
}

fn main() {
    // Create a small synthetic dataset for demonstration.
    let data = vec![
        DataPoint {
            features: vec![2.5, 1.5],
            label: 0,
        },
        DataPoint {
            features: vec![3.0, 1.0],
            label: 0,
        },
        DataPoint {
            features: vec![2.0, 1.0],
            label: 0,
        },
        DataPoint {
            features: vec![7.5, 6.5],
            label: 1,
        },
        DataPoint {
            features: vec![8.0, 7.0],
            label: 1,
        },
        DataPoint {
            features: vec![7.0, 6.0],
            label: 1,
        },
    ];

    // Hyperparameters for training the random forest.
    let num_trees = 5;
    let min_samples = 2;
    let max_depth = 3;

    // Train the Random Forest classifier.
    let forest = RandomForest::train(&data, num_trees, min_samples,
    ↪  max_depth);
```

```rust
    // Example test instance.
    let test_instance = vec![3.0, 1.2];
    let prediction = forest.predict(&test_instance);
    println!(
        "Predicted label for test instance {:?} is: {}",
        test_instance, prediction
    );
}
```

Chapter 60

Gradient Boosting Machines for Predictive Modeling

Mathematical Framework of Gradient Boosting

Consider a training dataset $D = \{(x_i, y_i)\}_{i=1}^{N}$, where each $x_i \in \mathbb{R}^d$ represents a feature vector and each corresponding label y_i is derived from the target space. The gradient boosting framework constructs an additive model of the form

$$F_M(x) = F_0(x) + \nu \sum_{m=1}^{M} h_m(x),$$

where $F_0(x)$ is the initial prediction, $h_m(x)$ denotes a weak learner applied at the mth iteration, and ν is a shrinkage parameter that controls the contribution of each successive learner. The optimization process is founded on minimizing an objective function defined as

$$\mathcal{L}(F) = \sum_{i=1}^{N} L\left(y_i, F(x_i)\right) + \sum_{m=1}^{M} \Omega\left(h_m\right),$$

where $L\left(y_i, F(x_i)\right)$ represents the loss incurred by the model prediction for the ith observation and $\Omega\left(h_m\right)$ is a regularization term that penalizes the complexity of the weak learner. The model is iteratively refined using functional gradient descent, with each step designed to compensate for the discrepancies between the current model output and the true target values.

Residual Fitting and Loss Minimization

At the core of the gradient boosting paradigm lies the sequential fitting of residuals, which are derived from the negative gradient of the loss function with respect to the model prediction. Given the current model $F_{m-1}(x)$, the negative gradient for the ith data point is computed as

$$r_i^{(m)} = - \left. \frac{\partial L\left(y_i, F(x_i)\right)}{\partial F(x_i)} \right|_{F=F_{m-1}}.$$

This quantity encapsulates the direction and magnitude of the requisite adjustments to the model output. Each weak learner $h_m(x)$ is subsequently trained to approximate this gradient information by minimizing a surrogate loss function. In the context of regression tasks, a common practice is to adopt the squared error loss, whereas classification tasks may require alternative loss functions such as the logistic loss. In each iteration, the optimization problem can be expressed as finding

$$h_m = \mathrm{argmin}_h \sum_{i=1}^{N} \left(r_i^{(m)} - h(x_i) \right)^2 + \Omega\left(h\right),$$

thereby ensuring that the learner closely mirrors the gradient of the loss while maintaining a controlled complexity through regularization.

Sequential Optimization and Regularization

The iterative update process intrinsic to gradient boosting is characterized by stagewise optimization. Each update modifies the current model according to the rule

$$F_m(x) = F_{m-1}(x) + \nu h_m(x),$$

where the learning rate ν serves to scale the corrective contribution of the weak learner. Such a formulation not only facilitates a gradual improvement in model accuracy but also acts as a regularization mechanism by limiting the magnitude of each update. The choice of ν is critical; a small value induces a more conservative update, thereby potentially requiring a larger number of iterations to achieve convergence, while a larger value may expedite convergence at the risk of overfitting.

Regularization is further enforced by incorporating complexity penalties into the objective function. The term $\Omega(h)$ quantifies the complexity of the weak learner, penalizing overly flexible models that may adapt excessively to noise within the training data. Additional regularization strategies, such as controlling the depth or number of leaves in tree-based weak learners, are commonly applied to maintain a balance between bias and variance. The combined effect of the learning rate and complexity penalties ensures that the ensemble of weak learners remains robust and generalizes well to unseen data.

Integration of Weak Learners via Sequential Aggregation

The final predictive model is obtained through the coherent integration of multiple weak learners, each contributing a fine-grained corrective adjustment. In a typical gradient boosting framework, the ensemble is represented by

$$F_M(x) = F_0(x) + \nu \sum_{m=1}^{M} h_m(x),$$

where each term $h_m(x)$ is a weak learner that is optimized sequentially to account for residual errors from the preceding iterations. The mechanism of sequential aggregation is predicated on the insight that a series of modest and targeted improvements can collectively yield a model with high predictive precision.

The heterogeneous nature of the weak learners results from the diverse aspects of the feature space that are emphasized during different iterations. This diversity is further enhanced by stochastic elements, such as subsampling of the training data or the random selection of candidate features, which serve to decorrelate the learners and enhance the overall stability of the ensemble. The aggregation process, therefore, embodies a robust synthesis of individual decision boundaries, each of which is calibrated to mitigate the errors not addressed by its predecessors. The cumulative structure of the ensemble thus emerges as a powerful predictive model, combining the strengths of iterative residual fitting with regularization strategies to effectively model complex and nonlinear relationships inherent in the data.

Rust Code Snippet

```
/// A simplified implementation of Gradient Boosting for regression
↪   with squared error loss.
/// The model follows the formulation:
///     F_M(x) = F_0(x) +  *  h(x)
/// where F(x) is initialized as the mean of targets, and each weak
↪   learner h(x)
/// is a constant fitted to the residuals r(m) = y - F(x).
///
/// In this example, we use a constant learner that approximates the
↪   residuals via their mean.
fn main() {
    // Sample dataset: feature vector 'x' (not used in constant
    ↪   prediction) and labels 'y'
    let x: Vec<f64> = vec![1.0, 2.0, 3.0, 4.0, 5.0];
    let y: Vec<f64> = vec![3.2, 4.8, 7.1, 9.0, 10.5];

    // Hyperparameters
    let num_iterations: usize = 10; // Number of boosting rounds (M)
    let learning_rate: f64 = 0.1;       // Shrinkage parameter ()

    // Initialize F(x) as the mean of target values y
    let f0: f64 = mean(&y);
    // Predictions vector initialized with F(x) for each data point
    let mut predictions: Vec<f64> = vec![f0; y.len()];

    // To store the weak learner parameter (constant value) at each
    ↪   iteration
    let mut weak_learners: Vec<f64> = Vec::new();

    println!("Initial Prediction (F): {:.4}", f0);
    println!("Starting training with {} iterations...\n",
    ↪   num_iterations);

    // Iterative boosting process: each iteration fits the residuals
    ↪   and updates predictions
    for m in 0..num_iterations {
        // Compute residuals: r^(m) = y - F(x)
        let residuals: Vec<f64> = y.iter()
                            .zip(predictions.iter())
                            .map(|(&yi, &fi)| yi - fi)
```

387

```rust
        .collect();

    // Fit weak learner h(x) by minimizing  (r^(m) - h(x))².
    // For a constant learner, the optimal h is simply the mean
    //    of the residuals.
    let h_m: f64 = mean(&residuals);
    weak_learners.push(h_m);

    // Update the model predictions:
    // F(x) = F(x) +  · h(x)
    for pred in predictions.iter_mut() {
        *pred += learning_rate * h_m;
    }

    // Optionally, compute the mean squared error loss to
    //    monitor convergence.
    let loss = mean_squared_error(&y, &predictions);
    println!("Iteration {:02}: h = {:.4}, Loss = {:.4}", m + 1,
    //    h_m, loss);
    }

    println!("\nFinal Predictions: {:?}", predictions);
    println!("Weak Learners (constants): {:?}", weak_learners);
}

/// Computes the mean of a slice of f64 numbers.
fn mean(values: &Vec<f64>) -> f64 {
    let sum: f64 = values.iter().sum();
    sum / (values.len() as f64)
}

/// Computes the Mean Squared Error between the true labels and
///    predictions.
fn mean_squared_error(y_true: &Vec<f64>, y_pred: &Vec<f64>) -> f64 {
    let error_sum: f64 = y_true.iter()
                            .zip(y_pred.iter())
                            .map(|(&yt, &yp)| (yt - yp).powi(2))
                            .sum();
    error_sum / (y_true.len() as f64)
}
```

Chapter 61

Collaborative Filtering and Recommendation Algorithms

Mathematical Foundations of Collaborative Filtering

Collaborative filtering is a methodology that leverages historical user interactions to infer latent preferences and generate personalized recommendations. Let $R \in \mathbb{R}^{m \times n}$ denote the user-item interaction matrix, where each entry r_{ij} represents the explicit or implicit feedback elicited from user i regarding item j. The inherent sparsity of R mandates that the majority of its entries remain unobserved, thereby necessitating the inference of missing values through latent factor models. The fundamental premise is that both users and items can be embedded into a low-dimensional latent space of dimension k, with $k \ll \min(m, n)$, such that the predicted interaction is modeled as

$$\hat{r}_{ij} \approx \mathbf{u}_i^{\top} \mathbf{v}_j,$$

where $\mathbf{u}_i \in \mathbb{R}^k$ represents the latent profile of user i, and $\mathbf{v}_j \in \mathbb{R}^k$ encapsulates the latent attributes of item j. This inner product formulation facilitates a parsimonious representation of the complex structure underlying user-item interactions.

User-Item Interaction Representation

The representation of user-item interactions is central to the efficacy of recommendation systems. In scenarios where explicit feedback is available, the entries of the matrix R capture numerical ratings provided by users; in contrast, implicit feedback systems record binary or count-based indicators of engagement, such as clicks or purchase events. The sparsity of R challenges direct modeling approaches, thereby motivating the projection of users and items into a unified latent space. By doing so, the system abstracts from the high-dimensional observed data to extract salient features that govern interaction patterns. This latent space transformation not only addresses the data sparsity problem but also enhances the system's ability to generalize to unobserved user-item pairs.

Matrix Factorization Techniques

Matrix factorization stands as a pivotal technique within collaborative filtering, enabling the discovery of latent factors that dictate user preferences and item characteristics. This approach seeks to approximate the interaction matrix R by factoring it into two lower-dimensional matrices, $U \in \mathbb{R}^{m \times k}$ and $V \in \mathbb{R}^{n \times k}$, such that

$$R \approx UV^{\top}.$$

In this formulation, the predictive rating for user i and item j is given by the dot product

$$\hat{r}_{ij} = \mathbf{u}_i^{\top} \mathbf{v}_j.$$

The estimation process involves minimizing the discrepancy between the observed ratings and the predictions by solving an optimization problem of the form

$$\min_{U,V} \sum_{(i,j) \in \mathcal{K}} \left(r_{ij} - \mathbf{u}_i^{\top} \mathbf{v}_j \right)^2 + \lambda \left(\|U\|_F^2 + \|V\|_F^2 \right),$$

where $\mathcal{K}$ denotes the set of index pairs corresponding to the observed entries in R, λ is a regularization parameter, and $\|\cdot\|_F$ represents the Frobenius norm. This framework not only aims to reduce the reconstruction error but also imposes a complexity penalty on the latent factors, thereby promoting generalizability.

Optimization and Regularization in Matrix Factorization

The estimation of latent factor matrices U and V is achieved through iterative optimization strategies that seek to minimize the prescribed objective function. Stochastic gradient descent (SGD) is a commonly adopted approach, wherein the latent factor vectors are updated by iteratively computing the gradients of the loss function with respect to each parameter. For an observed entry (i, j), the error is defined as

$$e_{ij} = r_{ij} - \mathbf{u}_i^\top \mathbf{v}_j,$$

and the subsequent updates for the latent factors are given by

$$\mathbf{u}_i \leftarrow \mathbf{u}_i + \eta \left(e_{ij} \mathbf{v}_j - \lambda \mathbf{u}_i \right),$$

$$\mathbf{v}_j \leftarrow \mathbf{v}_j + \eta \left(e_{ij} \mathbf{u}_i - \lambda \mathbf{v}_j \right),$$

where η represents the learning rate. An alternative method, alternating least squares (ALS), decomposes the optimization task into two subproblems, each solvable in closed form by alternately fixing one of the latent factor matrices while optimizing the other. The incorporation of regularization terms proportional to λ ensures that the model avoids overfitting by constraining the magnitude of the latent vectors, thereby balancing model fidelity with robustness against noise inherent in the sparse observations.

Evaluation Metrics and Mechanisms for Personalized Recommendations

Upon estimating the latent representations through matrix factorization, personalized recommendations are generated by predicting the preference of a user for an item via the computed inner product $\mathbf{u}_i^\top \mathbf{v}_j$. The quality of these predictions is evaluated using error metrics such as mean squared error (MSE) and root mean squared error (RMSE), which quantify the average deviation between the observed ratings and the predicted values. In contexts where the rank order of recommendations is paramount, ranking-based evaluation criteria—such as precision at k, recall, and normalized discounted cumulative gain (NDCG)—are employed to assess the efficacy of the recommendation rankings. The latent factor model thereby facilitates the identification of items most likely to align with the inferred preferences of individual users, culminating in a personalized recommendation mechanism that translates historical interaction data into actionable predictive insights.

Rust Code Snippet

```rust
use rand::Rng;
use std::f64;

// Define a structure for observed ratings
#[derive(Debug)]
struct Rating {
    user: usize,
    item: usize,
    rating: f64,
}

// MatrixFactorization encapsulates the latent factor model for
// ↪ collaborative filtering.
// It approximates the user-item interaction matrix R   U * V, where
// U  ^(m×k) and V  ^(n×k) are the user and item latent factor
// ↪ matrices respectively.
struct MatrixFactorization {
    n_users: usize,
    n_items: usize,
    n_factors: usize,
    ratings: Vec<Rating>,
    user_factors: Vec<Vec<f64>>, // U matrix: each row is a user's
    ↪ latent vector
    item_factors: Vec<Vec<f64>>, // V matrix: each row is an item's
    ↪ latent vector
}

impl MatrixFactorization {
    // Constructs a new MatrixFactorization model with random
    // ↪ initialization of latent factors.
    fn new(n_users: usize, n_items: usize, n_factors: usize,
    ↪ ratings: Vec<Rating>) -> Self {
        let mut rng = rand::thread_rng();
        let user_factors = (0..n_users)
            .map(|_| {
                (0..n_factors)
                    .map(|_| rng.gen::<f64>())
                    .collect::<Vec<f64>>()
            })
            .collect::<Vec<Vec<f64>>>();
        let item_factors = (0..n_items)
            .map(|_| {
                (0..n_factors)
```

392

```rust
                    .map(|_| rng.gen::<f64>())
                    .collect::<Vec<f64>>()
            })
            .collect::<Vec<Vec<f64>>>();
        MatrixFactorization {
            n_users,
            n_items,
            n_factors,
            ratings,
            user_factors,
            item_factors,
        }
    }

    // Computes the dot product between two vectors.
    fn dot(u: &Vec<f64>, v: &Vec<f64>) -> f64 {
        u.iter().zip(v.iter()).map(|(x, y)| x * y).sum()
    }

    // Predicts the rating for a given user and item as u * v.
    fn predict(&self, user: usize, item: usize) -> f64 {
        Self::dot(&self.user_factors[user],
        ↪   &self.item_factors[item])
    }

    // Trains the matrix factorization model using Stochastic
    ↪   Gradient Descent (SGD).
    // The update equations are:
    //   u ← u +  * (e * v   * u)
    //   v ← v +  * (e * u   * v)
    // where e = r - u * v is the prediction error.
    fn train(&mut self, epochs: usize, learning_rate: f64, lambda:
    ↪   f64) {
        for epoch in 0..epochs {
            let mut total_error = 0.0;
            // Iterate over each observed rating in the training
            ↪   data.
            for rating in self.ratings.iter() {
                let user = rating.user;
                let item = rating.item;
                let prediction = Self::dot(&self.user_factors[user],
                ↪   &self.item_factors[item]);
                let error = rating.rating - prediction;
                total_error += error * error;

                // Update latent factors for each dimension.
                for f in 0..self.n_factors {
                    let u_old = self.user_factors[user][f];
                    let v_old = self.item_factors[item][f];
                    self.user_factors[user][f] += learning_rate *
                    ↪   (error * v_old - lambda * u_old);
                    self.item_factors[item][f] += learning_rate *
                    ↪   (error * u_old - lambda * v_old);
```

```rust
            }
        }
        let rmse = (total_error / self.ratings.len() as
         ↪  f64).sqrt();
        println!("Epoch {}: RMSE = {:.4}", epoch + 1, rmse);
        }
    }
}

fn main() {
    // Simulate a small user-item rating matrix.
    // For explicit feedback, ratings represent numerical scores;
     ↪  here we use a 3-user x 4-item example.
    let ratings = vec![
        Rating { user: 0, item: 0, rating: 5.0 },
        Rating { user: 0, item: 1, rating: 3.0 },
        Rating { user: 0, item: 3, rating: 1.0 },
        Rating { user: 1, item: 0, rating: 4.0 },
        Rating { user: 1, item: 2, rating: 2.0 },
        Rating { user: 2, item: 1, rating: 1.0 },
        Rating { user: 2, item: 2, rating: 5.0 },
        Rating { user: 2, item: 3, rating: 4.0 },
    ];

    let n_users = 3;
    let n_items = 4;
    let n_factors = 2; // Latent space dimension k, where k <<
     ↪  min(n_users, n_items)

    // Initialize the Matrix Factorization model.
    let mut mf = MatrixFactorization::new(n_users, n_items,
     ↪  n_factors, ratings);

    // Set training hyperparameters.
    let epochs = 50;
    let learning_rate = 0.01;
    let lambda = 0.1;

    // Train the latent factor model via SGD.
    mf.train(epochs, learning_rate, lambda);

    // Generate personalized recommendations by predicting ratings
     ↪  for a specific user, e.g., user 0.
    println!("Predicted ratings for User 0:");
    for item in 0..n_items {
        let pred = mf.predict(0, item);
        println!("Item {}: {:.4}", item, pred);
    }
}
```

Chapter 62

Association Rule Mining using the Apriori Algorithm

Problem Formulation and Notation

Let $I = \{i_1, i_2, \ldots, i_n\}$ denote the finite set of items and $D = \{t_1, t_2, \ldots, t_m\}$ represent the transactional database, where each transaction t_j is a subset of I. An itemset is any subset $X \subseteq I$, and the support of an itemset is defined as

$$supp(X) = \frac{|\{t \in D : X \subseteq t\}|}{|D|}.$$

An itemset is classified as frequent if its support meets or exceeds a predetermined minimum support threshold σ, that is, if

$$supp(X) \geq \sigma.$$

The objective of association rule mining is to discover significant relationships among items by deriving rules of the form

$$X \to Y,$$

with $X, Y \subset I$ and $X \cap Y = \emptyset$. The quality of these rules is typically evaluated using metrics such as confidence, defined as

$$conf(X \to Y) = \frac{supp(X \cup Y)}{supp(X)},$$

and lift, given by

$$lift(X \to Y) = \frac{supp(X \cup Y)}{supp(X) \cdot supp(Y)}.$$

Frequent Itemset Discovery via Iterative Candidate Generation

The Apriori algorithm commences the mining process by determining the set of frequent 1-itemsets. Each individual item is evaluated based on its support within the transactional database. The inherent principle of downward closure, or the Apriori property, asserts that if an itemset is not frequent, then none of its supersets can be frequent. Following the identification of frequent 1-itemsets, subsequent iterations generate candidate itemsets of larger sizes. For any candidate itemset of size $k + 1$, every subset of size k must be frequent in order for the candidate to be considered viable. This iterative candidate generation continues until no new frequent itemsets are discovered, ensuring a comprehensive enumeration of all itemsets that satisfy the support criterion.

Efficient Candidate Generation and Pruning Strategies

The efficiency of the Apriori algorithm is largely attributed to its systematic candidate generation combined with rigorous pruning methodologies. When generating candidates, the algorithm utilizes the principle that for any candidate itemset C of size $k + 1$, every subset $c \subset C$ with $|c| = k$ must already be known to be frequent. Formally, if there exists any subset $c \subset C$ such that

$$supp(c) < \sigma,$$

then C is pruned from the candidate set. This property greatly reduces the computational burden by curtailing the exponential growth of the candidate itemset search space. Moreover, efficient scanning techniques of the transactional data, often supported by specialized data structures, further mitigate the computational expense associated with repeatedly verifying candidate supports. The combination of these strategies ensures that the algorithm scales efficiently even as the dimensionality of the data increases.

Association Rule Generation and Evaluation Metrics

Once all frequent itemsets have been identified, the next phase involves generating association rules from these itemsets. For any frequent itemset F that contains more than one item, possible association rules are constructed in the form

$$X \to Y,$$

where $X \cup Y = F$ and $X \cap Y = \emptyset$. The confidence of each rule is computed as

$$conf(X \to Y) = \frac{supp(F)}{supp(X)},$$

which quantifies the conditional probability that Y appears in a transaction given that X appears. In addition, the lift of a rule, defined as

$$lift(X \to Y) = \frac{supp(F)}{supp(X) \cdot supp(Y)},$$

serves as a measure of the degree to which the presence of X increases the likelihood of observing Y, relative to their independent occurrences. Only those rules that satisfy minimum thresholds for both confidence and lift are retained for further analysis. This dual-filtering mechanism enhances the robustness of the discovered rules by ensuring that they capture statistically significant relationships in the data.

Rust Code Snippet

```rust
use std::collections::{HashSet, HashMap};

/// Computes the support of an itemset within the transactional
↪    database.
///
/// The support is defined as:
///     supp(X) = |{t in D such that X  t}| / |D|
///
/// # Arguments
/// * `itemset` - A set of items (represented as &str).
/// * `transactions` - A vector of transactions, where each
↪    transaction is a HashSet of items.
fn support(itemset: &HashSet<&str>, transactions:
↪    &Vec<HashSet<&str>>) -> f64 {
```

```rust
    let count = transactions.iter().filter(|t|
    ↪  itemset.is_subset(t)).count() as f64;
    count / transactions.len() as f64
}

/// Generates candidate itemsets of size k+1 from current frequent
↪  itemsets of size k.
///
/// According to the Apriori property, every subset of a candidate
↪  itemset must be frequent.
/// This function performs the join and prune steps in candidate
↪  generation.
///
/// # Arguments
/// * `frequent_itemsets` - A vector of frequent itemsets (each as a
↪  HashSet of &str) of size k.
/// * `k` - The current size of the frequent itemsets.
///
/// # Returns
/// A vector of candidate itemsets of size k+1.
fn generate_candidates(frequent_itemsets: &Vec<HashSet<&str>>, k:
↪  usize) -> Vec<HashSet<&str>> {
    let mut candidates = Vec::new();
    let n = frequent_itemsets.len();
    for i in 0..n {
        for j in i+1..n {
            // Join step: Compute the union of two frequent
            ↪  itemsets.
            let union: HashSet<&str> = frequent_itemsets[i].union(
            &frequent_itemsets[j]).cloned().collect();
            if union.len() == k + 1 {
                // Prune step: Ensure every k-subset of the
                ↪  candidate is frequent.
                let mut all_subsets_frequent = true;
                for item in &union {
                    let mut subset = union.clone();
                    subset.remove(item);
                    if !frequent_itemsets.contains(&subset) {
                        all_subsets_frequent = false;
                        break;
                    }
                }
                if all_subsets_frequent &&
                ↪  !candidates.contains(&union) {
                    candidates.push(union);
                }
            }
        }
    }
    candidates
}
```

```
/// Implements the Apriori algorithm to discover all frequent
↪   itemsets in the transactional database.
///
/// An itemset is considered frequent if:
///     supp(X) >=
///
/// # Arguments
/// * `transactions` - A vector of transactions (each as a HashSet
↪   of &str).
/// * `min_support` - The minimum support threshold  (e.g., 0.4 for
↪   40% support).
///
/// # Returns
/// A vector containing all frequent itemsets.
fn apriori(transactions: &Vec<HashSet<&str>>, min_support: f64) ->
↪   Vec<HashSet<&str>> {
    let mut frequent_itemsets = Vec::new();

    // Generate frequent 1-itemsets.
    let mut candidate_1: HashMap<&str, usize> = HashMap::new();
    for transaction in transactions {
        for &item in transaction {
            *candidate_1.entry(item).or_insert(0) += 1;
        }
    }
    let total_transactions = transactions.len() as f64;
    let mut current_frequent: Vec<HashSet<&str>> =
    ↪   candidate_1.iter()
        .filter(|(_, &count)| (count as f64 / total_transactions) >=
        ↪   min_support)
        .map(|(&item, _)| {
            let mut set = HashSet::new();
            set.insert(item);
            set
        })
        .collect();
    frequent_itemsets.extend(current_frequent.clone());

    let mut k = 1;
    // Iteratively generate candidate itemsets and filter them by
    ↪   support.
    while !current_frequent.is_empty() {
        let candidate_itemsets =
        ↪   generate_candidates(&current_frequent, k);
        let mut next_frequent = Vec::new();
        for candidate in candidate_itemsets {
            // Calculate support for candidate itemset:
            // supp(candidate) = |{t in D such that candidate  t}| /
            ↪   |D|
            let supp = transactions.iter().filter(|t|
            ↪   candidate.is_subset(t)).count() as f64 /
            ↪   total_transactions;
            if supp >= min_support {
```

399

```rust
                next_frequent.push(candidate.clone());
                frequent_itemsets.push(candidate);
            }
        }
        current_frequent = next_frequent;
        k += 1;
    }

    frequent_itemsets
}

/// Generates association rules from a given frequent itemset.
///
/// For any frequent itemset F with |F| > 1, rules are of the form:
///     X -> Y  where X   Y = F and X   Y =
///
/// The confidence of a rule is computed as:
///     conf(X -> Y) = supp(F) / supp(X)
///
/// The lift of a rule is computed as:
///     lift(X -> Y) = supp(F) / (supp(X) * supp(Y))
///
/// Only rules with a confidence above the threshold are returned.
///
/// # Arguments
/// * `frequent_itemset` - A frequent itemset F (as a HashSet of
/// ↪ &str).
/// * `transactions` - The transactional database.
/// * `min_confidence` - The minimum confidence threshold for a
/// ↪ rule.
///
/// # Returns
/// A vector of tuples representing the rules:
/// (X, Y, confidence, lift)
fn generate_rules(
    frequent_itemset: &HashSet<&str>,
    transactions: &Vec<HashSet<&str>>,
    min_confidence: f64,
) -> Vec<(HashSet<&str>, HashSet<&str>, f64, f64)> {
    let mut rules = Vec::new();
    let total_transactions = transactions.len() as f64;

    // Convert the frequent itemset into a vector for subset
    // ↪ generation.
    let items: Vec<&str> =
    ↪ frequent_itemset.iter().cloned().collect();
    let n = items.len();

    // Iterate over all non-empty proper subsets of
    // ↪ frequent_itemset.
    for i in 1..(1 << n) - 1 {
        let mut x_set = HashSet::new();
        for j in 0..n {
```

400

```rust
            if (i >> j) & 1 == 1 {
                x_set.insert(items[j]);
            }
        }
        let y_set: HashSet<&str> =
        ↪ frequent_itemset.difference(&x_set).cloned().collect();
        let supp_f = transactions.iter().filter(|t|
        ↪ frequent_itemset.is_subset(t)).count() as f64 /
        ↪ total_transactions;
        let supp_x = transactions.iter().filter(|t|
        ↪ x_set.is_subset(t)).count() as f64 / total_transactions;
        let supp_y = transactions.iter().filter(|t|
        ↪ y_set.is_subset(t)).count() as f64 / total_transactions;

        let confidence = if supp_x > 0.0 { supp_f / supp_x } else {
        ↪ 0.0 };
        let lift = if supp_x * supp_y > 0.0 { supp_f / (supp_x *
        ↪ supp_y) } else { 0.0 };
        if confidence >= min_confidence {
            rules.push((x_set, y_set, confidence, lift));
        }
    }

    rules
}

fn main() {
    // Example transactional dataset.
    // Each transaction is represented as a HashSet of item names.
    let transactions: Vec<HashSet<&str>> = vec![
        ["Milk", "Bread", "Beer"].iter().cloned().collect(),
        ["Milk", "Bread"].iter().cloned().collect(),
        ["Milk", "Beer"].iter().cloned().collect(),
        ["Bread", "Beer"].iter().cloned().collect(),
        ["Milk", "Bread", "Beer"].iter().cloned().collect(),
    ];

    // Set minimum support and minimum confidence thresholds.
    let min_support = 0.4;    // e.g., itemset must appear in at
    ↪ least 40% of transactions.
    let min_confidence = 0.7; // e.g., rules must have at least 70%
    ↪ confidence.

    // Discover frequent itemsets using the Apriori algorithm.
    let frequent_itemsets = apriori(&transactions, min_support);
    println!("Frequent Itemsets:");
    for itemset in &frequent_itemsets {
        println!("{:?} with support {:.2}", itemset,
        ↪ support(itemset, &transactions));
    }

    // Generate and display association rules from each frequent
    ↪ itemset containing more than one item.
```

401

```
    println!("\nAssociation Rules:");
    for itemset in &frequent_itemsets {
        if itemset.len() > 1 {
            let rules = generate_rules(itemset, &transactions,
            ↪ min_confidence);
            for (x, y, conf, lift) in rules {
                println!("Rule: {:?} -> {:?} (Confidence: {:.2},
                ↪ Lift: {:.2})", x, y, conf, lift);
            }
        }
    }
}
```
___

Chapter 63

Markov Models for Predicting Sequential Data

Mathematical Foundations and Notation

Let the finite state space be denoted by $S = \{s_1, s_2, \ldots, s_N\}$, where each element s_i represents a distinct state in the system. A Markov chain is formally defined as a sequence of random variables $\{X_t\}_{t \geq 0}$ such that, for every time step $t \geq 0$, the following Markov property holds:

$$P(X_{t+1} = s_j \mid X_t = s_i, X_{t-1} = s_{i_{t-1}}, \ldots, X_0 = s_{i_0})$$

$$= P(X_{t+1} = s_j \mid X_t = s_i).$$

This property implies that the future evolution of the process depends solely on its present state and is independent of the path by which that state was reached. A trajectory or realization of the process may be represented as $(s_{i_0}, s_{i_1}, \ldots, s_{i_T})$ with each transition governed by conditional probabilities that encapsulate the dynamics of the sequential events.

State Transition Matrices: Structure and Computation

The dynamics of a Markov chain are succinctly captured by its state transition matrix, $P \in \mathbb{R}^{N \times N}$, where each entry P_{ij} is defined as

$$P_{ij} = P(X_{t+1} = s_j \mid X_t = s_i).$$

By construction, the matrix P is row-stochastic, meaning that for every state $s_i \in S$,

$$\sum_{j=1}^{N} P_{ij} = 1.$$

In practical applications, these transition probabilities are often estimated from empirical data by counting the observed transitions. If n_{ij} denotes the number of observed transitions from state s_i to state s_j, and $n_i = \sum_{j=1}^{N} n_{ij}$ is the total number of transitions from state s_i, then a maximum likelihood estimation for the transition probability is given by

$$P_{ij} = \frac{n_{ij}}{n_i} \quad \text{provided } n_i > 0.$$

The state transition matrix thus serves both as a compact representation of the sequential dependencies within the data and as a foundational tool for the construction of predictive models.

Probabilistic Simulation for Sequential Forecasting

Forecasting sequential events involves the use of probabilistic simulations in which future states are generated by iterative sampling from the state transition matrix. Starting from an initial state s_{i_0}, each subsequent state is determined by sampling from the discrete probability distribution specified by the row of P corresponding to the current state. More precisely, if the process is currently in state s_i, the next state s_j is chosen with probability P_{ij}, thereby yielding a simulated trajectory $(s_{i_0}, s_{i_1}, s_{i_2}, \ldots, s_{i_T})$.

This simulation framework provides numerous sample paths, each representing a realization of the underlying Markov process. Statistical analysis of these paths, including the computation of expected state frequencies, mean recurrence times, or the distribution of sojourn times, enables the characterization of the probabilistic behavior of the system. Through such iterative sampling procedures, the evolution of complex sequences is approximated, offering valuable insights into the likely future configurations of the process, and thereby supporting forecasting endeavors.

Modeling Temporal Patterns using Markov Chains

Temporal patterns in sequential data often exhibit stochastic variability that can be effectively modeled using the framework of Markov chains. The state transition matrix encapsulates the intrinsic probabilistic relationships between observable events, allowing for the compact representation of temporal dynamics. In many contexts, each state corresponds to a particular event or condition, and the transition probability P_{ij} provides an explicit measure of the likelihood that event s_j follows event s_i.

Extensions to the basic first-order Markov model permit the capture of more intricate temporal dependencies by either expanding the state space or by incorporating a finite history of previous states into the model. Despite such extensions, the first-order Markov assumption remains widely applicable due to its balance between model simplicity and descriptive power. The invariant or stationary distribution of the Markov chain, defined as the unique distribution π satisfying

$$\pi^\mathsf{T} = \pi^\mathsf{T} P \quad \text{with} \quad \sum_{i=1}^{N} \pi_i = 1,$$

provides additional insight into the long-term behavior of the system, although the primary focus here is on the sequential prediction of events based on the immediate probabilistic transitions.

By encoding the complete statistical properties of sequential transitions, Markov models offer a rigorous and efficient methodology for forecasting temporal patterns, facilitating both theoretical analysis and empirical prediction in complex data environments.

Rust Code Snippet

```rust
use rand::distributions::{Distribution, WeightedIndex};
use rand::thread_rng;

/// A struct representing a Markov Chain with a state transition
/// ↪ matrix and state names.
struct MarkovChain {
    /// The state transition matrix where each row corresponds to a
    /// ↪ current state and each column to the next state.
    /// Each row sums to 1.
    transition_matrix: Vec<Vec<f64>>,
    /// A list of state names.
    states: Vec<String>,
}

impl MarkovChain {
    /// Constructs a new MarkovChain instance ensuring that each row
    /// ↪ of the transition matrix sums to 1.
    fn new(transition_matrix: Vec<Vec<f64>>, states: Vec<String>) ->
    ↪ Self {
        for (i, row) in transition_matrix.iter().enumerate() {
            let sum: f64 = row.iter().sum();
            assert!(
                (sum - 1.0).abs() < 1e-6,
                "Row {} of the transition matrix must sum to 1. Got
                ↪ {}",
                i,
                sum
            );
        }
        MarkovChain {
            transition_matrix,
            states,
        }
    }

    /// Samples the next state given the current state index.
    ///
    /// Implements the equation:
    ///   next_state ~ P(current_state, *)
    ///
    /// Where P is the row of the state transition matrix
    /// ↪ corresponding to the current state.
    fn next_state(&self, current_state: usize) -> usize {
        let probabilities = &self.transition_matrix[current_state];
        let dist = WeightedIndex::new(probabilities)
            .expect("The probabilities must be non-negative and not
            ↪ all zero.");
        let mut rng = thread_rng();
        dist.sample(&mut rng)
    }
```

```rust
/// Simulates a Markov chain trajectory starting from the given
↪    state for a specified number of steps.
///
/// Returns a vector of state indices representing the path.
fn simulate(&self, start_state: usize, steps: usize) ->
↪    Vec<usize> {
    let mut state_sequence = Vec::with_capacity(steps + 1);
    let mut current_state = start_state;
    state_sequence.push(current_state);
    for _ in 0..steps {
        current_state = self.next_state(current_state);
        state_sequence.push(current_state);
    }
    state_sequence
}

/// Constructs a MarkovChain from observed transition counts.
///
/// Given a counts matrix where counts[i][j] is the number of
↪    transitions from state i to state j,
/// this function estimates the transition probabilities by the
↪    Maximum Likelihood Estimation:
///    P_ij = n_ij / n_i, where n_i = sum_j n_ij.
fn from_counts(counts: Vec<Vec<usize>>, states: Vec<String>) ->
↪    Self {
    let mut transition_matrix = Vec::new();
    for row in counts {
        let row_sum: usize = row.iter().sum();
        let row_prob: Vec<f64> = if row_sum > 0 {
            row.iter().map(|&count| count as f64 / row_sum as
↪                f64).collect()
        } else {
            // In the absence of observed transitions, assign a
↪                zero probability for all outcomes.
            vec![0.0; row.len()]
        };
        transition_matrix.push(row_prob);
    }
    MarkovChain {
        transition_matrix,
        states,
    }
}

/// Computes the stationary (invariant) distribution using the
↪    power iteration method.
///
/// The stationary distribution  satisfies:
///     = P, subject to sum_i _i = 1.
/// The iteration continues until the L1 difference between
↪    iterations is less than the specified tolerance
/// or until reaching max_iterations.
```

407

```rust
    fn stationary_distribution(&self, tolerance: f64,
    ↪  max_iterations: usize) -> Vec<f64> {
        let n = self.states.len();
        let mut dist = vec![1.0 / n as f64; n]; // Start with a
        ↪  uniform distribution.
        for _ in 0..max_iterations {
            let mut new_dist = vec![0.0; n];
            for i in 0..n {
                // Transition contribution from state i to all other
                ↪  states.
                for j in 0..n {
                    new_dist[j] += dist[i] *
                    ↪  self.transition_matrix[i][j];
                }
            }
            // Check convergence using the L1 norm of the
            ↪  difference.
            let diff: f64 = dist.iter()
                                .zip(new_dist.iter())
                                .map(|(a, b)| (a - b).abs())
                                .sum();
            if diff < tolerance {
                return new_dist;
            }
            dist = new_dist;
        }
        dist
    }
}

fn main() {
    // Define state names (for example: representing events A, B,
    ↪  and C).
    let states = vec!["A".to_string(), "B".to_string(),
    ↪  "C".to_string()];

    // Define a manually constructed state transition matrix.
    // Each row must sum to 1 and each element P[i][j] represents
    ↪  P(next_state = j | current_state = i).
    let transition_matrix = vec![
        vec![0.1, 0.6, 0.3],  // From state A
        vec![0.4, 0.4, 0.2],  // From state B
        vec![0.3, 0.3, 0.4],  // From state C
    ];

    // Create a MarkovChain instance.
    let markov_chain = MarkovChain::new(transition_matrix,
    ↪  states.clone());

    // Simulate a trajectory of 10 steps starting from state 0
    ↪  ("A").
    let simulated_indices = markov_chain.simulate(0, 10);
    println!("Simulated state indices: {:?}", simulated_indices);
```

```rust
    // Map the state indices to their corresponding names for
    ↪ clarity.
    let simulated_states: Vec<String> = simulated_indices
        .iter()
        .map(|&i| states[i].clone())
        .collect();
    println!("Simulated states: {:?}", simulated_states);

    // Example: Constructing the MarkovChain from empirical counts
    ↪ using Maximum Likelihood Estimation.
    let counts = vec![
        vec![5, 15, 10],  // Transition counts from state A.
        vec![8, 12, 5],   // Transition counts from state B.
        vec![7, 7, 16],   // Transition counts from state C.
    ];
    let markov_from_counts = MarkovChain::from_counts(counts,
    ↪ states.clone());
    println!("Transition matrix from counts: {:?}",
    ↪ markov_from_counts.transition_matrix);

    // Compute and display the stationary distribution for the built
    ↪ Markov Chain.
    let stationary = markov_chain.stationary_distribution(1e-6,
    ↪ 10000);
    println!("Stationary distribution: {:?}", stationary);
}
```

Chapter 64

Heuristic Optimization Techniques: Genetic Algorithms and Simulated Annealing

Mathematical Foundations of Heuristic Optimization

Heuristic optimization encompasses a class of algorithms devised to approximate solutions in scenarios where the search space is both large and complex, often characterized by numerous local extrema. In many optimization problems, an objective function $f : \mathbb{R}^n \to \mathbb{R}$ must be optimized over a high-dimensional domain. The landscape defined by f may exhibit steep gradients, flat plateaus, and discontinuities, rendering classical deterministic methods computationally infeasible or prone to premature convergence. Heuristic methods address these challenges by embedding stochastic components that facilitate global exploration while allowing for local exploitation.

Central to the formulation of these methods is the balance between diversification and intensification. Diversification encourages broad exploration of the solution space, whereas intensification refines the search within promising regions. Probabilistic models often underpin the acceptance criteria for candidate solutions, with formulations based on the Boltzmann distribution, such as an acceptance probability proportional to $\exp\left(-\Delta E/T\right)$, where T is a control parameter analogous to temperature, and ΔE represents the change in the objective function.

Genetic Algorithms: Evolutionary Computation for Search

Genetic algorithms (GAs) are population-based methods inspired by the principles of natural evolution and genetics. In a GA, candidate solutions are encoded as chromosomes, and a collection of these chromosomes constitutes a population that evolves over successive generations. The quality of each candidate is measured by a fitness function $F : S \to \mathbb{R}$ defined over the solution space S, and this fitness determines the likelihood of a solution being selected for reproduction.

Key operators in genetic algorithms include selection, crossover, and mutation. Selection mechanisms, such as tournament selection or fitness-proportionate selection, probabilistically favor candidates with higher fitness, thereby increasing their representation in subsequent generations. The crossover operator recombines segments of two or more parent chromosomes, thereby facilitating the exchange of genetic material and potentially synthesizing enhanced solutions. Mutation introduces random alterations to candidate solutions, ensuring the maintenance of genetic diversity within the population and mitigating the risk of convergence to sub-optimal regions. The interplay of these operators allows a GA to concurrently search multiple regions of the design space, progressively refining the population toward higher fitness while maintaining robustness against premature convergence.

Simulated Annealing: Probabilistic Escape from Local Optima

Simulated annealing (SA) is a single-solution based optimization technique that draws its inspiration from the annealing process in metallurgy. The algorithm commences with an initial candidate solution and iteratively explores its neighborhood according to a probabilistic acceptance rule. Given a current solution s and a neighboring solution s', the change in the objective function is defined as $\Delta f = f(s') - f(s)$. For minimization tasks, a candidate s' is accepted with probability

$$P = \min\left\{1, \exp\left(-\frac{\Delta f}{T}\right)\right\},$$

where T denotes a temperature parameter that decreases according to a scheduled cooling process. At high temperatures, the probability of accepting worse solutions is elevated, thereby allowing the algorithm to traverse the search space more freely. As T diminishes, the acceptance criterion becomes more conservative, promoting convergence as the search becomes increasingly localized.

The design of the cooling schedule is critical to the performance of simulated annealing. A well-chosen schedule ensures a gradual reduction in temperature that balances the exploration of distant regions of the space with the exploitation of local basins of attraction. In complex search spaces characterized by rugged objective landscapes, the probabilistic mechanism inherent in SA provides a means to overcome local optima, facilitating a more comprehensive exploration of the parameter space.

Heuristic Strategies for Model Parameter Tuning in Complex Search Spaces

The task of model parameter tuning frequently involves navigating a high-dimensional, non-convex search space. In this setting, candidate solutions correspond to distinct parameter sets whose evaluations are dictated by a performance metric closely related to the objective function. Both genetic algorithms and simulated annealing are well suited to this task due to their complementary search strategies.

Genetic algorithms leverage a population-based approach that inherently explores multiple regions of the parameter space simultaneously. Their reliance on selection, crossover, and mutation enables the aggregation of beneficial traits from disparate regions, which is particularly advantageous in avoiding stagnation in suboptimal regions. In contrast, simulated annealing provides a mechanism for fine-tuning parameter values through its controlled, probabilistic acceptance of non-improving moves. This capacity to accept temporary degradations in performance allows the algorithm to escape local minima and converge toward configurations that offer improved predictive performance.

By integrating these heuristic methods, model parameter tuning can be approached in a robust and adaptive manner. The selection of candidate solutions based on fitness criteria, the controlled recombination and variation in genetic algorithms, and the temperature-driven exploration in simulated annealing collectively create a powerful framework for traversing complex search spaces. Analytical tools, such as convergence analyses and sensitivity studies, are typically employed to assess both the quality of the optimized parameters and the resilience of the optimization process against the intricacies of the underlying objective landscape.

Rust Code Snippet

```
use rand::Rng;
use rand::seq::SliceRandom;

#[derive(Clone, Debug)]
struct Individual {
    genes: Vec<f64>,
    fitness: f64,
}

/// Objective function: Sphere function, f(x) = sum(x_i^2)
fn objective(genes: &Vec<f64>) -> f64 {
    genes.iter().map(|x| x * x).sum()
}

/// Simulated Annealing implementation.
/// This function minimizes the objective function using the
↪    acceptance
/// probability: P = min{1, exp(-f/T)} as described in the chapter.
fn simulated_annealing(initial: Vec<f64>, initial_temp: f64,
↪    cooling_rate: f64, iterations: usize) -> Vec<f64> {
    let mut current = initial.clone();
    let mut best = initial.clone();
    let mut current_temp = initial_temp;
    let mut best_obj = objective(&best);
    let mut rng = rand::thread_rng();

    for _ in 0..iterations {
        // Generate a neighbor by perturbing one random gene
        let mut neighbor = current.clone();
        let idx = rng.gen_range(0..neighbor.len());
        let change = rng.gen_range(-1.0..1.0) * 0.1; // small
        ↪    perturbation
        neighbor[idx] += change;
```

```rust
        let current_obj = objective(&current);
        let neighbor_obj = objective(&neighbor);
        let delta = neighbor_obj - current_obj;

        // Accept the neighbor if it improves the objective,
        // otherwise accept with probability P = exp(-f/T)
        if delta < 0.0 {
            current = neighbor.clone();
        } else {
            let acceptance_prob = (-delta / current_temp).exp();
            if rng.gen::<f64>() < acceptance_prob {
                current = neighbor.clone();
            }
        }

        // Update the best solution found so far
        if objective(&current) < best_obj {
            best = current.clone();
            best_obj = objective(&best);
        }

        // Cool down the temperature
        current_temp *= cooling_rate;
    }

    best
}

/// Tournament selection to choose a parent for Genetic Algorithm.
/// This function selects the best individual among a random sample
↪   (tournament)
/// from the current population.
fn tournament_selection(population: &Vec<Individual>,
↪   tournament_size: usize) -> Individual {
    let mut rng = rand::thread_rng();
    let mut best: Option<Individual> = None;
    for _ in 0..tournament_size {
        let candidate = population.choose(&mut rng).unwrap();
        best = match best {
            None => Some(candidate.clone()),
            Some(ref b) => {
                if candidate.fitness > b.fitness {
                    Some(candidate.clone())
                } else {
                    Some(b.clone())
                }
            }
        }
    }
    best.unwrap()
}
```

```rust
/// Single-point crossover for Genetic Algorithm.
/// It creates a new child by combining genes from two parents at a
↪   random crossover point.
fn single_point_crossover(parent1: &Vec<f64>, parent2: &Vec<f64>) ->
↪   Vec<f64> {
    let mut rng = rand::thread_rng();
    let len = parent1.len();
    if len == 0 {
        return vec![];
    }
    let crossover_point = rng.gen_range(1..len);
    let mut child = Vec::with_capacity(len);
    child.extend_from_slice(&parent1[0..crossover_point]);
    child.extend_from_slice(&parent2[crossover_point..len]);
    child
}

/// Mutation operator: Each gene has a chance (mutation_rate) to be
↪   perturbed by a small random value.
/// This maintains diversity in the population.
fn mutate(genes: &Vec<f64>, mutation_rate: f64) -> Vec<f64> {
    let mut rng = rand::thread_rng();
    genes.iter().map(|&gene| {
        if rng.gen::<f64>() < mutation_rate {
            gene + rng.gen_range(-0.5..0.5)
        } else {
            gene
        }
    }).collect()
}

/// Genetic Algorithm implementation.
/// This function evolves a population of individuals through
↪   selection,
/// crossover, and mutation, aiming to minimize the objective
↪   function.
fn genetic_algorithm(pop_size: usize, gene_length: usize,
↪   generations: usize, mutation_rate: f64, tournament_size: usize)
↪   -> Individual {
    let mut rng = rand::thread_rng();
    // Initialize population with random individuals
    let mut population: Vec<Individual> = (0..pop_size).map(|_| {
        let genes: Vec<f64> = (0..gene_length).map(|_|
        ↪   rng.gen_range(-10.0..10.0)).collect();
        // Fitness is defined as 1 / (1 + objective) to favor lower
        ↪   objective values.
        let fitness = 1.0 / (1.0 + objective(&genes));
        Individual { genes, fitness }
    }).collect();

    // Evolve population over generations
    for _ in 0..generations {
        let mut new_population = Vec::with_capacity(pop_size);
```

415

```rust
        while new_population.len() < pop_size {
            let parent1 = tournament_selection(&population,
            ↪  tournament_size);
            let parent2 = tournament_selection(&population,
            ↪  tournament_size);
            let child_genes = single_point_crossover(&parent1.genes,
            ↪  &parent2.genes);
            let mutated_genes = mutate(&child_genes, mutation_rate);
            let fitness = 1.0 / (1.0 + objective(&mutated_genes));
            new_population.push(Individual { genes: mutated_genes,
            ↪  fitness });
        }
        population = new_population;
    }

    // Return the best individual from the final population
    population.into_iter()
            .max_by(|a, b|
            ↪  a.fitness.partial_cmp(&b.fitness).unwrap())
            .unwrap()
}

fn main() {
    // Example usage of Simulated Annealing:
    // Starting from an arbitrary initial state in a 3-dimensional
    ↪  space.
    let initial_state = vec![5.0, -3.0, 2.0];
    let best_state_sa = simulated_annealing(initial_state, 100.0,
    ↪  0.99, 1000);
    println!("Best state found by Simulated Annealing: {:?}",
    ↪  best_state_sa);
    println!("Objective value: {}", objective(&best_state_sa));

    // Example usage of Genetic Algorithm:
    // Evolve a population of 50 individuals, each with 3 genes,
    ↪  over 100 generations.
    let best_individual = genetic_algorithm(50, 3, 100, 0.1, 3);
    println!("Best individual found by Genetic Algorithm: {:?}",
    ↪  best_individual.genes);
    println!("Fitness value: {}", best_individual.fitness);
}
```

Chapter 65

Convex Optimization Methods for Data Fitting

Mathematical Foundations of Convex Data Fitting

The data fitting problem is formalized as an optimization task in which the objective is to identify a parameter vector $\theta \in \mathbb{R}^n$ that minimizes a convex loss function. Such loss functions are typically constructed as the sum of squared residuals, as exemplified by

$$f(\theta) = \sum_{i=1}^{N} \big(y_i - \phi(x_i; \theta)\big)^2,$$

where $\{(x_i, y_i)\}_{i=1}^{N}$ denotes the set of observations and $\phi(x_i; \theta)$ represents the model prediction corresponding to the input x_i. The convexity of f is guaranteed under conditions where the mapping $\theta \mapsto \phi(x_i; \theta)$ interacts with the squared error in a manner that preserves convexity. Moreover, several problems include regularization terms, which are added to prevent overfitting and to imbue the solution with desired properties such as smoothness or sparsity. In these instances the objective is modified to

$$f(\theta) = \sum_{i=1}^{N} \big(y_i - \phi(x_i; \theta)\big)^2 + \lambda R(\theta),$$

where $R(\theta)$ is a convex regularizer and $\lambda > 0$ controls its influence.

The theoretical underpinnings of these formulations rely on principles from convex analysis. In particular, the requirement that any local minimum is also a global minimum follows from the convexity of f, a property that is further reinforced by attributes such as the Lipschitz continuity of the gradient $\nabla f(\theta)$ and the strong convexity of f in certain settings. The Hessian matrix $H = \nabla^2 f(\theta)$ provides critical insight into the curvature of the objective function and its conditioning, both of which play decisive roles in the design and analysis of optimization algorithms.

Gradient-Based Optimization Techniques for Data Fitting

Gradient-based methods leverage the differentiability of convex objective functions to iteratively approach a minimum by following the negative gradient direction. The classical update rule is given by

$$\theta^{(k+1)} = \theta^{(k)} - \alpha \nabla f(\theta^{(k)}),$$

where $\alpha > 0$ is the step-size parameter and k indexes the iteration. The convergence of this method is ensured under suitable assumptions pertaining to the smoothness of f, and the selection of α plays a pivotal role in balancing rapid descent with numerical stability.

When the gradient $\nabla f(\theta)$ is Lipschitz continuous with constant L, explicit bounds on the convergence rate can be established. Under strong convexity, the method exhibits a linear rate of convergence once the iterates approach the vicinity of the optimal solution. Furthermore, adaptive step-size strategies such as backtracking line search are often incorporated to dynamically adjust α, thereby ensuring sufficient decrease in the objective function at every iteration. Variants of the basic gradient descent algorithm may also integrate momentum terms, which combine past directional information to ameliorate oscillations and enhance convergence in ill-conditioned scenarios. In this context, the update rules are augmented to include an inertial component, leading to improved performance on high-dimensional data fitting tasks.

Interior-Point Methods for Convex Optimization in Data Fitting

Interior-point methods offer an alternative paradigm to gradient-based techniques, particularly when the data fitting problem involves inequality constraints or requires robust handling of barrier conditions. These methods reformulate the constrained optimization problem by embedding a barrier function into the objective, thereby transforming it into an unconstrained problem that is amenable to standard optimization techniques. A commonly used formulation incorporates a logarithmic barrier term, leading to a modified objective

$$\min_{\theta \in \mathbb{R}^n} \left\{ f(\theta) - \mu \sum_{j=1}^{m} \ln\big(g_j(\theta)\big) \right\},$$

where each function $g_j(\theta) \geq 0$ represents an inequality constraint and $\mu > 0$ is the barrier parameter.

The approach proceeds by solving a sequence of such unconstrained problems with gradually decreasing values of μ, thereby guiding the iterates along the so-called central path—a trajectory that satisfies perturbed Karush-Kuhn-Tucker conditions. At each iteration, Newton's method is applied to the modified objective, utilizing second-order derivative information from both the original loss function and the barrier terms. The efficacy of the Newton step within an interior-point framework is bolstered by a careful analysis of the search direction and the maintenance of strict feasibility with respect to the constraints.

The convergence theory for interior-point methods relies on the self-concordance properties of the barrier function, which ensure that the Newton steps lead to a rapid decrease in the duality gap. The polynomial-time convergence guarantees, as established in classical convex optimization literature, underscore the robustness of these techniques even in settings where the number of constraints is large relative to the dimensionality of θ. The interplay between the barrier parameter μ, the Newton update, and the central path forms the conceptual basis for the design of efficient interior-point algorithms tailored to complex data fitting problems.

Rust Code Snippet

```
//! This Rust snippet demonstrates a convex optimization approach
↪   for data fitting
//! using gradient descent and an interior-point method with a
↪   barrier term.
//!
//! The optimization problem is formulated as:
//!
//!   f() = _{i=1}^{N} (y_i - (x_i; ))^2 +  ||||^2,
//!
//! where (x; ) is a linear model: (x; ) = [0]*x + [1].
//!
//! The gradient descent update rule is implemented as:
//!
//!   ^(k+1) = ^(k) -  f(^(k))
//!
//! For constrained problems (e.g., enforcing [1] > 0), we add a
↪   logarithmic barrier:
//!
//!   f_barrier() = f() -  * ln([1])
//!
//! whose gradient includes an extra term: - / [1] for the
↪   intercept.
//!

// Prediction function: (x; ) = [0] * x + [1]
fn phi(x: f64, theta: &[f64]) -> f64 {
    theta[0] * x + theta[1]
}

// Compute the convex loss function:
// f() = (y_i - (x_i; ))^2 + ([0]^2 + [1]^2)
fn loss(data: &[(f64, f64)], theta: &[f64], lambda: f64) -> f64 {
    let sum_sq_error: f64 = data.iter().map(|&(x, y)| {
        let error = y - phi(x, theta);
        error * error
    }).sum();
    sum_sq_error + lambda * (theta[0] * theta[0] + theta[1] *
↪   theta[1])
}

// Compute the gradient of the loss function with respect to
// grad[0] = -2 *  x_i * (y_i - ([0]*x_i + [1])) + 2[0]
// grad[1] = -2 *  (y_i - ([0]*x_i + [1])) + 2[1]
fn gradient(data: &[(f64, f64)], theta: &[f64], lambda: f64) ->
↪   Vec<f64> {
    let mut grad0 = 0.0;
    let mut grad1 = 0.0;
    for &(x, y) in data.iter() {
        let prediction = phi(x, theta);
        let error = y - prediction;
```

```rust
        grad0 += -2.0 * x * error;
        grad1 += -2.0 * error;
    }
    grad0 += 2.0 * lambda * theta[0];
    grad1 += 2.0 * lambda * theta[1];
    vec![grad0, grad1]
}

// Standard gradient descent to minimize the convex loss.
// ^(k+1) = ^(k) -  * f(^(k))
fn gradient_descent(
    data: &[(f64, f64)],
    init_theta: &[f64],
    lambda: f64,
    alpha: f64,
    tol: f64,
    max_iter: usize,
) -> Vec<f64> {
    let mut theta = init_theta.to_vec();
    for iter in 0..max_iter {
        let grad = gradient(data, &theta, lambda);
        let theta_next: Vec<f64> = theta
            .iter()
            .zip(grad.iter())
            .map(|(&t, &g)| t - alpha * g)
            .collect();
        // Compute the Euclidean norm of the update difference
        let diff_norm = theta
            .iter()
            .zip(theta_next.iter())
            .map(|(a, b)| (a - b).powi(2))
            .sum::<f64>()
            .sqrt();
        theta = theta_next;
        if diff_norm < tol {
            println!("Converged in {} iterations", iter + 1);
            break;
        }
    }
    theta
}

// For a constrained optimization example, assume we require [1] >
↪   0.
// We modify the loss by adding a barrier term:
// f_barrier() = f() -  * ln([1])
fn loss_with_barrier(data: &[(f64, f64)], theta: &[f64], lambda:
↪   f64, mu: f64) -> f64 {
    if theta[1] <= 0.0 {
        return f64::INFINITY;
    }
    loss(data, theta, lambda) - mu * theta[1].ln()
}
```

```rust
// The gradient of the barrier-augmented loss function.
// For [1], an extra term - / [1] is added.
fn gradient_with_barrier(data: &[(f64, f64)], theta: &[f64], lambda:
↪    f64, mu: f64) -> Vec<f64> {
    let mut grad = gradient(data, theta, lambda);
    if theta[1] > 0.0 {
        grad[1] += -mu / theta[1];
    } else {
        grad[1] = f64::INFINITY; // Infeasible region
    }
    grad
}


// A simple interior-point method using gradient descent on the
↪    barrier-augmented loss.
// is decreased gradually to guide the solution toward the
↪    constrained optimum.
fn interior_point_method(
    data: &[(f64, f64)],
    init_theta: &[f64],
    lambda: f64,
    init_mu: f64,
    alpha: f64,
    tol: f64,
    max_iter: usize,
) -> Vec<f64> {
    let mut theta = init_theta.to_vec();
    let mut mu = init_mu;
    for _outer in 0..10 {
        for iter in 0..max_iter {
            let grad = gradient_with_barrier(data, &theta, lambda,
↪                mu);
            let theta_next: Vec<f64> = theta
                .iter()
                .zip(grad.iter())
                .map(|(&t, &g)| t - alpha * g)
                .collect();
            let diff_norm = theta
                .iter()
                .zip(theta_next.iter())
                .map(|(a, b)| (a - b).powi(2))
                .sum::<f64>()
                .sqrt();
            theta = theta_next;
            if diff_norm < tol {
                println!("Inner loop ( = {}) converged in {}
↪                    iterations", mu, iter + 1);
                break;
            }
        }
        // Decrease the barrier parameter to approach the original
↪            constrained problem.
```

```rust
            mu *= 0.1;
            if mu < 1e-6 {
                break;
            }
        }
        theta
    }

    fn main() {
        // Create a sample dataset with (x, y) observations.
        // For example, assume a true relationship: y = 2.0*x + 1.0,
        ↪   with slight noise.
        let data = vec![
            (0.0, 1.1),
            (1.0, 3.0),
            (2.0, 5.0),
            (3.0, 7.1),
            (4.0, 9.0),
        ];

        // Initial guess for parameters: [slope, intercept]
        let init_theta = vec![0.0, 0.0];
        let lambda = 0.1;     // Regularization parameter
        let alpha = 0.001;    // Learning rate for gradient descent
        let tol = 1e-6;       // Tolerance for convergence
        let max_iter = 10000;

        println!("Starting Gradient Descent Optimization
        ↪   (Unconstrained):");
        let theta_opt = gradient_descent(&data, &init_theta, lambda,
        ↪   alpha, tol, max_iter);
        println!("Optimized parameters: {:?}", theta_opt);
        println!("Final loss: {}\n", loss(&data, &theta_opt, lambda));

        // For the interior-point method, enforce the constraint [1] >
        ↪   0.
        // Use an initial guess with a positive intercept.
        let init_theta_ip = vec![0.0, 1.0];
        let init_mu = 1.0;    // Initial barrier parameter
        println!("Starting Interior-Point Optimization (with Barrier
        ↪   Method):");
        let theta_ip_opt = interior_point_method(&data, &init_theta_ip,
        ↪   lambda, init_mu, alpha, tol, max_iter);
        println!("Optimized parameters with barrier: {:?}",
        ↪   theta_ip_opt);
        println!("Final barrier-augmented loss: {}",
        ↪   loss_with_barrier(&data, &theta_ip_opt, lambda, init_mu));
    }
```

Chapter 66

Custom Macro Development for Data Processing DSLs in Rust

Foundations of Macro Systems in Rust

Macros in Rust provide a sophisticated meta-programming mechanism that performs compile-time code transformation through the manipulation of token trees. This mechanism is best understood as a function $T : \mathcal{T} \to \mathcal{T}$ defined on the space of abstract syntax trees $\mathcal{T}$, transforming high-level syntactic constructs into expanded, low-level representations. The design of such macros centers on the separation of syntax and semantics, enabling the encapsulation of recurring patterns that arise in data processing pipelines. In particular, the integration of domain-specific language (DSL) constructs within macros permits the expression of complex operations in concise forms, thereby reducing redundancy in codebases that address advanced analytics tasks.

At its core, the utility of custom macros in Rust lies in their ability to generate code that is both performant and type-safe. The system enforces hygienic expansion, ensuring that identifiers introduced within a macro do not interfere with those present in the surrounding context. This property preserves variable bindings

424

and maintains compiler guarantees, leading to robust integration within larger systems. By leveraging these theoretical underpinnings, macros serve as a foundation for constructing DSLs that capture the semantics of data manipulation and transformation operations.

Design Principles for Data Processing Domain-Specific Languages

The development of DSLs tailored to data processing tasks requires careful attention to syntax design, semantic clarity, and integration with existing abstractions. In this context, custom macros are employed to synthesize high-level constructs that encapsulate data operations such as filtering, mapping, and aggregation. The design process involves establishing a clear correspondence between DSL syntax and the underlying Rust constructs that execute efficient data transformations.

DSLs developed via custom macros are constructed to mirror mathematical formulations of data processing tasks. For instance, aggregate operations may be modeled in a manner analogous to summation defined by the operator Σ, while compositional pipelines evoke the concept of function composition $f \circ g$. By abstracting these operations through macro definitions, the resulting DSL exhibits both expressive power and clarity. Emphasis is placed on creating a syntactic structure that is both intuitive to domain experts and capable of succinctly representing complex processing patterns.

A defining characteristic of such DSLs is their ability to enforce semantic invariants at compile time. By encoding domain-specific constraints within the macro expansion process, it becomes possible to catch a broad class of errors early in the development cycle. This static validation not only enhances code reliability but also streamlines the iterative process of developing analytic systems that operate on large-scale data.

Macro Expansion, Hygiene, and Formal Semantics

A critical aspect of custom macro development is the precise control over macro expansion and the preservation of hygiene. The transformation function T must satisfy strict invariance conditions with respect to variable bindings, as captured by a binding relation B such that $B(T(t)) = B(t)$ for all token trees $t \in \mathcal{T}$. This formal criterion prevents unintended capture of identifiers and guarantees that macro-generated constructs remain isolated from external definitions.

Macro hygiene in Rust is maintained through a rigorous framework that assigns unique scopes to identifiers introduced during macro expansion. This approach minimizes side effects and ensures that macros remain composable regardless of the local context in which they are invoked. The formal semantics of such systems can be conceptualized in terms of rewriting rules that are both confluent and terminating, thereby providing strong correctness properties. These properties are fundamental when developing DSLs for data processing, as they safeguard the consistency of pattern substitutions and enforce predictable transformation outcomes.

Moreover, the macro system supports a tiered approach to expansion, where declarative rules are supplemented by procedural logic to handle complex syntactic patterns. The careful balance between simplicity in rule specification and the expressive requirements of a DSL compels developers to articulate transformation strategies that are both modular and amenable to static analysis. Such strategies enhance the overall reliability of the DSL and optimize the generated code for performance-critical data processing applications.

Integration of DSL Constructs in Data Processing Pipelines

Custom macros designed for DSL development play an instrumental role in the integration of advanced analytics within data processing pipelines. By encapsulating common operations and repetitive patterns, these DSL constructs promote code clarity and reduce boilerplate in scenarios that involve extensive data transformations. The macro-generated code effectively acts as a domain-specific interpreter, mapping high-level operations into optimized code sequences without compromising on performance.

In data-intensive applications, it is common to encounter recurring patterns such as iterative filtering, mapping, and reduction. Custom macros synthesize these patterns into abstract DSL constructs that can be composed in a manner analogous to mathematical function composition. Such composability is expressed through constructs that, at a higher level of abstraction, resemble pipelines of transformations. The macro system thus facilitates a seamless translation from declarative DSL expressions to efficient, low-level implementations that leverage Rust's performance characteristics.

Integration is further enhanced by the ability of custom macros to enforce invariants and static guarantees during the compilation process. By embedding domain-specific rules into the macro transformation process, the resultant DSL attains a level of rigor comparable to that observed in formal specification languages. This rigorous treatment ensures that advanced analytics workflows—often expressed through chains of data transformations—are both syntactically concise and semantically robust, yielding systems that are capable of handling complex data processing tasks with reliability and efficiency.

Rust Code Snippet

```
/*
    This comprehensive Rust code snippet demonstrates the
    ↪   implementation of a custom
    macro-based domain-specific language (DSL) for data processing
    ↪   pipelines.

    It illustrates key theoretical concepts from the chapter:

    1. Macro Transformation Function: T :  →
        - The macro transforms input token trees into expanded Rust
        ↪   code.
    2. Binding Invariance: B(T(t)) = B(t)
        - Macro hygiene guarantees that identifiers introduced during
        ↪   expansion do not
          conflict with those in the surrounding context.
    3. DSL Constructs for Data Processing:
        - The DSL supports operations such as filtering, mapping, and
        ↪   reduction.
    4. Function Composition (f  g):
        - A helper function that demonstrates composing two functions
        ↪   into one,
          capturing the idea of composing data transformations.

    The following code defines:
    - A 'compose' function implementing function composition.
    - A declarative macro 'dsl_pipeline!' that builds a pipeline from
    ↪   optional 'filter'
      and 'map' operations and a mandatory 'reduce' operation.
```

```
    - Example usages of the DSL and function composition in the
    ↪  'main' function.
*/

use std::iter::Iterator;

// Function composition: given f and g, (f  g)(x) = f(g(x))
fn compose<F, G, T, U, V>(f: F, g: G) -> impl Fn(T) -> V
where
    F: Fn(U) -> V,
    G: Fn(T) -> U,
{
    move |x| f(g(x))
}


// Declarative macro to build a data processing DSL pipeline.
// It accepts an input data expression and a series of optional
// ↪  operations.
// The macro expansion (representing the transformation function T:
// ↪  → ) preserves
// binding invariants (B(T(t)) = B(t)) by leveraging Rust's hygienic
// ↪  macro system.
macro_rules! dsl_pipeline {
    (
        data: $data:expr;
        $(filter: $filter:expr;)?
        $(map: $map:expr;)?
        reduce: $reduce:expr, init: $init:expr
    ) => {{
        let iter = $data.into_iter()
            $(.filter(|x| $filter(x)))?
            $(.map(|x| $map(x)))?;
        iter.fold($init, $reduce)
    }};
}

fn main() {
    // Sample dataset for processing.
    let data = vec![1, 2, 3, 4, 5, 6];

    // Using the DSL pipeline:
    // - filter: retain values greater than 2.
    // - map: multiply each value by 2.
    // - reduce: sum all values, starting from an initial
    // ↪  accumulator of 0.
    let result = dsl_pipeline! {
        data: data;
        filter: |x: &i32| *x > 2;
        map: |x: i32| x * 2;
        reduce: |acc, x| acc + x, init: 0
    };

    println!("Aggregated result: {}", result);
```

```rust
    // Demonstrate function composition: f  g.
    // Here, times_two multiplies an input by 2 and add_five adds 5.
    let times_two = |x: i32| x * 2;
    let add_five = |x: i32| x + 5;
    let composed = compose(add_five, times_two);
    println!("Composition result for input 3: {}", composed(3));
    // Explanation: composed(3) computes add_five(times_two(3)) =
    ↪   add_five(6) = 11.

    // Additional usage: DSL pipeline with only the reduce
    ↪   operation.
    let numbers = vec![10, 20, 30, 40];
    let sum = dsl_pipeline! {
        data: numbers;
        reduce: |acc, x| acc + x, init: 0
    };
    println!("Sum of numbers: {}", sum);
}
```

www.ingramcontent.com/pod-product-compliance
Lightning Source LLC
LaVergne TN
LVHW052056060326
832903LV00061B/2915

* 9 7 9 8 3 1 2 9 0 7 0 1 8 *